MW00987590

ONESELF AS ANOTHER

ONESELF AS ANOTHER

PAUL RICOEUR

Translated by Kathleen Blamey

The University of Chicago Press
Chicago and London

Paul Ricoeur is the John Nuveen Professor Emeritus in the Divinity School, the Department of Philosophy, and the Committee on Social Thought, University of Chicago. Among his many works is the three-volume *Time and Narrative,* also published by the University of Chicago Press.

The University of Chicago Press, Chicago 60637
The University of Chicago Press, Ltd., London
© 1992 by The University of Chicago
All rights reserved. Published 1992
Printed in the United States of America
00 99 98 97 96 95 94 93 92   5 4 3 2 1

ISBN (cloth): 0-226-71328-8

Originally published as *Soi-même comme un autre,*
© Editions du Seuil, March 1990.

Library of Congress Cataloging-in-Publication Data

Ricoeur, Paul.
    [Soi-même comme un autre.   English]
    Oneself as another / Paul Ricoeur ; translated by Kathleen Blamey.
    p.   cm.
    Translation of: Soi-même comme un autre.
    Includes bibliographical references and index.
    1. Self (Philosophy)   2. Identity (Psychology)   3. Ethics.
I. Title.
B2430.R553S6513   1992
126–dc20   92-107
                                                     CIP

To François Wahl
in gratitude and friendship

CONTENTS

vii

CONTENTS

ACKNOWLEDGMENTS

I would like to begin by thanking the University of Edinburgh in the person of its chancellor for the honor of giving the 1986 Gifford Lectures, under the title "On Selfhood: The Question of Personal Identity." These lectures formed the basis for the studies published here.

I would also like to express my gratitude to Professor Spaemann of the University of Munich, who permitted me to give a second version of the original lectures, also in 1986, within the framework of the Schelling Vorlesungen.

Allow me also to thank Professor Bianco of the University of Rome, "La Sapienza," who provided me the opportunity to develop the ethical part of my work in the teaching he entrusted to me in 1987.

I am grateful to my friends Jean Greisch and Richard Kearney for having allowed me to sketch out the ontological considerations with which this work concludes during the Cerisy Decade that they organized and chaired in the summer of 1988.

Finally, I wish to express to François Wahl, of the Éditions du Seuil, my profound gratitude for the help he gave me during the writing and production of this book. This work, as all my earlier books he has edited, is indebted, beyond anything I could express, to his rigorous mind and to his devotion to writing.

The Question of Selfhood

By the title *Oneself as Another,* I wish to designate the point of convergence between the three major philosophical intentions that influenced the preparation of the studies that make up this book.

The first intention was to indicate the primacy of reflective meditation over the immediate positing of the subject, as this is expressed in the first person singular: "I think," "I am." This initial intention draws support from the grammars of natural languages inasmuch as they allow the opposition between "self" and "I." This support takes different forms following the peculiarities of each language. Beyond the broad correlation between the French *soi,* the English *self,* the German *Selbst,* the Italian *se,* and the Spanish *sí mismo,* grammars diverge. But these divergences are themselves instructive, to the extent that each grammatical peculiarity sheds light on part of the essential meaning sought. With respect to French, *soi* is directly defined as a reflexive pronoun. It is true that the philosophical use of the term throughout these studies violates a restriction that has been stressed by grammarians, namely that *soi* is a third-person reflexive pronoun (himself, herself, itself). This restriction, however, is lifted if we compare the term *soi* to the term *se,* which itself is related to verbs in the form of the infinitive—we say *se présenter, se nommer.* This typical use verifies one of the teachings of the linguist G. Guillaume,[1] who observed that in the infinitive form, and also up to a certain point in the participle, the verb expresses its broadest meaning, before it is distributed among the tenses and the grammatical persons. *Se* then designates the reflexive character of all the personal pronouns, and even the impersonal pronouns, such as "each," "anyone," "one," to which I shall frequently refer in the course of these investigations. This detour by way of *se* is not gratuitous, insofar as the reflexive pronoun *soi* also attains the same timeless range when it is added to the *se* in the infinitive mode: *se décider soi-même.* (I am leaving aside for the moment the meaning attached to *même* in the expression *soi-*

---

1. G. Guillaume, *Temps et Verbe* (Paris: Champion, 1965).

1

même.) It is on the basis of this last-stated use—belonging admittedly to the "proper usage" of the French language—that my constant use of the term *soi* in a philosophical context depends, as a reflexive pronoun belonging to all the grammatical persons, not to mention the impersonal expressions cited above. In its turn, this value of an omnipersonal reflexive pronoun is also preserved when *soi* functions as the object of a noun: *le souci de soi* (care of the self)—to borrow Michel Foucault's magnificent title. There is nothing surprising in this turn of phrase, to the extent that the nouns that admit *soi* in the indirect case are themselves substantives derived from infinitives, as is seen in the equivalence of the following expressions: *se soucier de soi(-même)* and *le souci de soi*. The shift from one expression to the other is permitted by the grammatical capacity for nominalizing any element of language: do we not say "the drink," "the beautiful," "the bright today"? By virtue of the same grammatical capacity we can say "the self" (*le soi*), aligning this expression with the other nominalized forms of the personal subject pronouns: "the I," "the you," "the they," and so on. This nominalizing, less tolerated in French than in English or in German, becomes an abuse of language only when we forget the grammatical lineage starting from the indirect case registered in the expression *désignation de soi* (self-designation), itself derived through an initial nominalization of the reflexive infinitive *se désigner soi-même* (to designate oneself). We shall henceforth take this latter form as the canonical one.

The second philosophical intention, implicitly present in the title in the word "self," is to distinguish two major meanings of "identity" (the relationship between this "identity" and the term "self" will be discussed shortly), depending on whether one understands by "identical" the equivalent of the Latin *ipse* or *idem*. The equivocity of the term "identical" will be at the center of our reflections on personal identity and narrative identity and related to a primary trait of the self, namely its temporality. Identity in the sense of *idem* unfolds an entire hierarchy of significations, which we shall explicate in the fifth and sixth studies. In this hierarchy, permanence in time constitutes the highest order, to which will be opposed that which differs, in the sense of changing or variable. Our thesis throughout will be that identity in the sense of *ipse* implies no assertion concerning some unchanging core of the personality. And this will be true, even when selfhood adds its own peculiar modalities of identity, as will be seen in the analysis of promising. The equivocalness of identity concerns our title through the partial synonymy, in French at least, between "same" (*même*) and "identical." In its diverse uses,[2] "same" (*même*) is used in the context

2. The *Robert* dictionary places at the head of the entries under the adjective *même* absolute identity (the same person, one and the same thing), simultaneity (at the same time),

of comparison; its contraries are "other," "contrary," "distinct," "diverse," "unequal," "inverse." The weight of this comparative use of the term "same" seems so great to me that I shall henceforth take sameness as synonymous with *idem*-identity and shall oppose to it selfhood (*ipseity*), understood as *ipse*-identity. To what extent is the equivocalness of the term "same" reflected in the title *Oneself as Another* (*Soi-même comme un autre*)? Only indirectly, inasmuch as "oneself" (*soi-même*) is only an emphatic form of "self," the expression *même* serving to indicate that it is precisely a matter of the being or the thing in question. (There is thus hardly any difference between *le souci de soi* [care of the self] and *le souci de soi-même* [care of oneself], aside from the effect of emphasis I have just mentioned.) Nevertheless, the tenuous thread that connects *même*, placed after *soi*, to the adjective *même*, in the sense of identical or similar, has not been broken. Reinforcing is still marking an identity. This is not the case in English or in German, where "same" cannot be confused with "self," *der, die, dasselbe*, or *gleich* with *Selbst*, except in philosophies that expressly derive selfhood or *Selbstheit* from sameness, resulting from a comparison. Here, English and German are less sources of equivocation than French is.

The third philosophical intention—this one explicitly included in the title—is related to the preceding one, in the sense that *ipse*-identity involves a dialectic complementary to that of selfhood and sameness, namely the dialectic of *self* and the *other than self*. As long as one remains within the circle of sameness-identity, the otherness of the other than self offers nothing original: as has been noted in passing, "other" appears in the list of antonyms of "same" alongside "contrary," "distinct," "diverse," and so on. It is quite different when one pairs together otherness and selfhood. A kind of otherness that is not (or not merely) the result of comparison is suggested by our title, otherness of a kind that can be constitutive of selfhood as such. *Oneself as Another* suggests from the outset that the selfhood of oneself implies otherness to such an intimate degree that one cannot be thought of without the other, that instead one passes into the other, as we might say in Hegelian terms. To "as" I should like to attach a strong meaning, not only that of a comparison (oneself similar to another) but indeed that of an implication (oneself inasmuch as being other).

*

In all these considerations, we have drawn support from the suggestions of basic grammar, but it is also under the guidance of philosophical ques-

---

similitude (making "same" synonymous with "analogous," "similar," "like," "such as"), and equality (a like quantity).

tioning that I have identified the canonical forms that support the conceptual analysis in my own language. There now looms the task of providing the expression "oneself as another" with the philosophical developments that, without losing sight of the constraints and the suggestions of basic grammar, transcend the idioms of a single language.

It seemed to me that a brief confrontation with the double heritage—positive as well as negative—of the *philosophies of the subject* would form an appropriate introduction, making it clear why the quarrel over the cogito will henceforth be considered to have been superseded. To be sure, other discussions will arise in the course of this work in which the dialectic of *ipse*-identity and of *idem*-identity, that of the self and of its other, will play the major roles. But the polemic in which we shall then be engaged will be situated beyond the point at which our problematic will have parted ways with the philosophies of the subject.

I hold here as paradigmatic of the philosophies of the subject that the subject is formulated in the first person—*ego cogito*—whether the "I" is defined as an empirical or a transcendental ego, whether the "I" is posited absolutely (that is, with no reference to an other) or relatively (egology requiring the intrinsic complement of intersubjectivity). In all of these instances, the subject is "I." That is why I am considering here the expression "philosophies of the subject" as equivalent to "philosophies of the cogito." This is also why the quarrel over the cogito, in which the "I" is by turns in a position of strength and of weakness, seems to me the best way to bring out the problematic of the self, under the condition that my subsequent investigations confirm the claim that I formulate here, namely that the hermeneutics of the self is placed at an equal distance from the apology of the cogito and from its overthrow. The style specific to the hermeneutics of the self is best understood if one has first had a chance to take stock of the amazing oscillations that the philosophies of the subject appear to present, as though the cogito out of which they arise were unavoidably caught up in an alternating sequence of overevaluation and underevaluation. Should it be said of the "I" of these philosophies, as some have said of the father, that there is always either too much or too little of it?

1. The Cogito Is Posited

The cogito is without any genuine philosophical signification unless its positing is invested with the ambition of establishing a final, ultimate foundation. This ambition is responsible for the great oscillation that causes the "I" of the "I think" to appear, by turns, to be elevated inordinately to the heights of a first truth and then cast down to the depths of a vast illusion. If this ambition of establishing an ultimate foundation has seen itself radicalized from Descartes to Kant, then from Kant to Fichte, and finally to the Husserl of the *Cartesian Meditations,* it nevertheless seems to me that it is enough to focus on its birthplace, in Descartes himself, whose philosophy confirms that the *crisis* of the cogito is contemporaneous with the *positing* of the cogito.[3]

The foundational ambition belonging to the Cartesian cogito can be recognized from the outset in the hyperbolic character of the doubt that opens the area of investigation in the *Meditations.* The radical nature of the project[4] is thus of the same scope as the doubt, which includes within the domain of "opinion" common sense, the sciences—mathematical and physical—and even the philosophical tradition. More precisely, this radicality stems from the nature of a doubt that has no common measure with respect to doubts that might be exercised within the three areas just mentioned. The hypothesis of an all-encompassing ruse proceeds from a doubt that Descartes calls "metaphysical" in order to indicate the disproportion with regard to any internal doubt within a particular area of certainty. In order to dramatize this doubt, Descartes creates the incredible hypothesis of a great deceiver or an evil genius, an inverted image of a truthful God, itself reduced to the status of mere opinion.[5] If the cogito can arise out of this extreme condition of doubt, it is because someone is doing the doubting.[6]

To be sure, this subject of doubt is radically stripped of its anchorage when its own body is carried away in the destruction of all physical bodies. But someone still remains to say, "I would do well . . . to deceive myself and pretend for a considerable period that [my thoughts] are wholly false and imaginary" (*Med.,* p. 16; AT 9 : 16). Even the hypothesis of the evil genius is a fiction that I form. But what is this "I" who doubts, so uprooted with respect to the spatiotemporal bearings of my body? Displaced with respect to the autobiographical subject of the *Discourse on Method*—

3. René Descartes, *Meditations on First Philosophy,* trans. Donald A. Cress (Indianapolis: Hackett, 1979), hereafter referred to as *Med.* Reference will also be given to the standard French edition of Adam-Tannery (Paris: Garnier-Flammarion, 1979), using the abbreviation AT.

4. "I realized that for once I had to raze everything in my life, down to the very bottom, so as to begin again from the first foundations, if I wanted to establish anything firm and lasting in the sciences" (ibid., "First Meditation," p. 13; AT 9 : 13).

5. "How do I know that I am not deceived every time I add two and three?" (ibid., p. 14; AT 9 : 16).

6. "I will . . . apply myself earnestly and openly to the general destruction of my former opinions" (ibid., p. 13; AT 9 : 13).

whose trace remains in the opening lines of the *Meditations*[7]—the "I" who does the doubting and who reflects upon itself in the cogito is just as metaphysical and hyperbolic as is doubt itself with respect to all knowledge. It is, in truth, no one.[8]

What is there left to say about this free-floating "I"? In its very stubbornness to want to doubt, it confirms its will to certainty and to truth (we are not, at this stage, distinguishing between these expressions), thus giving doubt as such a kind of direction: in this sense, Cartesian doubt is not Kierkegaardian despair. Quite the opposite, the will to discover is what motivates it; what I want to discover is the truth of things themselves. What I doubt is, in fact, that things are actually as they seem. In this regard, it is not without importance that the hypothesis of the evil genius is that of the great deceiver. The deceit consists precisely in making seeming pass for "true being." Through doubt, "I will believe that none of those things . . . ever existed"; what I want to discover is "one thing that is certain and indubitable" (ibid., p. 17; AT 9:19).

The last remark is critical for our understanding the reversal of doubt into the certainty of the cogito in the "Second Meditation." In agreement with the ontological intention of doubt, the first certainty that derives from it is the certainty of my existence, implied in the very exercise of thought in which the hypothesis of the great deceiver consists: "Then there is no doubt that I exist, if he deceives me. And deceive me as he will, he can never bring it about that I am nothing so long as I shall think that I am something" (ibid.). This is indeed an existential proposition; the verb "to be" is taken here absolutely and not as the copula: "I am; I exist."[9]

The question "who?", related first to the question "who doubts?", takes on a new twist when it is connected to the question "who thinks?" and,

---

7. "Several years have now passed since I first realize how many were the false opinions that in my youth I took to be true" (ibid.).

8. This is why the "who" involved in doubt is oblivious to the lack of any sort of other, since, in losing its anchoring, it has left behind the speech conditions of dialogue. We cannot even say that it is a monologue, in the sense that a monologue presupposes an interruption of a dialogue.

9. The reader familiar with the *Discourse on Method* may be surprised not to find here the celebrated formula *Cogito ergo sum*. It is nevertheless implicit in the formula "I doubt, therefore I am." This is so in several ways: to begin with, doubting is thinking; next, the "I am" is connected to the doubt by a "therefore," reinforced by all the reasons for doubting, so that we should read: "To doubt, one must be." Finally, the first certainty is not on the order of feeling; it is a proposition: "Thus it must be granted that, after weighing everything carefully and sufficiently, one must come to the considered judgment that the statement 'I am, I exist' is necessarily true every time it is uttered by me or conceived in my mind" (*Med.*, p. 19; AT 9:19). Let us leave aside for the moment the restriction "every time it is uttered by me . . .", it will play a decisive role in what I shall later term the crisis of the cogito.

more radically, "who exists?" The utter indetermination of the answer—an indetermination inherited from the initial, hyperbolic nature of doubt—indicates that, in order to flesh out the certainty obtained, Descartes was forced to add to it a new question, namely that of knowing *what* I am.[10] The answer to this question leads to the more developed expression of the cogito: "I am therefore precisely only a thing that thinks; that is, a mind, or soul, or intellect, or reason—words the meaning of which I was ignorant before" (ibid., p. 19; AT 9:21). By the question "what?" we are led into a predicative investigation, concerning what "pertains to this understanding that I have of myself" or, even more clearly, to "its nature" (ibid., p. 19; AT 9:22).[11] At this point the "I" definitively loses all singular determination in becoming thought—that is to say, understanding. This, so to speak, epistemologizing tendency (reinforced by the celebrated development of the "Second Meditation," known by the name "piece of wax") is tempered by a "phenomenologizing" tendency, expressed in the enumeration that preserves the real internal variety of the act of thinking: "What is [a thing that thinks]? A thing that doubts, understands, affirms, denies, wills, refuses, and which also imagines and senses" (ibid.). This enumeration poses the question of the identity of the subject, but in a sense entirely different from the narrative identity of a concrete person. This can involve nothing but a kind of pointlike ahistorical identity of the "I" in the diversity of its operations; this identity is that of the *same* that escapes the alternatives of permanence and change in time, since the cogito is instantaneous.[12]

At the end of the "Second Meditation" the status of the meditating subject appears to have nothing in common with what, in the following investigations, I shall call the speaker, agent, character of narration, subject of moral imputation, and so forth. The subjectivity that posits itself through reflection on its own doubt, a doubt radicalized by the fable of the great deceiver, is a free-floating subjectivity that Descartes, preserving the substantialist vocabulary of the philosophies with which he believes he

10. "But I do not yet understand well enough who I am—I, who now necessarily exist"; "I know that I exist; I ask now who is this 'I' whom I know" (ibid., p. 19; AT 9:21). This shift from the question "who?" to the question "what?" is prepared by a use of the verb "to be," which oscillates between the absolute "I am, I exist," and the predicative "I am something." Something, but what?

11. Here there begins a new sifting of opinions by methodical doubt, one that runs parallel to the screening performed in the "First Meditation" but that includes this time the list of predicates attributable to the "I," certain of existing in the starkness of "I am."

12. The argument here deserves to be cited: "For it is so obvious that it is I who doubt, I who understand, I who will, that there is nothing through which it could be more evidently explicated" (*Med.*, p. 20; AT 9:22). The evidence here concerns the impossibility of dividing up any of the modes of knowledge that I have of myself, hence of my true nature.

has broken, will call a *soul*. But what he means is just the opposite: what tradition calls a soul is actually a *subject*, and this subject can be reduced to the simplest and barest act, the act of thinking. This act of thinking, as yet without any determined object, is sufficient to vanquish doubt because doubt already contains it. And since doubt is voluntary and free, thought posits itself in positing doubt. It is in this sense that the "I exist thinking" is a first truth—that is, a truth that nothing else precedes.

The question then arises whether, in Descartes himself, the "I exist thinking" maintains itself in this position of first truth immediately known by reflecting on doubt. This would be the case if, in the order of reasons, all other truths proceeded from the certainty of the cogito. But the objection formulated by Martial Gueroult in *Descartes' Philosophy Interpreted according to the Order of Reasons* continues to seem to me to be irrefutable. The certainty of the cogito gives a strictly subjective version of truth; the reign of the evil genius continues, with regard to whether certainty has any objective value. The fact that my soul is pure intelligence is certain, but it is only an internal necessity of science: "Although this science is as certain as the *Cogito* for my understanding, it has certainty only within it, that is, for my self enclosed within itself." The difficulty being as just stated, it seems that in Descartes "only the demonstration of God's existence will allow me to resolve the question."[13] However, this demonstration, as it occurs in the "Third Meditation," reverses the order of discovery, or *ordo cognoscendi*, which ought to be the only one, if the cogito were in every respect the first truth, to lead from the "I" to God, then to mathematical essences, then to sensible things and to bodies. The demonstration reverses it to the benefit of another order, that of the "truth of things," or *ordo essendi:* a synthetic order according to which God, a mere link in the first order, becomes the first ring. The cogito would be genuinely absolute in all respects if it could be shown that there is but one order, that in which it is indeed first, and that the other order, in which it is set back to second place, derives from the first. Now it does seem that the "Third Meditation" reverses the order by placing the certainty of the cogito in a subordinate position in relation to divine veracity, which is first in accordance with the "truth of the thing."[14]

---

13. Martial Gueroult, *Descartes' Philosophy Interpreted according to the Order of Reasons,* vol. 1, *The Soul and God,* trans. Roger Ariew (Minneapolis-University of Minnesota Press, 1984), pp. 52, 88.

14. There is no doubt that, for Descartes, this involved neither sophism nor circularity. But the price to pay is considerable. The argument rests on the distinction between two ways of characterizing ideas. With respect to their "formal being"—that is, as present in me, abstracting from their representative value—they are simply in me, all of the same level, for all are thought by me equally. As to their representative value, called "objective being," this

What is the result of this for the cogito itself? By a sort of rebound effect of the new certainty (namely that of the existence of God) on that of the cogito, the idea of myself appears profoundly transformed, due solely to my recognizing this Other, who causes the presence in me of its own representation. The cogito slips to the second ontological rank. Descartes does not hesitate to write: "Thus the [notion] of the infinite somehow exists in me prior to the [notion] of the finite, that is, the [notion] of God exists prior to the [notion] of myself" (*Med.*, "Third Meditation," trans. modified, p. 30; AT 9:36). One must therefore go so far as to say that, if God is the *ratio essendi* of myself, he thereby becomes the *ratio cognoscendi* of myself, since I am an imperfect being, a being who is lacking; the imperfection attaching to doubt is known only by the light of the idea of perfection. In the "Second Meditation" I knew myself as existing and thinking, but not yet as a finite and limited nature. This infirmity of the cogito is far reaching indeed: it is not related only to the imperfection of doubt but to the very precariousness of the certainty that conquered doubt, essentially to its absence of duration. Left to itself, the "I" of the cogito is Sisyphus condemned, from one instant to the next, to push up the rock of its certainty, fighting the slope of doubt. In contrast, because he maintains me in existence, God confers on the certainty of myself the permanence that it does not hold in itself. This strict contemporaneousness of the idea of God and the idea of myself, considered from the angle of the power to produce ideas, makes me say that "just as the idea of myself, [the idea of God] was born and produced with me when I was created" (ibid., trans. modified, p. 33; AT 9:41). Better: the idea of God is in me as the very mark of the author upon his work, a mark that assures the resemblance between us. I then have to confess that "I perceive this

---

presents varying degrees of perfection: equal as thoughts, ideas are no longer so with respect to what they represent. We know what follows: the idea of perfection, held to be synonymous with the philosophical idea of God, proves to carry with it a representative content disproportionate to my inner being, which is that of an imperfect being, since I am doomed to move toward the truth along the painstaking path of doubt. This, then, is the surprising situation: a content is greater than its container. The question then arises concerning the cause of this idea: with regard to all other ideas, I can claim to be the cause, for they do not possess more being than I do. Of the idea of God, however, I am not the "capable" cause. It remains that it has been placed in me by the very being that it represents. I shall not discuss here the innumerable difficulties that are connected to each of the moments of the argument: the legitimacy of distinguishing the objective being of ideas from their formal being, of considering the degrees of perfection of the idea as proportional to the beings represented in this way, of considering God as the cause of the presence of his own idea in us. I shall go right to the consequences that concern the cogito itself, surpassed in this way by the idea of infinity or of perfection incommensurable with its condition of finite being.

likeness . . . by the same faculty through which I perceive myself" (p. 33; AT 9:41).

It is hardly possible to push the fusion between the idea of myself and that of God any further. But what results from this for the order of reasons? The order now is no longer presented as a linear chain but as a loop; regarding this backward projection of the arrival point back onto the starting point, Descartes perceives only its benefits, namely the elimination of the insidious hypothesis of a deceitful God that nourishes the most hyperbolic doubt; the fantastic image of the great deceiver is conquered in me, as soon as the Other, actually existing and entirely truthful, takes its place. For us, however, as for the first ones to contradict Descartes, the question is whether, by giving the order of reasons the form of a circle, Descartes has not thereby turned the step that takes the cogito, hence the "I," out of its initial solitude into a gigantic vicious circle.

A set of alternatives then appears to open up: either the cogito possesses the value of a foundation, but it is a sterile truth which nothing can follow without breaking the order of reasons; or it is the idea of perfection that founds it in its condition of finite being, and the first truth loses its aura of first foundation.

These alternatives have been transformed into a dilemma by Descartes's heirs: on the one hand, Malebranche and, even more so, Spinoza, drawing the consequences of the reversal performed by the "Third Meditation," have taken the cogito to be no more than an abstract, truncated truth, stripped of any prestige. Spinoza is the most consistent here: in his *Ethics,* the discourse on infinite substance alone has foundational value; the cogito not only falls back to the second rank but loses its first-person formulation. In book 2 of the *Ethics* we therefore read, under axiom 2: "Man thinks." The axiom preceding this lapidary formula underscores even more heavily the subordinate character of the latter: "The essence of man does not involve necessary existence; that is, from the order of Nature it is equally possible that a certain man exists or does not exist."[15] Our problematic of the self draws away from the philosophical horizon. On the other hand, for the entire movement of idealism, through Kant, Fichte, and Husserl (at least the Husserl of the *Cartesian Meditations*), the only coherent reading of the cogito is that for which the alleged certainty of the existence of God is struck with the same seal of subjectivity as the certainty of my own existence; the guarantee of guarantees constituted by divine veracity then stands simply as an addendum to the primary certainty. If this is so, the cogito is not a first truth that would be followed by a second, a third, and

15. Baruch Spinoza, *The Ethics,* trans. Samuel Shirley (Indianapolis: Hackett, 1982), p. 64.

so on but the ground that grounds itself, incommensurable with all propositions, not only empirical ones but transcendental ones as well. In order to avoid slipping into a subjectivist idealism, the "I think" must be divested of any psychological resonance, all the more so of any autobiographical reference. It must become the Kantian "I think," which the transcendental deduction states must be able to accompany all my acts. The problematic of the self emerges magnified, in a sense, but at the price of the loss of its relation to the person who speaks, to the I-you of interlocution, to the identity of a historical person, to the self of responsibility. Must the exaltation of the cogito be paid at this price? Modernity is indebted to Descartes at least for having been placed before such formidable alternatives.

2. The Shattered Cogito

The shattered cogito: this could be the emblematic title of a tradition, one less continuous perhaps than that of the cogito, but one whose virulence culminates with Nietzsche, making him the privileged adversary of Descartes.

In order to understand the attack led by Nietzsche against the Cartesian cogito, in particular in the fragments of the last period, it is useful to return to some writings that are contemporary with the *Birth of Tragedy,* in which the plea against rhetoric is directed at subverting the claim of philosophy to set itself up as science, in the strong sense of a foundational discipline.[16]

The attack against the foundational claim of philosophy is based upon a critique of the language in which philosophy expresses itself. Now one has to admit that, except for Herder, the philosophy of subjectivity had utterly disregarded the mediating factor of language in the argumentation of the "I am" and the "I think." By emphasizing this dimension of philosophical discourse, Nietzsche brings to light the rhetorical strategies that have been buried, forgotten, and even hypocritically repressed and denied, in the name of the immediacy of reflection.

16. Two Nietzsche texts merit our attention in this regard. The first is *Course on Rhetoric,* the substance of a course taught in Basel during the winter term, 1872–73. *Course* is volume 5 of the Kroner-Musarion edition and appears in English translation by Carole Blair as "Nietzsche's Lecture Notes on Rhetoric," *Philosophy and Rhetoric* 16 (1983): 94–129. The second text, entitled "On Truth and Lies in a Nonmoral Sense," was written in the summer of 1873 and was intended to be part of a work that was to be called *Das Philosophenbuch* (The philosophers' book) and that was to serve as a theoretical complement to *Birth of Tragedy.* This text has been translated by Daniel Breazeale in *Philosophy and Truth: Selections from Nietzsche's Notebooks of the Early 1870s* (Atlantic Highlands, N.J.: Humanities Press, 1979), pp. 79–97.

The *Course on Rhetoric* proposes the novel idea that tropes—metaphors, synecdoche, metonomy—do not constitute ornaments added onto a discourse that is by right literal and nonfigurative but instead are inherent in the most basic linguistic functioning. In this sense, there is no nonrhetorical "naturalness" of language. Language is figurative through and through.[17]

"On Truth and Lies in a Nonmoral Sense" pushes to its furthest point the paradox of language that is figural through and through and thus reputed to be deceitful. It is a paradox in a double sense: first, in that from the opening lines, life, apparently taken in a referential and nonfigural sense, is taken as the source of the fables by which it sustains itself. Next, it is paradoxical in that Nietzsche's own discourse on truth as a lie ought to be drawn into the abyss of the paradox of the liar. But Nietzsche is precisely the thinker who assumed this paradox to the end, something missed by the commentators who take the apology of Life, of the Will to power, to be the revelation of a new immediacy, substituted in the very place and with the same foundational claims as the cogito. I do not mean to say by this that Nietzsche, in his effort to overcome nihilism, did not have some such reconstruction in mind. It matters, however, that this reconstruction remains at the mercy of a gesture of deconstruction to which the metaphysics that has preceded is subjected. In this sense, if the argument directed at the cogito can be interpreted as extending to the cogito itself the Cartesian argument of the evil genius, in the name of the figural and deceitful character of all language, it is not certain that, by placing himself under the paradox of the liar, Nietzsche managed to shelter his own philosophy from the effect of deconstruction unleashed by his rhetorical interpretation of all philosophy.

The initial paradox is that of an "illusion" serving as an "expedient" on behalf of preserving life.[18] Nature itself, however, has removed from man the power to decipher this illusion: "She threw away the key" ("On Truth and Lies," p. 80). Nevertheless, Nietzsche thinks that he possesses this key: it is the functioning of illusion as *Verstellung*. It is important to keep

17. *Course on Rhetoric* quotes favorably a passage from the writer Jean-Paul's *Vorschule der Aesthetik,* which concludes with the following statement: "Thus, with respect to spiritual relationships, each language is a dictionary of faded metaphors" (cited in Blair, "Nietzsche's Lecture Notes on Rhetoric," p. 123). Metaphor, here, appears to be the privileged form among all the tropes, but metonymy—substituting one word by another—is not thereby eliminated: substituting the effect by its cause (metalepsis) will become, in the fragments of *Will to Power,* the principal mechanism of the hidden sophism of the cogito.

18. The human intellect is said to belong to nature as an appanage of the clever beast who invented knowledge: "For this intellect has no additional mission which would lead it beyond human life" ("On Truth and Lies," p. 79).

the sense of displacement as part of the meaning of this process, which also signifies dissimulation, for it designates the secret of not only the linguistic but also the properly rhetorical functioning of the illusion. In this we return to the situation of Plato's *Cratylus* and to the confrontation expressed in the Socratic dialogue between a "natural" origin and a "conventional" origin of the designation of things by means of words. Nietzsche does not hesitate: the model, so to speak, is the liar who misuses language by repeated "arbitrary substitutions or even reversals of names" (p. 81). However, just as figurative language, in the preceding text, could no longer be opposed to any sort of literal language, the language of the liar no longer has as its reference a nondeceitful language, for language as such has come from these substitutions and inversions.[19]

In what sense is the Cartesian cogito intended here, at least obliquely? In the sense that it cannot constitute an exception to generalized doubt, to the extent that the same certainty that covers the "I exist," the "I exist-thinking," the formal reality of ideas and finally their representative value, is struck with the sort of tropological reduction pronounced here. In the same way that Descartes's doubt proceeded from the presumed absence of distinction between dreaming and waking, that of Nietzsche proceeds from the even more hyperbolic absence of distinction between lies and truth. This is indeed why the cogito has to succumb to this version (which is itself hyperbolic) of the evil genius, for what the latter could not encompass was the instinct for truth. Now this is precisely what has become "enigmatic." The evil genius proves to be even more clever than the cogito. As for Nietzsche's own philosophy, either it exempts itself from the universal reign of *Verstellung* (but through what higher ruse could it escape the sophism of the liar?), or else it succumbs to it (but then how can one justify the tone of revelation with which the will to power, the overman, and the eternal return of the same are proclaimed?). This dilemma, which does not seem to have kept Nietzsche from thinking and writing, has become that of his commentators, split into two camps: the faithful and the ironists.[20]

19. Whence the solemn tone of this declaration: "What then is truth? A movable host of metaphors, metonymies, and anthropomorphisms: in short, a sum of human relations which have been poetically and rhetorically intensified, transferred, and embellished, and which, after long usage, seem to a people to be fixed, canonical, and binding. Truths are illusions which we have forgotten as illusions; they are metaphors that have become worn out and have been drained of sensuous force, coins which have lost their embossing and are now considered as metal and no longer as coins" (ibid., p. 84).
20. French commentators line up generally in the second camp, accompanied by Paul de Man in his essay "Rhetoric of Tropes," in *Allegories of Reading* (New Haven: Yale University Press, 1979), pp. 103–18.

What has just been termed a tropological reduction [21] constitutes a very useful key for interpreting the frontal critique of the cogito that can be read in the fragments of the *Nachlass* scattered between 1882 and 1884. [22] The choice of fragments with the most obvious anticogito content raises only a corner of the veil cast over this gigantic endeavor, in which the critique of Christianity is found next to the development of the enigmatic themes of the will to power, the overman, and the eternal return. But the strict selection made here is faithful to my purpose, which is to show in Nietzsche's anticogito not the inverse of the Cartesian cogito but the destruction of the very question to which the cogito was held to give an absolute answer.

Despite the fragmentary nature of these aphorisms directed against the cogito, the constellation that they trace allows us to see in them the rigorous exercise of a hyperbolic doubt, where Nietzsche himself would be the evil genius. Consider this fragment from November 1887 to March 1888: "I am convinced of [*ich halte*] the phenomenalism of the *inner* world also: everything that reaches our consciousness is utterly and completely adjusted, simplified, schematized, interpreted, the *actual* process of inner 'perception,' the *relation of causes* between thoughts, feelings, desires, between subject and object, is absolutely concealed from us, and may be purely imaginary." [23]

---

21. In a study devoted to the work of Nietzsche, this tropological reduction would have to be completed with the genealogical reduction at work in the *Genealogy of Morals*. One would find here an alliance between medical symptomatology and textual deciphering. The critique of conscience at the end of the present work will allow me the opportunity to give full credit to this great text.

22. In the large octavo edition, prior to the Colli-Montinari edition, these fragments were grouped together in section 3 of a work that never saw the light of day and that had been carelessly placed under the title of *The Will to Power*. These fragments have now been put back in chronological order in Colli-Montinari's scholarly edition.

23. Nietzsche, *Will to Power*, vol. 15 of *Complete Works*, trans. Anthony M. Ludovici (Edinburgh: T. N. Fowlis, 1910), no. 477, p. 7. Following this quotation we read: "This '*inner* world of appearance' is treated with precisely the same forms and procedures as the 'outer' world. We never come across a single 'fact': pleasure and pain are more recently evolved intellectual phenomena. . . .

"Causality evades us; to assume the existence of an immediate causal relation between thoughts, as Logic does, is the result of the coarsest and most clumsy observation. There are *all sorts of passions* that may intervene between two thoughts: but the interaction is too rapid—that is why we *fail* to *recognize* them, that is why we actually *deny* their existence. . . .

"'Thinking,' as the epistemologists understand it, never takes place at all: it is an absolutely gratuitous fabrication, arrived at by selecting one element from the process and by eliminating all the rest—an artificial adjustment for the purpose of the understanding. . . .

"The 'mind' *something that thinks:* at times, even, 'the mind absolute and pure'—this

To proclaim the phenomenal character of the internal world is, first, to align it with the so-called external world, where phenomenality in no way means objectivity in a Kantian sense, but precisely "arrangement, simplification, schematization, interpretation." To understand this point, one must keep in mind the attack on positivism; where positivism says, There are only facts, Nietzsche says, There are no facts, only interpretations. In extending the critique to so-called internal experience, Nietzsche destroys in its principle the exceptional character of the cogito with respect to the doubt that Descartes directed to the distinction between the world of dreams and the world of waking. To assume the phenomenality of the internal world is, in addition, to align the connection of inner experience with external "causation," which is also an illusion that conceals the play of forces under the artifice of order. It is, as well, to posit an entirely arbitrary unity, that fiction called "thinking," apart from the bristling multiplicity of instincts. And finally, it is to imagine a "substratum of subject" in which the acts of thought would have their origin. This final illusion is the most dangerous, for it puts in action, in the relation between the actor and his or her deed, the sort of inversion between effect and cause that we related above to the trope of metonymy, in the figure of metalepsis. In this way we take as a cause, under the title of "I," what is the effect of its own effect. The argument obviously works only if one introduces causation, hence a certain discursivity, beneath the allegedly immediate certainty of the cogito. In the exercise of hyperbolic doubt, which Nietzsche carries to its limit, the "I" does not appear as inherent to the cogito but as an interpretation of a causal type. Yet we encounter our earlier tropological argument: as a matter of fact, placing a substance *under* the cogito or a cause *behind* it "is simply a grammatical habit, that of connecting an agent to every action." We slip back into the "inversion of words," denounced twenty years earlier.

I shall not consider any further these arguments in which one should see nothing other, in my opinion, than an exercise of hyperbolic doubt taken further than that of Descartes and turned against the very certainty that the latter believed he could eliminate from doubt. At least in these fragments, Nietzsche says nothing other than simply, I doubt better than Descartes. The cogito too is doubtful. It is in this hyperbolic mode that I understand statements such as this: "my hypothesis, the subject as multi-

---

concept is an evolved and second result of false introspection, which believes in 'thinking': in the first place an act is imagined here which does not really occur at all, *i.e.* 'thinking;' and, *secondly,* a subject-substratum is imagined in which every process of this thinking has its origin, and nothing else—that is to say, *both the action and the agent are fanciful*" (pp. 7–8).

plicity." Nietzsche does not dogmatically state here (although he does elsewhere) that the subject *is* multiplicity: he *is trying out* this idea; he is in a way playing with the idea of a multiplicity of subjects struggling among themselves, like so many "cells" rebelling against the ruling authority. He bears witness in this way to the fact that nothing resists the most fantastic hypothesis, at least as long as one remains within the problematic defined by the search for a certainty that would be an absolute guarantee against doubt.

3. Toward a Hermeneutics of the Self

Exalted subject, humiliated subject: it seems that it is always through a complete reversal of this sort that one approaches the subject; one could thus conclude that the "I" of the philosophies of the subject is *atopos,* without any assured place in discourse. To what extent can one say that the hermeneutics of the self developed here occupies an epistemological place (also an ontological place, as I shall state in the tenth study), situated beyond the alternative of the cogito and of the anticogito?

A rapid overview of the nine studies that together form the hermeneutics of the self can give the reader a general idea of the way in which philosophical discourse replies on the conceptual level to the three grammatical features mentioned above, namely the use of *se* and *soi* in indirect cases, the splitting of "same" into the domains of *idem* and *ipse,* and the correlation between the self and the other than self. To these three grammatical features correspond the three major features of the hermeneutics of the self, namely, the detour of reflection by way of analysis, the dialectic of selfhood and sameness, and finally the dialectic of selfhood and otherness. These three features of hermeneutics will be progressively uncovered, in the order in which they have just been listed, in the series of studies that form this work. I shall give an interrogative form to this perspective, introducing by means of the question "who?" all the assertions relating to the problematic of the self, and in this way giving the same scope to the question "who?" and to the answer—*the self.* Four subcategories will therefore correspond to four manners of questioning: Who is speaking? Who is acting? Who is recounting about himself or herself? Who is the moral subject of imputation? Let us look at this in greater detail.

The first subset (studies 1 and 2) belongs to a *philosophy of language,* from the twofold perspective of semantics and pragmatics. As early as these first studies, the reader will be confronted with an attempt to include within a hermeneutics of the self certain significant fragments of English-language analytic philosophy. Such a hermeneutics is heir, as we have seen, to the debates inherent in European philosophy (amusingly called Continental by the inheritors of a philosophy that, to begin with, was itself insular). These borrowings, which will continue in the second and third subsets, are not arbitrary; they do not result from some will a priori to engage in the reciprocal cross-fertilization of two largely alien traditions; even less do they represent some compulsive ambition to force a marriage between two families of minds who seldom frequent one another. *The recourse to analysis,* in the sense given to this term by analytic philosophy, *is the price to pay for a hermeneutics characterized by the indirect manner of positing the self.* By this first feature, hermeneutics proves to be a philosophy of detours: the detour by way of analytic philosophy quite simply seems to me to be the one richest in promises and in results. The driving force, however, lies indeed with the question "who?" This question divides itself into the twin questions: *Of whom* does one speak in designating persons, as distinct from things, in the referential mode? And *who* speaks by designating himself or herself as "locutor" (addressing an interlocutor)?

The second subset (studies 3 and 4) belongs to a *philosophy of action,* in the limited sense that this term has acquired principally in analytic philosophy. This subset has a complex relation with respect to the preceding one; in a sense, the latter serves as organon, to the extent that it is in statements—hence in propositions, in particular on the basis of verbs and action sentences—that we speak of action and to the extent that it is in speech acts that the agent of action designates himself or herself as the one who is acting. In another sense, the second subset annexes the first, inasmuch as speech acts are themselves action and, by implication, speakers are themselves actors. The questions "Who is speaking?" and "Who is acting?" appear in this way to be closely interconnected. Here again, the reader will be invited to participate in a constructive confrontation between analytic philosophy and hermeneutics. In fact, analytic philosophy will direct the wide detour by means of the questions "what?" and "why?", although it will be unable to follow all the way to the end the return route leading back to the question "who?"—*who* is the agent of action? Allow me to repeat that these long loops of analysis are characteristic of the indirect style of a hermeneutics of the self, in stark contrast to the demand for immediacy belonging to the cogito.

This sort of competition between analytic philosophy and hermeneutics continues in the third subset (studies 5 and 6), where the *question of personal identity* is posed at the point of intersection between the two philosophical traditions. The question of identity, tied to that of temporality, will be taken up at the point where it was left by *Time and Narrative* 3 under the title "narrative identity," but with the help of new resources obtained through the analysis of personal identity in terms of objective

criteria of identification. What has just been termed the competition between two philosophical traditions will be submitted to the arbitration of
the dialectic of *idem*-identity and *ipse*-identity, which we have cited as the
second grammatical feature of *soi-même*, in the reflexive character of the
self (*soi*). Thanks to this new development of the theme of narrative identity, the concept of action—which has, as we recall, the narrative as its
mimesis—will recover the full scope of meaning that belonged to the
Aristotelian concept of praxis, in contrast to the drastic limitations (although perhaps justified by the purpose of the analysis) placed upon human action by the semantics of action in the preceding subset. At the same
time, and correlatively, the subject of the action recounted will begin to
correspond to the broader concept of the *acting and suffering* individual,
which our analytic-hermeneutical procedure is capable of eliciting.

The fourth subset (studies 7, 8 and 9) will have the task of proposing a
final detour by way of the *ethical and moral determinations of action,* related
to the categories of the good and of the obligatory, respectively. In this
way, I shall bring to light the ethical and moral dimensions of a subject to
whom an action, whether good or not, whether performed out of duty or
not, can be imputed. If the first and second studies were the first to set the
process of analysis and reflection into operation, and if the fifth and sixth
studies focused in particular on the opposition between selfhood and
sameness, it is in the three ethical studies that the dialectic of the same and
the other will find its appropriate philosophical development. In truth, the
dialectic of oneself and the other will not have been entirely missing from
the earlier studies, nor from the dialectic of *idem* and *ipse*. Never, at any
stage, will the self have been separated from its other. It remains, however,
that this dialectic, the richest of all, as the title of the work recalls, will take
on its fullest development only in the studies in the areas of ethics and
morality. The *autonomy* of the self will appear then to be tightly bound up
with *solicitude* for one's neighbor and with *justice* for each individual.

The overview just presented of the studies that form this work gives an
idea of the gap that separates the hermeneutics of the self from the philosophies of the cogito. To say *self* is not to say *I*. The *I* is posited—or is
deposed. The *self* is implied reflexively in the operations, the analysis of
which precedes the return toward this self. Upon this dialectic of analysis
and reflection is grafted that of *idem* and *ipse*. Finally, the dialectic of the
same and the other crowns the first two dialectics. I shall conclude this
preface by underscoring the two features diametrically opposing, not
simply the immediacy of the *I am,* but also the ambition of placing it in
the position of ultimate foundation. Here I introduce these two complementary features briefly to complete the perspective I have just sketched.

The first feature concerns the *fragmentary* character of the series of studies I present here. It challenges the thesis of the indecomposable simplicity of the cogito, which is joined to that of its immediacy. We shall see that it challenges the hypothesis of reflective simplicity without thereby giving in to the vertigo of the disintegration of the self pursued mercilessly by Nietzschean deconstruction. Let us therefore carefully examine both aspects that are challenged.

The fragmentary character of these studies results from the analytic-reflective structure that imposes arduous detours on our hermeneutics, beginning as early as the first study. In introducing the problematic of the self by the question "who?", we have in the same stroke opened the way for the genuine polysemy inherent in this question itself: Who is speaking of what? Who does what? About whom and about what does one construct a narrative? Who is morally responsible for what? These are but so many different ways in which "who?" is stated. Now these different ways of posing the question "who?" do not escape a certain contingency of questioning, a contingency linked to that of the divisions produced in turn by the grammar of natural languages (some examples of this were given in the opening lines of this preface), ordinary language usage, and finally the emergence of philosophical questioning in the course of history. Hermeneutics is here raised to the historicality of questioning, from which the fragmentation of the art of questioning results.[24]

This fragmentation, however, has a thematic unity that keeps it from the dissemination that would lead the discourse back to silence. In a sense, one could say that these studies together have as their thematic unity *human action* and that the notion of action acquires, over the course of the studies, an ever-increasing extension and concreteness. To this extent, the philosophy that comes out of this work deserves to be termed a practical philosophy and to be taken as "second philosophy," in the sense that Manfred Riedel gives to this term,[25] following the failure of the cogito to be constituted as first philosophy and to resolve the question of determining an ultimate foundation. But the unity that the concern with human action confers to these studies as a whole is not the unity that an ultimate foundation would confer to a series of derivative disciplines. It is rather a merely analogical unity between the multiple uses of the term "acting," which, as we have just mentioned, receives its polysemy from the variety

24. This fragmentation justifies the preference for the title "study" rather than "chapter," given that each of our investigations constitutes a total part, permitting the reader to enter into this inquiry at any point.
25. Manfred Riedel, *Für eine zweite Philosophie, Vorträge und Abhandlungen* (Frankfurt: Suhrkamp, 1988).

and contingency of the questions that activate the analyses leading back to the reflection on the self.[26]

Even to speak of analogical unity is to say too much, for one could hesitate about the choice of the first or single term of reference. Does the primary sense of human action consist in the self-designation of a speaking subject? Or in the power to act, belonging to an agent of action? Or in the moral imputation of action? Each of these answers is legitimate. It will be objected that, along the way, we impose on the diversity of our studies on acting the following three-step rhythm: describing, narrating, prescribing. As we shall see, this threesome will allow us to assign to the narrative approach—which, in *Time and Narrative* 3, placed the notion of narrative identity at a sort of summit—a transitional and relational function between the description that prevails in the analytic philosophies of action and the prescription that designates all the determinations of action by means of a generic term, using the predicates "good" and "obligatory." This ordering, however, serves a merely didactic function, intended to guide the reader through the polysemy of action. Depending on the question asked, however, this threesome can be read in a different order. No approach is primary in every respect.

The perplexity created by this fragmentary style is by no means dispelled in the final study, of which I have as yet said nothing, a study whose exploratory nature I should like to underscore even now. In this study of an ontological style, what is at issue is indeed the analogical unity of human action. It is asked whether, in order to treat human action as a fundamental mode of being, hermeneutics can stand on the authority of the resources of past ontologies that could be, as it were, reawakened, liberated, regenerated at its contact. We shall ask principally whether the great polysemy of the term "being," according to Aristotle, can permit us to give new value to the meaning of being as act and potentiality, securing in this way the analogical unity of acting on a stable ontological meaning. But this reevaluation of a meaning of being, too often sacrificed to being-as-substance, can take place only against the backdrop of a plurality more radical than any other, namely that of the meanings of being. Moreover, it will quickly become apparent that the ontology of act and of potentiality will in turn open up variations of meaning difficult to specify because of their multiple historical expressions. Finally, and most especially, the dialectic of the same and the other, readjusted to the dimensions of our her-

---

26. By introducing the term "analogical unity" here, I am alluding to the problem posed by the heritage of the categories of being in Aristotle and to the interpretation that the Scholastics gave of the reference of the entire series to a first term (*pros hen*), held to be *ousia*, translated into Latin by *substantia*. Of course, I am applying the term "analogical unity" to a different problematic. I shall return to this question in the tenth study.

meneutic of the self and its other, will prevent on ontology of act and potentiality from becoming enclosed within a tautology. The polysemy of otherness, which I shall propose in the tenth study, will imprint upon the entire ontology of acting the seal of the diversity of sense that foils the ambition of arriving at an ultimate foundation, characteristic of cogito philosophies.

The second feature will widen the gap between this hermeneutic and cogito philosophies. It concerns the type of certainty to which the former may aspire and which distinguishes it in a decisive way from that attaching to the latter's claim of providing its own foundation. Over the course of the first studies, we shall see dawning, then taking on strength during the middle ones, and finally coming to full expression in the last ones, the notion of *attestation,* by which I intend to characterize the alethic (or veritative) mode of the style appropriate to the conjunction of analysis and reflection, to the recognition of the difference between selfhood and sameness, and to the unfolding of the dialectic of the self and the other—in short, appropriate to the hermeneutics of the self considered in its threefold structure. To my mind, attestation defines the sort of certainty that hermeneutics may claim, not only with respect to the epistemic exaltation of the cogito in Descartes, but also with respect to its humiliation in Nietzsche and his successors. Attestation may appear to require less than one and more than the other. In fact, compared to both of them, it too is properly *atopos.*

On the one hand, attestation does stand in greater opposition to the certainty claimed by the cogito than to the criterion of verification of objective science. The detour by way of analysis indeed imposes the indirect and fragmentary mode of any return to the self. In this sense, verification is included in the process of reflection as a necessary epistemic moment. What is set in opposition to attestation is fundamentally the notion of *epistēmē,* of science, taken in the sense of ultimate and self-founding knowledge. And in this opposition attestation appears to be less demanding than the certainty belonging to the ultimate foundation. Attestation presents itself first, in fact, as a kind of belief. But it is not a doxic belief, in the sense in which *doxa* (belief) has less standing than *epistēmē* (science, or better, knowledge). Whereas doxic belief is implied in the grammar of "I believe-that," attestation belongs to the grammar of "I believe-in." It thus links up with testimony, as the etymology reminds us, inasmuch as it is in the speech of the one giving testimony that one believes. One can call upon no epistemic instance any greater than that of the belief—or, if one prefers, the credence—that belongs to the triple dialectic of reflection and analysis, of selfhood and sameness, and of self and other.

It might be objected that this initial approach to attestation does not move as far away from the certainty of the cogito as it may at first seem: did not the hyperbole of the evil genius situate the problematic of the first truth in the dimension of deceit and veracity? And is not the entire Cartesian edifice of knowledge based upon the veracity of God? This is indeed true: in this sense, the problematic of attestation finds one of its sources in the Cartesian problematic of a deceitful God. But attestation cannot claim for itself the character of a guarantee attaching to the cogito through its allegedly demonstrating the existence of God, a guarantee that finally reabsorbs veracity into truth, in the strong sense of self-founding theoretical knowledge. In this respect, attestation lacks both this guarantee and the hypercertainty belonging to it. The other features of hermeneutics, mentioned earlier, confirm the weakness of attestation with regard to any radical foundational claim: the fragmentation that follows from the polysemy of the question "who?" (the contingency of the questioning itself resulting, let us repeat, from the history of philosophical systems as well as from the grammar of natural languages and ordinary language usage, to say nothing of the frequently aporetic nature of so many analyses yet to come) gives to attestation its own special fragility, to which is added the vulnerability of a discourse aware of its own lack of foundation. This vulnerability will be expressed in the permanent threat of suspicion, if we allow that suspicion is the specific contrary of attestation. The kinship between attestation and testimony is verified here: there is no "true" testimony without "false" testimony. But there is no recourse against false testimony than another that is more credible; and there is no recourse against suspicion but a more reliable attestation.

On the other hand—and now attestation is confronting the opposite side, that of the humiliated cogito—credence is also (and, we should say, nevertheless) a kind of trust, as the expression "reliable attestation" has just suggested. *Credence is also trust.* This will be one of the leitmotifs of our analysis: attestation is fundamentally attestation *of* self. This trust will, in turn, be a trust in the power to say, in the power to do, in the power to recognize oneself as a character in a narrative, in the power, finally, to respond to accusation in the form of the accusative: "It's me here" (*me voici!*), to borrow an expression dear to Lévinas. At this stage, attestation will be that of what is commonly called conscience and which in German is termed *Gewissen.* (This word is better than the French *conscience,* which translates both *Bewusstsein* and *Gewissen;* the German *Gewissen* recalls the semantic kinship with *Gewissheit,* "certainty.") And if one admits that the problematic of acting constitutes the analogical unity within which all of these investigations are grouped, attestation can be defined as the *assurance of being oneself acting and suffering.* This assurance remains the ultimate recourse against all suspicion; even if it is always in some sense received from another, it still remains *self*-attestation. It is self-attestation that, at every level—linguistic, praxic, narrative, and prescriptive—will preserve the question "who?" from being replaced by the questions "what?" or "why?" Conversely, at the center of the aporia, only the persistence of the question "who?"—in a way laid bare for lack of a response—will reveal itself to be the impregnable refuge of attestation.

As credence without any guarantee, but also as trust greater than any suspicion, the hermeneutics of the self can claim to hold itself at an equal distance from the cogito exalted by Descartes and from the cogito that Nietzsche proclaimed forfeit. The reader will judge whether the investigations that follow live up to this claim.

✳

To my readers I owe an explanation why I decided not to include in the present work the twin lectures with which I concluded the Gifford Lectures, delivered in Edinburgh in 1986. These lectures belonged to the biblical hermeneutics whose project I outlined in *From Text to Action.*[27] In the first, entitled "Le soi dans le miroir des Écritures" (The self in the mirror of Scripture), I interrogate, as Northrup Frye does in *The Great Code,*[28] the sort of teaching and summoning emanating from the symbolic network woven by Scripture, Jewish and Christian. The main emphasis was placed on "naming God," which, through a great variety of literary genres, distinguishes the kerygmatic dimension of these writings from the argumentative dimension of philosophy, within the poetic dimension to which it belongs. In the second lecture, entitled "Le soi mandaté" (The mandated self),[29] taking as my guide "narratives of vocations" of prophets and disciples in the Old and New Testament (or, as Paul Beauchamp calls them, *l'Un et l'Autre Testament*),[30] I explored the features by which the understanding of oneself best responded to the teaching and to the summoning which solicit the self in the manner of a call, imposing no constraints. The relation between call and response was therefore the strong connection between these two lectures.

Why, then, did I not keep them in this work, which itself developed

27. Paul Ricoeur, *From Text to Action,* trans. Kathleen Blamey and John Thompson (Evanston, Ill.: Northwestern University Press, 1991).

28. Northrup Frye, *The Great Code: The Bible and Literature* (New York: Harcourt Brace Jovanovich, 1982).

29. This lecture appears in *Revue de l'Institut catholique de Paris,* October–December 1988, pp. 83–99, under the title "Le sujet convoqé. A l'école des récits de vocation prophétique."

30. Paul Beauchamp, *L'Un et l'Autre Testament. Essai de lecture* (Paris: Éd. du Seuil, 1977).

out of the original Gifford Lectures? I plead more than simply the excuse that they would have made overly lengthy a work that was already voluminous, although this consideration did play an important role in my decision.

The primary reason for excluding them, which may be debatable and even perhaps regrettable, has to do with my concern to pursue, to the very last line, an autonomous, philosophical discourse. The ten studies that make up this work assume the bracketing, conscious and resolute, of the convictions that bind me to biblical faith. I do not claim that at the deep level of motivations these convictions remain without any effect on the interest that I take in this or that problem, even in the overall problematic of the self.[31] But I think I have presented to my readers arguments alone, which do not assume any commitment from the reader to reject, accept, or suspend anything with regard to biblical faith. It will be observed that this asceticism of the argument, which marks, I believe, all my philosophical work, leads to a type of philosophy from which the actual mention of God is absent and in which the question of God, as a philosophical question, itself remains in a suspension that could be called agnostic, as the final lines of the tenth study will attest. It is in an effort not to make an exception to this suspension that the sole extension given to the nine studies conducted within the dimension of a philosophical hermeneutics consists in an ontological investigation that involves no ontotheological amalgamations.

I should like to add to this principal reason another one concerning the relation that the exercises in biblical exegesis, upon which my interpretation of the "Great Code" is based, maintain with the studies collected here. If I defend my philosophical writings against the acccusation of cryptotheology, I also refrain, with equal vigilance, from assigning to biblical faith a cryptophilosophical function, which would most certainly be the case if one were to expect from it some definitive solution to the aporias that philosophy produces in abundance, mainly in relation to the status of *ipse*-identity on the practical, narrative, ethical, and moral planes.

It must first be said that the schema of question and answer does not hold between philosophy and biblical faith. If the lecture on the "mandated self" involves the notion of response, this is placed over and against the notion of call, not that of question. It is one thing to answer a question, in the sense of solving a problem that is posed; it is quite another to

---

31. I shall not conceal the enchantment exerted on me by this passage from the end of Bernanos's *Journal d'un curé de compagne:* "It is easier than one thinks to hate oneself. Grace means forgetting oneself. But if all pride were dead in us, the grace of graces would be to love oneself humbly, as one would any of the suffering members of Jesus Christ."

respond to a call, in the sense of corresponding to the manner of existing proposed by the "Great Code."

Next, it must be asserted that, even on the ethical and moral plane, biblical faith adds nothing to the predicates "good" and "obligatory" as these are applied to action. Biblical *agapē* belongs to an economy of the gift, possessing a metaethical character, which makes me say that there is no such thing as a Christian morality, except perhaps on the level of the history of *mentalités,* but a common morality (one that I attempt to articulate in the three studies devoted to ethics, morality, and practical wisdom) that biblical faith places in a new perspective, in which love is tied to the "naming of God." It is in this sense that Pascal placed charity on a level higher than that of bodies and of minds. If a dialectic of love and justice results from it, this in itself presupposes that each of the terms preserves its allegiance to the order to which it belongs. In this sense, the autonomy of the analyses I propose of the ethical and moral determinations of action is confirmed by a meditation grafted onto the poetics of *agapē* which is placed in parentheses voluntarily by the analyses of the present work.

Finally—and perhaps most of all—if, under the title of "mandated self" and "respondent," the determinations of the self in this work are found to be intensified and transformed by the recapitulation that biblical faith proposes, this recapitulation by no means serves as a sly revenge of the foundational ambition that my hermeneutical philosophy never ceases to combat. The reference of biblical faith to a culturally contingent symbolic network requires that this faith assume its own insecurity, which makes it a chance happening transformed into a destiny by means of a choice constantly renewed, in the scrupulous respect of different choices. The dependence of the self on a word that strips it of its glory, all the while comforting its courage to be, delivers biblical faith from the temptation, which I am here calling cryptophilosophical, of taking over the henceforth vacant role of ultimate foundation. In turn, a faith that knows itself to be without guarantee, following the interpretation given by the Lutheran theologian Eberhard Jüngel in *God as the Mystery of the World,*[32] can help philosophical hermeneutics to protect itself from the hubris that would set it up as the heir to the philosophies of the cogito and as continuing their self-foundational claim.

In these matters the present work recognizes that it belongs to what Jean Greisch has called the hermeneutical age of reason.[33]

---

32. Eberhard Jüngel, *God as the Mystery of the World* (Edinburgh: Clark, 1983).
33. Jean Greisch, *L'Âge herméneutique de la raison* (Paris: Éd. du Cerf, 1985).

"Person" and Identifying Reference

A Semantic Approach

In this first study, I shall begin with the most modest sense that can be given to the notion of *identification*. To identify something is to be able to make apparent to others, amid a range of particular things of the same type, of *which* one we intend to speak. It is along this path of identifying reference that we encounter the person for the first time, considering this term in an equally modest sense as globally distinguishing this entity from physical bodies. At this elementary stage, identifying is not yet identifying oneself but identifying "something."

1. Individual and Individualization

I want to establish here that the person is, to begin with, one of the things that we distinguish by means of identifying reference. To do this, I shall undertake a preliminary inquiry into the procedures by which we individualize "something" in general and consider it as an indivisible example within a species.[1] Language, indeed, is constituted in such a way that it does not condemn us to the choice, as Bergson long maintained, between the conceptual or the ineffable. Language contains specific connecting units that allow us to designate individuals. In speaking of individualization rather than of individual, I highlight the fact that the ascription of individualities can be based, depending on the various lexical resources of natural languages, on widely varying degrees of specification. One language may make finer dinstinctions than another in some particular area, and this corresponds to the respective features of each natural language; what is common to all is individualization, the operation rather than the result.

1. I propose the term "individualization" rather than "identification," more common to English than to French, to designate the procedure in question. Peter Strawson, however, to whom we shall give a great deal of credit in the second part of this study, has given the name *Individuals* (London: Methuen, 1957) to his own work on the identification of particulars. I want to take this opportunity to express my debt to the work of J. C. Pariente, *Le Langage et l'individuel* (Paris: A. Colin, 1973).

As a process, individualization may be broadly characterized as the inverse of classification, which eliminates the singular under the name of the concept. But if we simply stress the adjective "inverse," we then underscore two purely negative features of the individual, namely that it is a type that is neither repeatable nor divisible without alteration. These negations do indeed carry us to the side of the ineffable. But just because this is an inverse movement does not mean that language is without resources, as though it were limited to classification and predication. The individualizing intention begins where classification and predication leave off but draws support from these operations and, as we shall see, gives them new impetus. We individualize only if we have conceptualized.[2] And we individualize with a view to describing more. It is because we think and speak in concepts that language has to repair, as it were, the loss caused by conceptualization. In order to do this, however, it does not employ only the same procedures as those by which it conceptualizes, namely predication. What are these procedures?

Logicians and epistemologists group together under the common heading "individualization operators" procedures as different as definite descriptions (e.g., the first man to walk on the moon, the inventor of the printing press, proper names (Socrates, Paris, the moon), and indicators such as I, you, this, here, now. Let us stress that at this stage of our investigation, the human individual is accorded no privilege in any of the three classes of operators, not even in that of indicators, as we shall see in a moment. To designate one and only one individual is the individualizing intention. The privilege accorded the human individual in our choice of examples—the first man who . . . , Socrates, I, you, and so forth—comes from the fact that we are especially interested in individualizing the agents of discourse and of action. We do this by projecting the results of subsequent stages of the process of identification, which we shall discuss in later studies, back to the first stage considered.

A word about each of the three categories of operators: a definite description consists in creating a class that has but a single member through the intersecting of well-chosen classes (man, walk, moon). Logicians find an interest in this process for two reasons: (1) because it seems to be continuous with classification and predication, and (2) because it would appear to encourage the construction of a language free of proper names and indicators (i.e., free of personal and deictic pronouns), if indeed the other operators could be reduced to them. In fact, such a language can be

---

2. Characterizing individualization as the inverse of specification is to turn away from the direction taken by Leibniz with his "universal characters" (cf. Pariente, *Langage*, pp. 48ff., and Strawson, *Individuals*, pp. 117ff.).

constructed as Quine and others have shown. But as Pariente forcefully states, this is not a language that can be spoken in a concrete situation of interlocution; it is an artificial language that can only be written and read. In this respect, if definite descriptions resort to classification and predication procedures, this is with the aim, no longer of classifying, but of opposing one member of a class to all the others. The minimal otherness that is required designates *this* element of the class, but not the rest of the class. A single one set off from all the others. In this sense, the aim of definite descriptions is indeed ostensive, even if the procedure is predicative.

As for proper names, these are limited to singularizing an unrepeatable, indivisible entity without characterizing it, without signifying it on the predicative level, and so without giving any information about it.[3] From a purely logical point of view, abstracting from the role of appellation in the denomination of individuals (to which we shall return later), singular denomination consists in making a *permanent* designation correspond to the unrepeatable and indivisible character of an entity, regardless of its occurrences. The same individual is designated by the same name. How? Simply by assigning the same phonic chain to the same individual in all of its occurrences. But, you might say, there is no relation between the two terms of this bi-univocal relation. But precisely this designation, which is at once singular and permanent, is not intended for description but for empty designation. Almost meaningless (Pariente), the proper name admits all predicates and so calls for subsequent determination. Otherness, for a second time, is incorporated into designation: a single name, among the list of available names, permanently designates a single individual in opposition to all the others of the same class. Once again, the privilege accorded the proper names assigned to humans has to do with their subsequent role in confirming their identity and their selfhood.[4] And even if in ordinary language proper names do not completely fill their role,[5] at

3. For Frege's semantics, proper names in logic designate real beings. "Socrates" is the name of the real Socrates. The name is therefore a tag that is attached to the thing. We shall examine later the problem posed by the proper names of fictive beings, such as Hamlet and Raskolnikoff.

4. In fact, in ordinary language we are familiar not only with the proper names designating humans, because we are interested for other reasons too in a certain permanence belonging to peoples, families, and individuals, one which is constituted on another level than that on which the operators of individualization function. We name cities, rivers, and even stars in relation to human behavior with respect to them (inhabiting, navigating, relating labors and days in calendar time). In this sense, identifying by naming states more than individualizing.

5. The overdetermination alluded to in the previous note explains why common proper names are but rarely logically pure proper names. This is the case for family names: the rules of denomination connected to the matrimonial status of women in our culture, at least in

least their aim is indeed to designate in each case one individual to the exclusion of all the others in the class considered.

The third class of individualizing operators, that of indicators, contains the personal pronouns ("I", "you") and deictic terms, which group together demonstratives ("this," "that"), adverbs of place ("here," "there," "over there"), adverbs of time ("now," "yesterday," "tomorrow"), and verb tenses ("he came," "he will come"). Unlike proper names, these are intermittent indicators which—and this is of capital importance—designate in each case different things. What alone is determinant here is the relation to the utterance, taken as a fixed point. "Here" is any place close to the source emitting the message; "now" is any event that is contemporary with the message. "I" and "you," to be sure, stand out from the group as interlocutors, subjects of utterance. At this stage, however, an utterance is still treated as an event in the world—a bizarre sort of object, to be sure, yet one occurring in the external world. This is why, situated in relation to an utterance as an event, all the indicators are on the same level. In one phase of his work, Russell thus attempted to organize the indicators in relation to the "this," in opposition to their characterization from another point of view as "egocentric particulars." Pariente, however, is correct in saying that the reference point for a "this" and for an ego is *this* utterance; in this sense, I should say that the demonstrative attached to the utterance wins out over the ascription to a particular speaker and listener, to a particular place and time.[6]

I draw three conclusions from this preliminary analysis:

1. Individualization rests on specific designation procedures, distinct from predication, aiming at one and only one specimen, to the exclusion of all the others of the same class.

2. These procedures have no unity apart from this aim.

3. Alone among the operators of identification, the indicators aim at the "I" and the "you," but they do so by the same token as the deictic terms, because they retain their reference to the utterance, understood as an event in the world.

2. The Person as a Basic Particular

How are we to move from the individual at large to the individual that each of us is? In *Individuals,* P. F. Strawson develops a strategy which we

the predominant practice, result in the fact that Jeanne Dupont can designate two different people: the unmarried sister of Pierre Dupont and his wife.

6. The term *repérage* (reference point, location) is well chosen (Pariente opposes *repérer* to describing): it designates a very rudimentary stage, far removed from selfhood. It indicates a simple decentering of all the facts and states of things within the sphere of utterance, still considered an event in the world.

shall adopt as a general framework within which we shall later place new analyses, as we work toward a determination of the self that is increasingly ample and concrete. This strategy consists in isolating, among all the particulars to which we may refer in order to identify them (in the sense of individualizing given above), privileged particulars belonging to a certain type, which the author calls "basic particulars." Physical bodies and the persons we ourselves are constitute, in this masterful strategy, such basic particulars in the sense that nothing at all can be identified unless it ultimately refers to one or the other of these two kinds of particulars. In this way, the concept of person, just as that of physical body, is held to be a primitive concept, to the extent that there is no way to go beyond it, without presupposing it in the argument that would claim to derive it from something else.

If we had to provide an ancestor for this strategy, it would most certainly be Kant—not the Kant of the second *Critique,* but instead the Kant of the *Critique of Pure Reason.* What we are going to undertake is indeed a sort of transcendental deduction of the notion of person, by showing that if we did not have available to us the schema of thought that defines this notion, we could not engage in the empirical descriptions that we make in this regard in ordinary conversation and in the human sciences.

Let us note straightaway that this treatment of the person as a basic particular does not stress the capacity belonging to the person to designate himself or herself in speaking, as will be the case in later studies based on the power of the subject of utterance to designate itself; here, the person is one of the "things" about which we speak rather than itself a speaking subject. To be sure, the two approaches to the subject—that of identifying reference and that of self-designation—are not to be radically opposed to one another. They will be seen to intersect in two ways from the very outset of the analysis. First, it is within a situation of interlocution that speaking subjects designate to their interlocutors which particular they choose to speak about out of a range of particulars of the same type, and that they assure themselves through an exchange of questions and answers that their partners are indeed focusing on the *same* basic particular as they. The theory of basic particulars intersects a second time with that of self-reference in connection with the role that the former assigns to demonstratives, in the broad sense of the term, and among these to personal pronouns and possessive adjectives and pronouns; these expressions, however, are treated as indicators of particularity, hence as instruments of identifying reference. Nevertheless, despite the mutual overlapping between the two theoretical approaches, in the referential approach one is not concerned with the question of whether or not the self-reference implied in the speech situation or in the use of demonstratives is part of the meaning given to the thing to which one refers considered as a person. What matters here is instead the sort of predicates characterizing that particular we call a person. The person, therefore, remains on the side of the thing about which we speak rather than on the side of the speakers themselves who designate themselves in speaking.

One must not, of course, be misled by the use of the word "thing" to speak of persons considered as basic particulars. It simply serves to indicate the fact that our initial investigation of the notion of person belongs to the general problem of identifying reference. A "thing" is something we speak about. And we speak about persons, in speaking about entities that make up the world. We speak about them as "things" of a particular type.

We may wonder, though, if we can get very far in determining the concept of person without bringing in, at one time or another, the power of self-designation that makes the person not merely a unique type of thing but a self. We may even wonder whether persons can be distinguished from bodies if self-designation is not included in the very determination of the meaning ascribed to the sort of things to which identifying reference is directed. In Strawson's strategy, however, the recourse to self-designation is intercepted, so to speak, from the very start because of the central thesis that determines the criterion for identifying anything as a basic particular. This criterion is the fact that individuals belong to a single spatiotemporal schema, which, it is stated from the start, contains *us,* in which *we ourselves* take our place. The self is indeed mentioned in this passing remark, but it is immediately neutralized by being included within the same spatiotemporal schema as all the other particulars. I would readily say that, in *Individuals,* the question of the self is concealed, on principle, by that of the same in the sense of *idem.* What matters for unambiguous identification is that the interlocutors designate the same thing. Identity is described as sameness (*mêmeté*) and not as selfhood (*ipséité*). Having said this, I am not unaware of the advantage gained at the start by a problematic that prefers the question of the same over that of the self. It warns us, from the outset, against the possible drift toward private and nonpublic reference to which a premature recourse to self-designation might lead. By placing its main emphasis not on the *who* of the one speaking but on the *what* of the particulars about which one speaks, including persons, the entire analysis of the person as a basic particular is placed on the public level of locating things in relation to the spatiotemporal schema that contains it.

The primacy accorded in this way to the *same* in relation to the *self* is especially underscored by the cardinal notion of reidentification. For it is not only a matter of being certain that we are speaking of the same thing, but also that we can identify several occurrences of the thing as the same. Now this can be done only by means of spatiotemporal location: the thing remains the same in different times and places. Finally, the fundamental sameness is that of the spatiotemporal framework itself: we use the same framework on different occasions (Strawson, *Individuals*, p. 32). "Same" then means unique and recurrent. As to the manner in which we ourselves belong to the framework, this is not set up as a problem in itself. Yet, as will be confirmed by what follows, understanding the way in which our own body is at once a body like any other (situated among other bodies) and an aspect of the self (its manner of being in the world) is a problem of vast proportions. However, one might bluntly reply, in a problematic of identifying reference, the sameness of one's body conceals its selfhood. And this will be the case as long as the characteristics related to possessive pronouns and adjectives ("my," "mine") have not been connected to the explicit problematic of the self. This will happen only within the framework of the pragmatics of language.

3. Bodies and Persons

Strawson's second broad thesis in *Individuals* is that the first basic particulars are bodies, since these best satisfy the criteria of localization in the single spatiotemporal schema. Moreover, the criterion and what satisfies it appear to be so well suited to one another that one may venture to say that what solves the problem is also what allows us to pose it (p. 40). Strawson accurately observes that this mutual selection of the problem and its solution is characteristic of all transcendental arguments.

The priority given to bodies is of the highest importance for the notion of person. For, if it is true, as we shall state later, that the concept of person is a notion no less primitive than that of the body, this is to evoke not a second referent, distinct from the body, such as the Cartesian soul, but in a manner yet to be determined, a single referent possessing two series of predicates: physical predicates and mental predicates. The fact that persons are bodies *too* is a possibility that is held in reserve in the general definition of basic particulars, according to which the latter are bodies or possess bodies. Possessing bodies is precisely what persons do indeed do, or rather what they actually are.

The primitive notion of body reinforces the primacy of the category of sameness that we have just stressed: bodies are indeed eminently identifiable and reidentifiable as being the same.

The advantage of this new strategic decision is certain: to say that bodies are the first basic particulars is to eliminate, as possible candidates, mental events; that is, representations or thoughts, whose shortcoming is that they are private rather than public entities. Their lot, as specific predicates of persons, is simply postponed. They first had to be dislodged from the dominant position of ultimate reference, which they occupy in a sub-jectivist idealism.

The first corollary to this sort of disqualification of mental events as basic particulars is that the person cannot be held to be a pure consciousness to which would then be added, in a secondary role, a body, as is the case in all mind-body dualisms. Mental events and consciousness, in whatever sense the term is taken, may then figure only among the special predicates attributed to the person. This dissociation between the person as a public entity and consciousness as a private entity is of the greatest importance for what follows in our analyses.

A second corollary, and one of equal importance, is that the person to whom mental events and a consciousness are attributed, in the manner we shall discuss, is not expressed exclusively by the first and second person, singular pronouns, as would be the case in a theory of reflexive utterance. They are attributed to *someone,* who may also be a third person. If the person is that of which we speak, it is granted that in a speech situation, we may speak of the pain experienced by a *third* party, who is not one of the interlocutors.

Numerous difficulties, however, arise from this strategic decision to attack the problem of the person by way of that of objective bodies situated in one and the same spatiotemporal framework. First, the question of our own body returns to the forefront, no longer simply in terms of our belonging to a single spatiotemporal schema, but in terms of the relation of our own body to the objective world of bodies. In a strictly referential problematic, without explicit self-designation, there is not actually any problem of the lived body. One has to confine oneself to the following observation: "That which one calls one's body is, at least, a body, a material thing" (*Individuals,* p. 89). This is true, but the body is *mine* in a sense that assumes that the logical force of the self is acknowledged. Second, disqualifying mental events and consciousness from occupying the position of basic particulars, hence from that of logical subject, has as its counterpart the increased concealment of the question of the self. This difficulty is not foreign to the previous one, inasmuch as mental events pose the same sort of problem as one's own body, namely the close connection that appears to exist between possession and selfhood. But this difficulty implies something more: one does not see how the property of selfhood could be placed in a list of predicates ascribed to an entity, even one as original as the person. It would seem, instead, that this property is to be sought on the side of self-designation tied to utterance and not the side of the "thing" that serves as a term in an identifying reference. What poses a problem to us is rather understanding how the self can be at one and the same time a person of whom we speak and a subject who designates herself in the first person, while addressing a second person. This will pose a problem, for we must not allow a theory of reflexivity to rob us of the definite advantage of being able to consider the person as a third person, and not only as an I and a you. The difficulty will be instead understanding how the third person is designated in discourse as someone who designates himself as a first person. And this possibility of shifting self-designation from the first to the third person, however strange this may be, is doubtless essential for the sense we ascribe to the *consciousness* that we join to the very notion of mental event: for can we ascribe mental events to a third person without assuming what this third party *feels*? Now feeling does indeed seem to characterize a first-person experience. The notion of mental event thus must include both the predicates ascribed to a certain sort of entity and the self-designation that we first understand in the first person because of the self-designation that accompanies the act of utterance. I admit that at this stage of the analysis, we have no way of accounting for this strange structure belonging to mental events, which are at once predicable of persons and self-designating.

4. The Primitive Concept of Person

We shall now take up the demonstration of the *primitive* character of the notion of person. I shall retain three points here.

1. First, the notion of person is determined by means of the predicates that we ascribe to it. The theory of person is therefore contained within the general framework of the theory of predication applied to logical subjects. The person is thus in the position of a logical subject in relation to the predicates that are ascribed to it. This is the great strength of the approach to the person by way of identifying reference. It is now important to stress, however, that the question of the self continues to be hidden to the extent that the ascription of these predicates to the person carries with it no specific character to distinguish it from the common process of attribution. Strawson shows no surprise at the strange implications for a general theory of predication of the following statement: "We ascribe to ourselves certain things." I do not deny the force that this alignment of ascription to ourselves in accordance with the attribution to something may possess: the "we" here receives so little emphasis that it becomes the equivalent of "one." Ascribing is what is done by anyone, by each one, by one, in relation to anyone, each one, one. The force of this *each one* will have to be preserved, for it marks a designation that is distributive rather than anonymous, in an analysis of the self stemming from the theory of utterance.

2. Second, the strangeness related to the primitive notion of per-

son—or better, that which makes this notion a primitive one—consists in
the fact that the person is the "same thing" to which two different sorts of
predicates are ascribed: physical predicates which the person shares with
bodies, and mental predicates which distinguish it from bodies. Once
again we touch upon the force of the same in the sense of identical found
in *Individuals.* "One's states of consciousness, one's thoughts and sensations, are ascribed *to the very same thing* to which these physical characteristics, this physical situation, is ascribed" (*Individuals,* p. 89). Note how
skillfully the passive form of the proposition ("are ascribed") consolidates
the neutrality of the "one" of "one's states of consciousness, one's thoughts
and sensations," and, along with it, the insignificance of the subject of the
ascription as utterance and as speech act. When the self of ascription is
omitted, the field is open for the sameness of *the very same thing,* to which
physical and mental predicates are ascribed. It is this sameness that provides the force of the argument and that accounts for a portion of the
strangeness of our own concept of person.

The major advantage of this identity of ascription is, as we saw above,
that it eliminates, through a simple analysis of the grammar of our discourse on the person, the hypothesis of a double reference to the soul or
to consciousness, on the one hand, and to the body, on the other, of two
series of predicates. It is the same thing that weighs sixty kilograms and
that has this or that thought. The paradox of this kind of analysis is that it
is due to the neutralization of the specific character of ascription (that
which concerns its *sui*-referential character) that the central problem of the
person can be brought to the forefront, that is, the phenomenon of double
attribution without double reference: two series of predicates for one and
the same entity. Sameness and selfhood, one is tempted to say, are two
kinds of problems that mutually conceal one another. Or, to be more
precise, the problem of identifying reference, where the sameness of the
logical subject is promoted to the fore, requires merely a marginal sui-
reference to the "one," which is "each one."

In the same stroke, the question of the foundation of this sameness is
posed. Can we be content with the argument according to which our mental framework is constituted in such a way that we cannot make identifying
references to persons without assuming the identity of the predicates? May
we not seek to justify the well-suitedness of this structure of our thought
of our language by an analysis of the very conception of the person in its
psychophysical unity? Did we not take this unity for granted above, when
we spoke of the mutual fitness between the spatiotemporal schema and the
properties of bodies, considered as entities that are directly localizable,
discrete, continuous in space, and stable in time? Every effort to justify the

structure of thought that imposes the sameness of the subject of ascription unavoidably encounters the question of one's own body, as this has been evoked at each of the critical moments of the analysis. Even stranger than the notion of person is that of one's own body. The "dependence" mentioned in Strawson's paradoxical argument, where three distinct bodies are capable of being implied in sight (one body to open its eyes, another to direct the gaze, and a third to locate the place from which one sees [*Individuals*, pp. 90ff.]) seems to be considered an ordinary case of causal connection (p. 92). The argument is already somewhat unsatisfying when we are speaking of someone's body, even of each person's body; it is even less so when we introduce first-person possessive adjectives: *this body as mine*. After all, is the possession implied by the adjective "mine" of the same nature as the possession of a predicate by a logical subject? There is, to be sure, a semantic continuity between *own, owner,* and *ownership* (or *possession*), but it is relevant only if we confine ourselves to the neutrality of *one's own*. And even under this condition of the neutralization of the self, the possession of the body by someone or by each one poses the enigma of an untransferable property, which contradicts the common notion of property. This is indeed a strange attribution, that of a body which can never be made or taken away. We shall have to return later to this most peculiar strangeness.

3. The third point of the analysis of the primitive concept of person will pose the greatest difficulty to a theory of the self that is solely derived from the reflexive properties of utterance. It concerns another kind of sameness assumed by language and by thought when we characterize a particular thing as a person. It concerns the psychic predicates to the exclusion of the physical ones. It consists in the fact that the mental events, which we relegated above from the level of basic entities to that of predicates, have the remarkable property, precisely as predicates, of retaining the same sense whether they are attributed to oneself or to others, that is, to anyone else: "the ascribing phrases," Strawson says, "are used in just the same sense when the subject is another as when the subject is oneself" (*Individuals,* p. 99).

Here is a new case of sameness: not "the same thing" receiving two kinds of predicates, but "the same sense" ascribed to psychic predicates, whether they are ascribed to oneself or to someone else. Once again the logical force of the same eclipses that of the self, even though in the preceding statement it is a question of the subject and of oneself. However, in the philosophical context of identifying reference the status of the subject is specified solely by the nature of what is ascribed to it, namely psychic and physical predicates. This is why the personal pronouns "I" and "you" have not even to be mentioned; "oneself" is enough. Not even the suffix "-self" poses a problem, since "oneself" and "another" can be replaced by "someone" and "anyone else" (*Individuals,* p. 97).

I wish to state, one last time, the importance that must be attached to this thesis. First, as we shall later discuss at greater length, this double ascription to "someone" and to "anyone else" is what allows us to form the concept of mind, that is, the repertory of psychic predicates ascribable to each one. Let us state straightaway that the distributive character of the term "each one" is essential for understanding what I shall henceforth call "the psychic." Mental states are, to be sure, always those *of* someone, but this someone can be me, you, him, anyone. Next, whatever the true sense of the correlation "someone"–"anyone else" may be (and I shall return to this in a moment), it imposes a constraint from the start, one just as unavoidable as the necessity to consider the person from the outset as a "thing" that possesses a body; as we said, there is no pure consciousness at the start. We shall now add: there is no self alone at the start; the ascription to others is just as primitive as the ascription to oneself. I cannot speak meaningfully of my thoughts unless I am able at the same time to ascribe them potentially to someone else: "To put it briefly. One can ascribe states of consciousness to oneself only if one can ascribe them to others. One can ascribe them to others only if one can identify other subjects of experience. And one cannot identify others if one can identify them *only* as subjects of experience, possessors of states of consciousness" (*Individuals,* p. 100).

One may wonder once again, however, whether the constraint of this identical ascription is to be taken as a simple fact, whether it is an inexplicable condition of discourse itself, or whether we can account for it on the basis of a clarification of the terms "oneself" and "another." Yet one cannot help wondering whether the expression "my experiences" is equivalent to the expression "someone's experiences" (and correlatively, if the expression "your experiences" is equivalent to the expression "someone else's experiences"). The strictly referential analysis of the concept of person can manage to avoid mentioning "I-you," which belongs to the reflexive analysis of utterance, for a long time, but it cannot avoid it in the end. This analysis is forced to evoke it, at least marginally, once it inquires into the criteria for ascription in one situation or the other: ascribing a state of consciousness to oneself is *felt;* ascribing it to someone else is *observed.* This dissymmetry in ascription criteria leads to a shift in emphasis onto the suffix "-self" in the expression "oneself." To say that a state of consciousness is felt is to say that it is self-ascribable. Yet how can we fail to include in the notion of something self-ascribable the self-designation of a subject, who designates himself or herself as the possessor of this state of consciousness? Correlatively, how, in clarifying the expression "other-ascribable," can we fail to stress the otherness of the other, with all the paradoxes of ascribing to this other the power of self-designation on the very basis of external observation, if it is true, as Strawson grants, that this other must also be considered a *self-ascriber* (*Individuals*, p. 108). In view of these questions the thesis of the sameness of self-ascription and of ascription to someone else demands that we account for the equivalence between ascription criteria (whether experienced or observed); and, beyond this equivalence, that we account for the reciprocity that remains to be interpreted between someone who is me and another who is you. In other words, we have to acquire simultaneously the idea of reflexivity and the idea of otherness, in order to pass from a weak correlation between someone and anyone else, which is too easily assumable, to a strong correlation between belonging to the self, in the sense of mine, and belonging to another, in the sense of yours.

The task, it must be admitted, is not easy; the enrichment that the notion of person can receive from a reflexive theory of utterance cannot result from substituting a theory of utterance for a theory of identifying reference, under pain of ceding to the aporias of solipsism and to the impasses of private experience. The task will be, instead, to preserve the initial constraint of conceiving of the *psychic* as ascribable to each one, in this reconstruction of the logical force of "each one" on the basis of the opposition between "I" and "you," which underlies the strong opposition between oneself and someone else. In this sense, if a purely referential approach in which the person is treated as a basic particular is to be completed by another approach, it cannot be thereby abolished but will be preserved in this very surpassing.[7]

---

7. In this critical analysis of the notion of person from the perspective of identifying reference, I have not mentioned the suggestion Strawson makes at the end of his chapter on the concept of person, to shift "to a central position in the picture" (*Individuals*, p. 111) a certain class of psychic predicates which involve *doing something*. The privilege belonging to this class of predicates is that they, better than any others, exemplify the three major points of the basic concept of person. Action would thereby appear to offer, if not a reply, at least the beginning of a reply to the question "what (is) it in the natural facts that makes it intelligible that we should have this concept" (of person) (ibid.). The third study evaluates, not only the relevance of the notion of action for a theory of the person as a basic particular, but its ability to carry the analysis beyond this first theoretical framework. Before that, however, we must develop the other aspect of linguistic philosophy which then, taken as a whole, serves as the organon for the theory of action.

Utterance and the Speaking Subject
A Pragmatic Approach

In the preceding study we pursued as far as possible the first of the two main approaches to the problem of the self stemming from the philosophy of language—namely, that of identifying reference. Now we shall attempt a new breakthrough in the direction of the self by following the second path, that of *utterance,* the central element of which is today the theory of speech acts. In doing this, we move from a semantics, in the referential sense of the term, to a *pragmatics,* that is, to a theory of language as it is used in specific contexts of interlocution. This shift of approach should not, however, lead us to abandon the transcendental viewpoint: pragmatics is intended to undertake not an empirical description of acts of communication but an investigation into the conditions that govern language use in all those cases in which the reference attached to certain expressions cannot be determined without knowledge of the context of their use, in other words, the situation of *interlocution.*

This new type of investigation is all the more promising in that what it places at the center of the problem is not the statement but the utterance, the act of speaking itself, which designates the speaker reflexively. Pragmatics, therefore, puts directly on stage the "I" and the "you" of the speech situation.

At the end of this exploration of the ties between the act of utterance and the subject of this act, our problem will be to confront the respective contributions of our two series of inquiries, the referential inquiry and the reflexive inquiry, with an integrated theory of the self (at least on the linguistic level). It indeed quickly becomes apparent that pragmatics can no more be substituted for semantics than semantics could carry out its task without borrowing from pragmatics. Just as a complete determination of the person as a basic particular proved to be impossible without resorting to the capacity for self-designation belonging to the subjects of experience, in the same way the complete analysis of the reflexivity implied in acts of utterance can be carried through only if a particular kind of referential value can be attributed to this reflexivity. What will finally prove most fruitful for our investigation into the self are the mutual overlappings of the two disciplines. At first glance, the two approaches seem to impose discordant priorities: for the referential inquiry, the person is considered primarily in terms of the third person, the one of whom someone speaks. For the reflexive inquiry, however, the person is primarily an I who speaks to a you. The question will be finally to determine how the "I-you" of interlocution can be externalized in a "him" or a "her" without losing its capacity to designate itself, and how the "he/she" of identifying reference can be internalized in a speaking subject who designates himself or herself as an I. It is indeed this exchange between personal pronouns that seems to be essential to what I have just termed an integrated theory of the self on the linguistic level.

1. Utterance and Speech Acts

We have proof that the reflexive approach is not purely and simply opposed to the referential approach in the fact that we first encounter the phenomena requiring an explicit theory of utterance as additional complications along the path of the reference of certain statements. Under the evocative title *La Transparence et l'énonciation,* François Récanati introduces pragmatics by making reflexivity appear as a factor of opacity that interferes with the presumed transparency of a sense that, without it, would allow the referential intention to pass through.[1] It is not unimportant that reflexivity is first presented as an obstacle to the transparency sought in the act of referring to. If, with the ancients and again with the Port-Royal grammarians, the sign is defined as a thing that represents some other thing, then transparency consists in the fact that the sign, in order to represent, tends to fade away and so to be forgotten as a thing. This obliteration of the sign as a thing is never complete, however. There are circumstances in which the sign does not succeed in making itself absent as a thing; by becoming opaque, it attests once more to the fact of being a thing and reveals its eminently paradoxical structure of an entity at once present and absent. The major circumstance in which the sign's opacity is made evident is that in which the fact of utterance, by being reflected in the sense of the statement, comes to influence the referential intention itself.[2] The new turn taken by the theory of utterance with the analyses of speech acts, therefore, does not constitute anything radically new. It adds

1. François Récanati, *La Transparence et l'énonciation* (Paris: Éd. du Seuil, 1979).
2. "In the meaning of a statement," Récanati writes, "the fact of its utterance is reflected" (ibid., p. 7). Later we shall discuss the justification for this vocabulary of reflection in a context in which utterance (the act of uttering) is treated as an event in the world.

new life to a paradox well known to classical thinkers, resulting from the rivalry, in the same statement, between the representative intention of the statement and what the Port-Royal grammar called "virtual reflection." In modern terms, this paradox consists in the fact that the reflection of the act of utterance in the sense of the statement is an integral part of the reference of most of the statements of everyday life in the ordinary situation of interlocution.

The time has come to show in what way the *theory of speech acts* contributes to recognizing this factor of opacity belonging to the signs of discourse, and to specify the sort of subject that is fostered in this way. The ground will thus be prepared for a confrontation between the results attained along these two different lines of the philosophy of language as regards the self.

The theory of speech acts is well known. I shall, therefore, be brief in the sketch that follows of its development from Austin to Searle. The starting point was, as we know, the distinction established in the first part of *How to Do Things with Words* between two classes of statements, performatives and constatives.[3] The former are remarkable in that the simple fact of uttering them amounts to accomplishing the very thing that is stated. The example of promises, which will play a decisive role in the ethical determination of the self, is noteworthy in this regard. To say "I promise" is actually to promise, that is, to pledge to do something and (let us assume) to do for someone else what I say I shall do. (The French translation of Austin's book has the title *Quand dire, c'est faire*, "When saying is doing.") And notice how the "I" is marked at the start: performatives have the feature of "doing-by-saying" only when expressed by verbs in the first person singular of the present indicative. The expression "I promise" (or, more precisely, "I promise you") has the specific sense of promising which the expression "he promises" does not have, for the latter retains the sense of a constative (or, if one prefers, of a description).

The distinction between performative and constative, however, was to be surpassed by Austin himself, opening the path in this way for Searle's speech-act theory.[4] The initial opposition between two classes of statements is incorporated into a more radical distinction that concerns the hierarchical levels that can be discerned in all statements, whether constative or performative. It is of the utmost importance for the following discussion that these levels designate different *acts*. If saying is doing, it is indeed in terms of acts that we must speak of saying. Here resides the

3. J. L. Austin, *How to Do Things with Words* (Cambridge: Harvard University Press, 1962).

4. John R. Searle, *Speech Acts* (Cambridge: Cambridge University Press, 1969).

major point of intersection with the theory of action that will be developed later: in a manner that remains to be determined, language is included on the very plane of action.

What acts are interwoven in this way in the global act of saying? We are familiar with the cardinal distinction between locutionary act, illocutionary act, and perlocutionary act. The locutionary act is the predicative operation itself, namely saying something about something. It is not without importance that the term "act" is not reserved for the illocutionary level but is already applied to the locutionary plane: the fact is thereby stressed that *it is not statements that refer to something but the speakers themselves who refer in this way;* nor do statements have a sense or signify something, but rather it is the speakers who mean to say this or that, who understand an expression in a particular sense. In this way, the illocutionary act is joined to a more fundamental act—the predicative act. As its name indicates, the illocutionary act consists in what the speaker *does in* speaking. This doing marks the "force" in virtue of which the utterance "counts as" a statement, a command, a piece of advice, a promise, and so on. The notion of illocutionary force thus allows us to generalize beyond performatives, properly speaking, the implication of doing in saying. In the constatives themselves, a type of doing is included that most often remains unsaid but that can be made explicit by placing a prefix before the statement of the form "I affirm that," which is comparable to the "I promise that," the form in which all promises can be rewritten. There is nothing arbitrary about this procedure. It satisfies the substitution criterion established in logical semantics; that is, the two statements "the cat is on the mat" and "I affirm that the cat is on the mat" have the same truth value. But one has the transparence of a statement that is wholly traversed by its referential intention; the other has the opacity of a statement that refers reflexively to its own utterance. The prefix of explicit performatives thus becomes the model for the linguistic expression of the illocutionary force of all statements.

Now it is in prefixes such as these that the "I" is brought to expression. Moreover, in the "I" of the prefix we have a complex situation of interlocution which is shown to contribute to the complete sense of the statement. Facing the *speaker* in the first person is a *listener* in the second person to whom the former addresses himself or herself—this fact belongs to the situation of interlocution. So, there is not illocution without allocution and, by implication, without someone to whom the message is addressed. The utterance that is reflected in the sense of the statement is therefore straightaway a bipolar phenomenon: it implies simultaneously an "I": that speaks and a "you" to whom the former addresses itself. "I affirm that" equals "I declare to you that"; "I promise that" equals "I promise you that." In short, utterance equals interlocution. A theme begins to take shape in this way which will continue to take on greater dimensions in the studies that follow, namely that every advance made in the direction of the selfhood of the speaker or the agent has as its counterpart a comparable advance in the otherness of the partner. At the stage of our present study, this correlation does not yet take on the dramatic character which the polemical confrontation between two narrative programs will introduce at the heart of interlocution. Speech-act theory does not provide us in this respect with any more than the dialogic skeleton of highly diversified interpersonal exchanges.

An additional element can be supplied to this allocutive relation without leaving the plane of utterance, if the theory of speech acts is completed by the theory of utterance proposed by Paul Grice,[5] according to which all designation consists in an intention of meaning which implies in its aim the expectation that the interlocutor has on his or her side the intention of recognizing the primary intention for what it is meant to be. Interlocution, interpreted in this way, is revealed to be an exchange of intentionalities, reciprocally aiming at one another. This circularity of intentions demands that the reflexivity of utterance and the otherness implied in the dialogic structure of the intentional exchange be placed on the same level.

Such is, broadly speaking, the contribution of speech-act theory to the quest of the self. The question is now to prepare the awaited confrontation between referential theory and the theory of reflexive utterance by some critical remarks concerning the nature of the subject put into relief in this way by the theory of utterance.

2. The Subject of Utterance

We shall now turn a critical eye to the relation between the utterance and its utterer.

At first sight, this relation does not seem to cause any problem. If the reflection of the statement onto the act of utterance introduces some opacity into the referential intention that traverses the meaning of the utterance, it does not seem at first that the relation internal to the utterance between the speech act and its author is in itself opaque; there is no reason

---

5. H. Paul Grice, "Meaning," *Philosophical Review* 66 (1957): 377–88; "Utterer's Meaning and Intentions," ibid. 78 (1969): 147–77; "Utterer's Meaning, Sentence-Meaning, Word-Meaning," in *The Philosophy of Language,* ed. J. R. Searle (Oxford: Oxford University Press, 1977), pp. 54–70. These three articles are reprinted now in Paul Grice, *Studies in the Way of Words* (Cambridge: Harvard University Press, 1989), pp. 213–23, 86–116, 117–37, respectively.

to assume that the subject of the utterance constitutes the opacity of what is opaque.

Is not the implication of the utterer in the utterance unambiguously apparent in the substitution for all illocutionary acts of the formula developed for explicit performatives: "I assert that," "I command that," "I promise that"? Is it not in this very prefix that the "I" is marked, and is it not through this prefix that "I" attests to its presence in all utterance?[6]

In addition, thanks to this mention of the subject in the intentional prefix of extensional statements, it becomes possible to group together, as two partial wholes, coordinated under the aegis of pragmatics, the theory of speech acts, which we have just summed up, and the *theory of shifters* as indicators, which we have already mentioned under the title of identifying procedures, hence from the perspective of a referential semantics. This manner of classification proves to be beneficial for both of the partners. On the one hand, the analysis of speech acts finds in the functioning of shifters the complement necessary for anchoring, as it were, the utterer to the utterance. On the other hand, the shifters (e.g., "I," "this," "here," "now") are separated from the other two categories of identifying operators introduced in the first study, namely proper nouns and definite descriptions, which are related to semantics, while the first are maintained within the gravitational sphere of pragmatics.

Furthermore, at the same time as the indicators taken together are separated from the group of identifying operators, the "I" is promoted to the first order of shifters, which, considered outside of the reflexive relation of utterance, present no privileged order. Related to the act of utterance, the "I" becomes first and foremost among the indicators; it indicates the one who designates himself or herself in every utterance containing the word "I." The other indexes—that is, the deictic terms ("this," "here," "now") are grouped around the subject of utterance. "This" indicates every object situated in the neighborhood of the utterer; "here" is the very place where the utterer is; "now" designates any event that is contemporaneous with the utterance made by the utterer.

By becoming the pivotal point of the system of indicators, the "I" is revealed in all its strangeness in relation to every entity capable of being placed in a class, characterized, or described. "I" so little designates the referent of an identifying reference that what appears to be its definition—namely, "any person who, in speaking, designates himself or her-

6. It is a problem to know whether or not the connection between the "I" and the utterance that includes it belongs to the much broader problematic of attestation, which we briefly touched upon in the discussion of the relation of imputation of mental predicates to the entity of the person. The question will become increasingly more nuanced in the studies that follow.

self"—cannot be substituted for the occurrences of the word "I." There is
no equivalence from a referential point of view between "I am happy" and
"the person who designates himself in speaking is happy." The failure to
pass the test of substitution is decisive here; it confirms the fact that the
expression does not belong to the order of entities capable of being identified by the path of reference. The logical gap is therefore deep between
the indicative function which is that of the "I," on the one hand, and the
referent in the sense of the first study, on the other.[7]

The singular nature of the functioning of indicators, which reinforces
the theory of speech acts, is confirmed by a decisive feature with which we
shall conclude our review of the results of pragmatics concerning the positing of the subject in discourse. This feature seals the autonomy of the
present approach to the subject in relation to the previous approach by
way of identifying reference. The dichotomy between the two approaches
is marked in a spectacular way by their opposite manners of dealing with
personal pronouns. Whereas in the referential approach it is the third person that is privileged—or at least a certain form of the third person,
namely "he/she," "someone," "each one," "one"—the theory of indicators
in connection with the theory of speech acts not only privileges the first
and second persons but expressly excludes the third person. This brings to
mind Benveniste's anathema concerning the third person.[8] According to
him, only the first and the second persons deserve this name grammatically, the third person being the nonperson. The arguments in favor of this
exclusion can be narrowed down to a single one: "I" and "you" are sufficient to determine a situation of interlocution. The third person can be
anything about which someone is speaking—thing, animal, or human being: this is confirmed by the disparate uses of the pronoun "it" ("it is
raining," "it is necessary") as well as the multiplicity of third-person expressions ("one," "each one," "that one," etc.). If the third person is so
grammatically inconsistent, this is because it does not exist as a third person, at least in an analysis of language that takes as its basic unit the instance of discourse, as it is expressed in the sentence. There is no better
way of binding the first and second person to the event of utterance than
by excluding the third person from the field of pragmatics, where it (he,
she) is only spoken of, among other things.

Having said this, does the pact between utterance and the indicators
("I" and "you"), followed by the deictic terms ("this," "here," "now"), ren-

7. To this gap corresponds a difference, well known since Wittgenstein, between *describing* and *showing*. "I" can be indicated or shown, not referred to or described. We shall draw
some consequences from this later.

8. Emile Benveniste, *Problems in General Linguistics,* trans. Mary Elizabeth Meek (Coral
Gables, Fla.: University of Miami Press, 1977).

der impossible all discordance between the theory of utterance and that of its subject?

Two or three remarks made earlier, which may have passed unnoticed, should, however, have alerted us: the first concerns the key term in the theory of speech acts: the word "act," not "agent." Another remark concerns the illocutionary force of the act, that is, according to the definition given by G. Granger, "that which allows us to give messages specific communication functions or allows us to specify the conditions of their use."[9] "The illocutionary element," in Granger's prudent expression, can therefore be defined and submitted to a detailed topology, without there being any explicit mention of the author of discourse. At the price of this elision the transcendental conditions of communication can be entirely stripped of psychological import and held to be regulations of language (*langue*) and not of speech. But how far can this depsychologizing be taken, if an ego must still be taken into consideration?

A second remark that was not underscored adds to our puzzlement: the reflexivity in question up to now has been constantly attributed, not to the subject of utterance, but to the utterance itself: "In the meaning of a statement," Récanati writes, "the fact of its utterance is reflected" (*La Transparence et l'énonciation,* p. 7). This declaration should surprise us to the extent that it relates reflexivity to the utterance considered as a fact, that is, as an event produced in the world. What we earlier termed an act has become a fact, an event that takes place in a common space and in public time—in short, a fact occurring in the same world as the facts and states of the things that are cited referentially by declarative or assertive statements.

Finally, the fact that the sign is also a thing, which as we mentioned earlier marks the very opacity of the sign, is brought to the foreground by the reflection of the fact of the utterance in the meaning of the statement. Récanati's declarations are unequivocal in this respect: "A statement is something by reason of its utterance" (p. 26); and again: "The utterance is posited as a being" (p. 27). Ultimately, one would have to say that reflexivity is not intrinsically bound up with a self in the strong sense of self-consciousness. In the statement "in the meaning of a statement, the fact of its utterance is reflected," the expression "is reflected" could just as well be replaced by "is mirrored." The paradox we encounter here is that of a reflexivity without selfhood: a "self" without "oneself"; or, in other words, the reflexivity characteristic of the fact of utterance resembles an inverted reference, a retroreference, to the extent that the referral is made to the *factuality* that makes the statement "opaque." In the same stroke,

9. G. G. Granger, *Langages et épistémologie* (Paris: Klincksieck, 1979), p. 170.

instead of opposing a reflexivity hostile to any characterization in terms of reference and the intention of the extralinguistic fact, the opposition mentioned earlier between indicating or showing and describing opposes simply sui-reference and reference *ad extra*. But are reflexivity and sui-reference equivalent notions? Does not the "I" disappear as an I when the statement is attributed to two references moving in opposite directions— one reference pointing in the direction of the thing signified and another in the direction of the signifying thing? This shift was in fact contained in the definition of the sign handed down from the ancients: a thing that represents another thing. Now, how can an act be simply a thing? More important, how can the subject that refers and signifies be designated as a thing while remaining a subject? Have we not lost from sight two of the most precious conquests of the theory of utterance, namely:

1. that it is neither statements nor even utterances that refer but, as was recalled earlier, speaking subjects, employing the resources of the sense and the reference of the statement in order to exchange their experiences in a situation of interlocution;

2. that the situation of interlocution has the value of an event only inasmuch as the authors of the utterance are put on stage by the discourse in act and, with the utterers in flesh and blood, *their* experience of the world, *their* irreplaceable perspective on the world?

The drift of pragmatics toward a concept of sui-reference in which the main accent is placed on the *factuality* of the utterance can be canceled out only if we are willing to stop for a moment and consider a number of paradoxes, even aporias, that pragmatics runs up against, as soon as we put questions to it regarding the status of the subject of the utterance as such, and not simply regarding the act of utterance treated as a fact, as an event that occurs in the world, in this very world to which the things belong that we refer to in reference *ad extra*. Confronting these paradoxes and aporias is placing oneself in line with the question "who?"—who is speaking?—which opened the problematic of identification.

The first paradox is the following: the expression "I" is fraught with a strange ambiguity; Husserl spoke in this regard of a necessarily ambiguous expression. On the one hand, "I" as a personal pronoun belonging to the system of language is a member of the paradigm of personal pronouns. As such, it is an empty term which, unlike generic expressions that keep the same sense throughout different uses, designates in each instance a different person for each new use; "I" in this first sense applies to anyone who, in speaking, designates himself or herself and who, in assuming this word, takes charge of language as a whole, according to Benveniste's fine expression. As a vacant term of this sort, "I" is a migrating term; it is a position with respect to which several virtual utterers can be substituted for one another. Whence the term "shifter," which has been attributed to all similar terms, including the deictic series, for the sake of assigning the empty term to a single, current, actual utterer, who assumes *hic et nunc* the illocutionary force of the act of utterance. On the other hand, in the same stroke, we have moved from one sense of the expression "I" to the other. We are no longer stressing the *substitutable* aspect of the shifter, but instead the *fixation* that results from speaking. We have passed from the paradigmatic viewpoint, by virtue of which "I" belongs to the table of pronouns, to the syntagmatic viewpoint, by virtue of which "I" designates in each case only one person to the exclusion of any other, the one who is speaking here and now. Let us, along with Granger, call this referring to a nonsubstitutable position, to a unique center of perspective on the world, *anchoring*.[10] The paradox consists quite precisely in the apparent contradiction between the substitutable character of the shifter and the nonsubstitutable character of the phenomenon of anchoring.

To be sure, one can give an explanation for this first paradox without going outside of pragmatics; the solution proposed, however, will simply put off the difficulty, leaving it intact on a higher level. The explanation in question rests on the distinction introduced by Peirce between type and token, which we must be careful not to confuse with that between a genus and a particular, to the extent that it holds only in the case of indices.[11] The type concerns the order of "in each case"; the token is on the order of "a single time," on the plane of actual utterance. Between the two, all contradiction disappears if we are willing to consider that the type implies in its very notion a necessary choice between candidates for the job of speaking subject.[12] By reason of this necessary choice, the shifter takes on a distributive value in relation to all the instances of "in each case" that govern the exclusive attribution of the term "I" to a single, actual speaker. One can then say, without further paradox, that the actual anchoring of the token "I" is correlative to the substitutable character of the type "I" in the distributive and nongeneric sense of the constitution of the index. Here we meet up with Husserl: the amphibology of the "I" is that of a

10. Ibid., pp. 174–75. My explanation of the paradoxes related to the subject of utterance owes a great deal to this work.

11. Cf. Charles S. Peirce, *Collected Papers,* ed. Charles Hartshorne and Paul Weis (Cambridge: Harvard University Press, 1931–35), 4:537. See also C. S. Peirce, *Écrits sur le signe,* trans. G. Deledalle (Paris: Éd. du Seuil, 1978), p. 190.

12. Unlike the substitutability of the utterer characteristic of the shifter, Granger observes, "the fixation of the referral of each message constitutes a necessary choice, regulating communication" (*Langages et épistémologie,* p. 174).

necessarily *occasional* meaning. The term "occasional" has the very precise sense of connecting the "in each case" belonging to the type to the token's "a single time."

However, does the distinction between type and token do away with every paradox concerning the "I"? This becomes doubtful, if we consider that it is perfectly compatible with an interpretation of reflexivity in the sense of sui-reference, that is, in the sense of a referral to the factuality of a spatiotemporal event occurring in the world. It is with regard to the act of utterance, understood as a worldly fact, that one can say that it takes place only once and has no existence except in the instant in which the utterance is produced. We then speak of different occurrences of the same sign, which differ numerically only with respect to their spatiotemporal position, while illustrating the same type. The sign in question, however, is the act of utterance treated as a fact. The "I" is then intended only obliquely, that is, as an expression bearing internally the mark of an explicit performative of the form "I affirm that," "I order that," "I promise that."

The fact that the distinction between type and token concerns primarily the utterance rather than the utterer is confirmed by the highly technical analyses of those expressions termed *token-reflexives*. To be sure, these expressions are warrantable utterances within the theory of speech acts, but it can well be said of them that they refer to a fact that takes place in public space and time—in short, in the world.[13] In this way, one avoids the paradox that arises only when the subject of utterance is thematized in itself. Yet this paradox cannot remain hidden for long, once we confront the strangeness of the relation between a single speaker and the multiplicity of his or her utterances. If each of these constitutes a different event, capable of taking its place in the course of things in the world, is the subject common to these multiple events itself an event?[14] We recall Husserl's hesitation to thematize in a distinct way the *ego* of the *cogito cogitatum*. Nor have we forgotten the difficulties inherent in metaphoric expressions such as

13. Récanati, *La Transparence et l'énonciation*, pp. 153–71. In chapter 8 on the topic of token-reflexivity, the author writes, "Someone's utterance of this sentence [water boils at 100°C.], the fact that someone says this, is an event that occurs, as do all events, at a certain time and in a certain place: this spatiotemporally determined event is the saying, or the utterance. The fact of saying something is an event, like the fact of breaking one's leg, the fact of receiving a decoration, the fact of being born or dying. The expression 'the fact of saying' underscores the eventlike character of utterance, insofar as it is a fact: a fact is above all something that 'takes place,' or that 'is the case,' to use an English expression" (p. 153).

14. The question of the status of the event in an investigation of selfhood will return several times in the course of this work, in particular in the discussion of Donald Davidson's claims regarding action (third study) and those of Derek Parfit regarding personal identity (sixth study).

Ichstrahle, "ray of the self," or *Ichpol,* "the self as the identical pole of acts," which characterize the sort of radiation or emanation that defines the relation of the unique speaker to the multiplicity of speech acts.

It is here that the paradox is transformed into an aporia. The type-token relation is no longer of any help, any more than the relation between the "I" as shifter and the anchored "I." In question is the very notion of anchoring the token "I." Indeed, what sense are we to attach to the idea of a *singular perspective* on the world? The aporia that guides us here is the one Wittgenstein continually returned to from the *Tractatus* to the *Investigations* and the *Blue Notebook.* I shall call it the aporia of anchoring. The privileged point of perspective on the world which each speaking subject is, is the limit of the world and not one of its contents.[15] And yet, in a certain enigmatic way, after it appeared to be self-evident, the *ego* of the utterance appears *in the world,* as is confirmed by assigning a proper name to the one who proffers the discourse. Indeed, it is I, P.R., who am and am not the limit of the world. In this regard the following text from the *Blue Notebook* hoists the aporia high: "By *I* (in 'I see') I did not mean: Ludwig Wittgenstein, although, addressing someone else, I could say: 'It is now L.W. who is actually seeing,' except that this is not what I meant to say."[16] The lack of coincidence between the "I" as the world-limit and the proper name that designates a real person, whose existence is confirmed by public records, reveals the ultimate aporia of the speaking subject. The aporia remained hidden in one version of pragmatics, in which the reflexive referral aimed less at the *ego* of the utterance than at the *fact* of the utterance, considered an event in the world. Reflexivity could then, without any apparent difficulty, be assimilated to a subtle kind of reference, the reference to the world-event of utterance. The utterance was then aligned with the things in the world of which we speak. This assimilation

15. Granger states this well: "The referral to utterance is not of the same order as properly semantic referrals. The utterance then is not located *in* the world of which one speaks; it is taken as the limiting reference of this world" (*Langages et épistémologie,* p. 174). The restrictive clause with which this quotation ends will take on its full meaning only later, when we shall attempt to join together reflexivity and referentiality.

16. This text is cited by Granger (ibid., p. 175). Granger also quotes the following passage: "The word 'I' does not mean the same as 'L.W.' even if I am L.W., nor does it mean the same as the expression 'the person who is now speaking'. But that doesn't mean: that 'L.W.' and 'I' mean different things. All it means is that these words are different instruments in our language" (Ludwig Wittgenstein, *The Blue and Brown Books* [New York: Harper and Row, 1958], p. 67). In this aporia, Granger sees essentially the confirmation of the nonempirical character of the conditions of the possibility of communication: "If one adopts this view, one sees that the phenomenon of *anchoring,* taken as the privileged position of a center of perspective, indeed expresses a nonempirical condition of the complete communication of an experience" (*Langages et épistémologie,* p. 175).

is no longer possible, at least not without taking into consideration the aporia of anchoring, once the emphasis is placed on the act in the fact and on the "I-you" in the act.

3. The Intersection of the Two Paths of the Philosophy of Language

In order to resolve this aporia, it is necessary, in my opinion, to make the two paths of the philosophy of language converge—the path of identifying reference and that of the reflexivity of the utterance. At the end of the first path, as we recall, the person appeared as a basic particular, irreducible to anything else: it was the one of whom one spoke and to whom one attributes physical and mental predicates. At the end of the second path, the subject appeared as the couple made up of the one who is speaking and of the one to whom the former is speaking, to the exclusion of the third person, who has become a nonperson. The convergence of these two approaches is assured by the mutual borrowings which allow each to accomplish its own design. We recall that, according to the theory of identifying reference, the third person acquires its complete signification of person only if the attribution of mental predicates is "accompanied," to borrow Kant's expression, by the capacity for self-designation, transferred from the first to the third person, in the manner of a citation placed within quotation marks. The other, the third person, says in his or her heart: "I affirm that." The phenomenon of anchoring becomes comprehensible now only if the "I" of "I affirm that," "I order that," "I promise that," is extracted from the prefix of an action verb and posited for itself as a person—that is, as a basic particular amid all of the things of which one speaks. This assimilation between the "I" who is speaking to "you" and the "him/her" of whom one is speaking functions in an opposite direction to the assigning of the power of self-designation to "him" or "her." The comparison consists here in a unique type of objectification, namely the assimilation between the "I," subject of the utterance, and the person, the irreducible basic particular. The notion of sui-reference, whose coherence we questioned earlier, is in fact of a mixed nature, resulting from the interconnection of reflexivity and identifying reference.

Before raising the question whether this mixture of the reflexive "I" and the person referred to is not an arbitrary assimilation—in other words, whether it is any more than a fact of language, unavoidable perhaps, yet one that cannot be derived from anything on a basic level—it is important to show that the intersecting of these two paths of the philosophy of language does indeed govern the functioning of all the indexes and can be identified on the basis of highly precise linguistic operations.

The deictic "now" offers a good starting point for this demonstration, since the assimilation of the act of language to a fact was also a result of characterizing the utterance as an event, or an instance of discourse. In addition, I now have available a detailed analysis of temporal deictic terms borrowed from my earlier work, *Time and Narrative* 3. There I tried to show that what we designate by the term "now" results from the conjunction between the living present of the phenomenological experience of time and the indifferent instant of cosmological experience. Now this conjunction does not consist in a mere juxtaposition of the notions belonging to distinct universes of discourse; it rests on precise operations that assure what I called the inscription of phenomenological time onto cosmological time, the model of which is the invention of calendar time. From this inscription results a *dated now*. Without a date, the definition of the present is purely reflexive: what occurs now is any event that is contemporaneous with the moment when I speak; reduced to itself, the sui-reference of the moment of speech is simply the tautology of the living present. This is why it is always today for us. We step outside of the tautology by posing the question, What day is it? The reply consists in supplying a date, that is, in making the living present correspond with one of the days that can be counted on the calendar. The dated now is the complete sense of the deictic "now."

The same thing is true with respect to "here"; it is opposed to "there" as the place in which I am situated corporally. This absolute place has the same limit-of-the-world character as the *ego* of the utterance. The spatial metaphor of orientation in space is even at the source of the idea of the subject as the center of perspective itself not situated in the space occupied by the objects of discourse; absolutely speaking, "here," as the place where I am, is the zero point in relation to which all other places become near or far. In this sense, "here" is nowhere. And yet, the use of "here" in conversation implies a minimal topographical knowledge, thanks to which I can situate my "here" in relation to a system of coordinates, whose source-point is just as indifferent as the instant of cosmological time. The place functions therefore in the same way as the date, namely by inscribing the absolute "here" onto a system of objective coordinates. By virtue of this inscription, comparable to the phenomenon of dating, the complete signification of the deictic "here" is that of a *localized here*.

From the deictic terms "now" and "here," we can return to the indicators "I-you." The conjunction between the subject as the world-limit and the person as the object of identifying reference rests on a process of the same nature as inscription, illustrated by calendar dating and geographic localization. The fact that the phenomenon of anchoring is assimilable to an inscription is marvelously attested to by the expression that so intrigued

Wittgenstein, namely "I." The relation between the personal pronoun "I," taken as the subject of attribution, and the proper noun, as the designation of the token of a basic particular, is a relation of inscription in the institutional sense of the term. "I" is literally inscribed by virtue of the illocutionary force of a particular speech act—naming—onto the public list of proper names in accordance with the conventional rules that govern the attribution of family names and first names. (Thus, in France and in other countries, the family name is imposed by kinship rules—matrimonial rules, rules of filiation—and the first name is chosen, relatively freely, by the legal parents, hence by someone other than the person who bears the name; in this sense, naming is through and through an act of inscription.) The expression is so well chosen that what we call a birth certificate contains a triple inscription: a proper name conforming to the rules of naming that have just been mentioned, a date in accordance with the usage of the calendar, a birthplace conforming to the rules of localization in public space, the whole inscribed in public records. Inscribed in this way, the "I" is, in the proper sense of the term, registered. From this registration, there results the one who states, "I, so and so, born on . . . , at. . . ." In this way, "I" and "P.R." mean the same person. It is therefore not arbitrary that the person (object of identifying reference) and the subject (author of the utterance) have the same meaning; an inscription of a special kind, performed by a special act of utterance—naming—performs this conjunction.

On the threshold of our conclusion, one final question remains. Can this assimilation of the person of identifying reference to the reflexive, token "I" be founded on a more fundamental reality?

This can only be done, in my opinion, by stepping outside of the philosophy of language and inquiring into the kind of being that can lend itself in this way to a twofold identification—as an objective person and as a reflecting subject. The phenomenon of anchoring itself suggests the direction in which we must move; it is the direction indicated in the preceding analysis, namely the absolutely irreducible signification of one's own body. We recall that the possibility of attributing mental and physical predicates to the same thing seemed to us to be grounded in a twofold structure of the lived body, namely its status as an observable, physical reality and its belonging to what Husserl termed, in the "Fifth Cartesian Meditation," the "sphere of ownness" or of "what is mine." The same double allegiance of the lived body founds the mixed structure of "I so and so"; as one body among others, it constitutes a fragment of the experience of the world; as mine, it shares the status of the "I" understood as the limiting reference point of the world. In other words, the body is at once a fact belonging to the world and the organ of a subject that does not belong to the objects of which it speaks. This strange constitution of the lived body extends from the subject of utterance to the very act of utterance: as a voice proffered outside by breath and articulated by phonics and gesticulation, the utterance shares the fate of all material bodies. As the expression of a sense intended by a speaking subject, the voice is the vehicle of the act of utterance insofar as it refers to an "I," the irreplaceable center of perspective on the world.

These brief reflections anticipate the moment when we shall have to leave the plane of language, to which we have strictly confined ourselves in this first series of investigations. The strange status of one's own body arises out of a wider problematic, where the stakes are the ontological status of the being that we ourselves are, a being that comes into the world in the mode of incarnation.

An Agentless Semantics of Action

The two studies that follow concern the theory of action, in the restrictive sense this term has acquired in the English-language works classified under this title. They maintain a highly complex relationship with the preceding studies. On the one hand, the philosophy of language that has just been presented plays the role of organon with respect to the theory of action, inasmuch as this theory utilizes, in the descriptions it offers of action sentences, the now-classical analyses of identifying reference and of speech acts. On the other hand, actions are such remarkable entities, and the tie between action and its agent constitutes such an uncommon relation, that the theory of action has become something quite different from the simple application of the linguistic analysis sketched out above. Moreover, by achieving the autonomy of a separate discipline, the theory of action has made apparent, as a repercussion, new linguistic resources, in its pragmatic as well as its semantic dimension. In the same stroke, the difficulties, paradoxes, and aporias with which the preceding studies ended take on new proportions within the framework of the theory of action.

The complexity of the relation between the theory of language and the theory of action will be tested, first in the course of this study within the context of philosophical semantics, then in the next study within the context of the pragmatics of language. In each case, we shall sound out the enigma of the relation between the action and its agent, but with different resources resulting from the initial distinction between semantics and pragmatics. What does action, we shall ask, teach about its agent? And to what extent can what is learned in this way contribute to clarifying the difference between *ipse* and *idem*?

Two remarks must be made at the start of the present study. It must first be understood that, in a semantics of action, the agent of action can be dealt with in the same way that, in the analysis of basic particulars in our first study, the person of whom one is speaking could be designated as an entity to which predicates of different orders were ascribable. However, the explicit recourse of the reflexive nature of the utterance by which the subject of discourse designates himself or herself is not within the province of a semantics based on identifying reference. This first limitation must be recognized from the start, if we are not to be disappointed by the relatively sparse results of the theory of action—itself so rich in rigorous analyses—on the precise point of the conceptual determination of the agent of action. Actually, only at the end of the next study will it be possible to make the path of identifying reference intersect with the path of the self-designation of the speaking subject, and so to thematize in an explicit manner the self-reference of an acting subject.

The second limitation of the present inquiry concerns the relative narrowness of the field of examples covered by the concept of action. We shall, of course, consider chains of actions, mainly in connection with the analysis of practical reasoning, but we shall bracket the unifying principle that makes these action-chains into higher-order practical units, which, in a later study, we shall call *practices*. Now this second limitation has important consequences: by not speaking of those practices worthy of the name—techniques, crafts, arts, games—we shall also fail to take into consideration the processes of hierarchization among practices which allow us to speak of the narrative unity of a life. And bracketing in this way any principle characterizing such practices and any hierarchization among practices, we are led in turn to disregard the ethical predicates belonging to the family of the good and the just. Indeed, only these higher-order practical units explicitly assume, in addition to the logical connection which we shall discuss here, a teleological significance in accordance with the good and a deontological significance in accordance with the just. This second limitation is perfectly legitimate to the extent that the semantics of action is confined in principle to describing and analyzing utterances in which indivdiuals state their actions, and it excludes any prescriptive attitude toward what is permitted or forbidden. To this very extent, the agent of action will have little resemblance to a self who is responsible for both words and actions. So it should not be surprising to find the author of action appearing here as an ethically neutral agent, as free of blame as of praise.

1. The Conceptual Schema of Action and the Question "Who?"

At first glance, the inquiry appears promising in the effort to refer action to its agent. Action and agent belong to the same conceptual schema, containing notions such as circumstances, intentions, motives, deliberations, voluntary or involuntary motions, passiveness, constraints, intended or unintended results, and so on. The open-ended nature of this enumeration is less important here than its organization as a network. What is important in establishing the range of meaning of each of these terms is the fact that they all belong to the same network; the relations of intersignification thus guide the respective meanings, so that knowing how to use one of them is actually knowing how to use the entire network in a meaningful and appropriate manner. This is a coherent language game, in which the rules governing the use of one term are systematically related to the rules governing the use of another term. In this sense, the notional network of action shares the same transcendental status as the conceptual framework of basic particulars. Indeed, unlike the empirical concepts developed by the human sciences, from biology to sociology, the entire network serves to determine what "counts as" an action, for example, in the psychological sciences of behavior and in the social sciences of conduct. It is the specificity of this network in relation to the general determination of the concept of person, established in the first study, that will henceforth concern us.

An effective way of establishing the reciprocal determination of the notions belonging to this network of action is to identify the chain of questions that can be asked on the subject of action: who did or is doing what, with what design, how, in what circumstances, with what means and what results? The key notions of the network of action draw their meaning from the specific nature of the answers given to the specific questions, which are themselves cross-signifying: who? what? why? how? where? when?

One can see in what sense this method of analysis would appear to be promising: a privileged access to the concept of agent is afforded by the replies provided to the question "who?" What Strawson called the "same thing," to which are attributed both mental and physical predicates, is now someone in response to the question "who?" Now this question reveals a genuine affinity with the problematic of the self as we outlined it in the Introduction. In Heidegger, the investigation of "who?" belongs to the same ontological sphere as that of the self (*Selbstheit*).[1] Hannah Arendt, echoing Heidegger, links the question "who?" to a specific characteristic of the concept of action, which she contrasts to those of labor and work.[2] While labor is wholly externalized in the thing produced, and while the work changes culture through its embodiment in documents, monuments, and institutions in the space of appearing opened up by politics, action is that aspect of human doing that calls for narration. And it is the function of narration, in its turn, to determine the "who of action." Despite these

---

1. Martin Heidegger, *Being and Time,* trans. John Macquarrie and Edward Robinson (New York: Harper and Row, 1962), §§25, 64.
2. Hannah Arendt, *The Human Condition* (Chicago: University of Chicago Press, 1958), chap. 5, "Action."

obvious affinities, it is a mistake to believe that the theory of action can lead this far. In Heidegger, the dependence of the problematic of *Selbst* on the existential *Dasein* draws the "who?" within the same ontological field of gravity. As for Hannah Arendt's "who?" it is mediated by a theory of action that exceeds the limits of the present analysis and will only have a place much later, when we pass from action in the narrow sense to practice in the broad sense we announced above.

The contribution of the theory of action to the question "who?" is, in fact, a considerably more modest one. For the reasons I shall state, it often even marks a retreat in relation to Strawson's problematic, inasmuch as the latter squarely posed the question of attributing to "someone," considered to be the "same thing," predicates characteristic of the person. But this question of attribution tends to be relegated to the sidelines to make room for the much more important question of the relation between the questions "what?" and "why?" (*quoi? et pourquoi?*) which overrides the relation between the pair of questions "what?-why?" and the question "who?" The theory of action presents itself in the first place as a challenge to any determination of the Heideggerian "who?" At the end of this study our problem will be to turn this challenge to our advantage, by making the investigation into the "what?-why?" of action the grand detour at the end of which the question "who?" returns in force, strengthened by all the mediations traversed by the investigation of "what?-why?"

What explains the concealment of the question "who?" by the analyses of the replies to the questions "what?" and "why?"? It is not enough to say that, from the perspective of semantics, heavily dominated by the way in which discourse refers to something, one can scarcely expect to come across replies to the question "who?" which are able to escape being characterized as a something, understood as a component of the so-called real world. To be sure, the problematic of the event, which we shall discuss later, will amply verify this capture of the "who" by the "something." This explanation, however, is not sufficient inasmuch as nothing prevents the question "who?" from preserving an autonomy in relation to the questions "what?-why?" within the referential framework of something in general. As I have already stated in connection with Strawson, the replies specific to the question "who?" are of considerable interest, not in spite of, but owing to, the limitation of this referential framework. The question "Who did this?" can be answered by mentioning a proper name, by using a demonstrative pronoun (he, she, this one, that one), or by giving a definite description (so and so). These replies render something in general a someone. This is not negligible, even if this identification of the person as someone who acts (or undergoes) lacks the self-designation which is accessible only to the pragmatic approach, which points up the I-you relation of the speech situation. If, however, the referential approach of the agent of action cannot cross this threshold, it has at least the advantage of fanning out the full arc of personal pronouns—I, you, he, she, and so forth—and by so doing of granting the conceptual status of person to the grammatical third person. On the level of a simple semantics of action, the question "who?" admits of all the replies introduced by any of the personal pronouns: I do, you do, he does.[3] This undiscriminating acceptance of the three grammatical persons, in both singular and plural form, is the great strength of referential analysis.

So it is not the referential approach as such that prevents us from deploying the resources contained in the replies to the question "who?" in the field of human action. I shall therefore attempt in the following study to pursue the analysis I have just begun and to take up again, using the resources of the analysis of the replies to the questions "what?-why?" the problem left in abeyance at the end of this study, namely that of the ascription of action to its agent.

The occultation of the question "who?" can, in my opinion, be attributed to the orientation imposed by analytic philosophy on its treatment of the question "what?" by placing it in an exclusive relation to the question "why?" Despite the enormous differences which will progressively appear between different varieties of the analytic philosophies of action, they can all be said to share a common focus on the question of what "counts" as an action among the events in the world. It is in relation to the notion of *something that occurs* that one then strives to determine the descriptive status of actions. This orientation given to the question "what?" in relation to the notion of world-event contains potentially the effacement to the point of occultation of the question "who?", despite the stubborn resistance that the replies to this question oppose to their alignment with the strongly impersonal notion of event. The answers to the question "what?" applied to action do indeed tend to separate themselves from the answers required by the question "who?" as soon as the answers to the question "what?" (what action has been performed?) are submitted to an ontological category that is in principle exclusive of the category of selfhood, namely the event in general, the "something that occurs."[4]

This dissociation of the "what?" and the "who?", resulting in the shift

3. It will be the task of pragmatics to organize the list of personal pronouns in relation to the illocutionary force of different speech acts. Then we shall be able to say in a confession or a claim, "It is I who . . ."; in thanking or accusing, "You are the one who. . . ." These different pragmatic determinations, however, are all grafted upon the someone of referential analysis.

4. We shall return here to a discussion begun above concerning the epistemological and ontological status of events. Cf. the end of sec. 2 in the second study.

of the problematic of action to the side of an ontology of the anonymous event, was made possible by a coalition in the opposite direction between the question "what?" and the question "why?": in order to determine what counts as an action (the question "what?"), one sought in the explanation for the action (the question "why?") the very criterion for what deserves to be described as an action. The use of "why?" in the explanation of action thus became the arbiter of the description of what counts as action.

2. Two Universes of Discourse: Action vs. Event, Motive vs. Cause

For didactic reasons, I shall distinguish three levels in this capture of the "what?" by the "why?" and, finally, in the capture of the pair "what?-why?" by an ontology of the impersonal event. I shall not concern myself here with the chronology of the debate, even if the positions I shall refer to are staggered in time more or less in the order in which I shall present them. My points of reference shall remain nonetheless more theoretical than historical.

I shall characterize the first level in terms of two major arguments: the first concerns the "what?" of action in its specificity; the second, the relation, also considered a specific one, between the "what?" and the "why?"

1. With respect to the first point, it is noteworthy that it was believed that, by taking the notion of event as its term of reference, the theory of action preserved the specificity of human action. To be sure, this was done first of all in order to oppose action to event. We shall see later through what turnabout the opposition became an inclusion. However, to begin with, opposition prevailed. Events, the argument ran, simply happen; actions, on the other hand, are what make things happen. Between happening and making happen there is a logical gulf, as is confirmed by the relation of the two terms in opposition to the idea of truth: what happens is the object of an observation, hence of a constative utterance which can be true or false. What is made to happen is neither true nor false but makes the assertion of a certain occurrence true or false, namely the action once it is accomplished. As the French language expresses it, *L'action faite est devenue un fait* (the action accomplished has become a fact). But making it true results from doing it. From this opposition it results that the "logical force of an action" cannot be derived from any set of statements bearing on the events and on their properties.[5]

---

5. A detailed presentation of this argument can be found in A. I. Melden, *Free Action* (London: Routledge and Kegan Paul, 1961), and in Stuart T. Hampshire, *Thought and Action* (Notre Dame, Ind.: University of Notre Dame Press, 1983). A comparable argument

I do not underestimate the merits of this approach to the problem of action. Among these I am prepared to include the elimination of certain prejudices resulting from a poor construction of the concept of action by so many authors; this would include pseudoconcepts such as kinesthetic sensations which would allow us to know as an internal event our production of voluntary motions, and this would include as well alleged affective sensations, which would allow us to know our desires, also considered as internal events. The logical defect consists in the fact that internal observation, as alleged here, is constructed after the model of external observation. This prejudice serves as the unseen support for the vain search for some internal event. One can speak in this regard of a "contemplative" prejudice, which invites the following question: "How do you know that you are doing what you are doing?" The answer is: "You know it by doing it."

I would compare the distinction between making something happen and happening to the distinction made by G. E. M. Anscombe between knowing-how and knowing-that.[6] Knowing-how does indeed have something to do with the events which Anscombe says are "known without observation." And this notion, in turn, authorizes us to speak of "practical knowledge" with respect to them. Now before being applied to the notion of intention, which will be discussed later, the notion of events that are known without observation is applied to expressions as primitive as the position of my body and my limbs and the gestures I make. Knowledge of the gesture is in the gesture: "This knowledge of what is done is practical knowledge. . . . A man who knows how to do things has practical knowledge" (Anscombe, *Intention*, p. 48).

These are certainly very strong arguments, at first glance. Their defect, however (defect by omission, so to speak), is to be concentrated on the "what" of action without thematizing its relation to the "who." By the same token, these arguments will prove to be extremely vulnerable to a critique which will result in making action a species of the genus "event," rather than an alternative term. The irony is that it is the opposition be-

---

is developed by Arthur Danto in *Analytical Philosophy of Action* (Cambridge: Cambridge University Press, 1973). Danto, however, emphasizes mainly the isomorphism characterizing two series of statements: on the one hand, m knows that s by means of evidence e; on the other hand, m makes a happen by doing b. Between being true that s and making it true that a happens, a certain logical homogeneity remains.

6. G. E. M. Anscombe, *Intention* (London: Basil Blackwell, 1979). I shall not dwell on this point here, for the argument will be set in another conceptual framework, centered on the notion of intention, in which I see the second level of concealment of the problematic of the self to the benefit of the problematic of events.

tween action and event that has opened the way for the absorption of the first term by the second.

2. The same paradoxical turnabout will occur on the second front opened by the theory of action. The "what" of action, in fact, is specified in a decisive way by its relation to the "why?" To say what an action is, is to say why it is done. The relation of one question to the other is unavoidable: one can hardly inform anyone else about what one does without saying at the same time why one is doing it. Describing is beginning to explain, and explaining more is describing better. It is here that a new logical gulf opens up, namely the one between motive and cause. A motive, it is noted, is already a motive for acting. As such, it is logically implied in the notion of action done or to be done, in the sense that the motive cannot be mentioned without mentioning the action for which it is the motive. The notion of cause, at least in the Humean sense, generally taken as a term of reference, implies on the contrary a logical heterogeneity between cause and effect, to the extent that I can mention one without mentioning the other (hence, the match on the one hand and the fire on the other). The internal, necessary (and in this sense, logical) connection characteristic of motivation is incompatible with the extrinsic, contingent (and, in this sense, empirical) connection of causality. As we see, the argument claims to be logical and not psychological, in that it is the logical force of the motivational connection that prevents classifying the motive as a cause. Motive is better interpreted as a reason-for; not that every motivation is rational, for this might exclude desire. Every motive is a reason-for, in the sense that the connection between motive-for and action is a relation of mutual implication. This is verified, according to this school of thought, by the very grammar of the word "wanting," which has a broader use than the term "desire" and which can be expressed as what one would like to do (be or have), what one would willingly do, reserving for the term "desire" a more restricted field, primarily an alimentary or sexual sense. The grammar proper to the term "wanting" requires that wanting can be named only in connection with that toward which it tends, that is, the action itself; wanting is wanting-to-do, wanting-to-get. Wanting, the argument continues, can be prevented, forbidden, or repressed, but even then it cannot be understood in any sort of logical independence from acting. In every instance there is logical involvement between wanting and doing; wanting something logically implies getting it. "Logically" signifies that, to use my terminology, wanting and doing mutually belong to one another. Following a logical chain of involvement, we move from wanting to trying to do and, finally, to doing.

This grammar of wanting confirms the criticism made above of the "contemplative" notion of internal events, observable by an inner eye.

Wanting is not a tension that an internal impression could make apparent; a bad grammar of the word "wanting," treated as a substantive, is responsible for this interpretation of wanting as an internal event, logically distinct from the action mentioned in public language. The elimination of internal entities, begun on the level of the first argument opposing action to event, is thus continued on the level of the second argument opposing motive to cause.

A variant of the same argument deserves to be mentioned: to evoke the reason for an action is to try to place the action in a broader context, generally one composed of rules of *interpretation* and of norms of execution, which are assumed to be shared by the agent and the community with which the agent interacts. In this way, I ask you to consider my gesture—for instance, raising my hand—as a greeting, a prayer, hailing a taxi, and so on. Although this type of reasoning will be fully developed only within the framework of an analysis of the illocutionary force of an utterance (as greeting, praying, calling, etc.) and so belongs to the pragmatics of action, it does strengthen the opposition between the two opposing schemata of explanation, to the extent that only one of them can be considered a form of interpretation. At the same time, a certain proximity becomes apparent between this conceptual analysis of action and the hermeneutical tradition, when the latter opposes understanding to explanation and makes interpretation a development of understanding. Interpreting, we read in *Being and Time,* is developing understanding by saying as what (*als was*) we understand something.[7] This kinship is not surprising, inasmuch as action can be treated as a text and the interpretation of motives as a reading.[8] Relating an action to a set of motives is like interpreting a text or part of a text in accordance with its context.

3. The kinship between this second type of argument and the first is obvious: the opposition between motive and cause shows a strict parallel with the opposition between action and event. The explanation of action in terms of motives even reinforces the description of action as that which "makes (something) happen." Action and motive are together on one side, just as event and cause both lie on the other, as indeed the Humean tradition prepares us to admit. We may therefore say, in Wittgenstein's sense, that action and its motives on one side, and the event and its cause on the other, belong to two separate "language games," which we must be careful not to confuse. The philosophy of action thus has the task, at least in an initial phase, of restoring to these two language games their respective coherence and their mutual independence. And yet this clear distinction

7. Heidegger, *Being and Time,* par. 32.
8. Ricoeur, *From Text to Action,* pp. 144–67.

between the two universes of discourse has been unable to resist the assaults of a conceptual analysis which is more interested in the shades of meaning to be distinguished in each of the terms of these two language games; the result has been the constant encroachment of one on the other to the point of rendering problematic the very principle of their dissociation. I shall situate my own investigation at this stage of encroachment, before moving to the stage at which the language game of action and of the reasons for acting is swallowed up by that of events and causality.

Allow me first to state why the dichotomous approach was destined to be heavily nuanced before being bluntly rejected.

To begin with, phenomenologically speaking, the opposition between motive and cause is not obligatory (later on we shall see that it is contestable on the very plane of logic where it is asserted). It seems instead that the category of wanting offers itself as a mixed category, whose appositeness is missed as soon as, for logical reasons, one casts motive on the side of the reason for acting. Even if one is attempting by this to underscore the originality of the mode of implication between motive and action, the danger remains that the reason-for will be taken in the sense of a technological, strategic, or ideological type of rationalization and that what constitutes the very peculiarity of wanting—namely that it offers itself as a meaning which can be expressed both within the sphere of justification and as a force which can be transcribed, more or less analogously, as belonging to the sphere of physical energy—will go unnoticed. This mixed character of wanting, of desire—the semantics of which I attempted to work out in my book on Freud[9]—finds a reflection on the very plane where the theory of action has chosen to place itself, namely that of ordinary language. Do we not ask, What prompted you to do this or that? In English one even says, What "caused" you to act that way?

I see three types of situation in which this sort of question is justified by a response in terms of cause. The first would involve the question, What prompted you to do this or that? to which one could provide an answer stating neither an antecedent in the sense of a Humean cause nor a reason-for in the rational sense but an incidental impulse, or a drive (*Treib*), as it is called in psychoanalysis. In the second type of situation, to a slightly different question—What usually makes you act this way?—the response mentions a disposition, an enduring or even permanent tendency. The third type of situation concerns a question such as, What made you jump? to which you reply, A dog frightened me. Here you are not linking the how to the why but the object to the cause. It is the feature peculiar to

9. Ricoeur, *Freud and Philosophy: An Essay on Interpretation,* trans. Denis Savage (New Haven: Yale University Press), 1970.

emotion, from the perspective of its linguistic expression, that its object is its cause and vice versa. These three contexts can be grouped together under the generic heading of *affect,* or *passion* in the ancient sense of the term. Indeed, in these three contexts, a certain passivity does seem to correlate with the action of doing something. The mediation of this passivity appears to be essential to the relation of wanting to acting, which cannot be reduced to the justification a purely rational agent would give of his or her action. This would be, precisely, an action without any element of desire! This phenomenology of wanting, extended to include affect, compels us to say that even in the case of rational motivation, motives would not be motives for action if they were not also its causes.

This phenomenological justification will give a certain plausibility to the causalist thesis. The question will then be to know whether a causal model other than that of Hume is not required to parallel the idea of motive as it has been recast, which is reduced to that of reason-for. The point can be discussed only at the end of the itinerary which will have led to the absorption of the idea of motive into that of cause.

Finally, however, it is not only on the phenomenological level that the dichotomy between the two universes of discourse is open to criticism (and it has been criticized in the sense we shall state later), but also on the ontological level. The term absent from the entire discussion, and which later will become the term expressly excluded, is strangely enough that of "agent." Now it is the reference to the agent which prevents us from getting to the end of the twofold opposition between making happen and happening, and between motive and cause. The opposition is indeed plausible on the level of the pair "what?-why?" In Strawson's vocabulary, which I employed in the first study, it amounts to opposing mental predicates to physical predicates, under the condition that a place be made for the mixed case of desire with its double valence of force and meaning. But an erroneous conclusion has been drawn from a partially correct analysis. What has been lost from sight is the attribution to one and the same thing—I shall now say to the same agent—of both series of predicates. As a result of this single attribution, action is at once a certain configuration of physical movements and an accomplishment capable of being interpreted in terms of reasons for acting which explain it. Only the relation to the same basic particular justifies the fact that the two language games are no longer juxtaposed but superimposed, following the relation that prevails between the concept of person and that of body and which makes us say that persons are bodies as well. The conceptual analysis of the notion of person on the ontological level of ultimate entities therefore exerts a prior restraint on the semantics of action, which is asked to satisfy the requirements of the conceptual framework determining our reasoned and appropriate use of the term "person."

The fragile nature of the dichotomous theory of action as I have just presented it is explained, in my opinion, by its barely plausible phenomenological character and by its lack of attention to the constraints ensuing from the theory of basic particulars. It will therefore not be surprising to find that a complete reversal of the relation between action and event on the level of "what?" and of the relation between motive and cause on the level of "why?" will be tied to an even greater obliviousness with respect to the ontological constraints I have just mentioned, an obliviousness finalized by the substitution of a general ontology of events for the regional ontology of persons. But this twofold reversal—on the plane of the analysis of discourse and on that of basic entities—will not be examined immediately. Before considering the confusion of the universes of discourse to the advantage of the event and the cause, it is preferable to linger awhile on the intermediate level, that of their mutual encroachment.

3. The Conceptual Analysis of Intention

It is significant that the conceptual analysis of the notion of intention, which we have purposely held in reserve until now, is responsible for producing the sort of nuanced and many-leveled analysis inherited from the Wittgenstein of the *Philosophical Investigations,* which, prior to any head-on attack, contributed to eroding the overly symmetrical polarities.[10] Anscombe's book *Intention* provides in this regard the most elegant example of what I shall call, without any pejorative overtone, a conceptual impressionism, to distinguish it from the somewhat cubist version found in Donald Davidson's theory, which I shall analyze in the section that follows. We would certainly expect that a conceptual analysis of intention would lead from the pair "what?-why?" to the question "who?" Is not intention, phenomenologically speaking, the aiming of a consciousness in the direction of something I am to do? Curiously enough, conceptual analysis deliberately turns its back on phenomenology: intention, for it, is not intentionality in Husserl's sense. It does not testify to the self-transcendence of a consciousness. Following Wittgenstein in this,

10. Jean-Luc Petit shows in *L'Action dans la philosophie analytique* (Paris: P. U. F., 1991) that the so-called Oxford School essentially calls upon the traditional philosophy of common sense in order to fill in the gap asserted by the *Philosophical Investigations* (§§611–60) between the semantic level of language and the effective experience of action. The paradoxes of the *Investigations* henceforth occupy a strategic position in the analytic philosophy of action.

Anscombe is in no way interested in the phenomenon which would be accessible to private intuition alone and, hence, compatible only with a private, ostensive description. Now this would be the case if intention were taken in the sense of intention-to . . . This sort of intention turned toward the future and not verified by action itself is in principle accessible only to the very agent who expresses it. For a conceptual analysis that admits only the criterion of what is accessible to public language, the intention-to . . . is valid only as a *declaration* of intention. We have no idea what an undeclared intention might be. Now the surface grammar of declared intentions is not clearly defined: nothing distinguishes the intention for the future (I am going to take a walk) from that of an estimate of the future (I am going to be sick) or from that of an order (you are going to obey me). Beyond the surface grammar, what is missing is a criterion for the truth of the expression of intention, if the intuition of the meaning of "I intend to . . ." is held to be irreducible.

Is this to say that the conceptual analysis of intention is impossible? The obstacle can be overcome if, following common linguistic usage, we distinguish between three uses of the term "intention": having done or doing something intentionally, acting with a certain intention, intending to . . . . The third use alone contains an explicit reference to the future. Reference to the past, however, is most often found in the case of action done intentionally. More important, the third use is the only one that is amenable to analysis solely on the basis of its expression. The other two uses are secondary qualifications of an action that can be observed by everyone. One therefore begins with the adverbial usage of the term "intention" (whose adjectival equivalent is "intentional action"). This use involves no violation of the rules of description.

This manner of attacking the problem, which Anscombe calls a piecemeal approach, is most remarkable for our own investigation: by taking as the focus of the analysis of intention its averbial form, one therefore privileges the use that exemplifies in the least explicit way the relation of intention to the agent. As close as is the tie between the intention-to and the person to whom it belongs, so qualifying the action as intentional can be accomplished independently of any consideration of the relation of possession that attaches the action to the agent. The criterion of intentional—hence of the "what?" of action—is in fact the form assumed by certain responses given to the question "why?" In this sense, the "why?" controls the "what?" and, in so doing, leads away from any interrogation concerning the "who?"

The central thesis is stated in the following terms: "What distinguishes actions which are intentional from those which are not? The answer that I shall suggest is that they are the actions to which a certain sense of the

question 'Why?' is given application; the sense is of course that in which
the answer, if positive, gives a reason for acting."[11] In testing this criteria,
we observe the *esprit de finesse* of this analysis, which will erode the clear-
cut dichotomies of the preceding analysis and, paradoxically, will open the
way for the *esprit de géométrie* characterizing a theory of action diametrically opposed to the preceding one. Indeed, far from putting an end to the
debate, the *application* of the criterion for the question "why?" allows access to an extraordinarily diverse field of mixed examples and of counterexamples, when it does not lead readers into a labyrinth of analyses in
which they may find themselves quite lost. This concern with subtle distinctions is first expressed in the investigation of cases in which the question "why?" has no application. This precaution had already been taken by
Aristotle in his analysis of *proairesis* (preferential choice): the case of ignorance, the case of constraint. Anscombe refines this analysis: everything
depends on recognizing under what description of the action the agent
was unaware of what he was doing (he did not know that he was making
noise by sawing a board). But the principal victim is the clear-cut opposition between reason-for-acting and cause. Instead we are dealing with a
range of cases where the opposition holds only for the extreme cases. The
mixed examples are in this respect the most interesting ones. Thus, in
Anscombe's estimation, the entire problematic of causality is in a state of
total confusion; we must therefore confine ourselves to saying that in certain acceptable answers to the question "why?" we employ the term "cause"
in a meaningful way. As was stated earlier, we often do speak, and are
justified in speaking of, what prompted someone to act. Even the notion
of mental cause has its legitimate place in certain descriptions of intentional action (military music excites me, that is why I am marching in
step). The most frequent cases in which reason for acting and cause tend
to merge are cases of backward-looking motives (cases of vengeance or of
gratitude, for instance). In contrast, forward-looking motives correspond
instead to the notion of the intention with which one acts. We shall have
more to say about this later. But one can see how fluid the border is between reason-for-acting, forward-looking motive, mental cause, and cause
as such (a grimacing face made me jump). The criterion of the question
"why?" is therefore firm; its application surprisingly flexible.

What about the opposition between action and event, which, in the
preceding analysis, we brought out before that of motive and cause? Here
again, G. Elizabeth Anscombe's position is highly nuanced. On the one
hand, she staunchly asserts that intentional action is the object of description; the place occupied by the notion of action under a certain description

11. Anscombe, *Intention*, p. 9.

testifies to this. In this sense, the "what?" of the act depends upon knowledge that can be true or false. We shall return later to this insistence on description in analytic philosophy. On the other hand, intentional actions constitute a subclass of things known without observation: I do not say that I knew that I was doing this or that because I had observed it. It is in doing that one knows that one is doing something, what one is doing, and why one is doing it. This notion of nonobservational knowledge, which we have already discussed above, and which is also called practical knowledge (knowing-how and not knowing-that) incontestably brings Anscombe's position closer to that of the supporters of the duality of language games.

It is mistaken to believe, however, that the notion of practical knowledge involves taking into account the relation of action to its agent, even though in all of the cases examined, the action verb is preceded by a personal pronoun. Employing the criterion of the question "why?" and of the acceptable answers to this question privileges the objective side of action, namely the result obtained, which is itself an event. As Anscombe states in a not unparadoxical fashion, I do what happens. The obliteration of the agent of action is further reinforced by accentuating the objective side of the reason for acting. Returning to the analysis of wanting, started above, Anscombe considers systematically the gerund form (wanting), without ever taking into account the expression "I want"; thus she writes, "The primitive sign of wanting is trying to get" (*Intention*, p. 68; the grammatical gerund allows this elision of the subject of the verb expressed by the tenses). As for the most commonly cited species of wanting, namely desire, what counts for conceptual analysis is not the tension experienced by a subject affected in this way but the "character of desirability," that is, that by reason of which something is desirable. Why this emphasis placed on the objective side of desire? Two reasons are apparent. The first is the concern to account for the evaluative dimension that is inseparable from the descriptive dimension, without, however, introducing moral considerations into the conceptual analysis. The second reason is the concern to provide an intelligible transition between intentional action (in the sense of an action done intentionally) and action done with the intention to . . .

This second use of the word "intention" covers what above we called a forward-looking motive. By this it must be clearly understood, however, that no internal entity accessible to the agent alone is thereby introduced. The action is there, and in order to describe it, one explains it. Now explaining it by citing a subsequent result is simply engaging in practical reasoning, which gives a discursive complexity to the reason for acting at the same time that one places a character of desirability in the position of premise. Here we are on sure ground, a terrain staked out earlier by Aristotle under the heading of practical syllogism, even if modern interpretations have to be corrected, along with those of Aristotle himself (to the extent that Aristotle places the analysis in the service of morality and, especially, to the extent that it is by no means obvious that the conclusion of the practical syllogism is indeed an action). The error, Anscombe says, is to consider the practical syllogism a reasoning that proves, whereas it is a reasoning that leads to action. The virtue of practical reasoning, in fact, is to make a future state of affairs appear as a subsequent stage of a process in which the action considered is the earlier stage. In the expression "I am doing this in view of that," the emphasis is not placed on "I" but on "in view of," that is, on the relation of dependence between two states of affairs—one earlier, the other later.

Here the mutual implication between the question "what?" and the question "why?" is most vigorously at work in both directions: moving from description to explanation, but also in the opposite direction, from explanation to description, inasmuch as the order introduced between a series of reasons for acting by practical reasoning rebounds onto the very description of the action.[12]

---

12. I cite here the example that G. E. M. Anscombe's analysis has made famous. "A man is pumping water into the cistern which supplies the drinking water of a house. Someone has found a way of systematically contaminating the source with a deadly cumulative poison whose effects are unnoticeable until they can no longer be cured. The house is regularly inhabited by a small group of party chiefs, with their immediate families, who are in control of a great state; they are engaged in exterminating the Jews and perhaps plan a world war. The man who contaminated the source has calculated that if these people are destroyed, some good men will get into power who will govern well, or even institute the Kingdom of Heaven on earth and secure a good life for all the people; and he has revealed the calculation, together with the fact about the poison, to the man who is pumping. The death of the inhabitants of the house will, of course, have all sorts of other effects; e.g., that a number of people unknown to these men will receive legacies, about which they know nothing.

This man's arm is going up and down, up and down. Certain muscles, with Latin names which doctors know, are contracting and relaxing. Certain substances are getting generated in some nerve fibers—substances whose generation in the course of voluntary movement interests physiologists. The moving arm is casting a shadow on the rockery where at one place and from one position it produces a curious effect as if a face were looking out of the rockery. Further, the pump makes a series of noises, which are in fact beating out a noticeable rhythm" (*Intention*, p. 37).

The question raised by this example is the following: What is the man doing? What is *the* description of his action? Answer: the question admits of as many answers as the multiple layers of "in view of"; all these descriptions are equally valid. In particular, an action can be named by the first thing one does or by the final result intended. Whether the agent is mentioned in each question and in each answer is of no importance to the series of reasons for acting ordered in accordance with the intended results. Now it is this series of reasons for acting that alone allows us to answer the question whether there are four actions or four

The irony of the situation is that it is precisely this mutual implication between the question "what?" and the question "why?" that has contributed to obliterating the question "who?" I explain this initially surprising phenomenon in the following way. In my opinion, it is the exclusive concern with the truth of the description that tends to overshadow any interest in assigning the action to its agent. Assigning the action to an agent poses a problem of veracity and no longer a problem of truth, in the descriptive sense of the term. This is the problem we shall return to later on with the analysis of the declaration of intention which we have systematically set aside. This is also evident in the cases of false allegation, made about others or about oneself, misunderstandings of the author of the action about his or her own intentions, or simply hesitations, the inner debates Aristotle placed under the heading of deliberation. In this respect, the relation of means to end and the logic that belongs to it does not exhaust the meaning of the intention with which one acts. The latter, it seems to me, implies in addition the pure act of intending which has been cast out of first place. I am suggesting here that the question of veracity, distinct from that of truth, stems from a more general problematic of attestation, which is itself suited to the question of selfhood: lies, deceit, misunderstandings, and illusions all belong to this order. It is perhaps due to the very style of analytic philosophy and to its almost exclusive preoccupation with description, as well as with the truth claims appropriate to description, that it ignores problems pertaining to attestation. If the possibility of suspecting the veracity of a declaration of intention argues against its descriptive character and against the truth claim attaching to descriptions, this very possibility of suspicion proves by itself that the problem posed belongs to a phenomenology of attestation, which cannot be reduced to a criteriology suited to description. Tests of sincerity, as I shall state at greater length in the study devoted to narrative identity, are not verifications but trials that finally end in an act of trust, in a final testimony, regardless of the intermediary episodes of suspicion. Anscombe herself recognizes that there is a moment when only the person concerned can say what his or her intention is. But this saying is on the order of an avowal, an expression of internal testimony: when communicated, the avowal is or is not accepted. But it is never the equivalent of a public description; it is a shared confession. What Anscombe calls knowledge without observation belongs, it seems to me—and this in opposition to the author's will—to this order of attestation. I do agree that the attesta-

---

descriptions of a single action: pumping, filling the well, poisoning the inhabitants, setting off a war.

tion of the intentional aim is not the work of some "very queer and special sort of seeing eye in the middle of the acting" (*Intention*, p. 57). Precisely, attestation escapes sight, if sight is expressed in propositions held to be true or false. Veracity is not truth, in the sense of the adequation of knowledge to its object.[13]

Because of the inability to thematize this attestation Anscombe's conceptual analysis is unable to account in any detail for the third use of the term "intention": the intention to . . . We recall the arguments used to dislodge this use—the major one from the phenomenological point of view—from first place at the outset of the inquiry and to relegate it to third place. Returning to this use at the end of her discussion, Anscombe confines herself to stating that the criterion for the question "why?" and for the corresponding answers also holds for the intention of a proposed action. This amounts to saying that the mark of the future, which intention shares with predictions or estimations of the future (this is going to happen), is not a distinguishing factor; only the explanation by reasons counts. From this point of view, it is unimportant whether or not the intention is fulfilled, whether the explanation is confined to a simple "because I felt like it, that's all." The analysis has merely eliminated what I shall call the intention of the intention, namely the specific leap toward the future, where the thing that is to be done is to be done by me, the same one (*ipse*) as he who says that he will do it.[14] In other words, what is eliminated is the one who, in intending, places this intention on the path of promising, even if the firm intention lacks the conventional and public framework of explicit promising.

In conclusion, the intention to . . . , relegated to the third rank by conceptual analysis, returns to the first rank in a phenomenological perspective. What remains is to say in what sense the attestation of the intention to . . . is at the same time the attestation of the self.

4. Semantics of Action and Ontology of Events

The third stage of the capture of the "what?" by the "why?"—with its corollary, the almost complete elision of the question "who?"—is attained by a theory of action in which the pair of questions "what?" and "why?"

13. The question of attestation (and the related one of veracity) will slowly make its way from study to study, until it is confronted head-on in the tenth study.

14. We find the trace of this problem in Anscombe herself, for instance when she defines the declaration of intention as "a description of something future in which the speaker is some sort of agent, which description he justifies (if he does justify it) by reasons for acting, reasons why it would be useful or attractive if the description came true, not by evidence that it is true" (*Intention*, p. 6).

is swallowed up by an *ontology of the impersonal event,* which makes actions themselves a subclass of events. This twofold logical and ontological re- duction is performed with remarkable vigor by Donald Davidson in the series of articles collected in the volume titled, significantly, *Actions and Events.*[15]

The theory opens with an apparent paradox. Although it begins by stressing the distinctive teleological character of action among all other events, this descriptive feature is quickly subordinated to a *causal* concep- tion of explanation. In this subordination lies the decisive move of David- son's theory of action, as hatchet-carved—as square-cut, if I may say so—as Elizabeth Anscombe's analyses appeared impressionistic. In David- son's strategy, causal explanation serves in its turn to insert actions into an ontology, not a hidden one but a declared ontology, which makes the notion of events, in the sense of incidental occurrences, a class of irre- ducible entities placed on an equal footing with substances in the sense of fixed objects. This ontology of the event, by nature impersonal, in my opinion structures the entire gravitational sphere of the theory of action and prevents an explicit, thematic treatment of the relation between action and agent, which the analysis nevertheless continually approaches. In this failure to return action to the agent, I see an impetus, as if by default, to seek in another sort of ontology, one more consonant with the search for the self, the genuine place of linkage between the action and its agent.

1. Proceeding in order, I shall conduct the analysis within the limits of the group of essays devoted to the relation between intention and action, taking as my guide the first of these essays, "Actions, Reasons, and Causes" (1963).[16] This essay, at once a kickoff and a master stroke, gave rise to a realignment of the entire philosophy of action, henceforth compelled to take a position with regard to this new state of affairs. This first essay— later, I shall discuss the important revision it was to undergo fifteen years later in the final essay of the group, titled "Intending" (1978)[17]—does not present in a thematic manner the ontological basis of the theory of action in an ontology of events but presupposes it on every page. The essay is limited to reducing teleological explanation, which one is tempted to as- sociate with the description of action in terms of intention which is itself teleological, to the rigorousness of causal explanation. In fact, the interest and, up to a certain point, the paradoxical nature of Davidson's theory is that it begins by recognizing the teleological nature of action on the descriptive level. What distinguishes action from all other events is, pre-

---

15. Donald Davidson, *Essays on Actions and Events* (Oxford: Clarendon Press, 1980).
16. Ibid., pp. 3–19.
17. Ibid., pp. 83–102.

cisely, intention. Of course, actions are events, inasmuch as their description designates something that happens, as is suggested by the grammar of verbs; but no grammar allows us to decide between verbs that do not designate actions, such as "err," and verbs that do designate actions, such as "strike" or "kill." In this sense, the distinction between making happen and happening, which was so heavily underscored by the preceding authors, falls within the boundary of events. It is intention that constitutes the criterion distinguishing action from all other events.

In what sense, however, are we to take the word "intention"? In his first essay Davidson assumes for himself the distinction proposed by Elizabeth Anscombe between several linguistic uses of the term "intention": the intention with which (something is done), intentionally, intention to (do something). The strategy he adopts in 1963 consists in privileging (he does it as well!) the adverbial use of "intention" (X does A intentionally) and in subordinating to it the substantive form (A has the intention to do X in circumstances Y), while "the intention with which (something is done)" continues to be considered a simple discursive extension of the adverb "intentionally." Several reasons support this strategy. First, by treating the intention as an adverb modifying the action, it is possible to subordinate it to the description of the action as a completed event. It is noteworthy that in most of the canonical examples submitted to the logical analysis of action sentences, the verbs are stated in a past tense: "Brutus killed Caesar" and so on. This will be a source of difficulty in the analysis of intending to (do something), where the orientation toward the future is so strongly marked, while the past form of the action-event is barely in evidence. Another argument: Davidson shares with all of analytic philosophy a profound mistrust of those mysterious entities called volitions, without, however, rejecting the notion of mental event, since desires and beliefs which will be placed in the position of causal antecedent are indeed mental events. But these mental events are not incompatible with a physicalist approach, which I shall not discuss here. So it is not the notion of mental event that is troublesome but the sort of event that cannot be set within the framework of antecedent causality as this will be developed later. Finally, the ability to enter into a causalist schema is the reason for privileging the adverbial use of the term "intention." It is this inscription of the teleology of the descriptive level within the causality of the explanatory level that I should now like to establish.

Actually, with intention taken in the adverbial sense, description amounts to explanation. Describing an action as having been done intentionally is explaining it by the reason the agent had to do what she did. In other words, it is giving an explanation in the form of a *rationalization;* it is saying that the alleged reason rationalizes the action. Given this, Davidson's thesis is developed in two stages: first, making explicit what is meant by rationalizing; then, showing that rationalization is a subset of causal explanation. Someone can be said to have a reason to do something if, on the one hand, he has a certain "pro-attitude"—that is, a favorable attitude, an inclination of the agent with respect to actions of a certain sort (understanding by "inclination" something broader than desire or wanting), and where a favorable attitude includes obligations, the agent's public and private goals, and, on the other hand, the agent has a belief (knowledge, perception, observation, memory) that his action belongs to this category of action. (Note that the agent is mentioned here. But will the agent be thematized as such?) In short, an intentional action is an action done "for a reason." The term "primary reason" will be given to the ensemble constituted by the favorable attitude and the belief: "To know a primary reason why someone acted as he did is to know an intention with which the action was done."[18]

On the basis of this equation between the reason for doing and the intention with which one does something, Davidson establishes his major claim, according to which explanation by reasons is a subset of causal explanation. This is, for him, first of all a common-sense claim: do we not ask what led or caused someone to do what he or she did? Moreover, this claim is in keeping with the ontology of events as a whole. What indeed is causality if not a relation between individual, discrete events? In contrast to the argument referred to in the preceding paragraph, reason and action most certainly are events, because of their character of incidence (a disposition becomes a reason for acting only by becoming suddenly a means of access); furthermore, they are distinct events that can be named and described separately, hence serious candidates for the role of cause and effect. In this respect, the mental event, considered from the angle of incidence, is entirely parallel to the sudden fissure that transforms the faulty construction of a bridge into an event that causes a catastrophe.

Let us also add, and this is a finer point, that a causal theory should not be confused with a nomological theory: it is not necessary to know a law in order to affirm a causal connection, which, as has been stated, governs particular events. This dissociation between causal explanation and nomological explanation avoids the major obstacle raised in analytic philosophy to a causal interpretation of the explanation of action by reasons. Now this is, at the very least, a plausible undertaking.[19] In *Time and Narra-*

18. Ibid., p. 7.
19. Davidson concedes that this is a weak version of the Humean definition of causation. To be sure, the latter takes into account singular events, since it invokes only the resemblance between what it calls "objects." In addition, however, it maintains regularity within repeti-

tive 1,[20] I myself defended the notion of singular causal explanation on the plane of historical knowledge, following in this Max Weber and Raymond Aron. Moreover, I expressed above my own doubts regarding a purely dichotomous treatment of the conceptual pair "motive-cause." But I confined myself then to a simple inventory of the linguistic situations in which it seemed legitimate to treat motives as causes. I should like to push the argument further and propose an interpretation of motivation which at the same time satisfies phenomenological intuition and offers an alternative to Davidson's causalist theory, which remains basically a Humean theory. If, as we have been saying, the phenomenology of wanting demands a new model of the idea of motivation that will take into account the dimension of passivity correlative to the action of doing, a similar overhaul of the idea of cause that dissociates it from the Humean model would also appear to be necessary. On the one hand, it does seem that the prestige of this model has prevented the acknowledgment of cases where motive and cause are indiscernible, namely all those involving the old idea of efficient cause—even the idea of disposition, restored to a place of

---

tion; causation can be observed without knowing the underlying law. In an essay devoted to Davidson's work, P. F. Strawson reinforces Davidson's position, in a way, though, that might ultimately weaken it ("Causation and Explanation," in *Essays on Davidson and Actions and Events*, ed. Bruce Vermazen and Merrill B. Hintikka [Oxford: Clarendon Press, 1985]). Strawson observes that on the simple level of ordinary observation the phenomenon of production (the "making happen" discussed time and again in analytic philosophy) lends itself to typification, from which emerge certain regularities that, in turn, on another level of explanatory language, evoke genuine laws. In this way, the tractor is seen to pull or push just as we may pull or push using our arms. This is the case of all mechanical transactions, to use Strawson's expression. The thesis incorporating teleology in the causation between particular events then is in danger of losing not only its paradoxical character but even its power of discrimination. As other authors have so often stressed, the notion of cause fans out with such polysemy that one can no longer tell if it is the result of incipient anthropomorphism that we see the bulldozer push, as we might push a rock through a series of repeated efforts, or if it is by means of a transfer from things to ourselves that we apply a mechanical model to our own action. In any event, Strawson denies that this question of priority is of any immediate interest by situating the major split, not between human causation (whether this lies in physical effort or in weighing motives) and material causation, but between the natural character of the causal relation between events and particular circumstances and the nonnatural character of the explanatory relation that links together not the events themselves but the fact that they happen. According to Strawson, facts designate states of affairs, which themselves do not occur, strictly speaking, but are simply exemplified by individual occurrences. I shall not let myself be drawn here into the dispute initiated by Strawson concerning the relation between (atemporal) states of affairs and (ephemeral) events. Davidson devotes two essays to this question in *Actions and Events:* "Events as Particulars" (1970) and "Eternal vs. Ephemeral Events" (1971), pp. 181–203.

20. Ricoeur, *Time and Narrative* 1, trans. Kathleen McLaughlin and David Pellauer (Chicago: University of Chicago Press), 1984.

honor by Ryle in *The Concept of Mind.*[21] On the other hand, one could certainly argue that the idea of efficient cause, driven out of physics by Galileo's revolution, has simply returned to its old source, to its native land, in the experience of desire. But we could not be satisfied with an analysis that would be limited to restoring an archaic meaning of cause in order to make room for experiences in which motive is actually lived as cause. It is the very grammar of the notions of drive, disposition, and emotion—in short, the grammar of the concept of affect—which requires that we articulate the intentional character of action onto a type of causal explanation that conforms to it. This can only be teleological explanation.[22]

What is teleological explanation? It is an explanation in which the order is itself a factor in the production of an event; it is a self-imposed order. To say that an event occurs because it is intended as an end is not to have recourse to a hidden entity, whether *virtus dormitiva* or other, but to describe a system and a system law, such that in this system an event occurs because the conditions that produced it are those required to produce this end. Or, to quote Charles Taylor, "This means that the condition of the event's occurring is that a state of affairs obtain such that it will bring about the end in question, or such that this event is required to bring about that end" (*Explanation*, p. 9). So to say that an animal stalks its prey is to say that the sort of action described as stalking is that which, within the animal's repertoire of available behaviors, is required to satisfy its hunger. One thus postulates no prior or internal entity; one simply says that the fact for an event to be required to obtain a given end is a condition for the appearance of that event. The fact that a system-state and its environment are such that they require a given event (a particular behavior—here, stalking) in order that a certain result be produced, is perfectly observable, just as is the fact that this antecedent condition can be established independently of the material proof produced by the event itself.

It is now the task of the semantics of action to establish the correlation between the form of the law appropriate to teleological explanation and the descriptive features that have led us to say that a motive fulfills its functions only if it is a cause as well. Between ordinary language and teleological explanation, an interesting two-way correlation then appears. In one direction the form of teleological explanation is the implicit sense of the explanation of action in terms of its dispositions. In this case we can speak of a transcendental deduction of teleological explanation by reason

21. Gilbert Ryle, *The Concept of Mind* (London: Hutchinson's University Library, 1949).

22. I owe the following analysis to Charles Taylor in his work *The Explanation of Behaviour* (London: Routledge and Kegan Paul, 1954).

of the feature belonging to ordinary language made possible by this explanation. Classifying an action as *intentional* is determining by what type of law it is to be explained and, by the same token, ruling out a certain type of explanation. In other words, it is deciding on the form of the law that governs the action and at the same time ruling out the possibility that this is a mechanical law. Here, describing and explaining coincide. The descriptive class is the same thing as the style of explanation: the question "why?" is realized in the question "what?" A statement of the goal amounts to a description; explanation is a redescription of the goal in view of which (something is done). The epistemology of teleological causality is thus the explanation of the unsurmountable nature of ordinary language. However, in the opposite direction, if teleological explanation makes explicit the form implicit in the description of ordinary language (disposition to do something), the latter in turn adds to the form of explanation the reference to a phenomenological feature of the experience of action, one that is not contained in this form (which, as such, is reduced to the law of a system); this is why there is more in phenomenological description than in teleological explanation. To the general notion of explanation in terms of a goal, human experience adds that of the conscious orientation of an agent capable of recognizing herself as the subject of her acts. Experience is here not only the application of a law; it makes this application specific by designating the intentional core of an action that is consciously directed.

The alternative interpretation I am proposing here of the relations between causality and motivation does not, in my opinion, cover only the adverbial use of the notion of intention but opens up a new career for the notion intention-to.

2. The true problem raised by Davidson's analysis of action is actually not, in my opinion, knowing whether the reasons for acting, in the case in which intention is taken adverbially, are or are not causes, but whether one is justified in considering the substantive use of intention—"the intention to (do something)"—as derivative with respect to its adverbial use.

It has already been noted that the expression "the intention with which an action is done" spontaneously replaces one of the grammatical forms of the past tense. So it is not surprising that the action-event is considered as something completed; what is surprising, however, is that verb tense is never itself the object of any separate analysis. But this cannot be omitted with the expression "the intention to . . . ," which as we shall see later has a strongly marked orientation toward the future. It may then be wondered whether the *temporal* dimension should not be taken into account in the analysis of intention and whether the intention-with-which, whose character of pastness has remained unmarked, is not in this respect a weak,

even mutilated, form of intention-to, for which the delay between intention and action is essential. Now a null delay is not a nondelay but a sort
of simultaneous accompanying. If we ask someone after the fact why he
did this or that intentionally, he will answer by raising the intention with
which he acted to the level of an intention-to: the reason for his action is
the intention-to, which he would have formed if he had thought about it,
if he had had the time to deliberate.

Now this initial attenuation, that of the temporal dimension, is not
unrelated to a second one, that of the reference to the *agent* in formulating
the action-event and its reason-cause; without being entirely neglected,
the attribution of the action and its reasons to an agent is never thematized; it too remains unmarked.[23] It is even absent from the formula which
is the focus of commentary for the entire essay: "C2. A primary reason for
an action is its cause" (Davidson, *Essays*, p. 12).[24] Would it not then be a
perverse effect caused by the alignment with the underlying ontology of
events to conceal the ascription of the action to its agent, to the extent

23. The agent is named by Davidson in proposition C1: "R is a primary reason why an
agent performed the action A under the description *d* only if R consists of a pro-attitude of
the agent towards actions with a certain property, and a belief of the agent that A, under the
description *d*, has that property" (*Essays*, p. 5). One can catch the moment when the reference
to the agent is attenuated in the following statement: "To know a primary reason why someone acted as he did is to know an intention with which the action was done" (p. 7). Practical
syllogisms constructed on this basis indeed mention only the desirability characterizing the
pro-attitude, to borrow E. Anscombe's happy expression in *Intention*.

24. This attenuation is confirmed in the reference to the agent in the essay devoted to
the concept of agency (Davidson, *Essays*, pp. 43–61). Given the title—"Agency"—one
might expect an analysis of the agent's power to act. There is nothing of the sort; instead it
is solely a matter of the distinguishing criterion of action properly speaking ("deeds and
doing") in relation to events which are but mere happenings, when the intentional character
appears to be lacking. The principal counterexample considered here is that of mistakes. An
admiral actually sinks the *Bismarck* when he meant to sink the *Tirpitz;* Hamlet kills Polonius,
thinking he is striking an intruder behind the curtain. The property of constituting an action
and not just some sort of happening (which is equivalent to the term "agency" in this context) poses a problem, to the extent that no one can doubt that the event considered—sinking
a ship, killing a man—is an action, although at first glance it lacks any apparent intentional
character. Can there be agency without intention? it is asked. The entire analysis, conducted
with great subtlety, consists in showing by simple analysis of the logical form of action
sentences that the criterion for action remains intention: "A man is the agent of an act if
what he does can be described under an aspect that makes it intentional" (p. 46). Does he
speak of the agent's intention? Not at all; everything rests on the split between the reason of
the pro-attitude and the belief accompanying it, on the one hand, and, on the other, the
reality of the actual effect substituted for the expected effect. It is noteworthy, nonetheless,
that Davidson cannot avoid distinguishing in this context between event causality and agent
causality in order to account for this substitution. But, to my knowledge at least, nowhere
does he develop this distinction, one borrowed moreover from I. Thalberg (p. 52).

that it is not relevant to the notion of event, whether it be produced or brought about by persons or by things?

This suspicion finds confirmation in the treatment of "pure intention," that is, not accompanied by action—"intending," as cited in the title of the 1978 essay, hence fifteen years after "Actions, Reasons, and Causes." Following the strategy adopted in the first essay, all the uses of the notion of intention should be derivable from the adverbial use: "I was wrong," Davidson confesses in the introduction to his collection of essays (p. xiii). It did not escape Davidson's attention that intending-to presents new and original features, precisely the orientation toward the future, the delay in accomplishing, even the absence of accomplishing, and, at least silently, the implication of the agent. However, the new thesis is that these features require no fundamental revision of causal explanation in terms of favorable attitudes and beliefs but only the addition of a supplementary factor incorporated into the well-established notion of reason for acting. This supplementary factor must not fraudulently reintroduce some mysterious act of a volitional sort. With extreme caution several candidates are examined: cannot the formation process of the intention be treated as an action? This is plausible. But what is a nonobservable action? Might action be assimilated into a kind of speech act, like a promise (or a command)? This is equally plausible. But intention lacks the system of conventions, the character of obligation by which the agent would be bound and the public character of a declaration—all features that distinguish promises as particular speech acts. What if intention is reduced to the belief that one does indeed want something or that one will do this or that if certain conditions are satisfied, or that one could do such and such if one wanted to? Here, we are certainly closer to the goal. But the analysis holds at best only for conditional intentions, where the conditions invoked are of the order of external circumstances. There remains the solution consisting in taking up again the analysis of "pro-attitude" in the form of the canonical analysis of wanting.

The earlier analysis in fact neglected the evaluative component, hence the role of *judgment* in the formation of wanting. Now, "forming an intention" is also "arriving at a judgment." But there are two sorts of judgment: on the one hand, the judgment that can be called prima facie, which corresponds to desire—for example, eating something sweet—and which is none other than the consideration of desirability, to borrow once again Anscombe's term;[25] on the other hand, all-out judgment, unconditional

25. "Let us call judgements that actions are desirable in so far as they have a certain attribute, prima facie judgements" (Davidson, *Essays*, p. 98).

judgment, which can conclude a process of practical reasoning. This is a supplementary judgment in which desirability suffices to govern action. Judgment that pleads solely in favor of an action is one thing; judgment that engages action and is sufficient for it is something else again. The formation of an intention is just this unconditional judgment. The advantage of this theory is that it remains within the confines of the earlier analysis of the reason for acting, while respecting the distinction between intention and mere wanting. This allows the introduction, as a new element in the analysis of intentional action, of unconditional judgment. Thus "intending and wanting belong to the same genus of pro-attitudes expressed by value judgements" (Davidson, *Essays,* p. 102). Having said this, the causal explanation of intention is safe and sound.

In my opinion, Davidson has underestimated the unsettling effect that this addition of all-out judgment imposes on the earlier analysis. The problematic that has been shunted aside up to now—namely the temporal component of delay and the reference to the agent whose intention it is—returns in full force under the cover of all-out judgments. Thus the last sentence of the essay reads: "Pure intendings constitute a subclass of the all-out judgements, those directed to future actions of the agent, and made in light of his beliefs" (ibid.). For with the delay there appears not only the character of anticipation—the intention's empty sighting, as one would say in a Husserlian perspective—but also the prospective character of the very condition of agency, as one would say in a Heideggerian perspective. Concerning the quality of anticipation belonging to intention, it is the intention-to and not its adverbial form that constitutes the basic usage of the concept of intention. In the case of action done intentionally, the temporal dimension of intention is simply attenuated and as if covered over by the almost simultaneous accomplishment. But as soon as we consider actions which, as we say, take time, anticipation operates during the entire unfolding of the action. Is there any sort of extended gesture that I could accomplish without anticipating in some sense its continuation, its completion or interruption? Davidson himself considers the case in which, writing a word, I anticipate the action of writing the next letter while still writing the present letter. How could we fail to recall, in this connection, the famous example of reciting a poem described in Augustine's *Confessions?* The entire dialectic of *intentio* and *distentio,* constitutive of temporality itself, is summed up here: I intend the poem in its entirety while reciting it verse by verse, syllable by syllable, the anticipated future transiting through the present in the direction of a completed past.

Concerning the projective character affecting the agent as such, it is still the "intention to" that constitutes the basic usage of the notion of intention. In its adverbial usage intention appears as a simple modification of action, which can be treated as a subclass of impersonal events. The same can no longer be said, however, with respect to "the intention-to," which refers directly to the agent to whom it belongs. By the same token, the question of priority (on the phenomenological level, between the multiple uses of the notion of intention) refers us to the underlying ontological problem, that of knowing whether an ontology of events is capable of taking intention into account as it belongs—and through it, action itself—to people.

3. These are the ontological stakes at issue in the series of essays appearing under the heading "Event and Cause," which compose the second section of *Actions and Events*. The bulk of the argument is devoted to justifying the claim according to which events—and among these, actions—are as deserving as substances of being called primitive entities, if we term "entities" the realities that give a truth value to the propositions referring to them. This Fregean criterion of assigning existence is common to any number of schools of analytic philosophy. They differ from one another only in their application of this criterion, which is basically in terms of the logical analysis of the sentences or propositions which are the support for a truth claim. In this regard, the comparison between Strawson's claim in *Individuals,* which we took as our guide in the preceding chapter, and Davidson's in *Actions and Events* is of the highest interest. It directly concerns the status of the agent of action on the ontological plane. In *Individuals,* the distinction between the two kinds of basic particulars—bodies and persons—was made on the basis of the attribution on each side of different series of predicates, mental predicates and physical predicates. In this way the agent of action is recognized as an ultimate particular, even if the agent as such is not yet a self, in the strong sense I am attributing to this term, but only as one of the "things" about which we speak. With Davidson, the split imposed by "the logical form of action sentences" (the title of the first essay in this section) passes between substances, or *fixed entities,* and events, or *transitory entities.* Now this split—and this is my major concern—not only does not promote any advance in the ontology of the agent but contributes in a certain sense to concealing it. In fact, persons in Strawson's sense are more on the side of substance, to the extent that it is to them that action-events happen. In the logical analysis of the sentence "Pierre struck a blow," what matters is that the verb "to strike" is said of both Pierre and the blow. The blow is in the position of a particular event. Pierre is in the position of substance, not so much as a person distinct from material things (bodies, in Strawson's vocabulary), but as bearer of the event. What matters here is that the event

possess the same ontological dignity as substance, whether the latter be a thing or a person.[26] To complete the occultation of the specific problematic of the agent, the assimilation of "primary reasons" (pro-attitudes and beliefs) to mental events results in the notion of person being torn between event and substance without ever being relevant in itself. In fact, when the emphasis is placed on the bearer of the event, the person is substance without any special privilege; but when it is the notion of mental events belonging to the person that is emphasized, this notion tends to fade away into the mass of events, that is, into the tumult of everything that happens.

The reasons Davidson advances to say why events should be treated as substances deserve to be taken into consideration, especially in view of the prudence and modesty with which the claim is presented. The logical form of action sentences exerts a constraint that is hardly open to dispute. If the explanation of action by reasons is a species of causal explanation and if causality operates between particular events, then actions must indeed be events, and these events must exist in order to assure the truth value of the propositions which refer to them. This vigorous claim is reinforced by the many parallels that the analysis of the logical form of action sentences discovers between substances and events. How, for example, could one say that a certain action is amenable to several descriptions (we have encountered innumerable times the expression: such and such an action under a description *d*), if it did not constitute a particular entity? In respect of this, the analysis of excuses, begun by Austin, and that of mistakes, outlined above, lead back by way of other paths to the notion of a plurality of descriptions of a certain action performed. The same can be said of "variable polyadicity" (to use Anthony Kenny's phrase),[27] by reason of which it is always possible to add to an action statement the mention of the recipient, the place, the time, the means, and other circumstances, without altering the truth value of the reference to the given action. In an even more striking way, could one speak of the numerical identity of a single

26. I shall not enter here into Davidson's discussion of Strawson's claim that events are conceptually dependent on objects; the analysis of the example just cited invites the conclusion that "neither the category of substance nor the category of change is conceivable apart from the other" (Davidson, *Essays*, p. 175). I shall also leave aside the discussion of another view hostile to the ontology of events, namely Roderick Chisholm's position that events are simply exemplifications of states of affairs which are held to be the true entities at issue (in "States of Affairs Again," *Noûs* 5, no. 2 [1971]: 179–89). Both of these discussions, found in two essays in the second section, unfold within the same parameter, that defined by the truth claims related to the "logical form of action sentences."

27. Anthony Kenny, *Action, Emotion, and Will* (London: Routledge and Kegan Paul, 1963).

action or of the qualitative identity between two actions? The question of identity is so central to the plea for an ontology of events that it provides the major argument in the essay titled "The Individuation of Events" (Davidson, *Essays,* pp. 163–80). The essay begins by asking, "When are events identical, when distinct? What criteria are there for deciding one way or the other in particular cases?" (p. 163). The answer is that the criteria for deciding identity are the same for events and for objects/substances. Could an action take place several times (recurrence of an occurrence), could one name an action (one, a few, all), if actions were not events which could be said to exist on an equal footing with material objects (and, we might add, with persons viewed as substances)? Everything contributes to the claim that events are individuated just as are singular substances. It is then possible to conclude that "the individuation of events poses no problems worse in principle than the problems posed by individuation of material objects; and there is as good reason to believe events exist" (p. 180).

The disappearance of any reference to persons, in the final assertion cited, is not accidental and should catch our attention. The question raised is this: is not an ontology of events, founded on the sort of logical analysis of action phrases conducted with the rigor and subtlety of Davidson's analysis, condemned to conceal the problematic of the agent as the *possessor* of his or her action? An indication of this occultation is provided by the discussion alluded to concerning the identity between events. From start to finish it is a matter only of identity in the sense of *idem* and not of identity in the sense of *ipse,* which would be the identity of a self.[28] In my opinion, this occultation of the question of the agent is the accumulated result of a series of strategic choices, all of which are open to question.

First, the priority given to "the intention-with-which" in relation to "the intention-to" has allowed the attenuation, without ever eliminating it entirely, of the temporal dimension of anticipation which accompanies the agent's projecting himself ahead of himself. It is the task of an explicit

28. Cf. the definition: "Events are identical if and only if they have exactly the same causes and effects" (Davidson, *Essays,* p. 179). Regardless of other conditions of sameness (same place, same time), the sameness of causal relations is the sole condition which is itself always sufficient to establish the sameness of events. There is a close connection between these identity criteria and positing an entity. As we read in "The Individuation of Events," "Quine has quipped: 'No entity without identity' in support of the Fregean thesis that we ought not to countenance entities unless we are prepared to make sense of sentences affirming and denying identity of such entities. But then more obvious still is the motto: 'No identity without an entity', and its linguistic counterpart: 'No statement of identity without singular terms'" (p. 164). We are placing ourselves firmly within the framework delimited by Frege; that is, we hold that all sentences that resemble one another in their truth claims name the same thing ("same" in the sense of *idem*).

phenomenology of the project, similar to the one I once sketched out at the beginning of *The Voluntary and the Involuntary,* to bring to the level of language what lies unexpressed in this initial choice.[29]

Next, the inclusion of teleological explanation by reasons within causal explanation has sealed the effacement of the subject to the benefit of a relation between impersonal events. An epistemological analysis is required to establish the rights of *teleological causality* and to show the latter's affinity with the phenomenological moment of intentionality, once it has been elicited. We made a first step in this direction above.

Finally, it is important to ask ourselves whether the incapacity of an ontology of events to account for the imputation of action to its agent does not result from the way in which this ontology is introduced. It would seem as though the search for symmetry between the incident nature of events and the permanence of substance prevented Davidson from pursuing the confrontation made by Strawson in *Individuals* between the basic particulars distinguished as persons and as things. The question of the agent is no longer relevant in the search for this symmetry between event and substance. To reply to this challenge on the ontological level where it is posed, one would have to introduce the question of the mode of being of the agent on some basis other than that of the analysis of the logical form of action sentences, without in any way denying the validity of this approach, so typical of analytic philosophy, on its own terrain. This would, I think, constitute a different ontology, one in harmony with the phenomenology of intention and with the epistemology of teleological causality referred to a moment ago. This different ontology would be that of a being in the making, possessing de jure the problematic of selfhood, just as the problematic of sameness belongs de jure to the ontology of events.

To the next study will fall the task of exploring the resources of the notion of *ascription* of action to an agent, left in abeyance at the end of the first study, from the perspective of this different ontology.[30] We can also

29. *Freedom and Nature: The Voluntary and the Involuntary,* trans. E. V. Kohak (Evanston, Ill.: Northwestern University Press), 1966.

30. Are these two ontologies mutually exclusive? I do not think so; they are, in my opinion, simply different by reason of their starting points, which themselves cannot be compared. Would Davidson be as conciliatory toward this different ontology as I am in respect of his ontology? I do not know. I draw some indication of this, however, from the modesty of his position as expressed in the following text which I cite at length: "We have learned to be wary, however, of what the surface of language suggests, especially when it comes to ontology. . . . So events as particulars may not, after all, be basic to our understanding of the world. How can we tell?

"We would be better placed to judge if we had a coherent, comprehensive account of the

expect that the epistemological role of *attestation,* mentioned several times already, will pass to the forefront with the analysis of ascription. Neither ascription nor its attestation can have a place in a semantics of action that has been doomed by its strategy to remain an agentless semantics of action.

---

conditions under which our common beliefs (or believed-true sentences) are true. If we were in command of such a theory and that theory called for a domain of particular events, while our best efforts found no theory that worked as well without events, then we would have all the reason we could have for saying events exist; we would have all the reason we could have for saying that we do say that events exist.

"We don't begin to have such a comprehensive theory, of course, but we can learn by trying" (*Essays,* pp. 181–82).

From Action to the Agent

The purpose of this study is to reconsider the question of the relation of action to its agent after the disappointing results of the preceding study. To do this, let us move back to an earlier stage. We noted at the start of the first study that the questions "Who? What? Why?", applied to the semantic field of action, form a network of interrelated meanings such that our ability to reply to any one of these questions implies our ability to reply to any other belonging to the same sphere of sense. The preceding study, which was based upon a semantics of discourse, followed this network in one direction only, leading us away from the question "who?" and directing us instead toward the pair "what?-why?" Is it possible, basing our inquiry on a pragmatics of discourse, to follow the chain of questions in the opposite direction—in other words, to move back from the pair "what?-why?" to the pivotal question "who?"? The major obstacle up to now has been the attraction exerted on the logical analysis of action sentences by an ontology of events which blocks the return path toward the question "who?" In this stymied situation it may well seem opportune to return to Strawson's analyses at the point where we left them at the end of the first study. In fact, each of the three claims we cited in Strawson's analysis points in its own way, and with increasing force, to a single linguistic phenomenon which, following Strawson himself, I shall designate by the term "ascription." Let me recall the three claims:

1. Persons are basic particulars in the sense that all *attribution* of predicates is made, ultimately, either in respect of bodies or of persons. The attribution of certain predicates to persons cannot be translated in terms of attribution to bodies.

2. It is "to the same things"—persons—that we *attribute* psychological predicates and physical predicates; in other words, the person is the sole entity to which we ascribe both series of predicates. There is thus no reason to posit dual entities corresponding to the dualism of mental and physical predicates.

3. Mental predicates, such as intentions and motives, are directly *at-*

tributable to oneself and to someone else; in both instances, the term retains the same sense.

It is therefore this threefold attribution that we are terming *ascription*. This term designates henceforth the critical point of our entire enterprise: the question is whether ascribing an action to an agent is not such a peculiar type of attribution that it calls into question the apophantic logic of attribution. Then, if the semantics of action stumbles over the question of the relation of the action to the agent, this is perhaps not only because an opposing ontology—the ontology of anonymous events—poses an obstacle to identifying persons as basic particulars but also because ascription poses a problem for the semantics of action which it is poorly equipped to solve. Will pragmatics be more useful in dealing with it?

1. An Old Problem and a New Problem

The difficulty confronting us is not new. It has been formulated since antiquity, by philosophers lacking the analytic resources available to us, and yet with a talent for linguistics that cannot help but amaze us.

Without treating this relation thematically, Aristotle, well before the Stoics, made it apparent that action *depends* on the agent, in a specific sense of the relation of dependence. Aristotle is one of the first, after the Sophists perhaps, to verify and codify the relevance of the linguistic choices made by orators, tragic poets, and magistrates, and also those made in ordinary usage, whenever it is a matter of submitting action and the agent to moral judgment. The care that Aristotle takes in making distinctions and providing definitions merits that we examine these by paying particular attention to the linguistic resources at work.

Aristotle, as has often been stated, did not have available in his *Ethics* a unified concept of will, as will be found in Augustine, Descartes and the Cartesians, Kant, and Hegel. Nevertheless, in order to have a point of anchorage on the level of action for his detailed study of virtue, that is, of the features of excellence belonging to action, he undertakes in book 3 of the *Nichomachean Ethics* [1] an initial distinction pairing actions performed despite oneself (*akōn, akousios*) with those performed freely (*hekōn, hekousios*),[2] then makes a finer distinction within this first circle of those

---

1. *Ethica Nichomachea*, English translation by W. D. Ross, in *The Basic Works of Aristotle*, ed. Richard McKeon (New York: Random House, 1941), hereafter referred to as *E.N.*

2. Here, I am following the translation of Gauthier-Jolif (Louvain: Publications univérsitaires de Louvain; Paris: Nauwelaerts, 1958) rather than that of Tricot (Paris: Vrin, 1987), who translates *akōn-hekōn* by "involuntary-voluntary." One could, in a more striking way, oppose "unwilling" (*contre-gré*) to "willing" (*plein gré*). [Translator's note: Ross, in his English translation, uses the opposition "involuntary-voluntary."]

actions expressing a choice—more precisely a preferential choice (*proairesis*), which is priorly determined through deliberation (*bouleusis*). This relation between the preferred and the predeliberated (*probebouleumenon*) will serve as the base for a definition of virtue that involves other differential features that I shall discuss in another study.[3]

How, on this base, is the relation of action to its agent to be stated? The most concise expression of this relation is found in a formula that makes the agent the principle (*arkhē*) of his actions, but in a sense of *arkhē* that authorizes us to say that the actions depend on (preposition *epi*) the agent himself (*autō*) (*E.N.* 3.1.1110a17).

The agent relation is thus expressed by the conjunction between the generic concept of principle and one of the deictic pronouns belonging to the family of the self (*le soi*), which will be enumerated later, through the mediation of one privileged preposition and of some others with similar senses. The simultaneous presence of these three components is essential to the Aristotelian interpretation of what today we term "ascription." These three components of ascription take on an ever more precise sense as the analysis progresses from the plane of the voluntary and the involuntary to the plane of preferential choice, where the relation between the theory of action and ethical theory is much closer.

Beginning with involuntary actions, characterized by compulsion or ignorance, Aristotle declares: "That is compulsory of which the moving principle is outside, being a principle in which nothing is contributed by the person who is acting or feeling the passion" (*E.N.* 3.1.1110a1–3).[4] In contrast, when a man acts voluntarily, "the principle that moves the instrumental parts of the body in such actions is in him [*en autō*], and the things of which the moving principle is in a man himself [*en autō*] are in his power [*ep' autō*, or as rendered in French, *dépend de lui*] to do or not to do" (1110a16–18).[5] Note that at this stage of the analysis the preposition "in" (*en*) prevails over the preposition "on" (*epi*). This will no longer be the case in the more precise analysis (closer to ethics, Aristotle will say) of preferential choice. But the linguistic and conceptual analysis of the voluntary and the involuntary already permits an emphasis on the con-

---

3. "Virtue, then, is a state of character concerned with choice, lying in a mean, i.e. the mean relative to us, this being determined by a rational principle by which the man of practical wisdom [*phronimos*] would determine it" (*E.N.* 2.6.1106b36–1107a2).

4. Cf. also *E.N.* 3.1.1110b15–17, which concludes the chapter with a discussion of the involuntary: "The compulsory, then, seems to be that whose moving principle is outside, the person compelled contributing nothing."

5. Later in *E.N.*, Aristotle says, "The voluntary would seem to be that of which the moving principle is in the agent himself, he being aware of the particular circumstances of the action" (3.1.1111a22–23).

junction between the notion of principle and a pronoun answering the question "who?" ("we," "someone," "each one," and summed up in the term *autos*, "himself"). Now this conjunction poses a considerable problem from the time of the analysis of the pair *akōn-hekōn*, to the extent that the notion of principle, considered in isolation, is not sufficient to *mark* the premoral sense of voluntary in the broad sense (as what is done freely, willingly—*de plein gré*) and a fortiori the sense better suited to the ethical field of preferential choice (or decision) in the strict sense of the term. "Principle" indeed is common to all investigations of first things, whatever they may be. It therefore cannot serve to distinguish between the physical and the ethical spheres. In this way, it is because nature is the principle of motion that one may attempt to clarify the notion of motion, which is the primary design of the *Physics*.[6] If the notion of principle can be shared in this way by physics and ethics, it is because in both we find becoming, change, and motion—events, according to our modern thinkers. By the same token, the notion of principle is not by itself sufficient to specify the tie between the action and the agent. Nor has the more specific notion of internal or immanent principle any value of discrimination: what, in fact, distinguishes natural beings (animals and their parts, plants, simple primary bodies, and all beings of the same kind) from the products of art (let us say artificial beings) is precisely that they contain in themselves a principle of motion and of rest.[7]

So if it is neither the term "principle" nor even the preposition "in" which specifies the relation of action to the agent, what alone can do this is the conjunction between the principle and one of the terms which answers to the question "who?" ("we" etc.). *A principle that is a self, a self that is a principle*—this is the characteristic trait of the relation we are looking for. With respect to this relation, unparalleled on the plane of physics,

6. We read in the *Physics,* book 3, in the opening lines of chapter 1: "Nature has been defined as a 'principle of motion and change', and it is the subject of our inquiry. We must therefore see that we understand the meaning of 'motion'; for if it were unknown, the meaning of 'nature' too would be unknown" (*Physica,* trans. R. P. Hardie and R. K. Gaye, in *The Basic Works of Aristotle,* ed. McKeon, 200b12–15). Concerning this, see A. Mansion, *Introduction à la physique aristotélicienne* (Paris: Vrin, 1973), pp. 49–79. Mansion recalls that the expression appearing in 184a15–16, *ta peri tas arkhas,* has the same extension as the classic *peri phuseōs,* handed down from the pre-Socratics. Hence, Aristotle speaks of "the principles of natural objects which are subject to generation" (191a3). As the first book of the *Physics* teaches, these principles are matter, form, and privation.

7. The full and precise definition of *phusis* is found in *Physics* 2.1.192b20: "Nature is a source or cause of being moved and of being at rest in that to which it belongs primarily, in virtue of itself and not in virtue of a concomitant attribute." Cf. Mansion, *Introduction,* p. 99. In other words, the internal tendency to change is what fundamentally distinguishes nature from art.

the subtle shift from the preposition *en* (in) to the preposition *epi* (depends on us, is in our power) has a definite significance. One could say that *en* marks the continuity between physics and ethics, a continuity more visible in the wide-ranging class of voluntary or involuntary acts, whereas the preposition *epi* confirms the specificity of the ethical plane, more evident in the narrower class of acts that are chosen, decided upon after deliberation.[8] Apart from this subtle variation, it is the function of these prepositions to connect the principle to the personal pronoun. This produces a twofold effect: by placing the paradigmatic "us" in the position of object of the verb, the preposition places the self in the position of principle; furthermore, by modifying the principle by the dependence on "us," it displaces the notion of principle from the physical plane to the ethical plane. This is the essential point: the sort of short circuit established between *arkhē* and *autos* results in each of these terms being interpreted in relation to the other. The entire enigma which the moderns have placed under the heading of ascription resides in this mutual interpretation.[9]

With the analysis of *proairesis,* of preferential choice (or decision), the ethical determination of the principle of action wins out over its physical determination. Here we reach the core of what is properly human in voluntary action, of which Aristotle says that it is "most closely bound up with virtue" (W. D. Ross), or "essentially proper to" virtue (Voilquin)[10] or "closely related to" the latter (Tricot) or possessing a "closer tie" with it (Gauthier-Jolif) (*E.N.* 3.2.1111b5). It is indeed preferential choice that makes human action worthy of praise or blame, inasmuch as it is what allows us "to discriminate characters better than actions do" (ibid.). With regard to choice it is said, more forcefully and precisely than with regard to the voluntary, that it "seems to relate to things that are in our power [*ta eph' hēmin,* or 'to things that depend on us']" (1111b30). To be sure, in the analysis that follows, the main emphasis is not placed on this tie of dependence (Tricot), on what is in our power (Ross, Gauthier-Jolif), but on the deliberation that precedes choice: the pre-ferred, Aristotle notes,

8. Later in connection with friendship (seventh study, sect. 2), I shall discuss a more subtle play between the nonreflexive pronoun *autos* and the reflexive *heauton*. (Must one be the friend of oneself in order to be someone else's friend?) This play is anticipated in book 3 of the *Nichomachean Ethics,* on the occasion of a remarkable observation: "Now of all of these no one could be ignorant unless he were mad, and evidently also he could not be ignorant of the agent; for how could he not know himself [*heauton*]?" (3.1.1111a8).

9. The variations in the French translations attest to the unusual situation created by the conjunction of principle and of self through the auspices of a particular preposition; thus Tricot translates *eph' hēmin* by *dépend de nous;* Gauthier-Jolif prefers *est en notre pouvoir* [as does Ross, "in our power"]. With the introduction of the word "power" we are set on the track of a development that we shall investigate at the end of this study.

10. Aristotle, *Ethique à Nicomaque,* trans. A. Voilquin (Paris: Garnier, 1963).

expresses the pre-deliberated. In this way Aristotle anticipates all the analyses we have considered above in which the "what?-why?" relation tends to marginalize the "what?-who?" relation by neutralizing the explicit reference to an agent. Aristotle, however, wastes no time in specifying that, of all the things about which we do not deliberate (eternal things, the weather, other people's government, etc.), none "can be brought about by [*dia*] our own efforts" (3.3.1112a30). "We deliberate about things that are in our power [*tōn eph' hēmin*] and can be done. . . . Now every class of men deliberates about the things that can be done by their own effort [*peri tōn di' hautōn praktōn*]" (1112a30–34).[11] The canonical definition of preferential choice admirably expresses this subtle attribution of the action to the agent through the predeliberated: "The object of choice being one of the things in our own power which is desired after deliberation, choice will be deliberate desire of things in our own power; for when we have decided as a result of deliberation, we desire in accordance with our deliberation" (1113a9–11).[12]

I do not wish to conclude this review of Aristotle's terminological and grammatical choices without mentioning some other expressions that underscore the enigmatic character of this relation between action and the agent. Two of these are clearly metaphoric. The first makes a comparison between principle and paternity. The context of this metaphoric tie is the refutation of the proverb stating that "no one [*oudeis*] is voluntarily wicked nor involuntarily happy" (*E.N.* 3.5.1113b14–15). To accept this aphorism would be, Aristotle says, to "deny that man is a moving principle or begetter of his actions as of children" (1113b18–19). The second metaphor is a political one; the reference to mastery appears clearly in the following text: "We are masters [*kurioi*] of our actions from the beginning right to the end" (1114b31–32). Taken together, these two metaphors mark in an oblique manner the originality of the ascription of action to its agent with respect to ordinary attribution to a logical subject. Could one

11. There are a number of terminological and grammatical remarks that might be made here. Let us note, in particular, the use of the passive voice in expressing what, in Husserlian terms, could be called the *noema of action:* the "realized" (which in turn calls for the preposition *dia,* similar to *epi*). Let us note too a different grammatical construction found a few lines later: "It seems, then, as has been said, that man is a moving principle of actions; now deliberation is about the things to be done by the agent himself [*tōn hautō praktōn*]" (*E.N.* 3.3.1112b31–32). Let us note, finally, the use of the distributive form "each" (*hekastoi*) and the recourse to the term "man," equivalent to "we" in the other texts cited. Finally, the play between the nonreflexive pronoun (*autos*) and the reflexive (*hautōn, hautō*) continues.

12. The second part of the sentence quoted shifts the emphasis onto the decision-deliberation relation, hence onto what-why; this relation, however, does not erase the prior emphasis on the fact that the object of deliberate desire depends on us, hence on the power we possess with respect to these things.

not say that the tie between principle (*arkhē*) and self (*autos*) is itself profoundly metaphoric, in the sense of "seeing-as," which I discuss in *The Rule of Metaphor*?[13] Does not ethics, in fact, demand that we "see" the principle "as" self and the self "as" principle? In this sense the explicit metaphors of paternity and of mastery would be the only way of putting into linguistic form the tie arising out of the short circuit between principle and self.

Let us consider the final indirect approach to ascription found in Aristotelian philosophy. To express the sort of collaboration (or better yet, synergy) between our choices and nature, in forming dispositions (*hexeis*) which together form our character, Aristotle forges the expression "co-responsible" (*sunaition*): "If, then, as is asserted, the virtues are voluntary (for we are ourselves somehow partly responsible [*sunaitioi pōs*] for our states of character, and it is by being persons of a certain kind that we assume the end to be so and so), the vices also will be voluntary; for the same is true of them: (3.5.1114b20–25). Aristotle's intention is certainly to extend the responsibility for our acts to our dispositions, hence to the whole of our moral personality; the intention is also to confine it within the limits of partial responsibility. The language used to express this cannot help but be unusual (*aition* rather than *aitia*, the addition of *sun* and the nuance of *pōs*).[14] Here, too, one would be tempted to say, words are lacking.

A leap across the centuries will make this apparent to us.

I should like to show that the modern theory of action gives to ascription a meaning distinct from attribution, a meaning that transforms the particular case into an exception and that places it on the same side—namely, on the side of pragmatics—as the capacity to designate oneself, a capacity related, as we know, to the theory of utterance and to speech acts. This distinct meaning is indicated, in Strawson's own work, by the features brought out by Aristotle. The author of *Individuals* indeed observes that the physical and mental characteristics *belong* to the person, that the latter *possesses* them. Now what an owner has is said to be his or her own in contrast to what belongs to someone else and which, for this reason, is said to be foreign to the former. In turn, that which is one's "own" governs the sense that we attribute to the adjectives and pronouns we term "pos-

13. *The Rule of Metaphor,* trans. Robert Czerny with Kathleen McLaughlin and John Costello (Toronto: University of Toronto Press), 1977.

14. Concerning the expression *sunaition,* see W. F. R. Hardie, *Aristotle's Ethical Theory* (Oxford: Oxford University Press, 1981), pp. 177–81. Chapter 8, devoted to the distinction between the voluntary and the involuntary, and chapter 9, dealing with choice and the origination of action, offer a thorough review of the problem discussed here from the perspective of the relation between action and the agent.

sessive": my-mine, your-yours, her-hers, and so forth, without forgetting the impersonal form "one's own" or the distributive "each," as in the expression "to each his own," upon which the ethics of the just will be constructed, as we shall see later.

The question is whether or not these expressions, often idiomatic, rest on universal meanings which deserve to be classified as transcendentals on the same order as those we assigned to the semantic field of action. There is every indication to think so. It is noteworthy that ascription marks the reference of all the terms of the conceptual network of action to its pivotal point: "who?" Moreover, we determine the answer to the question "who?" by obtaining an answer to the chain of questions "what?" "why?" "how?" and so on. Let us verify this for the two questions that we were concerned with in the preceding study—"what?" and "why?"

It is first with reference to *action* itself that we say it is mine, yours, his or hers, that it depends on each of us, that it is in our power. Then, of *intention* we say that it is someone's intention, and of someone we say that he or she intends to do something. We can, to be sure, understand the intention as such, but if we have severed it from its author to examine it, we then give it back to the latter by attributing it to him or to her. Moreover, this is just what the agent does when he or she considers the options that are open and when the agent deliberates, to use Aristotle's expression. Ascription consists precisely in this reappropriation by the agent of his or her own deliberation: making up one's mind is cutting short the debate by making one of the options contemplated one's own. As concerns the notion of *motive,* to the extent that it is distinguished from the intention with which one acts, principally as a retrospective motive, the fact of its belonging to an agent is just as much a part of the meaning of the motive as its logical tie to the action of which it is the cause. It can legitimately be asked: "Why did A do X?" "What made A do X?" To mention the motive is to mention the agent as well. This relation has something particularly strange, even paradoxical about it. On the one hand, searching for the author is a *terminable* investigation which stops with the designation of the agent, usually by citing his or her name: "Who did that? So and so." On the other hand, searching for the motives of an action is an *interminable* investigation, the chain of motivations losing itself in the unfathomable haze of internal and external influences: psychoanalysis has a direct relation to this situation. Nevertheless, this does not keep us from tying the interminable investigation of motives to the terminable investigation of the agent; this strange relation is part and parcel of our concept of ascription. So it is in terms of the entire network crisscrossing the semantics of action that we understand the expression "agent." With this remark let us recall that mastering the entire network is comparable to learning a language and that understanding the word "agent" is learning to place it correctly in that network.

2. The Aporias of Ascription

If things seem relatively simple as long as we remain on the level of generalities concerning the interconnections of meaning that tie together all the terms of the network, and in particular the "who?" the "what?" and the "why?" of action, how is one to explain the resistance, within the semantics of action as such, to any closer investigation of the relation of ascription? It is not enough to blame the adverse ontology of events, which we have shown obstructs efforts to pursue the relations between action and agent. One may wonder whether one does not have to step outside the framework of the semantics of action, within which Strawson's theory of basic particulars is developed. The person, as a referential term, remains one of the "things" about which we speak. In this sense the theory of basic particulars finally remains captive to an ontology of "something in general" which, faced with the demand for recognition of the *ipse,* develops a force of resistance comparable, although set forth in a somewhat different way, to that of the ontology of events.

Does this mean that the pragmatics of discourse, centered on utterance and open to the self-designation of the utterer, is of any greater help? Yes, most probably. But only up to a certain point, since designating oneself as agent means something more than designating oneself as speaker. This gap between the two degrees of self-designation will make apparent the aporias proper to ascription. The latter, as is generally the case with the most intractable aporias, do not imply any condemnation of the philosophy that discovers them. Quite the opposite, they are all to its credit, as I have shown elsewhere.[15]

1. The *first difficulty* can be perceived in the extension of the third of Strawson's theses as these were enumerated above, namely that it is part of the meaning of practical predicates, just as it is of all mental predicates, to be attributable to someone other than oneself, once they are attributable to oneself, and to keep the same meaning in both situations of attribution. It is worth noting that, unlike the other two theses considered, the attribution is made not only to the "same thing"—hence under the heading of something in general—but to oneself and to another (self-ascribable versus other-ascribable). The relation of "who?" to "what?" is laid bare here. Now the strangeness of this relation deserves that we stop and attend to

---

15. *Time and Narrative* 3 is entirely constructed around the relation between an aporetics of temporality and the response of a poetics of narrativity.

it. Splitting ascription in this way between oneself and another suggests that ascription compensates in a way for an inverse operation, consisting in suspending the attribution to someone, for the sole purpose of giving a descriptive tenor to the action predicates which are thus placed, if I may say so, in reserve with respect to attribution. It is the relation between the splitting in two of actual attribution and the possibility of maintaining it in suspension that causes a problem. Now it is a surprising phenomenon, which, on the scale of an entire culture, takes on considerable proportions, that we never cease to add to the repertoire of thoughts, in the broad sense of the term, including cognitions, volitions, and emotions, whose meaning we understand without taking into account the differences between the persons to whom they are attributed. This is what is confirmed by the various treatises on the passions from book 2 of Aristotle's *Rhetoric,* passing by way of the medieval and classical treatises (Saint Thomas Aquinas, Descartes, Spinoza, etc.).[16]

Not only are mental phenomena, which classical authors called affections and actions, attributable to everyone, to anyone, but their meaning can be understood outside of any explicit attribution. It is quite precisely in this form that they enter the thesaurus of mental significations. It can even be said that this aptitude of mental predicates for being comprehensible in themselves, while suspending any explicit attribution, constitutes what can be called "the mental." Literature will later give us a striking example of the understanding we have of mental states which are not attributed to anyone or which are suspended from attribution, to the extent that this understanding is the condition for their attribution to fictional characters. This possibility of naming mental phenomena and of understanding their meaning, abstracting from their attribution, precisely defines their status as predicate: "The mental" is the repertoire of mental predicates available for a given culture.

16. Thus we read in article 1 of Descartes's *Treatise on the Passions:* "On proceeding to do so, I observe that whatever occurs in the way of novelty or change, is by the philosophers ordinarily termed a passion in respect of the subject to which it happens and an action in respect of what causes it to happen. Though agent and patient are often very different, the action and the passion are thus always one and the same thing. We are allowing it these two names because of the two diverse subjects to which we can refer it" (*Descartes, Philosophical Writings,* trans. Norman Kemp Smith [New York: Modern Library, 1958], pp. 265–66). This is why the passions can be enumerated without consideration of persons. To be sure, passions are called passions of the *soul.* But the word "soul" introduces no difference between "I" and "you." This is why the "we" that enters into the definition of each of the passions designates anyone to whom the passions are attributed. We can read on this point articles 53, 56, 57, 61, which give definitions of the primary passions and the relations of each one to an undetermined "we." In this context, "we" means no more than "one" or "each one." Thus one can, without any particular qualms, speak of the soul in the third person.

This suspending of the attribution of practical predicates to a specific agent reveals the particularity of the relation between the question "who?" and the pair of questions "what?-why?" It indeed belongs to the nature of this relation to be capable of being suspended in this way, and ascription is understood in correlation with this suspension. By the same token, it is then understandable that the theory of action developed in the preceding study could include a methodical *epokhē* of the question of the agent, without appearing to do violence to experience and to its expression on the level of ordinary language. The attraction exerted by causalist epistemology and by the ontology of events on the logical analysis of action sentences was favored, and in a sense encouraged, by the point of least resistance of the conceptual network of action at the suture between the question "who?" and the block of other questions to which the phenomenon of action gives rise. The attention given to the content of our intentions and to their motivation tends by itself to separate the "what?" of the thing to be done and the "why?" of the thing done from the "who?" of the action and of the reason for acting. This separation has the twofold effect—on the one hand, of helping to incorporate the meaning of intentions and motives into the repertoire of mental phenomena, without our having to specify to whom these phenomena belong, and on the other hand, of making even more enigmatic the appropriation which removes the suspension of ascription.

This may, in fact, offer a series of degrees. Between the total suspension of attribution and the actual attribution to this or that agent, at least three degrees may be distinguished: that of *one,* completely anonymous, the absolute antithesis of the self; that of *someone* in the sense of anyone, hence in the sense of an individuation admitting of indifferent substitution; that, finally, of *each one,* which implies an operation of distribution of distinct "shares," as is suggested by the juridical adage "To each his own" (*suum cuique*). These intermediary phases of neutralized attribution are precisely those which assure the permutation sought by Strawson between self-ascription and other-ascription. From this dialectic of suspension and appropriation it results that the first aporia of ascription cannot be resolved within the framework of the theory of identifying reference. In order to move from the suspension of ascription, through neutralized ascription, to actual and singular ascription, an agent must be able to *designate himself or herself* in such a way that there is a genuine *other* to whom the same attribution is made in a relevant manner. We must then move out of the semantics of action and enter into pragmatics, which takes into account propositions whose meaning varies with the position of the speaking subject and which, to this very extent, implies a face-to-face speech situation of an "I" and a "you." But if the recourse to the pragmatics of discourse is necessary, is it sufficient to account for the particularities of self-designation as agent? This is the question raised by the other aporias of ascription.

2. The *second difficulty* concerns the status of ascription in relation to description. If ascribing is not describing, is this not by virtue of a certain affinity, which remains to be clarified, with prescribing? Now prescription applies simultaneously to agents and to actions. It is to someone that it is prescribed to act in accord with this or that rule of action. In this way is determined simultaneously what is permitted and what is not with regard to actions, and what is blameworthy and praiseworthy with regard to agents. A double presupposition is thereby assumed, namely that actions are capable of being submitted to rules and that agents can be held responsible for their actions. The term "imputation" can be used to designate the act of holding an agent responsible for actions which themselves are considered to be permissible or not permissible.

This sort of analysis can be referred to Aristotle, who, as we saw above, directly links preferential choice to the idea of praise and blame. For him, the criteria of the voluntary—and all the more so, those of choice—are from the start criteria of moral and juridical imputation. Compulsion and ignorance have an explicit value of excuse, of discharge from responsibility. If the voluntary deserves praise and blame, the involuntary calls for pardon and pity (it is true, nevertheless, that Aristotle does not specify what is the precise domain of the courts and what the province of purely moral evaluation). Whence the ingenious idea of considering imputation, not as an operation added onto ascription, but of the same nature as the latter. In this way, H. L. A. Hart proposes to interpret propositions in ordinary language of the type "he did that," along the lines of judicial decisions, where a judge rules, for example, that this is a valid contract, or that this is a murder and not an assassination.[17] According to Hart, the transition from ordinary language propositions, without moral or legal coloration, to judicial decisions is assured by propositions of an intermediary status of the form "this is mine (yours, his, hers)," that is, propositions which make demands, confer, transfer, recognize—in short, attribute rights. From this comparison between imputation and the attribution of rights results, by contrast, the complete break between ascribing and describing. Ascribing, according to Hart, is the result of a specific process in which opposing claims are confronted and in which one of them is defeated, not because the positive core of good or bad intention has been reached but because the excuses considered acceptable in similar cases have been ex-

17. H. L. A. Hart, "The Ascription of Responsibility and Rights," *Proceedings of the Aristotelian Society* 49 (1948): 171–94.

hausted. Dismissibility—defeasibility—thus becomes a criterion of any claim to ascribe an action to an agent.

The intention that guides this assimilation of ascription and moral and legal imputation is most legitimate: it tends to widen the gap separating ascription in the moral sense from attribution in the logical sense. This gap concerns as well the sense assigned to the words "possess" and "belong to," as well as to the deictic group of the family of possessive adjectives and pronouns. The agent, we said, is the possessor of his or her actions, which are therefore his or her own. It belongs to someone, we also said, to do this rather than that. Ownership has always been a legal problem, as indeed we find in the school of natural law, in the Kantian philosophy of private right, entirely focused on the distinction between mine and yours in the *Metaphysics of Morals,* and in the theory of abstract right in Hegel's *Philosophy of Right.*[18]

It can be doubted, however, that moral and legal imputation constitutes the strong form of a logical structure, whose weak form would be ascription. This is so for three reasons.

First reason: legal statements do not readily apply to actions as simple—some would say, as outrageously banal—as those that the grammar and logic of action sentences like to describe, in their legitimate intention not to let the moral, political, or ideological interest the reader might have in the content of the actions considered interfere with their propositional structure. The moral or legal imputation really enters into the equation only when one considers complex actions—those action chains, as we shall call them in the sixth study on practices. Now the rules of complexification that preside over the composition of these practices belong to a different type of investigation than that which still directs the semantics of action sentences, even if pragmatics adds a complexity of its own to this semantics. We must therefore postpone the study of moral and legal imputation until after the study devoted to practices.

Second reason: if we remain within the framework prescribed by pragmatics, it does seem that properly legal statements apply in a selective way to actions considered from the perspective of what is blamable and punishable. What is blamable are bad actions considered from a verdict of condemnation. Legal imputation is thus placed within a category of speech acts, namely that of "verdictives," which go beyond the simple ascription of an action to an agent. Submitting an action to a verdict of condemnation is submitting it to an accusatory procedure which has its own constitutive rules, just as do all speech acts. If ascription appears to be an

18. Even the ownership of one's own body can be held to involve legal questions (*Hegel's Philosophy of Right,* trans. T. M. Knox [Oxford: Clarendon Press, 1952], pars. 47–48).

operation prior to any accusatory utterance of the class of verdictives, is the distinctive feature of ascription to be sought on the plane where speech acts are distinguished from one another?

Third reason: what the assignation of responsibility in the ethico-legal sense appears to presuppose is of a different nature than the self-designation of a speaker, namely a causal tie (one that remains to be determined) related to the power to act. The action must be able to be said to depend on the agent in order to be blamable or praiseworthy. Thus, in the *Nichomachean Ethics,* before his theory of virtue, Aristotle, as we saw above, develops an analysis of a fundamental act: preferential choice. Here a power to act is expressed which is even more primitive than the blamable or praiseworthy character (today we should say "verdictible" character) of the action produced. We are thus sent back to a specific analysis of the power to act, centered on the causal efficiency of this power. It is here that the tie of action to its agent adds a new and properly practical dimension to the self-designation of a speaker and to the designation of his or her interlocutor as other than self.

3. But what is meant by the "power to act"? It is here that we encounter the *third aporia* which seems to confound our concept of ascription. To say that an action depends on its agent is to say in an equivalent fashion that it is in the agent's power.[19] With the notion of power returns the old idea of efficient causality which the Galilean revolution had cast out of physics. Is it permissible to say that with ascription efficient causality simply returns to its place of origin, to its native land, namely the living experience of the power to act? To authorize this rehabilitation, is it sufficient to argue from the real polysemy of the notion of causality, which numerous contemporary authors have willingly recognized, either to justify a reformulation of causality appropriate to the human sciences, in particular to historiography, as is seen in Collingwood,[20] or to justify its definitive elimination from the scientific field in favor of the ideas of laws or functions, as we see in Russell?[21]

However, restoring efficient causality for the sole benefit of ascription may well appear a weak argument, as does any appeal to something as a primitive datum (*fait primitif*). I am not rejecting the notion of primitive datum. At a much later stage of the investigation, I shall oppose the modest avowal of a few primitive data, inherent in the construction of a fundamental anthropology to the Promethean ambition of an ultimate

19. Cf. in Sec. 1 above my remarks concerning the French translation of Aristotle's *eph' hēmin.*

20. Cf. *Time and Narrative* 1 : 252 n. 7.

21. Ibid., p. 113.

foundation based upon the model of the Cartesian cogito and its successively more radical formulations.[22] One must not surrender one's arms, however, without a fight. This is why I want to give the form of an aporia to the admission that the agent's power of acting is, in the final analysis, to be considered a primitive datum. A primitive datum does not mean a raw datum. Quite the opposite, a primitive datum should be recognizable only at the end of a labor of thinking, of a dialectic—that is, of a conflict of arguments, which has been developed rigorously.

In my opinion, this dialectic passes through two stages: a *disjunctive* stage, at the end of which we observe the necessarily antagonistic character of the original causality of the agent in relation to the other modes of causality; and a *conjunctive* stage, at the end of which we recognize the necessity to coordinate in a synergistic way the original causality of the agent with the other forms of causality. Only then will the primitive datum of what we must call not simply the power to do but *initiative,* in the strong sense of the word, be recognized.

In its disjunctive phase, our dialectic unavoidably encounters the famous Kantian argument of the "Third Conflict of the Transcendental Ideas."[23] I am not proposing here any new interpretation of the Kantian antinomy of the causality of freedom and of causality in accordance with the laws of nature. My ambition is to bring to light, with the help of the Kantian dialectic, some of the strong points of our analysis of ascription, perhaps even eliciting some new ones.

Let us begin by stressing the *necessarily* dialectical character of the notion of power of acting—in other words, the *necessarily* antithetical formulation of the very question itself. I shall recall Kant's statement of the thesis of the causality of freedom: "Causality in accordance with the laws of nature is not the only causality from which the appearances of the world can one and all be derived. To explain these appearances it is necessary to assume that there is also another causality, that of freedom" (A444, B472).[24] Now our discussion of the analytic theory of action has constantly confronted us with an antithetical formulation similar to Kant's.

22. Cf. below, tenth study.

23. A certain recognition of the antagonistic character of causality can be found in the Aristotelian analysis with which we began this study. If there are things that depend on us, there are also others which belong to causes traditionally placed under the heading of nature, necessity, and chance (*E.N.* 3.3.1112a31–32). After affirming that man is the principle and begetter (father) of his actions as he is of his children, Aristotle adds: "But if these facts are evident and we cannot refer actions to moving principles other than those in ourselves, the acts whose moving principles are in us must themselves also be in our power and voluntary" (3.5.1113b18–19). Thus the "on us" is dialectically opposed to the "causes other than ourselves" within the field of application of the notion of principle.

24. Immanuel Kant, *The Critique of Pure Reason,* trans. Norman Kemp Smith (New York: St. Martin's Press, 1965), p. 409.

We have not forgotten the opposition between the event that happens and the event that one brings about or the opposition between cause and motive in the dichotomous phase of the theory of action. The objection might be raised here that, in a subsequent phase, this dichotomous aspect has been overcome. Nothing of the sort! We later saw the antithesis reappear in other, more subtle forms, whether this was in Anscombe, with the opposition between knowledge by observation and knowledge without observation, or in Davidson himself, with the distinction between event agency and agent agency.[25] It is in the polarity between ascription and description, however, that the antithetical formulation of the problem finds its culmination, leading us to say along with Kant that "causality in accordance with the laws of nature is not the only causality."

Let us now consider the argument of the "Thesis" in the Kantian antinomy of freedom and determinism. What is given to our reflection here is what Kant terms "an absolute spontaneity of the cause" and which he defines as the power to begin "of itself" (*von selbst*) "a series of appearances, which proceeds in accordance with laws of nature" (A447, B475).[26] In the "Observation" following the "Proof," Kant notes that this absolute spontaneity of action is the "proper ground of its imputability" (A448, B476).[27] So we were indeed correct in seeking in imputation, in the moral and legal sense of the term, the original stratum of a power of acting. What in the analytic theory of action corresponds to the Kantian notion of absolute spontaneity? It is the now-classical notion, following A. Danto, of "basic actions." Recall the definition that Danto gives of basic actions: these are actions which require no other intermediary action one would have had to perform in order to do this or that. To eliminate from the definition of action the clause "in order to . . ." is to allege, under the heading of basic action, a kind of causality that would be defined in and of itself. Basic actions are those actions which belong to the repertoire of what each of us knows how to do without resorting to any intermediary action of an instrumental or strategic nature that one would have to have learned beforehand. In this sense the concept of basic action designates a primitive datum. It is to the theory of action what basic particulars are to the theory of identifying reference. We see why this is so: the original concept of a basic action holds in the practical order the place that evidence occupies in the cognitive order. Arthur Danto argues that we all know in a direct and intuitive way that there are basic actions and what actions are basic actions.[28]

25. Cf. n. 24 above in the third study.

26. Kant, *Critique of Pure Reason*, p. 411.

27. Ibid., p. 412.

28. Arthur Danto, "Basic Actions," *American Philosophical Quarterly* 2, no. 2 (1965): 141–48.

The connection between this final assertion and the Kantian antithetical argument remains hidden as long as it has not been placed back in the conflictual field of causality. For it is indeed as a *beginning* of a causal series that the notion of basic action acquires its problematic character, while at the same time escaping the charge of being a weak argument. In its negative form, the idea of beginning implies that the movement of thought is halted in its pursuit of a prior cause. It is this halt that the Kantian antithesis denounces as an illegitimate exemption from laws; at this precise point the necessary "conflict of transcendental ideas" is born. The theory of action cannot ignore this antithetical character of the notion of beginning, which may well remain hidden in a naive approach to the concept of basic action. In truth, this notion leaves unexplored the question of attribution to an agent. And this is why its antithetical character goes unperceived. In contrast, the antinomy moves to the forefront when the answers to the question "who?" are confronted with the answers to the question "why?" We then noted with surprise that, if the search for the motives of an action is interminable, the search for its author is terminable: the answers to the question "who?", whether they contain a proper name, a pronoun, or a definite description, put an end to the inquiry. It is not that the investigation is arbitrarily interrupted, but the answers that terminate the investigation are considered to be sufficient by the one who gives them and acceptable as such by the one who receives them. "Who did that?" someone asks. "So and so," someone answers. The agent thereby proves to be a strange cause indeed, since naming him or her puts an end to the search for the cause, a search which continues along another line—that of motivation. In this manner, the antithetical of which Kant spoke penetrates the theory of action at the very point where acting and the reasons for acting are joined.

However, we have not yet reached what is essential in Kant's argument. The idea of an absolute beginning is not only justified by a negative argument (it is not necessary to move back up the causal chain). It is given even stronger justification by the positive argument which constitutes the very core of the proof. Without a beginning in the series, Kant argues, the series of causes would not be complete; it therefore belongs to the idea of beginning that it assures the "completeness of the series on the side of the causes that arise the one from the other" (A446, B474).[29] This seal of completeness imprinted on the idea of serial causality is essential to the formulation of the antinomy. The unlimited openness of the causal process presented in the antithesis is opposed to the very idea of the completeness of a causal series. But the Kantian argument itself is not yet complete. In

29. Kant, *Critique of Pure Reason*, p. 410.

the "Observation" following the "Proof" of the thesis, Kant distinguishes two types of beginning: one which would be the beginning of the world, the other which is a beginning in the midst of the world. The latter is the beginning related to freedom. Kant concedes that this is the source of misunderstanding: did we not above call spontaneity "absolute," that is nonrelative? How can we now speak of a "relatively first" beginning? [30] Answer: an absolute beginning with respect to a particular series of events, liberty is only a relative beginning with respect to the entire course of the world. Kant specifies: "For the absolutely first beginning of which we are here speaking is not a beginning in time, but in causality" (A450, B478). [31] There follows the example of the man who arises from his chair "in complete freedom, without being necessarily determined thereto by the influence of natural causes" (ibid.). And Kant repeats: "Accordingly, in respect of causality though not of time, [this act] must be entitled an absolutely first beginning of a series of appearances" (ibid.). This distinction between a beginning *of* the world and a beginning *in* the world is essential to the notion of a practical beginning taken from the point of view of its function of completeness. The practical beginning *in medias res* exerts its function of completeness only on determined series of causes, which it helps to distinguish from other series initiated by other beginnings.

This integrating function of the beginning in relation to a determined series of causes finds an interesting confirmation in our earlier analyses, at the same time as the Kantian analysis reveals their implicitly antithetical character.

The theory of action encounters the problem of the relation between a beginning and a complete series in its own terms. It first encounters this problem in the provisional framework of the theory of descriptions. The initial problem, as we showed above, is to identify and to name the actions belonging to a practical chain. The question is then whether this is the "true" description in this complex case. We recall Anscombe's example: men, moving their arms, work a pump, which pumps poisoned water up to a higher floor; in doing this, they kill those involved in a conspiracy and contribute to the success of a revolutionary movement. What exactly are these men doing? If the various answers given are equally acceptable, this is because, in Anscombe's words, the first gesture—which is in fact a basic action in accordance with Danto's criteria—"swallows" the chain of events which result from it, down to the last with which the story ends. For the logic of practical reasoning, the series, in Kant's terms, is unified by a tie of implication of the means-to-end type. From the causal perspective,

30. Ibid., p. 413.
31. Ibid., p. 414.

however—the perspective of events rather than of intentions—the unification of the series is assured by the capacity of integration and summation
exerted by the beginning itself on the series in question, the intentional
aim of this beginning traversing the entire series.[32]

These hesitations in the description, which do not actually constitute
an aporia, lead us to the threshold of a genuine difficulty, when we move
from the description of "what?" to the ascription to a "who?" The problem
then takes the following form: *how far* does the efficiency of the beginning
extend, and consequently *how far* does the agent's responsibility extend,
considering the unlimited nature of the series of physical consequences?
This problem is thus the inverse of that of basic actions: then, we asked if
it was necessary to halt the ascending series of causes somewhere along
the way; now, we are asking where the descending series of effects should
be halted. If the causality of the agent was seen as a plausible stopping
point in the backward movement through the series of causes, the diffuse
efficient causality of the beginning seems limitless on the side of the effects.
This problem, which can be called the *bearing* of the beginning, has a close
connection with the Kantian notion of a "relatively first beginning," "as a
series occurring in the world." When the beginning of action does not
coincide with that of the world, it then indeed takes its place in a constellation of beginnings, which each have a bearing; these have then to be
evaluated in comparison with one another. In the case of each beginning,
it is legitimate to ask about what could be called the confines marking the
domain of that beginning. This question opens a very real problem, one
well known to judges, whether involved in sentencing or not, and to his-
torians as well. An agent is not *in* the far distant consequences as he or she
is in a sense *in* his or her immediate act. The problem is then to delimit
the sphere of events for which the agent can be held responsible. This is
by no means easy, for several reasons. First, if we follow only a single
series, the effects of an action are in a sense separated off from the agent,
just as this occurs in language to living speech through the mediation of
writing. In these effects the laws of nature take control of what follows
from our initiatives. In this way action has effects that are unintended,
even perverse. Now separating what belongs to the agent from what belongs to the chains of external causality proves to be a highly complex
operation. It is necessary to separate the intentional segments capable of
being formalized in practical syllogisms from those segments which could
be called systemic, to the extent that they express the structure of dynamic
physical systems. However, as I shall state later, continuation, as that

---

32. We shall return to this question of the integral unity of a series later, when we discuss
the narrative unity of a life and the narrative identity of a character.

which prolongs the energy of the beginning, expresses the entanglement of these two modes of connection; without this entangling, acting could not be said to produce changes in the world.

Another sort of entanglement, however, makes it difficult to attribute to a particular agent a determined series of events. It is the way the actions of each one of us are intertwined with the actions of everyone else. We have insisted elsewhere, following W. Schapp, on the idea, proper to the narrative field, of "being entangled in stories"; [33] the action of each person (and of that person's history) is entangled not only with the physical course of things but with the social course of human activity. How, in particular, are we to distinguish in a group action what belongs to each of the social actors? This difficulty, like the preceding one, concerns the historian no less than the judge, when it is a matter of designating the authors distributively, assigning to each participant a distinct sphere of action. Here, attributing is distributing. We must not be afraid to say that determining the end point where the responsibility of an agent ends is a matter of decision and not some fact to be established. It is here that Hart's thesis gains credibility, according to which attributing an action to an agent resembles an adjudication by which a judge attributes to the parties in conflict what properly belongs to each.[34] Ascription tends once again to merge with imputation in a conflictual situation between rival claims. Nevertheless, the fact that the historian too may have to determine the share of responsibility of the various actors participating in a complex action makes one think that this delimiting of the respective spheres of responsibility does not necessarily include an aspect of incrimination or condemnation. Raymond Aron, following Max Weber, was not wrong to distinguish between historical responsibility and moral responsibility.[35] What they have in common is precisely their illustration of the Kantian notion of a relatively first beginning. This notion implies a multiplicity of agents and of beginnings of actions, which can be identified only in terms of the distinct series of actions assigned to each one. Now the conflictual structure of this assigning cannot be eliminated; delimiting the bearing of a responsible decision contributes to the closure effect, without which it would be impossible to speak of a complete series. This closure effect, which is essential to the thesis of the causality of freedom, contradicts the limitless openness of the series of causes required by the antithesis in the Kantian antinomy.

Having said all this, is it possible to remain at the stage of antinomies in our understanding of what is meant by the power to act? Kant himself

33. W. Schapp, *In Geschichten verstrickt* (Wiesbaden: B. Heyman, 1976).
34. See Hart, "Ascription."
35. *Time and Narrative* 1:260 n. 11.

does not do so. After having said and repeated that the "Thesis" and "Antithesis" of the beginning, like the "Thesis" and "Antithesis" of the other three cosmological antinomies, may well be "commanded to keep the peace before the tribunal of reason" (A501, B529),[36] Kant finally reserves a different fate for the transcendental ideas he terms "mathematical," which are related to the finite or infinite extension of the world and the finite or infinite division of matter (the first and second cosmological antinomies). For the latter, the skeptical solution is definitive. The same is not true of the transcendental ideas termed "dynamical," which concern the relatively first beginning, that of human actions, and the absolute beginning of the world as a whole. The solution of the first two antinomies was a skeptical solution, because "in the mathematical connection of the series of appearances no other than a sensible condition is admissible, that is to say, none that is not itself part of the series" (A530, B558).[37] The solution of the third and fourth antinomies, however, may consist in maintaining the "Thesis" and the "Antithesis" side by side. Indeed, "in the dynamical series of sensible conditions, a heterogeneous condition, not itself a part of the series, but purely intelligible, and as such outside the series, can be allowed. In this way reason obtains satisfaction and the unconditioned is set prior to the appearances, while yet the invariably conditioned character of the appearances is not obscured, nor their series cut short, in violation of the principles prescribed by the understanding" (A531, B559).[38] It results that the thesis and the antithesis can both be held to be true, on the condition that they are maintained on different levels. We are familiar with what follows: freedom as a pure transcendental idea, without any connection to appearances, constitutes the ultimate sense of the faculty of beginning a causal series oneself. Upon this transcendental freedom is founded the practical concept of freedom—that is, independence of the will in relation to the coercion of sensuous impulses (A532, B560).[39] But what is transcendental freedom? It is intelligible freedom, if by intelligible is meant "whatever in an object of the senses is not itself appearance" (A538, B566).[40] And note the passage that follows: "If, therefore, that which in the sensible world must be regarded as appearance has in itself a faculty which is not an object of sensible intuition, but through which it can be the cause of appearances, the causality of this being can be regarded from two points of view. Regarded as the causality of a

36. Kant, *Critique of Pure Reason*, p. 446.
37. Ibid., p. 463.
38. Ibid.
39. Ibid., p. 465.
40. Ibid., p. 467.

thing in itself, it is intelligible in its action; regarded as the causality of an appearance in the world of sense, it is sensible in its effects" (ibid.).[41]

I should like to suggest here another outcome of the antinomy, one toward which Kant himself, in a sense, leans, when he writes: "There is nothing to prevent us from ascribing to this transcendental object, besides the quality in terms of which it appears, a causality which is not appearance, although its effect is to be met with in appearance" (A538–39, B566–67).[42] What is this effect that is met with in appearance? Kant calls it "character," distinguishing between empirical character and intelligible character. Could one not say, in a nonphenomenalist sense of the term "appearance" (that is, in the sense of what shows itself), the phenomenon or appearance of acting requires the union of thesis and antithesis in a phenomenon—in the sense I have just mentioned—specific to the practical field, which could be termed *initiative?*[43]

Thinking initiative, reflecting on this notion, is the task that is set before us at the end of the present study. Initiative, we shall say, is an *intervention* of the agent of action in the course of the world, an intervention which effectively causes changes in the world. If, at the present stage of our investigation, we can represent this grasp of the human agent on things, within the course of the world, as Kant himself says, only as a conjunction between several sorts of causality, this must be frankly recognized as a constraint belonging to the structure of action as initiative. In this respect, Aristotle opened the way with his notion of *sunaition,* which makes the agent a partial and contributing cause in forming dispositions and character. We recall, however, the prudence with which Aristotle introduced this mixed notion, which he nuances with "partly," "in some sense" (*pōs*). It is indeed "in some sense" that causalities are composed. We have ourselves several times encountered the necessity of turning to this type of union; it ultimately results from the very necessity of joining "who?" to the "what?" and the "why?" of action, a necessity stemming from the in-

41. Ibid.
42. Ibid., pp. 467–68.
43. Compare this with the "Explanation of the Cosmological Idea of Freedom in Its Connection with Universal Natural Necessity" (A542–57, B570–85, pp. 469–79). Kant speaks here of a causality which "would be the action of a cause which, in respect of appearances, is original, and therefore, as pertaining to this faculty, not appearance but intelligible; although it must otherwise, in so far as it is a link in the chain of nature, be regarded as entirely belonging to the world of sense" (A544, B572, p. 471). But for Kant the sole criterion of the reality of intelligible freedom is the ability of action to submit itself to rules, to obey or not to obey duty. I want to resist this moral solution here, as I consider it premature at this point, and shall instead look to the phenomenon of the power to act for a way out of the antinomy.

tersignifying structure of the conceptual network of action. In accordance
with this demand, it seems necessary not to confine our analysis to opposing the terminable character of the inquiry concerning the agent to the
interminable character of the inquiry into the motives. The power to act
consists precisely in the connection between these two inquiries and reflects the necessity to tie "who?" to "why?" through the "what?" of action.
The course of motivation, however, does not take us out of what could,
with all due precaution, be called the plane of "mental facts." It is on the
course of "external" nature that the power of acting exerts its hold.

The best representation of a conjunction such as this seems to me to be
that suggested by G. Von Wright in *Explanation and Understanding* in the
form of a quasi-causal model.[44] I have considered this model elsewhere in
the framework of an investigation devoted to explanation in history.[45] But
in fact, over and beyond the epistemology of historical knowledge, I was
concerned with accounting for the general phenomenon of intervention.
The model proposed is a mixed one, in the sense that it joins together
teleological segments amenable to practical reasoning with systematic segments amenable to causal explanation. What matters here and what poses
a problem are precisely the points of suture between the two. Indeed,
every result of a practical syllogism is a real action which introduces a new
fact into the world order, and this in turn sets off a causal series. Among
the effects of this series are new facts which are then assumed as circumstances by the same agent or by other agents. Now what makes this linking
of means and ends fundamentally possible? Essentially, it is the agent's
capacity to make one of the things he or she knows how to do (knows he
or she is able to do) coincide with an initial system-state, thereby determining the system's conditions of closure.[46] According to Von Wright's
own words, this conjunction occurs only if we feel confident on the basis
of past experience to be able to set in motion a dynamic system such as
this. With the idea of "setting a system in motion," the notions of action
and causality are joined to one another, Von Wright says. But to what
extent do they overlap with one another?

    44. G. Von Wright, *Explanation and Understanding* (London: Routledge and Kegan
Paul, 1971).
    45. *Time and Narrative* 1 : 132–43. Here I am leaving aside the narrative interpretation
which I then proposed of the series of causes and ends in the model termed "quasi-causal."
    46. Let me recall in this connection the terms of my presentation in *Time and Narrative:*
"Action realizes another noteworthy type of closure, in that it is in doing something that an
agent learns to 'isolate' a closed system from its environment and to discover the possibilities
of development inherent to this system. The agent learns this by setting the system in motion,
beginning from some initial state the agent has 'isolated.' It is this setting things in motion
that constitutes interference, at the intersection between one of the agent's abilities and the
resources of the system" (ibid., p. 135).

It is noteworthy that in an analysis like this, which I am presenting in an outrageously abbreviated form, the two components—systemic and te-leological—remain distinct from one another, even if they are intertwined. Does not this powerlessness to overcome the discontinuity (on the epis-temological plane) between these dissimilar components of intervention provide a prime indication that it will have to be in a type of discourse different from the one we employ here that the "I can" will be able to be recognized as the very *origin* of the connection between the two orders of causality? What would make this discourse based on the "I can" a different discourse is, in the last analysis, its reference to an ontology of *one's own body,* that is of *a* body which is also *my* body and which, by its double allegiance to the order of physical bodies and to that of persons, therefore lies at the point of articulation of the power to act which is ours and of the course of things which belongs to the world order. It is only in this phenomenology of the "I can" and in the related ontology of the body as one's own that the status of primitive datum accorded to the power to act would be established definitively.

At the close of this investigation devoted to the relation between action and its agent, it is important to sketch out the paths opened by the series of aporias to which the phenomenon of ascription has given rise. No ac-commodation for the aporia as an aporia should transform lucid reflection into self-consenting paralysis. The phenomenon of ascription constitutes, in the final analysis, only a partial and as yet abstract determination of what is meant by the ipseity (the selfhood) of the self. From the aporetics of ascription, there can and should result an impetus to break out of these limits in the search for richer and more concrete determinations to char-acterize the ipseity of the self. Each of these aporias of ascription points toward a specific supersession of the strictly linguistic viewpoint.

The first aporia still appeals to a transition internal to the linguistic viewpoint, namely the transition from semantics to pragmatics. What, in fact, distinguishes ascription from the simple attribution of a predicate to a logical subject is the agent's power to designate herself by designating her other. The Strawsonian consideration concerning the identity of sense which mental predicates maintain in self-ascription and even in other-ascription already tends in the direction of this sort of shift to the linguistic operations in which these two types of designation—self-designation and other-designation—predominate in a speech situation. For this reason, the first aporia was not fruitless.

Nor does the second aporia end at an impasse. The difficulties we faced in our effort to distinguish between ascription and imputation led us to think that the gap between them had to be bridged by an investigation into practical modalities which, by their complexity and organization, exceeded the limits of the theory of action itself, at least in the limited sense in which it has been understood up to now. It will be the task of an inquiry into praxis and practices to find the points of anchorage of a properly ethical evaluation of human action in the teleological and deontological sense—in other words, in accordance with the good and the obligatory. Only then will we be able to take account of the articulation of ascription and imputation in the moral and legal sense.

The third aporia generated by the notion of the power to act, and so by the causal efficiency assigned to the agent of action, may have seemed to be the most intractable. And indeed it is. Returning to the third Kantian antinomy has certainly heightened the appearance of a difficulty with no way out. And yet we did not fail to assert that the antinomy belongs to an antithetical strategy intended to combat the accusation of being a weak argument leveled, as it should be, against any alleged primitive datum. Yet it is indeed a matter of a primitive datum, namely the assurance that the agent has the power to do things, that is to produce changes in the world. The passage from the disjunctive to the conjunctive stage of the dialectic had no aim other than to carry to a reflective and critical level what was already precomprehended in this assurance of being able to do something. To speak of assurance is to say two things. It is, first of all, to bring to light, on the epistemological plane, a phenomenon we have already glimpsed several times, that of attestation. We are assured with a certainty that is not a belief, a *doxa* inferior to knowledge, that we can perform those familiar gestures that Danto roots in basic actions. But admitting a primitive datum attested in the certainty of being able to act has not simply an epistemological side, it has an ontological side as well. The primitive datum of the power-to-act is part of a constellation of primitive data that belong to the ontology of the self, to be sketched out in the tenth study. What we have just said of the phenomenology of the "I can" and of the neighboring ontology of one's own body already points in the direction of this ontology of the self. It will only be at the end of a long journey through and beyond these philosophies of subjectivity that we shall be able to establish the concrete ties by which this phenomenology of "I can" and this ontology of one's own body are related to an ontology of the self, as an acting and suffering subject. In this sense, the third aporia of ascription will in reality be superseded only at the end of our undertaking.

FIFTH STUDY

Personal Identity and Narrative Identity

With the discussion of the relations between agent and action, an initial series of studies, placed under the aegis of the analytic conception of language, has reached its end. The first two studies were confined to the resources that semantics and pragmatics, considered in succession, offered to the analysis of action and of the complex relations between action and the agent. In the course of this analysis, it appeared that the theory of action, despite its dependence in principle on the theory of language, constituted an autonomous discipline by reason of the features peculiar to human action and of the originality of the tie between action and its agent. In order to secure its autonomy, this discipline appeared to us to require a new alliance between the analytic tradition and the phenomenological and hermeneutical tradition, once it had been recognized that the major issue resided less in determining what distinguishes actions from other events occurring in the world than in determining what specifies the self, implied in the power-to-do, at the junction of acting and the agent. Thus liberated from its initial subservience, the theory of action assumed the role of a propaedeutic to the question of selfhood. In return, the question of the self, taking over the lead from that of action, gives rise to considerable reshufflings on the plane of human action itself.

Looking back, the greatest lacuna in our earlier studies most obviously concerns the *temporal* dimension of the self as well as of action as such. Neither the definition of the person from the perspective of identifying reference nor that of the agent in the framework of the semantics of action, considered nonetheless an enrichment of the first approach, has taken into account the fact that the person of whom we are speaking and the agent on whom the action depends have a history, are their own history. The approach to the self along the second line of the philosophy of language, that of utterance, has also failed to give rise to any particular reflection concerning the changes that affect a subject capable of designating itself in signifying the world. What has been omitted in this way is not just one

113

important dimension among others but an entire problematic, namely that of *personal identity,* which can be articulated only in the temporal dimension of human existence. In order to fill this major lacuna I propose to reconstruct here a theory of narrative, no longer considered from the perspective of its relation to the constitution of human time, as I did in *Time and Narrative,* but from that of its contribution to the constitution of the self. The extremely lively contemporary debates on the question of narrative identity in the field of Anglo-American philosophy seem to me to offer an excellent opportunity to confront head-on the distinction between sameness and selfhood, continually presupposed in the earlier studies but never treated thematically. I hope to show that it is within the framework of narrative theory that the concrete dialectic of selfhood and sameness — and not simply the nominal distinction between the two terms employed up until now — attains its fullest development.[1]

Once the notion of narrative identity has been confronted with — and has, I believe, emerged victorious from — the puzzles and the paradoxes of personal identity, it will be possible to develop, in a less polemical and more constructive way, the thesis announced early on in the Introduction to this work, namely that narrative theory finds one of its major justifications in the role it plays as a middle ground between the descriptive viewpoint on action, to which we have confined ourselves until now, and the prescriptive viewpoint which will prevail in the studies that follow. A triad has thus imposed itself on my analysis: describe, narrate, prescribe — each moment of the triad implying a specific relation between the constitution

1. The notion of narrative identity, introduced in *Time and Narrative* 3, responds to a different set of problems: at the end of a long voyage through historical narrative and fictional narrative, I asked whether there existed a structure of experience capable of integrating the two great classes of narratives. I then formed the hypothesis according to which narrative identity, either that of a person or of a community, would be the sought-after place of this chiasm between history and fiction. Following the intuitive preunderstanding we have of these things, do we not consider human lives to be more readable when they have been interpreted in terms of the stories that people tell about them? And are not these life stories in turn made more intelligible when the narrative models of plots — borrowed from history or from fiction (drama or novel) — are applied to them? It therefore seems plausible to take the following chain of assertions as valid: self-understanding is an interpretation; interpretation of the self, in turn, finds in the narrative, among other signs and symbols, a privileged form of mediation; the latter borrows from history as well as from fiction, making a life story a fictional history or, if one prefers, a historical fiction, interweaving the historiographic style of biographies with the novelistic style of imaginary autobiographies. Lacking in this intuitive apprehension of the problem of narrative identity was a clear comprehension of what is at stake in the very question of identity applied to persons or communities. The question of the interconnection of history and fiction shifted attention away somewhat from the considerable difficulties pertaining to the question of identity as such. These difficulties are examined in the present study.

of action and the constitution of the self. Now narrative theory would not be able to perform this mediation — that is, to be more than one segment interposed in the sequence of separate studies — if it could not be shown, on the one hand, that the practical field covered by narrative theory is greater than that covered by the semantics and pragmatics of action sentences and, on the other hand, that the actions organized into a narrative present features that can be developed thematically only within the framework of ethics. In other words, narrative theory can genuinely mediate between description and prescription only if the broadening of the practical field and the anticipation of ethical considerations are implied in the very structure of the act of narrating. For the moment, let it suffice to say that in many narratives the self seeks its identity on the scale of an entire life; between the brief actions, to which our earlier analyses were confined (conforming to the constraint of the grammar of action sentences), and the *connectedness of life*, of which Dilthey speaks in his theoretical writings on autobiography, we find staggered degrees of complexity which carry the theory of action to the level required by narrative theory.[2] In the same way, I would say, anticipating the course of these studies, there is no ethically neutral narrative. Literature is a vast laboratory in which we experiment with estimations, evaluations, and judgments of approval and condemnation through which narrativity serves as a propaedeutic to ethics. It is to this double gaze, looking backward in the direction of the practical field and ahead in the direction of the ethical field, that the sixth study will be devoted, a study whose close solidarity with the present one I should here like to indicate.

1. The Problem of Personal Identity

The problem of personal identity constitutes, in my opinion, a privileged place of confrontation between the two major uses of the concept of identity, which I have evoked many times without ever actually thematizing

2. Analytic philosophy of action has often been reproached for the poverty of the examples it cites. For my part, I do not decry this thinness in the use of examples; by bracketing ethical and political considerations, analytic philosophy of action has succeeding in concentrating on the grammatical, syntactic, and logical constitution of action sentences. And we are indebted to this very asceticism of the analysis, even in the internal critique we made of this theory of action. We had no need to restore to action either the complexity of everyday practices or the teleological and deontological dimension required by a moral theory of imputation in order to sketch the initial outlines of a theory of selfhood. The simplest actions — those, let us say, corresponding to Danto's basic actions — are sufficient to make apparent the enigma of sameness, in which are summed up *in nuce* all the difficulties following from a theory of selfhood.

them. Let me recall the terms of the confrontation: on one side, identity as *sameness* (Latin *idem*, German *Gleichheit*, French *mêmeté*); on the other, identity as *selfhood* (Latin *ipse*, German *Selbstheit*, French *ipséité*). Selfhood, I have repeatedly affirmed, is not sameness. Because the major distinction between them is not recognized — as the second section will verify — the solutions offered to the problem of personal identity which do not consider the narrative dimension fail. If this difference is so essential, one might ask, why was it not treated in a thematic manner earlier, since its ghost has continually haunted the preceding analyses? The reason is that it is raised to the level of a problem only after the temporal implications have themselves moved to the forefront. Indeed, it is with the question of *permanence in time* that the confrontation between our two versions of identity becomes a genuine problem for the first time.

1. At first sight, in fact, the question of permanence in time is connected exclusively to *idem*-identity, which in a certain sense it crowns. It is indeed under this heading alone that the analytic theories that we will examine later approach the question of personal identity and the paradoxes related to it. Let us recall rapidly the conceptual articulation of sameness in order to indicate the eminent place that permanence in time holds there.

Sameness is a concept of relation and a relation of relations. First comes *numerical* identity: thus, we say of two occurrences of a thing, designated by an invariable noun in ordinary language, that they do not form two different things but "one and the same" thing. Here, identity denotes oneness: the contrary is plurality (not one but two or several). To this first component of the notion of identity corresponds the notion of identification, understood in the sense of the reidentification of the same, which makes cognition recognition: the same thing twice, *n* times.

In second place we find *qualitative* identity, in other words, extreme resemblance: we say that *x* and *y* are wearing the same suit — that is, clothes that are so similar that they are interchangeable with no noticeable difference. To this second component corresponds the operation of substitution without semantic loss, *salva veritate*.

These two components of identity are irreducible to one another, as are in Kant the categories of quantity and quality. But they are not thereby foreign to one another; it is precisely to the extent that time is implied in the series of occurrences of the same thing that the reidentification of the same can provoke hesitation, doubt, or contestation; the extreme resemblance between two or more occurrences can then be invoked as an indirect criterion to reinforce the presumption of numerical identity. This is what happens when we speak of the physical identity of a person. We have no trouble recognizing someone who simply enters and leaves, appears, disappears and reappears. Yet doubt is not far away when we compare a present perception with a recent memory. The identification of an aggressor by a victim from among a series of suspects who are presented affords an initial opportunity to introduce doubt; and with the distance of time, it grows. Hence a defendant appearing in court may object that he is not the same as the one who was incriminated. What happens then? One compares the individual present to the material marks held to be the irrecusable traces of his earlier presence in the very places at issue. It happens that this comparison is extended to eyewitness accounts, which, with a much greater margin of uncertainty, are held to be equivalent to the past presentation of the individual examined. The question of knowing whether the person here present in court and the presumed author of an earlier crime are one and the same individual may then remain without any sure answer. The trials of war criminals have occasioned just such confrontations along with, as we know, the ensuing risks and uncertainties.

The weakness of this criterion of similitude, in the case of a great distance in time, suggests that we appeal to another criterion, one which belongs to the third component of the notion of identity, namely the *uninterrupted continuity* between the first and the last stage in the development of what we consider to be the same individual. This criterion is predominant whenever growth or aging operate as factors of dissemblance and, by implication, of numerical diversity. Thus, we say of an oak tree that it is the same from the acorn to the fully developed tree; in the same way, we speak of one animal, from birth to death; so, too, we speak of a man or of a woman — I am not saying of a person — as a simple token of a species. The demonstration of this continuity functions as a supplementary or a substitutive criterion to similitude; the demonstration rests upon the ordered series of small changes which, taken one by one, threaten resemblance without destroying it. This is how we see photos of ourselves at successive ages of our life. As we see, time is here a factor of dissemblance, of divergence, of difference.

This is why the threat it represents for identity is not entirely dissipated unless we can posit, at the base of similitude and of the uninterrupted continuity, a principle of *permanence in time*. This will be, for example, the invariable structure of a tool, all of whose parts will gradually have been replaced. This is also the case, of supreme interest to us, of the permanence of the genetic code of a biologic individual; what remains here is the organization of a combinatory system. The idea of structure, opposed to that of event, replies to this criterion of identity, the strongest one that can be applied. It confirms the relational character of identity, which does not appear in the ancient formulation of substance but which Kant reestablishes by classifying substance among the categories of relation, as the condition of the possibility of conceiving of change as happening to something which does not change, at least not in the moment of attributing the accident to the substance; permanence in time thus becomes the transcendental of numerical identity.[3] The entire problematic of personal identity will revolve around this search for a relational invariant, giving it the strong signification of permanence in time.

2. Having performed this conceptual analysis of identity as sameness, we can now return to the question that directs the present study: Does the selfhood of the self imply a form of permanence in time which is not reducible to the determination of a substratum, not even in the relational sense which Kant assigns to the category of substance; in short, is there a form of permanence in time which is not simply the schema of the category of substance? Returning to the terms of the opposition which has repeatedly appeared in the earlier studies, we ask, Is there a form of permanence in time which can be connected to the question "who?" inasmuch as it is irreducible to any question of "what?"? Is there a form of permanence in time that is a reply to the question "Who am I?"?

It will immediately be apparent that this is a difficult question indeed if we consider the following reflection. When we speak of ourselves, we in fact have available to us two models of permanence in time which can be summed up in two expressions that are at once descriptive and emblematic: *character* and *keeping one's word*. In both of these, we easily recognize a permanence which we say belongs to us. My hypothesis is that the polarity of these two models of permanence with respect to persons results from the fact that the permanence of character expresses the almost complete mutual overlapping of the problematic of *idem* and of *ipse*, while faithfulness to oneself in keeping one's word marks the extreme gap between the permanence of the self and that of the same and so attests fully to the irreducibility of the two problematics one to the other. I hasten to complete my hypothesis: the polarity I am going to examine suggests an intervention of narrative identity in the conceptual constitution of per-

3. In Kant, the shift of the idea of substance from the ontological to the transcendental domain is marked by the simple correspondence between the category, its schema, and the principle (or first judgment). To substance, the first category of relation, corresponds the schema, which expresses its temporal constitution, namely: "permanence [*Beharrlichkeit*] of the real in time, that is, the representation of the real as a substrate of empirical determination of time in general, and so as abiding while all else changes" (*Critique of Pure Reason*, A143, B183, p. 184). To the schema of substance corresponds the principle expressing its relational constitution, namely ("The First Analogy of Experience"): "All appearances contain the permanent [*das Beharrliche*] (substance) as the object itself, and the transitory as its mere determination" (A182, p. 212). And in the second edition: "In all change of appearances substance is permanent [*beharrt*]; its quantum in nature is neither increased nor diminished" (B224, p. 212).

sonal identity in the manner of a specific mediator between the pole of character, where *idem* and *ipse* tend to coincide, and the pole of self-maintenance, where selfhood frees itself from sameness. But I am running ahead of myself!

What are we to understand by *character*? In what sense does the term possess at once a descriptive and an emblematic value? Why do we say that it adds self-identity to identity of the same? What is it that allows self-identity to betray itself under the identity of the same and so prevents assigning the identity of character purely and simply to that of the same?

By "character" I understand the set of distinctive marks which permit the reidentification of a human individual as being the same. By the descriptive features that will be given, the individual compounds numerical identity and qualitative identity, uninterrupted continuity and permanence in time. In this way, the sameness of the person is designated emblematically.

This is not the first time that I have encountered the notion of character along my path. In the days when I was writing *The Voluntary and the Involuntary*, I placed character under the heading of "absolute involuntary" in opposition to the "relative involuntary" of motives in the area of voluntary decision and to powers in that of voluntary motion. As an absolute involuntary, I assigned it, along with the unconscious and with being alive, symbolized by birth, to that level of our existence which we cannot change but to which we must consent. And even then, I underscored the immutable nature of character as a finite, unchosen perspective through which we accede to values and to the use of our powers.[4] Ten

---

4. This immutability of character, which I shall nuance as I proceed, served during that same period as a warning to a particular discipline, termed "characterology," whose approximateness, even arbitrariness, we are in a position to measure much better today. What nevertheless interested me in this perilous enterprise was the claim to give an objective equivalent to this layer of our subjective existence. This is what today I shall term the inscription of character in Sameness. Characterology, indeed, attempted to treat character as a portrait painted from outside; it sketched out this portrait by means of a series of correlations between a small number of invariants (activity, emotivity, primariness/secondariness) in such a way as to draw, using this combinatory of distinctive features, a typology capable of relatively pertinent refinements. Regardless of the simplifications and ossification of this characterology, today fallen into disfavor, its very ambition testifies to the emblematic value of character as fate. The very word "fate," which unavoidably recalls Heraclitus's famous saying linking character (*ēthos*) and *daimōn* (Diels/Kranz, *Die Fragmente der Vorsokratiker*, B119), is sufficient to alert our attention, for it is related not to an objectivizing but to an existential problematic. Only a freedom is or has a fate. This simple remark restores to the determinations put forward by characterology the equivocalness that makes it partake simultaneously of two orders, that of objectivity and that of existence. A portrait painted from outside? But also a manner of being that is one's own. A combinatory of permanent features? But an indivisible style. A type? But an unsubstitutable singularity. A constraint? But a fate that I am, the very one to which I must consent.

years later, I returned to this fascinating theme of character in *Fallible Man,* but in a somewhat different context. This time, it was no longer in relation to the polarity of the voluntary and the involuntary but in connection with the Pascalian theme of the "disproportion," the noncoincidence between the finite and the infinite. Here, character appeared to me as my manner of existing in accordance with a finite perspective affecting my opening to the world of things, ideas, values, and persons.[5]

In a certain sense, I am still pursuing the investigation in this direction. Character still appears to me today as the other pole in a fundamental, existential polarity. But instead of conceiving of character, in a framework of perspective and of opening, as the finite pole of existence, I am interpreting it here in terms of its place in the problematic of identity. This shift of emphasis has as its principal advantage the fact of putting into question the immutable status of character, taken for granted in the earlier analyses. In fact, this immutability proves to be of a most peculiar sort, as is attested by the reinterpretation of character in terms of acquired disposition. With this notion, the *temporal* dimension of character allows itself

---

5. *Fallible Man,* trans. Charles A. Kelbley (New York: Fordham University Press, 1986). This notion of perspective was expressly shifted from the theoretical plane — from the Husserlian phenomenology of perception, to be precise — to the plane of practice. It thus served to sum up all the aspects of practical finiteness (the receptive nature of desire, the perseverance of habits), which enables me to underscore for the first time the nature of character as a finite totality: in this way, I spoke of character as a "limited openness of our field of motivation taken as a whole" (p. 60). This second version of character in *Fallible Man* confirmed, in a sense, the sameness of character, perhaps at the expense of an excessive insistence on its immutability, authorized by my reading and approbation of some brilliant texts written by Alain. I therefore went so far as to say that, unlike the perspective of perception, which I can change by moving from one place to another, "there is no movement by which I could change the zero origin of my total field of motivation" (p. 62). My birth, I also said, is the "already-there-ness of my character" (p. 63). In this way, character could be defined in broad strokes as an immutable and inherited nature (ibid.). However, at the same time, my adherence to the perspective of a movement of opening in terms of which I defined the act of existing forced me to place character on the plane of existence, stressing nowadays its quality of being "mine," its "mineness." "Character is the finite openness of my existence taken as a whole" (p. 58). Character, I would say today, is sameness in mineness. In *Fallible Man,* the basic reason for which character had to be placed on the side of lived experience, despite its presumed immutability, was its contrast with the pole of infinity, which I considered to be represented by the notion of happiness, from a perspective at once Aristotelian and Kantian. The opening with respect to which character marked a closing, a constitutive partiality, was the intention of happiness. This opposition was justified in the framework of an anthropology attentive to this question, on the one hand, by the *fault* (*faille*) in existence, which makes the "fall" into evil possible, and, on the other hand, by its prompting us to interpret the disproportion responsible for fallibility in terms of the pair "finite-infinite." The main advantage was to shift all of the weight onto the third term, the place of the existential fault. The present study will place narrativity in a comparable position of mediation between two extremes.

to be thematized at last. Character, I would say today, designates the set of lasting dispositions by which a person is recognized. In this way character is able to constitute the limit point where the problematic of *ipse* becomes indiscernible from that of *idem*, and where one is inclined not to distinguish them from one another. It is therefore important to ask ourselves about the temporal dimension of the disposition, which will later set character back upon the path of the narrativization of personal identity.

The first notion related to that of disposition is habit, with its twofold valence of habit as it is, as we say, being formed and of habit already acquired.[6] Now these two features have an obvious temporal significance: habit gives a history to character, but this is a history in which sedimentation tends to cover over the innovation which preceded it, even to the point of abolishing the latter. Ravaisson was the first to express astonishment, in his famous treatise *De l'habitude*, at this force of habit, in which he saw the return from freedom to nature. It is this sedimentation which confers on character the sort of permanence in time that I am interpreting here as the overlapping of *ipse* by *idem*. This overlapping, however, does not abolish the difference separating the two problematics: precisely as second nature, my character is me, myself, *ipse*; but this *ipse* announces itself as *idem*. Each habit formed in this way, acquired and become a lasting disposition, constitutes a *trait* — a character trait, a distinctive sign by which a person is recognized, reidentified as the same — character being nothing other than the set of these distinctive signs.

Second, we may relate to the notion of disposition the set of *acquired identifications* by which the other enters into the composition of the same. To a large extent, in fact, the identity of a person or a community is made up of these identifications with values, norms, ideals, models, and heroes, *in* which the person or the community recognizes itself. Recognizing oneself *in* contributes to recognizing oneself *by*. The identification with heroic figures clearly displays this otherness assumed as one's own, but this is already latent in the identification with values which make us place a "cause" above our own survival. An element of loyalty is thus incorporated into character and makes it turn toward fidelity, hence toward maintaining the self. Here the two poles of identity accord with one another. This proves that one cannot think the *idem* of the person through without considering the *ipse*, even when one entirely covers over the other. Thus are

---

6. Aristotle was the first to have tied character to habit by means of the quasihomonymy between *ēthos* (character) and *ethos* (habit, custom). From the term *ethos* he passes to *hexis*, an acquired disposition, which is the basic anthropological notion upon which his ethics is built, inasmuch as virtues are just such acquired dispositions, conforming to the right rule and under the control of the judgment of *phronimos*, of the prudent man. Cf. *E.N.* 3.2.1112a13ff.; 6.2.1139a23–24; 6.13.1144b27.

incorporated into the traits of character the aspects of evaluative preference which define the moral aspect of character, in the Aristotelian sense of the term.[7] This occurs through a process comparable to that of habit formation, namely through the internalization which annuls the initial effect of otherness, or at least transfers it from the outside to the inside. The Freudian theory of the supergo has to do with this phenomenon, which gives internalization an aspect of sedimentation. In this way, preferences, evaluations, and estimations are stabilized in such a way that the person is recognized in these dispositions, which may be called evaluative. This is why behavior that does not correspond to dispositions of this sort makes us say that it is not in the character of the individual in question, that this person is not herself or even that the person is acting completely out of character.

By means of this stability, borrowed from acquired habits and identifications — in other words, from dispositions — character assures at once numerical identity, qualitative identity, uninterrupted continuity across change, and, finally, permanence in time which defines sameness. I would say, barely skirting paradox, that the identity of character expresses a certain adherence of the "what?" to the "who?" Character is truly the "what" of the "who." It is no longer exactly the "what" external to the "who," as was the case in the theory of action, where one could distinguish between what someone does and the one who does something (and we saw the riches and the pitfalls of this distinction, which leads directly to the problem of ascription). Here it is a question of the overlapping of the "who" by the "what," which slips from the question "Who am I?" back to the question "What am I?"

However, this overlapping of *ipse* by *idem* is not such that it makes us give up all attempts to distinguish between them. The dialectic of innovation and sedimentation, underlying the acquisition of a habit, and the equally rich dialectic of otherness and internalization, underlying the process of identification, are there to remind us that character has a history which it has contracted, one might say, in the twofold sense of the word "contraction": abbreviation and affection. It is then comprehensible that the stable pole of character can contain a narrative dimension, as we see in the uses of the term "character" identifying it with the protagonist in a story. What sedimentation has contracted, narration can redeploy. And it is dispositional language — for which Gilbert Ryle pleads in *The Concept of Mind* — which paves the way for this narrative unfolding. The fact that character must be set back within the movement of narration is attested to by numerous vain debates on identity, in particular when they concern the

---

7. On evaluation considered as the threshhold to ethics, see the seventh study.

identity of a historical community. When Fernand Braudel treats *L'Identité de la France*, he attempts, of course, to point out lasting, even permanent, distinctive traits by which we recognize France as a quasicharacter. But separated from history and geography, something the great historian is careful not to do, these traits are solidified and lend themselves to exploitation by the most harmful ideologies of "national identity." It will be the task of a reflection on narrative identity to balance, on one side, the immutable traits which this identity owes to the anchoring of the history of a life in a character and, on the other, those traits which tend to separate the identity of the self from the sameness of character.

3. Before setting out on this path, it is important to make the argument in favor of the distinction between the identity of the self and the identity of the same on the basis of the use we make of the notion of identity in the contexts in which the two sorts of identity cease to overlap, and even dissociate entirely from one another, baring in a sense the selfhood of the self, severed from its base in sameness. There is, in fact, another model of permanence in time besides that of character. It is that of keeping one's word in faithfulness to the word that has been given. I see in this keeping the emblematic figure of an identity which is the polar opposite of that depicted by the emblematic figure of character. Keeping one's word expresses a *self-constancy* which cannot be inscribed, as character was, within the dimension of something in general but solely within the dimension of "who?" Here, too, common usage is a good guide. The perseverance of character is one thing,[8] the perseverance of faithfulness to a word that has been given is something else again. The continuity of character is one thing, the constancy of friendship is quite another. In this regard, Heidegger is right to distinguish the permanence of substance from *self-subsistence* (*Selbst-Ständigkeit* — which Martineau has aptly translated in French as *maintient de soi* rather than as *constance à soi,* as I did in *Time and Narrative* 3).[9] This major distinction remains, even if it is not certain that "anticipatory resoluteness" in the face of death exhausts the sense of self-constancy.[10] This attitude thus expresses a certain existential investment of the transcendentals of existence which Heidegger terms "existentialia," among which we find selfhood. Other attitudes — situated at the

---

8. It is noteworthy that Kant denotes substance (the first category of relation) by the term *Beharrliche* (that which persists) (cf. n. 3 above).

9. "Ontologically, Dasein is in principle different from everything that is present-at-hand or Real. Its 'subsistence' [*Bestand*] is not based on the substantiality of a substance but on the '*Self-subsistence*' [*Selbst-Ständigkeit*] of the existing Self, whose Being has been conceived as care" (*Being and Time*, p. 351).

10. "Existentially, '*Self-constancy*' signifies nothing other than anticipatory resoluteness" (ibid., p. 369).

same juncture of the existentiell and the existential, as all the Heideggerian analyses revolving around Being-toward-death — reveal just as much about the fundamental conjunction between the problematic of permanence in time and that of the self, inasmuch as the self does not coincide with the same. In this respect, keeping one's promise, as was mentioned above, does indeed appear to stand as a challenge to time, a denial of change: even if my desire were to change, even if I were to change my opinion or my inclination, "I will hold firm." It is not necessary, for the promise to be meaningful, to place keeping one's word within the horizon of Being-toward-death. The properly ethical justification of the promise suffices of itself, a justification which can be derived from the obligation to safeguard the institution of language and to respond to the trust that the other places in my faithfulness. This ethical justification, considered as such, develops its own temporal implications, namely a modality of permanence in time capable of standing as the polar opposite to the permanence of character. It is here, precisely, that selfhood and sameness cease to coincide. And it is here, consequently, that the equivocalness of the notion of permanence in time is dissipated.

This new manner[11] of opposing the sameness of character to the constancy of the self in promising opens *an interval of sense* which remains to be filled in. This interval is opened by the polarity, in temporal terms, between two models of permanence in time — the perseverance of character and the constancy of the self in promising. It is therefore in the sphere of temporality that the mediation is to be sought. Now it is this "milieu" that, in my opinion, the notion of narrative identity comes to occupy. Having thus situated it in this interval, we will not be surprised to see narrative identity oscillate between two limits: a lower limit, where permanence in time expresses the confusion of *idem* and *ipse;* and an upper limit, where the *ipse* poses the question of its identity without the aid and support of the *idem.*

First, however, we must examine the claims of theories of personal identity which do not consider either the distinction of *idem* and *ipse* or

11. The manner is new, if one compares it to the strategy developed in my earlier works. In *The Voluntary and the Involuntary* mediation was not a major problem; I then confidently spoke about the reciprocity of the voluntary and the involuntary and unconcernedly quoted Maine de Biran's statement "Homo simplex in vitalitate, duplex in humanitate." At the very most, it could be said that the relative voluntariness of motivation and powers occupied the middle ground between the two extremes of project and character. In *Fallible Man,* which was wholly constructed upon the "disproportion" of human beings, the question of the third term, the privileged place of fragility, became the central issue of the entire enterprise. Having posited the problem in terms of the finite and the infinite, I saw in the respect of the moral person, the union of particularity and universality represented in Kant by the idea of humanity, the third term required by the disproportion between character and happiness.

the resources offered by narrativity to resolve the paradoxes of personal identity, which these same theories have the advantage of presenting clearly and forcefully.

2. The Paradoxes of Personal Identity

1. The lesson that, without the guideline of the distinction between two models of identity and without the help of narrative mediation, the question of personal identity loses itself in labyrinthine difficulties and paralyzing paradoxes was first taught to philosophers of the English language and of analytic formation by Locke and Hume.

From the former, the tradition retained the equation between personal identity and memory. But one must realize at what price of inconsistency in the argument and of unlikelihood in the order of consequences this equation was paid. Lack of consequence in the argument, first: at the beginning of the famous chapter 27 of the *Essay concerning Human Understanding* (2d ed., 1694),[12] titled "Identity and Diversity," Locke introduces a concept of identity which seems to escape our alternatives of sameness and selfhood; after having said that identity results from a comparison, Locke introduces the singular idea of the identity of a thing with itself (of "sameness with itself"). It is indeed by comparing a thing with itself in different times that we form the ideas of identity and diversity; "When therefore we demand whether anything be the same or no, it refers always to something that existed such a time in such a place, which it was certain at that instant, was the same with itself" (p. 207). This definition seems to join together the characters of sameness by virtue of the operation of comparison and those of selfhood by virtue of what was instantaneous coincidence, maintained through time, of a thing with itself. But what follows in the analysis decomposes the two valences of identity. In the first series of examples — a ship which has been rebuilt in all of its parts, the oak tree which has grown from an acorn to a tree, animals and men whose development we follow from birth to death — sameness prevails. The element all these examples have in common is the permanence of their organization, which involves no substantialism, according to Locke. But just when he reaches personal identity, which Locke does not confuse with the identity of a man, he assigns "sameness with itself" alleged by the general definition to instantaneous *reflection*. There remains simply to extend the privilege of reflection from the instant to the duration; for this, it is enough to consider memory as the retrospective expan-

12. John Locke, *An Essay concerning Human Understanding* (New York: World Publishing, 1964).

sion of reflection as far as it can extend in the past. By reason of this mutation of reflection into memory, "sameness with itself" can be said to extend through time. Thus, Locke thought he could introduce a caesura in his analysis without having to give up his general concept of the sameness of a thing with itself. And yet the turn to reflection and memory did, in fact, mark a conceptual reversal in which selfhood was silently substituted for sameness.

It is not, however, on the level of the argument's coherence that Locke produces the principal difficulty: the tradition has credited him with inventing a *criterion* of identity, namely mental identity, to which may henceforth be opposed the criterion of corporeal identity, to which, in fact, the first series of examples belonged, governed by the permanence of an organization observable from outside. A discussion of the various criteria of identity will then occupy the forefront, where we will witness opposing and equally plausible pleas in favor of one or the other. Thus, to Locke and his partisans will be regularly opposed the aporias of an identity hinging on the testimony of memory alone; psychological aporias concerning the limits, the intermittence (during sleep, for example), and the failings of memory, but also more properly ontological aporias: rather than saying that a person exists inasmuch as that person remembers, is it not plausible, Butler will ask,[13] to assign the continuity of memory to the continuous existence of a soul-substance? Without having foreseen it, Locke revealed the aporetic character of the very question of identity. Attesting to this more than anything else are the paradoxes he assumed unflinchingly but which his successors have transformed into proofs of undecidability. For instance, he offers the case of a prince whose memory is transplanted into the body of a cobbler; does the latter become the prince whom he remembers having been, or does he remain the cobbler whom other people continue to observe? Locke, consistent with himself, decides in favor of the first solution. But modern readers, more sensitive to the collision between two opposing criteria of identity, will conclude that the case is undecidable. In this way, the era of *puzzling cases* began, despite Locke's assurances. We will return to this later.[14]

13. Joseph Butler, "Of Personal Identity," in *The Analogy of Religion* (1736), reprinted in *Personal Identity,* ed. John Perry (Berkeley: University of California Press, 1975), pp. 99–106.

14. It is not in Locke but in his successors that the situation created by the hypothesis of transplanting one and the same soul into another body began to appear more undetermined rather than simply paradoxical, that is, contrary to common sense. For how could the prince's memory not affect the cobbler's body, his voice, his gestures, and his poses? And how could one situate the expression of the habitual character of the cobbler in relation to that of the prince's memory? What has become problematic after Locke, and which was not so for him,

With Hume opened the era of doubt and suspicion. It is a strong concept of the relation of identity which Hume posits at the beginning of the analysis in his *Treatise of Human Nature,* book 1, part 4, section 6 (1739): "We have a distinct idea of an object that remains invariable and uninterrupted through a supposed variation of time; and this idea we call that of *identity* or *sameness.*"[15] So there is no ambiguity here; there exists but a single model of identity: sameness. Like Locke, Hume runs through a series of typical examples of ships and plants, animals and humans. Unlike Locke, however, he introduces, beginning in his first examples, *degrees* in assigning identity, depending, for instance, on whether the mutations of a material or living being are more or less extensive, more or less sudden. The question of identity thus from the outset escapes answers that are black or white. But, more especially, unlike Locke, Hume does not overturn his criteria of assigning identity when he moves from things and animate beings to the self. And, as a good empiricist, he requires for every idea a corresponding impression ("It must be some one impression that gives rise to every real idea"),[16] and since, when he "enters most intimately into" himself, he finds only a diversity of experiences and no invariable expression relative to the idea of a self, he concludes that the latter is an illusion.

This conclusion, however, does not end the debate but serves instead to open it. What is it, asks Hume, that gives us such a strong inclination to superimpose an identity on these successive perceptions and to assume that we possess an invariable and uninterrupted existence during the entire course of our life? It is in his explanation of the illusion of identity that Hume unfolds the nuances which, after having made a profound impression on Kant, have left such a lasting mark on subsequent discussions. Two new concepts enter on stage here, imagination and belief. To *imagination* is attributed the faculty of moving easily from one experience to another if their difference is slight and gradual, and thus of transforming diversity into identity. *Belief* serves here as a relay, filling in the deficiencies of the impression. In a culture like the one to which Hume still belongs, avowing that an idea rests on a belief and not on an impression does not entirely discredit this idea; beliefs have a place and a role which philosophy

---

is the possibility of distinguishing between two criteria of identity: the identity termed mental and that termed corporeal, as though the expression of memory were not itself a bodily phenomenon. In fact, the defect inherent in Locke's paradox, besides the possible circularity of the argument, is an imperfect description of the situation created by the imaginary transplant.

15. David Hume, *A Treatise of Human Nature* (New York: Penguin Books, 1969), p. 301.

16. Ibid., p. 299.

marks out. Nevertheless, to say that belief engenders fictions is to an-
nounce the time when belief will have become unbelievable. Hume does
not yet take this step and suggests that the unity of personality can be
assimilated to that of a republic or a commonwealth whose members unceasingly change but whose ties of association remain. It will be left to
Nietzsche to complete the move into suspicion. With him, the violence of
denial will replace the subtlety of insinuation.

It will be objected: Was not Hume seeking what he could not hope to
find — a self which was but sameness? And was he not presupposing the
self he was not seeking? Let us read his main argument: "For my part, when
I enter most intimately into what I call *myself*, I always stumble on some
particular perception or other, of heat or cold, light or shade, love or hatred,
pain or pleasure. I can never catch *myself* at any time without a perception,
and can never observe anything but the perception."[17] Here, then, is *someone* who claims to be unable to find anything but a datum stripped of
selfhood; *someone* who penetrates within himself, seeks and declares to have
found nothing. At least, observes Chisholm in *Person and Object*,[18] *someone*
is stumbling, observing a perception. With the question Who? — who is
seeking, stumbling, and not finding, and who perceives? — the self returns
just when the same slips away.

In the discussion that follows, we shall repeatedly encounter a similar
paradox. I will not stop here to consider the question of whether the best
criterion of identity is of a bodily or a psychological nature. I have several
reasons for this.

First, I do not want to leave the impression that the psychological criterion has any particular affinity for selfhood and the corporeal criterion
for sameness. If memory has an affinity for selfhood, a matter I will return
to later, the psychological criterion cannot be reduced to memory; all that
has been said above about character supplies sufficient proof for this. Now,
as we have seen, the fact of character is what makes us most inclined to
think of identity in terms of sameness. Character, we said, is the self under
the appearances of sameness. In the opposite direction, the corporeal criterion is not by nature foreign to the problematic of selfhood, to the extent
that my body's belonging to myself constitutes the most overwhelming
testimony in favor of the irreducibility of selfhood to sameness.[19] Even to

17. Ibid., p. 300.

18. Roderick Chisholm, *Person and Object: A Metaphysical Study* (London: Allen and
Unwin, 1976), pp. 31–41.

19. The confrontation between the corporeal criterion and the psychological criterion
has given rise to a considerable body of literature in English. The following collections of
essays may be consulted: Amelie Oskenberg Rorty, ed., *The Identities of Persons* (Berkeley:
University of California Press, 1976); John Perry, ed., *Personal Identity* (Berkeley: University

the extent to which a body continues to resemble itself — even here, this is not really the case. One has only to compare two self-portraits of Rembrandt — it is not the sameness of my body that constitutes its selfhood but its belonging to someone capable of designating himself or herself as the one whose body this is.

Next, I have the gravest doubt concerning the use of the term "criterion" in the framework of the present discussion. A criterion is what allows us to distinguish the true from the false in competing truth claims. Now the question is precisely whether selfhood and sameness lend themselves in the same way to the test of truth claims. In the case of sameness, the term "criterion" has a very precise sense: it designates the tests of verification or falsification of statements concerning identity as a relation: the same as (we recall the assertion made by Locke and by Hume that identity results from a comparison; in Kant, too, substance is the first category of relation). One can then legitimately term a criterion the test of the truth of assertions concerning sameness. Is the same thing true with respect to selfhood? Is my body's belonging to myself on the order of a criteriology? Does it not come instead within the province of *attestation*?[20] Is memory — the alleged psychological criterion of choice — the criterion of anything at all? Does memory not also come within the province of attestation? Can we speak of a criterion in the order of attestation? We might hesitate here: the answer will be no, if criterion is identified with the test of verification or falsification; yes, if we admit that attestation lends itself to a truth test of another order than the test of verification or falsification. This discussion will lead nowhere until the distinction between the two problematics of selfhood and sameness has been firmly established and until the entire spectrum of relations, extending from their superimposition to their disjunction, has been reviewed. This can occur only at the end of our reflections on narrative identity.

2. So, rather than entering into a discussion of the criteria of personal identity, I have deliberately chosen to wrestle with a major work which, transcending the debate on the respective merits of the psychological criterion and the corporeal criterion, addresses itself directly to the *beliefs* that we ordinarily attach to the claim of personal identity. This outstanding work is Derek Parfit's *Reasons and Persons*. I have found in it the most

of California Press, 1975); and the works of Sidney Shoemaker, *Self-Knowledge and Self-Identity* (Ithaca: Cornell University Press, 1963), and of Bernard Williams, *Problems of the Self* (Cambridge: Cambridge University Press, 1973).

20. This is not the first time that the epistemological status of attestation moves into the foreground; cf. the end of the third study above. The connection between selfhood and attestation will be directly addressed in the tenth study.

formidable adversary (not an enemy — far from it!) to my thesis of narrative identity, in that these analyses are situated on a plane where identity can signify only sameness, to the express exclusion of any distinction between sameness and selfhood, and hence of any dialectic — narrative or other — between sameness and selfhood. The work recalls that of Locke — due less to the place occupied by memory in it than to its recourse to puzzling cases — and that of Hume, in its skeptical conclusion. The famous puzzling cases which serve as truth tests throughout Parfit's book do indeed lead us to think that the very question of identity can prove to be meaningless, to the extent that, in the paradoxical cases at least, the answer is undetermined. The question for us will be whether, as in the case of Hume, Parfit was not looking for something he could not find, namely a firm status for personal identity defined in terms of sameness, and whether he does not presuppose the self he was not seeking, principally when he develops, with uncommonly vigorous thinking, the moral implications of his thesis and then writes of it: "Personal identity is not what matters."[21]

Parfit attacks the basic beliefs underlying our use of identity criteria. For didactic purposes, our ordinary beliefs regarding personal identity can be arranged in three series of assertions. The first concerns what we are to understand by identity, namely the separate existence of a core of permanence; the second consists in the conviction that a determined response can always be given concerning the existence of such permanence; and the third states that the question posed is important if the person is to claim the status of a moral subject. Parfit's strategy consists in the successive dismantling of these three series of assertions, which are less juxtaposed than superimposed on one another, from the most obvious to the most deeply concealed.

Parfit's first thesis is that common belief has to be reformulated in terms that are not its own, namely in terms of the inverse thesis, which he holds to be the only true one and which he calls the reductionist thesis. The adverse thesis will therefore be called the nonreductionist thesis. According to the reductionist thesis, identity through time amounts, without remainder, to the fact of a certain connectedness between events, whether these be of a physical or mental nature. The two terms employed here must be properly understood: by "event," we are to understand any occurrence capable of being described *without* it being explicitly affirmed that the experiences that make up a personal life are the possession of that person,

---

21. Derek Parfit, *Reasons and Persons* (Oxford: Oxford University Press, 1986), p. 255 and passim. One will note that Parfit sometimes writes: "Our identity is not what matters" (p. 245 and passim), an expression that will not fail to reintroduce the question of ownership.

without it being affirmed that this person exists. It is under the condition of an impersonal description such as this that any search for connections can be undertaken, whether this be on the physical or corporeal level or on the mental or psychic level.

The reductionist thesis therefore reintroduces into the debate the neutral notion of *event* which we first confronted within the framework of the theory of action when we considered Donald Davidson's theses concerning the relation between action and events.[22] As in Davidson, the category of event appears to be primitive, that is, not dependent on the category of substantial entity, unlike the notion of state, which, it seems, has to be the state of some entity. Once the notion of event is taken in this broad sense, including mental events and physical events, the reductionist thesis can then be formulated: "A person's existence just consists in the existence of a brain and body, and the occurrence of a series of interrelated physical and mental events."[23]

What does the reductionist thesis exclude? Precisely: "that we are separately existing entities" (p. 210). In relation to simple mental or psychological continuity, the person constitutes "a separate further fact." Separate, in what sense? In the sense that the person is distinct from his brain and his experiences. For Parfit, the notion of spiritual substance, with which he identifies the pure Cartesian ego, is doubtless only one of the versions of the nonreductionist thesis, but it is the best-known one, even if a materialist version is equally conceivable. Essential to it is the idea that identity consists in an additional fact in relation to physical and/or mental continuity: "I call this the *Further Fact View*" (ibid.).

Before proceeding any further, it is important to underscore the point that it is the reductionist thesis which establishes the terms of reference in which the adverse thesis is then formulated, namely the vocabulary of events, of facts, described in an impersonal manner; in relation to this basic vocabulary, the adverse thesis is defined both by what it denies (reductionism) and by what it adds (the further fact). In this way, the central

22. See above, third study, sec. 4.
23. Parfit, *Reasons and Persons,* p. 211. Parfit does admit two versions of the reductionist thesis: according to the first, a person is simply what has just been stated; according to the second, a person could be considered a distinct entity without that entity having a separate existence. The latter version credits the analogy proposed by Hume between the person and a republic or commonwealth; in this way, one says that France exists but not Rusitania, although the former does not exist separately apart from its citizens and its territory. It is the second version that Parfit adopts for his notion of person. In his eyes, it does not violate the reductionist thesis. In the second version, the person can be mentioned without involving any claim of existence.

phenomenon which the theory reduces is, in my opinion, eluded, namely that someone possesses her body and her experience. The choice of the event as the term of reference expresses (better, accomplishes) this evasion (better, this elision) of mineness. And it is in the vocabulary of the event, resulting from just such an elision, that the existence of the person appears as a further fact. The thesis said to be nonreductionist is thus made parasitic on the reductionist thesis, set up as the basic unit. Now, the entire question is to know whether mineness belongs to the range of facts, to the epistemology of observable entities, and, finally, to the ontology of events. We are thus carried back once again to the distinction between two problematics of identity, that of *ipse* and that of *idem*. It is because he neglects this possible dichotomy that Parfit has no other recourse than to consider as superfluous, in the precise sense of the word, the phenomenon of mineness in relation to the factual character of the event.

The failure to recognize this produces as its corollary the false appearance that the thesis called nonreductionist finds its most remarkable illustration in the spiritual dualism to which Cartesianism is itself all too rapidly assimilated. As far as I am concerned, what the reductionist thesis reduces is not only, nor even primarily, the mineness of experience but, more fundamentally, that of my own body. The impersonal character of the event marks above all the neutralization of one's own body. Thereafter, the true difference between the nonreductionist thesis and the reductionist thesis in no way coincides with the so-called dualism between spiritual substance and corporeal substance, but between my own possession and impersonal description. To the extent that the body as my own constitutes one of the components of mineness, the most radical confrontation must place face-to-face two perspectives on the body — the body as mine, and the body as one body among others. The reductionist thesis in this sense marks the reduction of one's own body to the body as impersonal body. This neutralization, in all the thought experiments that will now appear, will facilitate focusing on the brain the entire discourse on the body. The *brain,* indeed, differs from many other parts of the body, and from the body as a whole in terms of an integral experience, inasmuch as it is stripped of any phenomenological status and thus of the trait of belonging to me, of being my possession. I have the experience of my relation to my members as organs of movement (my hands), of perception (my eyes), of emotion (the heart), or of expression (my voice). I have no such experience of my brain. In truth, the expression "my brain" has no meaning, at least not directly: absolutely speaking, there is a brain in my skull, but I do not feel it. It is only through the global detour by way of my body, inasmuch as my body is also a body and as the brain is contained in this body, that I can say: "my brain." The unsettling nature of this expression is reinforced by the fact that the brain does not fall under the category of objects perceived at a distance from one's own body. Its proximity in my head gives it the strange character of nonexperienced interiority.

Mental phenomena pose a comparable problem. In this respect, the most critical moment in the entire enterprise can be held to occur in the attempt to dissociate the psychological criterion from the trait of belonging to me (*appartenance mienne*). If, Parfit judges, the Cartesian cogito obviously cannot be stripped of the trait of being in the first person, the same thing is not true of identity defined by mental or physical continuity. One must therefore be able to define *mnemonic* continuity without any reference to mine, yours, his, or hers. If one could, one would genuinely be rid of the trait of belonging to me — in short, of "one's own." One could do this if one were able to create a replica of the memory of someone in the brain of someone else. (This, of course, involves manipulations of the brain, but later we will see the place that such manipulations and other similar operations hold in the imaginary experiences constructed by Parfit.) Memory can then be held to be equivalent to a cerebral trace. We will speak in this sense of memory traces. There is then nothing in the way of building a replica of these traces. On this basis, we can define a broad concept of *quasi memory*, of which ordinary memory would be a subclass, namely that of the quasi memories of our own past experiences (p. 220). But can what is one's own be a particular case of the impersonal? In fact, all of this was granted when we agreed to substitute for one's own memory the notion of mnemonic trace, which indeed belongs to the problematic of neutral events. This initial slippage authorizes treating the specific connection between past experience and present experience in terms of causal dependence.

The case of memory is only the most striking case in the order of psychic continuity. What is at issue is the ascription of thought to a thinker. Can one substitute, without any semantic loss, "the thinking is that . . ." (or "thought is occurring") for "I think"? Self-ascription and other-ascription, to return to Strawson's vocabulary, seem untranslatable into the terms of impersonal description.

The second belief Parfit attacks is the belief that the question of identity is always determinable, hence that all apparent cases of indeterminacy can be decided by yes or by no. In truth, this belief is found to underlie the preceding one: it is because we take aberrant cases to be determinable that we seek the stable formula of identity. In this respect, the invention of puzzling cases with the help of science fiction, where the indecidability of the question of identity is attested to, exercises such a decisive strategic function that Parfit begins the third part of his book, which deals with personal identity, by presenting the most troubling of these puzzling cases. Thus from the very beginning, the author insinuates the vacuity of a question which would give rise to such indetermination in the response. I have nevertheless preferred to begin by presenting the reductionist thesis because it does, in fact, govern the construction and selection of the puzzling cases.

In a sense, the question of identity has always stimulated an interest in paradoxical cases. Religious and theological beliefs about the transmigration of souls, immortality, and the resurrection of the flesh have not failed to intrigue the most speculative of minds (we find testimony to this in Saint Paul's response to the Corinthians in 1 Cor. 15:35ff.). We saw above in what way Locke makes use of a troubling imaginary case, not, to be sure, to undermine belief, but in order to put to the test of paradox his own thesis on the equation between personal identity and memory. It was his successors who transformed Locke's paradox into a puzzling case. The literature of personal identity is full of inventions of this sort: transplanting, bisecting brains, duplicating the cerebral hemispheres, and so on, to say nothing of the cases offered by clinical observations of split personalities, cases familiar to the general public. I too will be led to assign a considerable place to the equivalent of Parfit's puzzling cases within the framework of a narrative conception of personal identity. The confrontation between the two sorts of puzzling cases will even be one of the strong points of the argument on behalf of my own thesis. Let us confine ourselves for the moment to the following observation: this striking continuity in the recourse of imagination to cases capable of paralyzing reflection allows us to see that the question of identity constitutes a privileged place of aporias. Perhaps we must conclude, not that the question is an empty one, but that it can remain a question without an answer: this is precisely what is at stake in this singular strategy.

It is important to underscore vigorously that Parfit's selection of puzzling cases is governed by the reductionist hypothesis that has just been discussed. Take, for instance, the fictional experience of teletransportation which opens the third section of *Reasons and Persons* in grand style. The author proposes two versions of it; in both cases, an exact copy is made of my brain. This copy is transmitted by radio to a receiver placed on another planet, where a replicator reconstitutes an exact replica of me on the basis of this information, identical in the sense of exactly similar as to the organization and sequence of states of affairs and events. In the first case, my brain and my body are destroyed during my space voyage. The question is whether I survived in my replica or whether I died. The case is undecidable: with respect to numerical identity, my replica is other than I; with respect to qualitative identity, it is indistinguishable from me, hence substitutable. In the second case, my brain and my body are not destroyed, but my heart is damaged; I encounter my replica on Mars, I coexist with it; it knows that I am going to die before it does and attempts to console me by promising that it will take my place. What can I expect from the future? Am I going to die or survive in my replica?

What presupposition grounds the construction of this puzzling case and a good many others, each more ingenious than the next? First of all, these are imaginary cases which remain conceivable, even when they may not be technically realizable. It is enough that they be neither logically nor physically impossible. The question will be whether they do not violate a constraint of another order, concerning human rootedness on this earth. We will return to this later when the science fiction scenarios will be compared with literary fictions of a narrative sort. In addition, these are highly technological manipulations performed on the brain, taken as equivalent to the person. It is here that the reductionist thesis exercises its control; in an ontology of events and an epistemology of the impersonal description of identity-bearing sequences, the privileged place of occurrences in which the person is mentioned, without any distinct existence being explicitly claimed, is the brain. It is clear that Parfit's fictions, unlike the literary fictions of which we will speak later, concern entities of a manipulable nature from which the question of selfhood has been eliminated as a matter of principle.

The conclusion Parfit draws from the indecidability of his puzzling cases is that the question posed was itself empty. If one holds that identity means sameness, this conclusion is irresistible; in fact, in the most troublesome cases none of the three solutions envisaged is plausible. They are:

1. no person exists who is the *same* as me;

2. I am the *same* as one of the two individuals resulting from the experiment;

3. I am the *same* as both individuals.

The paradox is indeed a paradox of sameness: it was necessary to maintain as equivalent the question Am I going to survive? and the question Will there be a person who will be the *same* person as I? In this predetermined framework, resolving the paradox is dissolving the question — in short, considering it to be empty. If, through a sort of debatable extrapolation, Parfit grants the puzzling cases such a major role, it is because they dissociate the components that in everyday life we take as indissociable and whose connectedness we even take to be noncontingent, namely the overlapping between psychological (and possibly corporeal) connectedness,

which can, if need be, involve an impersonal description, and the feeling
of belonging — of memories, in particular — to someone capable of designating himself or herself as their owner. It will be one of the functions of
the subsequent comparison between science fiction and literary fiction to
place back on the drawing board the question of the presumed contingency
of the most fundamental traits of the human condition. Among these, there
is at least one which, in the imaginary experiences of teletransportation,
seems irrefutable, namely the *temporality,* not of the voyage, but of the
teletransported voyager. As long as we consider only the adequation of the
replica of the brain, the only thing that counts is the structural identity,
comparable to that of the genetic code, preserved throughout experience.[24]
As for me, the one who is teletransported, something is always happening
to me; I am afraid, I believe, I doubt, I wonder if I am going to die or
survive — in short, I am worried about myself. In this respect, the shift in
the discussion from problems of *memory* to problems of *survival* marks the
appearance on the stage of a dimension of historicality which, it would
seem, is quite difficult to describe in impersonal terms.[25]

   The third belief that Parfit submits to his virulent critique concerns the
judgment of importance which we attach to the question of identity. I have
already quoted his remarkable expression: "Identity is not what matters."
The tie between the belief attacked here and the preceding belief is this: if
indecidability seems unacceptable to us, it is because it troubles us. This is
clear in all the bizarre cases in which survival is at issue: What is going to
happen to me? I ask. Now if we are troubled, it is because the judgment
of identity seems important to us. If we give up this judgment of importance, we cease to be troubled. Presented with the options opened by the
puzzling cases, we are ready to concede that we know all there is to know
about the case in question and to stop the investigation there: "Even when
we have no answer to a question about personal identity, we can know
everything about what happens" (p. 266).

   This attack on what matters occupies, in fact, a central strategic position

   24. One may well, however, object to the very construction of the imaginary case that,
if the replica of my brain were a complete replica, it would have to contain, in addition to the traces of my past history, the mark of my history to come woven out of
chance encounters. But this condition would indeed appear to violate the rules of what is
conceivable: from the time of the separation of myself and my replica, our histories distinguish us and make us unsubstitutable. The very notion of replica is in danger of losing all
meaning.
   25. Concerning the problem of survival, in the sense of persisting into the future after an
experience of radical alteration of personal identity, cf. in Perry, *Personal Identity,* sec. 5, "Personal Identity and Survival" (articles by Bernard Williams and Derek Parfit), pp. 179–223;
in Rorty, *Identity of Persons,* articles by David Lewis, "Survival and Identity," pp. 18–40, and
Georges Rey, "Survival," pp. 41–66.

in Parfit's entire work. I have neglected to state that the problem of identity discussed in the third part of the book is destined to resolve a moral problem posed in the two preceding parts, namely the problem of the *rationality* of the ethical choice posed by the utilitarian ethics which predominates in the English-language world. Parfit attacks the most egotistic version of it, which he terms the "self-interest theory."[26] What is at stake here is indeed the self in its ethical dimension. Parfit's thesis is that the argument between egoism and altruism cannot be decided on the level where it unfolds if one has not first taken a position on the question of what sort of entities persons are (whence the title of the work *Reasons and Persons*). The valid reasons for ethical choices pass by way of the dissolution of false beliefs concerning the ontological status of persons. So, at the end of the third part of the work we return to the question raised in the first part. And now the entire weight of the ethical questions falls back upon the question of identity. The latter then becomes a genuinely axiological issue. The judgment of what matters is a judgment that ranks in the hierarchy of evaluations. But which identity — identity in what sense of the term — are we asked to renounce? Is it the sameness that Hume held impossible to find and little worthy of our interest? Or mineness, which, in my opinion, constitutes the core of the nonreductionist thesis? Actually, everything leads me to think that Parfit, by reason of not distinguishing between selfhood and sameness, aims at the former through the latter. This is far from uninteresting, for the sort of Buddhism insinuated by Parfit's ethical thesis consists precisely in not making any difference between sameness and mineness. In doing this, does he not risk throwing out the baby with the bathwater? For, as much as I am willing to admit that imaginative variations on personal identity lead to a crisis of selfhood as such — and problem cases in the narrative order which we shall consider later will certainly confirm this — I still do not see how the question "who?" can disappear in the extreme cases in which it remains without an answer. For really, how can we ask ourselves about *what* matters if we could not ask *to whom* the thing mattered or not? Does not the questioning about what matters or not depend upon self-concern, which indeed seems to be constitutive of selfhood? And when we move from the third level to the second, and then to the first level of beliefs sifted out by the critique, do we not continue to move within the element of belief, of the belief concerning what *we* are? The tenacity of personal pronouns, even in the statement of the reductionist thesis from which we started, reveals

26. Parfit sums it up in the following terms: The Self-interest theory "*S* gives to each person this aim: the outcomes that would be best for himself, and that would make his life go, for him, as well as possible" (*Reasons and Persons,* p. 3).

something more profound than the rhetoric of argumentation: it marks the resistance of the question "who?" to its elimination in an impersonal description.[27]

In the last analysis, it is a matter of changing the conception we have about "ourselves, and about our actual lives" (p. 217). It is "our view" of life that is at issue.

It will be objected here to my plea on behalf of the irreducibility of the trait of mineness and, by implication, of the very question of selfhood that Parfit's quasi Buddhism does not leave even the assertion of selfhood intact. What Parfit asks is that we concern ourselves less with ourselves, with our aging and our death among other things, that we attach less importance to the question of "whether experiences come within the same or different lives" (p. 341); hence, that we take an interest in the "experiences" themselves rather than in "the person, the subject of experiences" (ibid.); that we place less emphasis on differences between ourselves at different periods and others who have had experiences similar to our own; that we ignore as much as possible the boundaries between lives by giving less importance to unity of each life; that we make the very unity of our life more a work of art than a claim to independence. Is it not to the very neutralization of the question of selfhood, beyond the impersonal observation of the connectedness of a life, that Parfit, the moralist, invites us? Does not Parfit oppose *carefreeness* (which, after all, was also preached by Jesus in his Sermon on the Mount) to *care?* I well understand the objection. But I think that it can be incorporated into the defense of selfhood in its confrontation with sameness. What Parfit's moral reflection provokes is, finally, a crisis *within* selfhood. The crisis consists in the fact that the very notion that my experiences belong to me has an ambiguous sense; there are different types of ownership (what I have and who I am). What Parfit is aiming at is precisely the egotism that nourishes the thesis of self-interest, against which his work is directed. But is not a moment of self-dispossession essential to authentic selfhood? And must one not, in order to make oneself open, available, belong to oneself in a certain sense? We have already asked: Would the question of what matters arise if there were no one to whom the question of identity mattered? Let us now add: if my

27. One would have to cite here in their entirety the provisional conclusions reached in ibid., pp. 216 and 217, where what is in question are "our brains," "our thoughts and our actions," "our identity." The substitution of deictic forms other than personal pronouns and adjectives ("this person's brain," "these experiences") changes nothing here, considering the constitution of the deictic forms themselves. In this regard, the most astonishing expression is the one that sums up the claim as a whole: "My claim [is] that we could describe our lives in an *impersonal* way" (p. 217).

identity were to lose all importance in every respect, would not the question of others also cease to matter?[28]

We will encounter these same questions at the end of our plea on behalf of a narrative interpretation of identity; the latter, we shall see, also has its bizarre cases which reshape the assertion of identity in the form of a question — and at times of a question without an answer: Who am I, actually? It is here that narrative theory, called upon to wrestle with Parfit's questions, will be invited, in its turn, to explore its common boundary with ethical theory.

28. Concerning the kinship between Parfit's theses and Buddhism, see ibid., p. 280; Matthew Kapstein, "Collins, Parfit, and the Problem of Personal Identity in Two Philosophical Traditions — A Review of *Selfless Persons*," *Feature Book Review*, offprint.

The Self and Narrative Identity

The present study is closely linked to the preceding one. Its tone, however, is different. Up to now, narrative identity has been treated only polemically and, overall, in a more defensive than constructive manner. Two positive tasks remain to be accomplished.

The first task is to carry to a higher level the dialectic of sameness and selfhood implicitly contained in the notion of narrative identity. The second is to complete this investigation of the narrated self by exploring the mediations that narrative theory can perform between action theory and moral theory. This second task will itself have two sides to it. Returning to our triad — describing, narrating, prescribing — we shall ask first what *extension of the practical field* is called for by the narrative function, if the action described is to match the action narrated. We shall then examine in what way narrative, which is never ethically neutral, proves to be the first *laboratory of moral judgment*. The reciprocal constitution of action and of the self will be pursued on both sides of narrative theory, in the practical as well as the ethical sphere.

1. Narrative Identity and the Dialectic of Selfhood and Sameness

The genuine nature of narrative identity discloses itself, in my opinion, only in the dialectic of selfhood and sameness. In this sense, this dialectic represents the major contribution of narrative theory to the constitution of the self.

The argument will proceed in the following way:

First, I shall begin by showing, in a continuation of the analyses in *Time and Narrative,* how the specific model of the interconnection of events constituted by emplotment allows us to integrate with permanence in time what seems to be its contrary in the domain of sameness-identity, namely diversity, variability, discontinuity, and instability.

Second, I shall then show how the notion of emplotment, transposed from the action to the characters in the narrative, produces a dialectic of the character which is quite clearly a dialectic of sameness and selfhood; returning, at this time, to the strategy of puzzling cases in analytic philosophy, I shall make room, within the space of the imaginative variations opened up by the dialectic of selfhood and sameness, for limiting cases at the point of dissociation between two modalities of identity, worthy of competing with Parfit's undecidable cases; a remarkable opportunity will thus arise to confront the respective resources of literary fiction and of science fiction concerning the eminently problematic character of personal identity.

1. When Dilthey formed the concept of *Zusammenhang des Lebens* (the connectedness of life), he spontaneously held it to be equivalent to the concept of a life history. It is this preunderstanding of the historical significance of connectedness that the narrative theory of personal identity attempts to articulate, at a higher level of conceptuality. Understood in narrative terms, identity can be called, by linguistic convention, the identity of the *character*. This identity will later be placed back into the sphere of the dialectic of the same and the self. But before this, I shall show how the identity of the character is constructed in connection with that of the plot. This derivation of one identity in relation to the other, merely indicated in *Time and Narrative*, will be clarified here.

Let us first recall what was meant in *Time and Narrative* by identity on the level of emplotment. It can be described in dynamic terms by the competition between a demand for concordance and the admission of discordances which, up to the close of the story, threaten this identity. By concordance, I mean the principle of order that presides over what Aristotle calls "the arrangement of facts." By discordances, I mean the reversals of fortune that make the plot an ordered transformation from an initial situation to a terminal situation. I am applying the term "configuration" to this art of composition which mediates between concordance and discordance. To extend the validity of this concept of narrative configuration beyond Aristotle's privileged example — Greek tragedy and, to a lesser degree, epic poetry — I propose to define discordant concordance, characteristic of all narrative composition, by the notion of the synthesis of the heterogeneous. By this I am attempting to account for the diverse mediations performed by the plot: between the manifold of events and the temporal unity of the story recounted; between the disparate components of the action — intentions, causes, and chance occurrences — and the sequence of the story; and finally, between pure succession and the unity of the temporal form, which, in extreme cases, can disrupt chronology to the point of abolishing it. These multiple dialectics do no more, in my opinion, than make explicit the opposition, already present in the domain of tragedy according to Aristotle, between the episodic dispersal of the narrative and the power of unification unfurled by the configuring act constituting *poiēsis* itself.

It is to narrative configuration understood in this sense that one must compare the sort of connectedness claimed by an impersonal description. The essential difference distinguishing the narrative model from every other model of connectedness resides in the status of *events,* which we have repeatedly made the touchstone of the analysis of the self.[1] Whereas in a causal-type model, event and occurrence are indiscernible, the narrative event is defined by its relation to the very operation of configuration; it participates in the unstable structure of discordant concordance characteristic of the plot itself. It is a source of discordance inasmuch as it springs up, and a source of concordance inasmuch as it allows the story to advance.[2] The paradox of emplotment is that it inverts the effect of contingency, in the sense of that which could have happened differently or which might not have happened at all, by incorporating it in some way into the effect of necessity or probability exerted by the configuring act.[3] The inversion of the effect of contingency into an effect of necessity is produced at the very core of the event: as a mere occurrence, the latter is confined to thwarting the expectations created by the prior course of events; it is quite simply the unexpected, the surprising. It only becomes an integral part of the story when understood after the fact, once it is transfigured by the so-to-speak retrograde necessity which proceeds from the temporal totality carried to its term. This necessity is a narrative necessity whose meaning effect comes from the configurating act as such; this narrative necessity transforms physical contingency, the other side of physical necessity, into narrative contingency, implied in narrative necessity.

1. Cf. the discussion of Davidson in the third study and that of Parfit in the fifth study. I am not contesting what these theories have established, namely that, as occurrences, events have the right to an ontological status at least equal to that of substance, nor do I contest that they can be the object of an impersonal description. I am saying that, by entering into the movement of a narrative which relates a character to a plot, the event loses its impersonal neutrality. By the same token, the narrative status conferred upon the event averts the drift of the notion of event which would make it difficult, if not impossible, to take the agent into account in the description of the action.

2. I find here something of Walter Benjamin's *Ursprung,* a surging forth that cannot be reduced to what is ordinarily understood by *Entstehung,* and even less so by *Entwicklung.* And yet, even though the surging forth of the narrative event cannot be coordinated with some totality, it does not exhaust itself in its effect of rupture, of caesura; it contains potentialities for development that have to be "saved." This *Rettung* of the *Ursprung* — a central theme in Benjamin — is, in my opinion, the workings of the plot. The plot "redeems" the origin of the "fall" into meaninglessness. Cf. Jeanne-Marie Gagnebin, "Histoire, mémoire et oubli chez Walter Benjamin" (unpublished text).

3. Concerning the necessity or probability that Aristotle attaches to the *muthos* of tragedy or of the epic, cf. the texts of Aristotle cited in *Time and Narrative* 1:40–41.

From this simple reminder of the notion of emplotment, and before any consideration of the dialectic of characters which is its corollary, it results that the narrative operation has developed an entirely original concept of dynamic identity which reconciles the same categories that Locke took as contraries: identity and diversity.

The decisive step in the direction of a narrative conception of personal identity is taken when one passes from the action to the character. A character is the one who performs the action in the narrative. The category of character is therefore a narrative category as well, and its role in the narrative involves the same narrative understanding as the plot itself. The question is then to determine what the narrative category of character contributes to the discussion of personal identity. The thesis supported here will be that the identity of the character is comprehensible through the transfer to the character of the operation of emplotment, first applied to the action recounted; characters, we will say, are themselves plots.

Let us recall briefly in what way narrative theory accounts for the correlation between action and character.

The correlation between story told and character is simply postulated by Aristotle in the *Poetics*. It appears as such a close correlation there that it takes the form of a subordination. It is indeed in the story recounted, with its qualities of unity, internal structure, and completeness which are conferred by emplotment, that the character preserves throughout the story an identity correlative to that of the story itself.[4]

Contemporary narrative theory has attempted to give to this correlation the status of a semiotic constraint, already implicit in a sense in Aristotle's conceptual analysis of *muthos* into its "parts." Propp gave the impetus to this investigation on a level of abstraction which I discuss in *Time and Narrative* 2 and will not repeat here.[5] The author of *Morphology of the Folk-*

---

4. I began to underscore this primacy of emplotment (*muthos*) over character in *Time and Narrative* 1 (p. 37). In the series marking the six "parts" of tragedy according to Aristotle, the plot comes first before the characters and the thought (*dianoia*), which, with the plot, constitutes the "what" imitated by the action. Aristotle pushes this subordinate status to the point of declaring: "Tragedy is essentially an imitation not of persons but of actions and life, of happiness and misery. All human happiness or misery takes the form of action; the end for which we live is a certain kind of activity, not a quality. . . . Besides this, a tragedy is impossible without action, but there may be one without Character" (*Poetics* [*De Poetica*], trans. Ingram Bywater, in *The Basic Works of Aristotle*, ed. McKeon, 7.1450a16–24). This last hypothesis will concern us later on, when we discuss the disappearance of the character in some contemporary works.

5. In *Time and Narrative* 2, I am careful to underscore the kinship of meaning between narrative *intelligence*, immanent in the competence of the spectator, the listener, or the reader, and narratological *rationality*, which I take to be derived from the former. This problem of preeminence does not concern me here. I am instead looking to narrative theory for a confir-

tale begins by distinguishing a series of "functions" — recurrent segments of actions and characters — allowing him to define folktales in terms of the sequence of functions alone. However, when he is about to consider the synthetic unity of this chain, he has to take into account the role played by the characters. He is thus the first to attempt a typology of these roles, established solely on the basis of their recurrence.[6] The list of roles is not independent of the list of functions; they intersect at a number of points, which Propp called spheres of action: "Many functions logically join together into certain spheres. These spheres in toto correspond to their respective performers" (p. 79); "The problem of the distribution of functions may be resolved on the plane of the problem concerning the distribution of the spheres of action among the characters" (p. 80). Quoting these statements of Propp in *Time and Narrative* 2 : 37, I ask whether every plot does not proceed from a mutual genesis involving the development of a character and that of a story. I adopt Frank Kermode's axiom that developing a character is recounting more.[7]

This is what Claude Bremond has clearly shown in his *Logique du récit;* according to him, a *role* can be defined only by "the attribution of some possible, actual, or completed predicate-process to a subject-person."[8] In this attribution we see the narrative solution to the problem of ascribing action to an agent, which was discussed in the preceding studies. The elementary sequences of a narrative already contain this correlation. In addition, the reference in the very definition of "role" to the three stages of possibility, of passing to action or not, of completion or incompletion, immediately situates the role within an action dynamics. On the basis of this definition of elementary sequence, it becomes possible to draw up a full repertoire of roles, by taking into account a series of enrichments bearing on both the subject-person and the predicate-process. It is noteworthy that the first great dichotomy is that of *sufferers,* those affected by processes of modification or conservation, and, in correlation with them, of agents who initiate these processes. Bremond thus takes into account our preunderstanding that stories are about agents and sufferers. For my part,

mation of the preunderstanding that we have, on the level of narrative intelligence, of the coordination between plot and character.

6. Vladimir Propp, *Morphology of the Folktale,* 1st ed., trans. Laurence Scott; 2d ed., rev. and ed. Louis A. Wagner (Austin: University of Texas Press, 1968). Here is Propp's list: the villain, the donor (or provider), the helper, the sought-for person, the dispatcher, the hero, and the false hero. Cf. *Time and Narrative* 2 : 36.

7. Frank Kermode, *The Genesis of Secrecy: On the Interpretation of Narrative* (Cambridge: Harvard University Press, 1979), pp. 75–99.

8. Claude Bremond, *Logique du récit* (Paris: Éd. du Seuil, 1973), 134.

I never forget to speak of humans as acting and suffering. The moral problem, as we saw in an earlier study, is grafted onto the recognition of this
essential dissymmetry between the one who acts and the one who undergoes, culminating in the violence of the powerful agent. Being affected by
a course of narrated events is the organizing principle governing an entire
series of roles of sufferers, depending on whether the action exerts an influence or whether its effect is to make matters better or worse, to protect
or to frustrate. A remarkable enrichment of the notion of role concerns its
introduction into the field of evaluations through the actions which have
just been enumerated, then into the field of retributions, where the sufferer
appears as the beneficiary of esteem or as the victim of disesteem, depending on whether the agent proves to be someone who distributes rewards
or punishments. Bremond rightly observes that it is only on these levels
that agents and sufferers are raised to the rank of persons and of initiators
of action. In this way, through the roles related to the domain of rewards
and punishments, the close connection between the theory of action and
ethical theory which we evoked above is witnessed on the plane of the
narrative.

It is with Greimas's *actantial* model that the correlation between plot
and character is carried to its most radical position, prior to all sensible
figuration. For this reason, one does not speak here of "character" but of
actant, in order to subordinate the anthropomorphic representation of the
agent to the position of the operator of actions along the narrative course.
The radicalization occurs along two different lines — on the side of the
actant and on that of the narrative course. Along the first line, to the actual
list of characters found in Russian folktales, according to Propp, Greimas
substitutes a model based upon three categories: desire (the principle of
the quest of a real object, a person, or a value), communication (the principle of all relations between a sender and a receiver), and action properly
speaking (the principle of all oppositions between helpers and opponents).
This provides a model that, unlike Propp's, starts with possible relations
between actants and then moves in the direction of a rich combinatory of
actions, whether these are called contracts, tests, quests, or struggles.
Along the second line, that of narrative courses, I would like to emphasize
the place occupied on a plane intermediary between that of deep structures
and the figurative plane by a series of notions which have a place only in a
narrative conception of the connectedness of life: first, that of a *narrative
program,* then that of a *polemical* relation between two programs, from
which results the opposition between subject and antisubject. We find
again here what was precomprehended on the plane of simple narrative
intelligence, namely that action is interaction and that interaction is competition among projects which themselves are by turn opposing and con-

vergent. Let us also add to this all the translations or transfers of objects/ values which narrativize the exchange. Finally, one would have to take into account the topology underlying the change of "place" — initial and terminal places of transfer — on the basis of which one can then speak of a "sequence of performances."[9]

If we reconnect the two lines of analysis which I have just broadly outlined (referring to *Time and Narrative* 2:44–60), we see the mutual reinforcement of a semiotics of the actant and a semiotics of narrative courses, to the point at which the narrative appears as the path of the character and vice versa. In concluding with this theme of the necessary correlation between plot and character, I would like to underscore one category which Greimas's work on *Maupassant* stressed,[10] although it was present in the earliest actantial model, namely the category of sender. The pair sender/ receiver is an extension of that of mandate in Propp or of inaugural contract in Greimas, the contract by reason of which the hero receives the competence to act. The senders — who may be individual, social, or even cosmic entities, as we see in the short story "Two Friends" — stem from what in *Maupassant* Greimas terms a "proto-actantial" status (p. 45).[11]

It has not been unavailing to recall in what way the narrative structure joins together the two processes of emplotment, that of action and that of the character. This conjunction is the true response to the aporias of ascription referred to as early as the first study. It continues to be true that, from a paradigmatic viewpoint, the questions "who?" "what?" "why?" and so on can denote separate terms in the conceptual network of action. But from a syntagmatic viewpoint, the responses to these questions form a chain that is none other than the story chain. Telling a story is saying who did what and how, by spreading out in time the connection between these various viewpoints. It is also true that one can describe separately the mental predicates considered outside of their attribution to a person (which is the very condition for any description of the "mental"). It is in the narrative, however, that attribution is reestablished. In the same way, the articulation between plot and character permits us to conduct together an inquiry that is infinite on the level of the search for motives and an inquiry

9. In the case of Greimas, just as in that of Propp and Bremond, I shall not go into the epistemological difficulties tied to the enterprise of dechronologizing narrative structures. Once again, I am interested here solely in what legitimates the *correlation* between the plot and the character, intuitively understood on the level of narrative intelligence alone.

10. A. J. Greimas, *Maupassant: The Semiotics of Text. Practical Exercises,* trans. Paul Perron (Amsterdam, Philadelphia: John Benjamins, 1988).

11. A good synthesis of the semiotic approach to the category of character can be found in the article by Philippe Hamon, "Statut sémiologique du personnage," in *Poétique du récit,* Roland Barthes et al. (Paris: Éditions du Seuil, 1977).

that is, in principle, finite on the level of attribution to someone. The two inquiries are interwoven in the twofold process of identification, involving plot and character. Even the fearsome aporia of ascription has a replica in the dialectic of character and plot. Confronted with the third Kantian antinomy, ascription appears to be torn between the thesis, which posits the idea of beginning a causal series, and the antithesis, which opposes to the former the idea of a sequence without beginning or interruption. The narrative resolves the antinomy in its own way, on the one hand, by granting to the character an initiative — that is, the power to begin a series of events, without this beginning thereby constituting an absolute beginning, a beginning of time — and on the other hand, by assigning to the narrative as such the power of determining the beginning, the middle, and the end of an action. By making the initiative belonging to the character coincide in this way with the beginning of the action, the narrative satisfies the thesis without violating the antithesis. Under its multiple aspects, it constitutes the *poetic reply* provided by the notion of narrative identity to the aporias of ascription. I am purposefully returning to the term "poetic reply" that was used in *Time and Narrative* 3 to express the relation between the aporias of time and the narrative function. I said then that the narrative function did not provide a speculative response to these aporias but made them productive on another order of language. In the same way, the dialectic of character and plot makes the aporias of ascription productive, and narrative identity can be said to provide a poetic reply to them.

2. From this correlation *between* action and character in a narrative there results a dialectic *internal* to the character which is the exact corollary of the dialectic of concordance and discordance developed by the emplotment of action. The dialectic consists in the fact that, following the line of concordance, the character draws his or her singularity from the unity of a life considered a temporal totality which is itself singular and distinguished from all others. Following the line of discordance, this temporal totality is threatened by the disruptive effect of the unforeseeable events that punctuate it (encounters, accidents, etc.). Because of the concordant-discordant synthesis, the contingency of the event contributes to the necessity, retroactive so to speak, of the history of a life, to which is equated the identity of the character. Thus chance is transmuted into fate. And the identity of the character emploted, so to speak, can be understood only in terms of this dialectic. The thesis of identity which Parfit calls nonreductionist receives more than an assist from this dialectic, something more like a complete overhaul. The person, understood as a character in a story, is not an entity distinct from his or her "experiences." Quite the opposite: the person shares the condition of dynamic identity peculiar to the story recounted. The narrative constructs the identity of the character, what can

be called his or her narrative identity, in constructing that of the story told. It is the identity of the story that makes the identity of the character.

This dialectic of discordant concordance belonging to the character must now be inscribed within the dialectic of sameness and of selfhood. The necessity of this reinscription imposes itself as soon as the discordant concordance of the character is confronted with the search for permanence in time attached to the notion of identity, a confrontation that brings out the equivocalness we made apparent in the preceding study: on one side, we said, there is the sameness of character; on the other, the ipseity, or selfhood, of self-constancy. We have now to show how the dialectic of the character comes to be inscribed in the interval between these two poles of permanence in time in order to mediate between them.

This mediating function performed by the narrative identity of the character between the poles of sameness and selfhood is attested to primarily by the *imaginative variations* to which the narrative submits this identity. In truth, the narrative does not merely tolerate these variations, it engenders them, seeks them out. In this sense, literature proves to consist in a vast laboratory for thought experiments in which the resources of variation encompassed by narrative identity are put to the test of narration. The benefit of these thought experiments lies in the fact that they make the difference between the two meanings of permanence in time evident, by varying the relation between them. In everyday experience, as we have said, these meanings tend to overlap and to merge with one another; in this way, counting on someone is both relying on the stability of a character and expecting that the other will keep his or her word, regardless of the changes that may affect the lasting dispositions by which that person is recognized. In literary fiction, the space of variation open to the relations between these two modalities of identity is vast. At one end, the character in the story has a definite character, which is identifiable and reidentifiable as the same: this may well be the status of the characters in fairy tales in our folklore. The classic novel — from *La Princesse de Clèves* or the eighteenth-century English novel to Dostoyevsky and Tolstoy — can be said to have explored the intermediary space of variations, where, through transformations of the character, the identification of the same decreases without disappearing entirely. We approach the opposite pole with the so-called novel of apprenticeship and move even closer with the stream-of-consciousness novel. The relation between the plot and the character appears to be inverted here: just the opposite of the Aristotelian model, the plot is placed in the service of the character. It is here that the identity of the character, escaping the control of the plot and of its ordering principle, is truly put to the test. We thus reach an extreme pole of variation where the character in the story ceases to have a definite character. It is at this pole that we encounter limiting cases in which literary fiction lends itself to a confrontation with the puzzling cases of analytic philosophy. The conflict between a narrativist version and a nonnarrativist version of personal identity will culminate in this confrontation.

The lesson that narrativity also has its unsettling cases is taught to perfection by contemporary plays and novels. To begin with, these cases can be described as fictions of the loss of identity. With Robert Musil, for example, *The Man without Qualities* — or more precisely, without properties (*ohne Eigenschaften*) — becomes ultimately nonidentifiable in a world, it is said, of qualities (or properties) without men. The anchor of the proper noun becomes ridiculous to the point of being superfluous. The nonidentifiable becomes the unnamable. To see more clearly the philosophical issues in this eclipse of the identity of the character, it is important to note that, as the narrative approaches the point of annihilation of the character, the novel also loses its own properly narrative qualities, even when these are interpreted as above in the most flexible and most dialectical manner possible. To the loss of the identity of the character thus corresponds the loss of the configuration of the narrative and, in particular, a crisis of the closure of the narrative.[12] We therefore find a sort of rebound effect of the character on the plot. It is the same sort of schism, to use Frank Kermode's term in *The Sense of an Ending*,[13] that affects both the tradition of the plot carried to its ending, which stands as a closure, and the tradition of the identifiable hero. The erosion of paradigms (again, Kermode's term) strikes both the figuration of the character and the configuration of the plot. Thus, in the case of Robert Musil, the decomposition of the narrative form paralleling the loss of identity of the character breaks out of the confines of the narrative and draws the literary work into the sphere of the essay. Nor is it by chance that so many contemporary autobiographies, that of Michel Leiris for example, deliberately move away from the narrative form and move into the literary genre with the least configuration — the essay.

What, however, is meant here by loss of identity? More precisely, what modality of identity is involved here? My thesis is that, set back in the framework of the dialectic of *idem* and *ipse,* these unsettling cases of narrativity can be reinterpreted as exposing selfhood by taking away the support of sameness. In this sense they constitute the opposite pole to that of the totally identifiable hero, formed by the superimposition of selfhood upon sameness. What is now lost, under the title of "property," is what

12. Concerning this crisis of closure, cf. *Time and Narrative* 2:19–28.

13. Frank Kermode, *The Sense of an Ending: Studies in the Theory of Fiction* (Oxford: Oxford University Press, 1966).

allowed us to equate the character in the story with lasting dispositions or character.

But what is selfhood, once it has lost the support of sameness? A comparison with Parfit's puzzling cases will enable us to make this more precise.

Literary fictions differ fundamentally from technological fictions in that they remain imaginative variations on an invariant, our corporeal condition experienced as the existential mediation between the self and the world. Characters in plays and novels are humans like us who think, speak, act, and suffer as we do. Insofar as the body as one's own is a dimension of oneself, the imaginative variations *around* the corporeal condition are variations on the self and its selfhood. Furthermore, in virtue of the mediating function of the body as one's own in the structure of being in the world, the feature of selfhood belonging to corporeality is extended to that of the world as it is inhabited corporeally. This feature defines the terrestrial condition as such and gives to the Earth the existential signification attributed to it in various ways by Nietzsche, Husserl, and Heidegger. The Earth here is something different, and something more, than a planet: it is the mythical name of our corporeal anchoring in the world. This is what is ultimately presupposed in the literary narrative as it is subjected to the constraint making it a mimesis of action. For the action "imitated" in and through fiction also remains subjected to the constraint of the corporeal and terrestrial condition.

What the puzzling cases render radically contingent is this corporeal and terrestrial condition which the hermeneutics of existence, underlying the notion of acting and suffering, takes to be insurmountable. What performs this inversion of meaning by which the existential invariant becomes a variable in a new imaginary montage? This is done by technology; better, beyond available technology, this is the realm of conceivable technology — in short, the technological dream. In this dream, the brain is taken to be the substitutable equivalent of the person. The brain is the point of application of advanced technology. In experiments of bisection, transplantation, reduplication, and teletransportation, the brain represents the human being as the object of manipulations. This technological dream, illustrated by cerebral manipulations, is of a piece with the impersonal treatment of identity on the conceptual level. In this sense, one may say that the imaginative variations of science fiction are variations with regard to sameness, while those of literary fiction concern selfhood, or more precisely, selfhood in its dialectical relation to sameness.

The real difficulty, then, does not lie within either of the fields of imaginative variations but, if one may say so, *between* them. Are we capable of conceiving of (I do not say of realizing) variations such that the corporeal and terrestrial condition itself becomes a mere variable, a contingent variable, if the teletransported individual does not transport with himself some residual traits of this condition, without which he could no longer be said to act or to suffer, even if it were only the question of knowing if and how he is going to survive?

Perhaps this second-order difficulty cannot be decided one way or the other on the level of the imaginary. It perhaps requires the aid of the ethical level, which we shall come to in the final section of this study, when we confront narrative identity, oscillating between sameness and selfhood, and ethical identity, which requires a person accountable for his or her acts. It is in relation to this capacity for imputation that cerebral manipulations can be said to undermine personal identity and so to violate a right — the right of the person to his or her physical integrity. However, in order that the capacity for imputation, whose significance is purely moral and legal, not be arbitrarily assigned to persons, must not the existential invariant of corporeality and worldliness, around which revolve all the imaginative variations of literary fiction, be itself taken as indispensable on an ontological plane? Is not what is violated by the imaginary manipulations of the brain something more than a rule, more than a law; is it not the existential condition of the possibility for rules or laws as such, that is, finally, for precepts addressed to persons as acting and suffering? In other words, is not what is inviolable the difference between the self and the same, even on the plane of corporeality?

I will leave in suspension what I have just called a second-order difficulty. For if an imaginary system which respects the corporeal and terrestrial condition as an invariant has more in common with the moral principle of imputation, would not any attempt to censure that other imaginary, the one which renders this very invariant contingent, be in its turn immoral from another point of view for the reason that it would prohibit dreaming? It will perhaps one day be necessary to forbid actually doing what today science fiction is limited to dreaming about. But have not dreams always transgressed into the realm of the forbidden? So let us dream along with Parfit. But let us simply express the wish that the manipulative surgeons in these dreams never have the means — or, more especially, the right — to perform what is perfectly permissible to imagine.[14]

14. I have not yet said my final word on Parfit. Later we shall ask whether a certain convergence of the literary fictions which I assign to selfhood and those of science fiction (which, in my opinion, concern only sameness) is not reconstituted when one takes into account the ethical implications of narrativity. There is perhaps for us, too, a way of saying that identity is not what matters.

2. Between Description and Prescription: Narration

There remains, in the second section of this inquiry, the need to justify the assertion advanced already in the Introduction and repeated at the beginning of the fifth study, namely that narrative theory occupies a central position in the course of our investigation as a whole between the theory of action and ethical theory. In what sense, then, is it legitimate to see in the theory of plot and of character a meaningful transition between the ascription of action to an agent who has the capacity to act and its imputation to an agent who has the obligation to act?

The question, it is clear, has two aspects to it; with regard to the first one, which concerns the preceding "logico-practical" studies, it is important to show to what extent the connection revealed by narrative theory between plot and character, in addition to the new light it sheds on the difficulties attaching to the relation between the action and its agent, calls for a considerable extension of the field of practice, if the action described is to match the action recounted. With regard to the second aspect, oriented toward the "moral" studies that will follow, the question instead revolves around the *supports* and *anticipations* that narrative theory offers to ethical questioning. The relation between plot and character sheds new light on the relation between action and its agent only at the expense of an extension of the field of practice beyond the action segments that logical grammar confines most readily to action sentences, and even beyond the action chains, whose sole interest consists in the mode of logical connection stemming from a theory of praxis. It is noteworthy that Aristotle, to whom we owe the definition of tragedy as the imitation of action, understands by action a connection (*sustasis, sunthesis*) of incidents, of facts, of a sort susceptible to conforming to narrative configuration. He specifies: "The most important of the six [parts of tragedy] is the combination of the incidents of the story. Tragedy is essentially an imitation [*mimēsis*] not of persons but of action and life [*bion*], of happiness and misery. All human happiness or misery takes the form of [*en*] action; the end [*telos*] for which we live is a certain kind of activity [*praxis tis*], not a quality [*ou poiotēs*]. Character gives us qualities, but it is in our actions — what we do — that we are happy or the reverse."[15] There is no better way of saying that any revision in the relation between action and agent requires along with it a revision in the very concept of action, if it is to be carried to the level of narrative configuration on the scale of an entire life.

By revision we are to understand much more than a lengthening of the connections between action segments as they are shaped by the grammar

---

15. Aristotle, *Poetics* 6.1450a15–19.

of action sentences. A hierarchy of units of praxis must be made to appear, each unit on its own level containing a specific principle of organization, integrating a variety of logical connections.

1. The first composite units are those deserving the name of *practices*. In French, the form of the verb "to practice" (*pratiquer*), in expressions such as "to practice a sport," "practice medicine," and so forth, is more common than the substantive form "practice" used in English.

The most familiar examples are professions, the arts, and games.[16] We may have an initial idea of what these practices are by starting from the description of basic actions in the analytic theory of action. We recall that Danto defined a basic action by extracting from ordinary actions the relation "in order to (do something)." What remain are basic actions, namely those actions that we know how to perform and that we do indeed perform without first having to do something else in order to be able to do what we do. These are, broadly speaking, gestures, postures, elementary corporeal actions that, to be sure, we learn to coordinate and to master but the basics of which we do not really learn. In contrast, all the rest of the practical field is constructed on the relation "X in order to do Y": to do Y, one must first do X. It might then be objected that the concept of practice is superfluous. To have the concept of action match that of practice, is it not enough, on the one hand, to lengthen the chains of means and ends, as E. Anscombe does in the famous example in *Intention* discussed above, and, on the other hand, to coordinate with one another the segments of physical causality and intentional segments, formalized into practical syllogisms, in a composite model, like the one proposed, for instance, by G. Von Wright in *Explanation and Understanding*? One would then obtain long action-chains in which the passage from the systemic point of view to the teleological point of view would be assured at each point in the chain by the fact that the agent is capable of considering the effects of causation for the circumstances of decision making, while, in return, the intended or unintended results of intentional actions would become new states of affairs entailing new causal series. This intermingling of finality and causation, of intentionality and systemic connections, is certainly constitutive of these long actions known as practices. What is lacking, however, is the unity of configuration that sets apart a profession, an art, or a game in these long action-chains.

A second kind of connection helps to define practices as second-order units. These are no longer linear relations like the ones we have just examined but nesting relations. The vocabulary attaching to our repertoire

16. In the next chapter I shall show in what sense the choice of these first units of praxis conforming to that made by Aristotle also agrees with his teleological version of ethics.

of powers wonderfully expresses these relations involving subordination more than coordination. The work of a farmer, for instance, includes subordinate actions, such as plowing, planting, harvesting, and so on in descending order, until one reaches basic actions such as pulling or pushing. Now this series of nesting relations — hence relations of subordination of partial actions to a global action — is joined with the relations of coordination between systemic and teleological segments only to the extent that both sorts of connection are unified under the laws of meaning that make the work of farming a practice. The same thing can be said with respect to other practices. Just as farming (but not plowing — and starting up the tractor even less so) is a practice, in the sense of a profession, in the same way, household management — in the Greek sense of *oikos,* to which we owe the word "economy" — or holding public office in the government (an example to which we shall return later) denotes as many practices, whereas the subordinate behaviors, such as putting together a menu or giving a speech at a public gathering, do not merit this title. Likewise painting is a practice, both a profession and an art, but not applying a spot of color to a canvas. One final example will put us on the path of a helpful transition: shifting the position of a pawn on the chessboard is in itself simply a gesture, but taken in the context of the practice of the game of chess, this gesture has the meaning of a move in a chess game.

The last example testifies to the fact that the unit of configuration constitutive of a practice is based upon a particular relation of meaning, that expressed by the notion of constitutive rule, which was borrowed precisely from game theory before being extended to the theory of speech acts and then integrated, as I am doing here, in the theory of praxis. By constitutive rule is meant those precepts whose sole function is to rule that, for instance, a given gesture of shifting the position of a pawn on the chessboard "counts as" a move in a game of chess. The move would not exist, with the signification and the effect it has in the game, without the rule that "constitutes" the move as a step in the chess game. The rule is constitutive in the sense that it is not something added on, in the manner of an external condition applied to movements which would already have their own meaning (as are traffic lights in relation to drivers who each have their own destination). The rule, all by itself, gives the gesture its meaning: moving a pawn; the meaning stems from the rule as soon as the rule is constitutive, and it is so because it constitutes meaning, "counting as." The notion of constitutive rule can be extended from the example of games to other practices, for the simple reason that games are excellent practical models. Thus John Searle was correct to extend the notion to the area of speech acts inasmuch as these, too, are actions or phases of greater practices. Illocutionary acts, such as promising, ordering, warning, and noting, are distinguished from one another by their "force," which is itself constituted by the rule that says, for example, that promising is placing oneself under the obligation to do tomorrow what today I say I shall do.

It is important to take note of the fact that constitutive rules are not moral rules. They simply rule over the *meaning* of particular gestures and, as was stated above, make a particular hand gesture "count as" waving hello, voting, hailing a taxi, and so on. To be sure, constitutive rules point the way toward moral rules to the extent that the latter govern conduct capable of conveying meaning. But this is only a first step in the direction of ethics. Even the constitutive rule of promising, as it was discussed above, has not as such a moral signification, although it contains the reference to an obligation. It is confined to defining what "counts as" a promise, what gives it its illocutionary "force." The moral rule, which can be termed the rule of faithfulness, according to which one must keep one's promises, alone has a deontological status.[17]

The introduction of the notion of constitutive rule at this stage of the investigation has another advantage besides introducing specific relations of meaning into the structure of practices; it has the further advantage of underscoring the *interactive* character belonging to most practices. This character is not stressed in the analytic theory of action because action sentences are taken out of their social environment. It is only in the pragmatic framework that the one who receives the sense assigned to an action sentence by a sender incorporates himself or herself into the meaning of the sentence. Even then, interlocution constitutes only the verbal dimension of action. Practices are based on actions in which an agent takes into account, as a matter of principle, the actions of others. It is in these terms that Max Weber successively and conjointly defined the terms of action and social action at the beginning of his great work *Economy and Society:* "In 'action' [*Handeln*] is included all human behavior when and in so far as the acting individual attaches a subjective meaning to it. Action in this sense may be either overt or purely inward or subjective; it may consist of positive intervention in a situation, or of deliberately refraining from such intervention [*Unterlassen*] or passively acquiescing in the situation [*Dulden*]. Action is social in so far as, by virtue of the subjective meaning [*gemeinten Sinn*] attached to it by the acting individual (or individuals), it takes account of [*Bezogen wird*] the behavior of others and is thereby oriented in its course."[18]

To refer to, to take account of, the conduct of other agents is the most

17. See below, the eighth study.

18. Max Weber, *Economy and Society,* ed. Guenther Roth and Claus Wittich (Berkeley: University of California Press, 1978), 1:1, §1.

general and most neutral expression that can cover the multitude of interactions encountered on the level of these units of action, known as practices. These interactions can themselves be placed as intentional actions
taken in their subjective meaning, under the heading reserved for them by
Max Weber. The "open," "external" ways of taking account of the conduct
of other agents is found in interactions ranging from conflict, through
competition, to cooperation. Interaction itself becomes an "internal" —
internalized — relation, for example, in the relation of learning as it shades,
little by little, into acquired competence; one can, therefore, play alone,
garden alone, do research alone in a laboratory, in the library, or in one's
office. These constitutive rules, however, come from much further back
than from any solitary performer; it is from someone else that the practice
of a skill, a profession, a game, or an art is learned. And the apprenticeship
and training are based on traditions that can be violated, to be sure, but
that first have to be assumed. Everything we have said elsewhere about
traditionality and about the relation between tradition and innovation takes
on meaning here in the framework of the concept of internalized interaction. I should like to add to this canonical example of interaction, in
which the reference to others has itself become internalized, the subtle
example that Hegel brings to mind in chapter 5 of the *Phenomenology
of Spirit:* it corresponds to the moment when consciousness makes an
assessment of the disproportion between the work, as limited, determined
actuality, and the power of *bringing something about,* which bears the universal destiny of effectuating reason. Just when the work is separated off
from its author, its entire being is gathered up in the signification that the
other grants it. For the author, the work as an index of individuality and
not of universal vocation, is quite simply relegated to the ephemeral.[19] The
way the work has of taking its meaning, its very existence as work, only
from the other underscores the extraordinary precariousness of the relation between the work and the author, the mediation of the other being
so thoroughly constitutive of its meaning.

Would it amount to giving in at last to the spirit of geometry if we were
to make a parallel with the ways in which an agent subjectively under-

19. "The work *is,* i.e. it exists for other individualities, and is for them an alien reality,
which they must replace by their own in order to obtain through *their* action the consciousness of *their* unity with reality; in other words, *their* interest in the work which stems from
their original nature, is something different from this work's *own* peculiar interest, which
is thereby converted into something different. Thus the work is, in general, something perishable, which is obliterated by the counter-action of other forces and interests, and really
exhibits the reality of the individuality as vanishing rather than as achieved" (G. W. F. Hegel,
Phenomenology of Spirit, trans. A. V. Miller [Oxford: Clarendon Press, 1977], chap. 5,
pp. 243–44).

stands action in terms of interaction using the negative mode of omission (*Unterlassen*) and of submission (*Dulden*)? In truth, omitting, enduring, and suffering, are as much data of interaction as data of subjective understanding. Both terms remind us that on the level of interaction, just as on that of subjective understanding, not acting is still acting: neglecting, forgetting to do something, is also letting things be done by someone else, sometimes to the point of criminality; as for enduring, it is keeping oneself, willingly or not, under the power of the other's action; something is done to someone by someone; enduring becomes being subjected, and this borders on suffering. At this point the theory of action is extended from acting to suffering beings. This addition is so essential that it governs a large part of the reflections on power as it is exerted by someone on someone, as well as the reflections on violence as the destruction by someone else of a subject's capacity to act; by the same token, it leads to the threshold of the idea of justice, as the rule aiming at the equality of the patients and agents of action.[20] In fact, every action has its agents and its patients.

Such, then, are some of the complexities of action brought to our attention by the narrative operation, by the very fact that it remains in a mimetic relation with respect to action. This is not to say that practices as such contain ready-made narrative scenarios, but their organization gives them a prenarrative quality which in the past I placed under the heading of *mimesis*₁ (narrative prefiguration). This close connection with the narrative sphere is reinforced by the forms of interaction proper to practices. It is to the latter that the narrative gives the polemical form of a competition between narrative programs.

2. The same relation between praxis and narrative is repeated on a higher level of organization: we recalled the text of Aristotle's *Poetics* in which he compares *praxis* and *bios:* "Tragedy is essentially an imitation [*mimēsis*] not of persons but of action and life." Before considering what MacIntyre calls "the narrative unity of a life,"[21] thus giving a narrative coloration to the Diltheyan expression "the connectedness of a life," it is worthwhile to pause on an intermediate level between practices — professions, games, arts — and the global project of an existence. We shall term "life plans" those vast practical units that make up professional life, family life, leisure time, and so forth. These life plans take shape — a shape that is mobile and, moreover, changeable — thanks to a back-and-forth movement between more or less distant ideals, which must now be speci-

20. See the eighth study below.

21. Alasdair MacIntyre, *After Virtue: A Study in Moral Theory* (Notre Dame, Ind.: University of Notre Dame Press, 1981).

fied, and the weighing of advantages and disadvantages of the choice of a particular life plan on the level of practices. In the study that follows, the properly ethical applications of this shaping of life plans will be developed, and at that time I shall return, under the guidance of Gadamer, to the Aristotelian analysis of *phronēsis* and of the *phronimos*. Here I shall attempt to bring to light the simple fact that the practical field is not constituted from the ground up, starting from the simplest and moving to more elaborate constructions; rather it is formed in accordance with a twofold movement of ascending complexification starting from basic actions and from practices, and of descending specification starting from the vague and mobile horizon of ideals and projects in light of which a human life apprehends itself in its oneness. In this sense, what MacIntyre calls "the narrative unity of a life" not only results from the summing up of practices in a globalizing form but is governed equally by a life project, however uncertain and mobile it may be, and by fragmentary practices, which have their own unity, life plans constituting the intermediary zone of exchange between the undetermined character of guiding ideals and the determinate nature of practices. In fact, it may happen that in this exchange the global project is the first to be clearly outlined, as in the case of a precocious or compelling vocation, and that, under the pressure of this constraint from above, the practices lose the clear outlines assigned to them by tradition and repeated in the process of apprenticeship. The practical field then appears to be subjected to a twofold principle of determination by which it resembles the hermeneutical comprehension of a text through the exchange between the whole and the part. Nothing is more propitious for narrative configuration than this play of double determination.

3. Now is the time to say something about the notion of "the narrative unity of a life" which MacIntyre places above the notions of practices and of life plans. It must be said that in his work this notion does not denote the last stage in the development of praxis. In a deliberately ethical perspective, which will be ours only in the following study, the idea of gathering together one's life in the form of a narrative is destined to serve as a basis for the aim of a "good" life, the cornerstone of his ethics, as it will be of ours. How, indeed, could a subject of action give an ethical character to his or her own life taken as a whole, if this life were not gathered together in some way, and how could this occur if not, precisely, in the form of a narrative?

I am pleased to find this felicitous encounter between my analyses in *Time and Narrative* and those in *After Virtue*. However, I should not want to identify without any further examination MacIntyre's approach and my own. MacIntyre is mainly considering stories told in the thick of everyday activity and does not attach any decisive importance, at least with respect to the ethical investigation he is conducting, to the split between literary fictions and the stories he says are enacted. In my own treatment of the mimetic function of narrative, the break made by the entry of narrative into the sphere of fiction is taken so seriously that it becomes a very thorny problem to reconnect literature to life by means of reading. For Mac-Intyre, the difficulties tied to the idea of a refiguration of life by fiction do not arise. However, he does not draw any benefit, as I try to do, from the double fact that it is in literary fiction that the connection between action and its agent is easiest to perceive and that literature proves to be an immense laboratory for thought experiments in which this connection is submitted to an endless number of imaginative variations. This advantage of a detour by way of fiction does, it is true, have another side to it. And here a difficulty unknown to MacIntyre arises, namely: how do the thought experiments occasioned by fiction, with all the ethical implications that will be discussed below, contribute to self-examination in real life?[22] If the gap is as great as it seems between fiction and life, how have we, in our own passage through the levels of praxis, been able to place the idea of the narrative unity of a life at the summit of the hierarchy of multiple practices? One might have thought that the gap had been bridged by the theory of reading that I proposed in *Time and Narrative* 3, with the intention of placing in contact the world of the text and the world of the reader.[23] However, the very act of reading gives rise to obstacles on the return path from fiction back to life, obstacles we shall discuss below.

What is to be said, first of all, about the relation between author, nar-

---

22. As Louis O. Mink, the great theorist of the historical narrative, states: "Stories are not lived but told" ("History and Fiction as Modes of Comprehension," *New Literary History* 1 (1970): 557–58. On Louis O. Mink, cf. *Time and Narrative* 1:155–61. Mink's major essays on the philosophy of history have been collected by Brian Fay et al. in a posthumous volume entitled *Historical Understanding* (Ithaca: Cornell University Press, 1987).

23. I shall retain here from the analyses conducted in *Time and Narrative* 3 the fact that reading, far from being a lazy imitation, is at its best a struggle between two strategies, the *strategy of seduction* pursued by the author in the guise of a more or less trustworthy narrator, with the complicity of the "willing suspension of disbelief" (Coleridge) that marks the entry into reading, and the *strategy of suspicion* pursued by the vigilant reader, who is not unaware of the fact that she brings the text to meaningfulness thanks to its lacunae, whether these be intended or not. To these remarks from *Time and Narrative*, I shall add here that the possibility of applying literature to life rests, with respect to the dialectic of the character, upon the problem of "identification-with," which above we stated was one of the components of character. Through the aspect of identifying with the hero, the literary narrative contributes to the narrativization of character. Concerning this theme, see H. R. Jauss, "La Jouissance esthétique dans les expériences fondamentales de la *poiēsis*, de l'*aisthēsis* et de la *catharsis*," *Poétique* 39 (1979). What follows is to be situated within the framework of the struggle between the two strategies proper to the act of reading and under the heading of the narrativization of character (and of identification-with, which is one of its components).

rator, and character, whose roles and voices are quite distinct on the plane of fiction? When I interpret myself in terms of a life story, am I all three at once, as in the autobiographical narrative?[24] Narrator and character, perhaps, but of a life of which, unlike the creatures of fiction, I am not the author but at most, to use Aristotle's expression, the coauthor, the *sunaition*.[25] However, even given this reservation, does not the notion of author suffer from equivocalness when we pass from writing to life?

Another difficulty: on the very plane of the narrative form, held to be similar in fiction and in life, major differences affect the notions of beginning and end. In fiction, to be sure, neither the beginning nor the end are necessarily those of the events recounted, but those of the narrative form itself. Thus *Remembrance of Things Past* begins with the famous sentence: "For a long time I used to go to bed early [*Longtemps, je me suis couché de bonne heure*]." This "for a long time," followed by a compound past tense, refers to a quasi-immemorial, earlier time. Nevertheless, this sentence is the first of the book and serves as its narrative beginning. The same thing is true of the conditional future tenses at the end of "Time Regained," which open onto an undetermined future, in which the writing of this work is invoked to ward off the approach of death. And yet there is a final page that stands as the narrative's end.[26] It is this closure — this literary closure, if one likes — that is lacking in what A. MacIntyre in *After Virtue* called the narrative unity of life and that he considers to be a condition for projecting the "good life." Life must be gathered together if it is to be placed within the intention of genuine life. If my life cannot be grasped as a singular totality, I could never hope it to be successful, complete. Now there is nothing in real life that serves as a narrative beginning; memory is lost in the hazes of early childhood; my birth and, with greater reason, the act through which I was conceived belong more to the history of others — in this case, to my parents — than to me. As for my death, it will finally be recounted only in the stories of those who survive me. I am always moving toward my death, and this prevents me from ever grasping it as a narrative end.

24. Cf. P. Lejeune, *Le Pacte autobiographique* (Paris: Éd. du Seuil, 1967).

25. Cf. above, the fourth study, sec. 1. In *After Virtue*, MacIntyre sees no difficulty in joining together the features of fictional narratives and those belonging to narratives of a life. For him, life histories are "enacted narratives." However, after saying that "what I have called a history is an enacted dramatic narrative in which the characters are also the authors," MacIntyre has to concede that by reason of the dependency of the actions of some people on the actions of others, "the difference between imaginary characters and real ones is not in the narrative form of what they do; it is in the degree of their authorship of that form and of their own deeds" (p. 215).

26. In *Time and Narrative* 2:21ff., I discussed the problem of the distinction between the closure of the narrative and the double-ended opening of the series of what is said.

To this basic difficulty is added another, which is not unrelated to it. Along the known path of my life, I can trace out a number of itineraries, weave several plots; in short, I can recount several stories, to the extent that to each there lacks that "sense of an ending" so stressed by Kermode.

Let us go further: whereas every novel unfolds a textual world of its own, preventing us most often from relating to one another the incommensurable plots of different works (with the exception perhaps of certain series such as novels of successive generations: Thomas Mann's *Buddenbrooks*, Roger Martin du Gard's *Men of Good Will*, after the model of the stories placed end-to-end in the biblical narratives of the Patriarchs), in our experience the life history of each of us is caught up in the histories of others. Whole sections of my life are part of the life history of others — of my parents, my friends, my companions in work and in leisure. What we said above about practices and about the relations of apprenticeship, cooperation, and competition that they include confirms this entanglement of the history of each person in the histories of numerous others. This is the very point stressed so forcefully by MacIntyre, embroidering, although probably unaware of it, on what Wilhelm Schapp had already written under the title *In Geschichten verstrickt:* caught up, entangled in histories.[27] It is precisely by reason of this entanglement, as much as by being open-ended on both sides, that life histories differ from literary ones, whether the latter belong to historiography or to fiction. Can one then still speak of the narrative unity of life?

Final objection: in self-understanding, *mimēsis praxeōs* appears able to cover only the past phase of life and to have to be joined to anticipations and projects following a schema similar to that proposed by R. Koselleck in *Futures Past,* where the dialectic of "the space of experiences" and the "horizon of expectation" relates the selection of narrated events to the anticipations belonging to what Sartre called the existential project of each of us.[28]

All these arguments are perfectly acceptable: the equivocalness of the notion of author, the "narrative" incompleteness of life, the entanglement of life histories in a dialectic of remembrance and anticipation. Nevertheless, they do not seem to me to be such as to abolish the very notion of the *application* of fiction to life. The objections are valid only in opposition to a naive conception of *mimēsis,* the very one that is spotlighted in certain fictions, like the first *Don Quixote* or *Madame Bovary*. These are less to be refuted than to be incorporated in a more subtle, more dialectical com-

---

27. Cf. *Time and Narrative* 1:74–75.
28. Reinhart Koselleck, *Futures Past: The Semantics of Historical Time,* trans. Keith Tribe (Cambridge: MIT Press, 1985). Cf. *Time and Narrative* 3:208–16.

prehension of *appropriation*. It is within the framework of the struggle, mentioned earlier, between the text and the reader that the preceding objections are to be reintroduced. But should not the equivocalness of the author's position be preserved rather than dissipated? By narrating a life of which I am not the author as to existence, I make myself its coauthor as to its meaning. Moreover, it is neither by chance nor by error that, in the opposite sense, so many Stoic philosophers interpreted life itself, life lived, as playing a role in a play we have not written and whose author, as a result, retreats outside of the role. These exchanges between the multiple sense of the term "author" and "authorship" contribute to the wealth of meaning of the very notion of agency discussed in the fourth study.

As for the notion of the narrative unity of a life, it must be seen as an unstable mixture of fabulation and actual experience. It is precisely because of the elusive character of real life that we need the help of fiction to organize life retrospectively, after the fact, prepared to take as provisional and open to revision any figure of emplotment borrowed from fiction or from history. In this way, with the help of the narrative beginnings which our reading has made familiar to us, straining this feature somewhat, we stabilize the real beginnings formed by the initiatives (in the strong sense of the term) we take. And we also have the experience, however incomplete, of what is meant by ending a course of action, a slice of life. Literature helps us in a sense to fix the outline of these provisional ends. As for death, do not the narratives provided by literature serve to soften the sting of anguish in the face of the unknown, of nothingness, by giving it in imagination the shape of this or that death, exemplary in one way or another? Thus fiction has a role to play in the apprenticeship of dying. The meditation on the Passion of Christ has accompanied in this way more than one believer to the last threshold. When F. Kermode or W. Benjamin utter the word "consolation" in this regard, one must not cry self-delusion too hastily. As a form of counterdesolation, consolation can be a lucid manner — just as lucid as Aristotelian *katharsis* — of mourning for oneself. Here, too, a fruitful exchange can be established between literature and being-toward-death.

Is the intertwining of life histories with one another hostile to the narrative understanding nourished by literature? Or does it not find in the framing of one narrative within another, examples of which abound in literature, a model of intelligibility? And does not each fictive history, in confronting the diverse fates belonging to different protagonists, provide models of interaction in which the entanglement is clarified by the competition of narrative programs?

The final objection rests on a misunderstanding which is not always easy to dispel. One may well believe that the literary narrative, because it is retrospective, can inform only a meditation on the past part of our life. The literary narrative is retrospective only in a very particular sense: it is simply in the eyes of the narrator that the events recounted appear to have occurred in the past. The past of narration is but the quasi past of the narrative voice.[29] Now among the facts recounted in the past tense we find projects, expectations, and anticipations by means of which the protagonists in the narrative are oriented toward their mortal future: the final, powerfully forward-looking pages of *Remembrance of Things Past*, mentioned earlier in connection with the open closure of the fictional narrative, attest to this. In other words, the narrative also recounts care. In a sense, it only recounts care. This is why there is nothing absurd in speaking about the narrative unity of a life, under the sign of narratives that teach us how to articulate narratively retrospection and prospection.

The conclusion of this discussion, then, is that literary narratives and life histories, far from being mutually exclusive, are complementary, despite, or even because of, their contrast. This dialectic reminds us that the narrative is part of life before being exiled from life in writing; it returns to life along the multiple paths of appropriation and at the price of the unavoidable tensions just mentioned.

3. The Ethical Implications of the Narrative

Turning to the second aspect of our investigation, what have we to say about the relations between narrative theory and ethical theory? Or, to return to the terms proposed above: in what way does the narrative component of self-understanding call for, as its completion, ethical determinations characteristic of the moral imputation of action to its agent?

Here again, the notion of narrative identity helps to clarify the relations between narrativity and ethics that were simply anticipated without being made explicit in what has preceded. However, we have to admit that, here too, it brings new difficulties related to the confrontation between the narrative version and the ethical version of selfhood.

The fact that the narrative function is not without ethical implications is already implied by the rootedness of the literary narrative in the ground of the oral narrative on the plane of the prefiguration of the narrative. In his well-known essay entitled "The Storyteller,"[30] Walter Benjamin recalls

29. Concerning this interpretation, admittedly exploratory in nature, cf. *Time and Narrative* 2:88–99, in particular pp. 98–99.

30. Walter Benjamin, "Der Erzähler, Betrachtungen zum Werk Nicolaj Lesskows," in *Illuminationen* (Frankfort: Ed. Suhrkamp, 1969); English translation by Harry Zohn, "The Storyteller," in *Illuminations* (New York: Schocken Books, 1969), pp. 83–109.

that, in its most primitive form, still discernible in the epic and already in the process of extinction in the novel, the art of storytelling is the art of exchanging *experiences;* by experiences, he means not scientific observations but the popular exercise of practical wisdom. This wisdom never fails to include estimations, evaluations that fall under the teleological and deontological categories that will be developed in the next study; in the exchange of experiences which the narrative performs, actions are always subject to approval or disapproval and agents to praise or blame.

Might it be said that the literary narrative, on the level of narrative configuration properly speaking, loses its ethical determinations in exchange for purely aesthetic determinations? This would be to misunderstand aesthetics itself. The pleasure we take in following the fate of the characters implies, to be sure, that we suspend all real moral judgment at the same time that we suspend action itself. But in the unreal sphere of fiction we never tire of exploring new ways of evaluating actions and characters. The thought experiments we conduct in the great laboratory of the imaginary are also explorations in the realm of good and evil. Transvaluing, even devaluing, is still evaluating. Moral judgment has not been abolished; it is rather itself subjected to the imaginative variations proper to fiction.

Because of these exercises in evaluating in the dimension of fiction, the narrative can finally perform its functions of discovery and transformation with respect to the reader's feelings and actions, in the phase of the refiguration of action by the narrative. In *Time and Narrative* 3, I even ventured to say that the narrative form intended to be the most neutral in this regard, namely historiographic narrative, never reaches the zero degree of valuation. Without displaying a personal preference for the values of this or that epoch, the historian who wants to be motivated by curiosity more than by the taste for commemoration or loathing, will nevertheless be carried back by this very curiosity to the way in which the people involved aimed at, reached, or missed what they held to constitute the true life. At least in the mode of imagination and of sympathy the historian brings back to life ways of evaluating which continue to belong to our deepest humanity. In this, history is reminded of its indebtedness to people of the past. And in certain circumstances — in particular when the historian is confronted with the horrible, the extreme figure of the history of victims — the relation of debt is transformed into the duty never to forget.[31]

---

31. I shall consider the problem from the inverse perspective in the next study. If stories told offer so many bases for moral judgment, is this not because this judgment needs the art of storytelling in order to schematize, as it were, its aim? Beyond the rules, norms, obligations, and legislating that constitute what can be called morality, there is, as we shall state

I do not, however, wish to end this study with the certainties attaching to the ethical implications of the narrative function. Just as certain difficulties appeared when we examined the first aspect of narrative identity, difficulties arising at the point of the intersection of narrative theory and the theory of action, so too symmetrical difficulties emerge at the point where narrative theory follows the curve of ethical theory. These difficulties have to do with the distinct, even opposite, fate of *identity,* the guiding theme of the present study on both levels. In the section dealing with the problematic of identity, we admitted that selfhood-identity covered a spectrum of meanings, from the pole where it overlapped with identity as sameness to the opposite pole, where it is entirely distinct from the latter. The first pole appeared to us to be symbolized by the phenomenon of character, by which the person can be identified and reidentified. As for the second pole, it appeared to us to be represented by the essentially ethical notion of self-constancy. Self-constancy is for each person that manner of conducting himself or herself so that others can *count on* that person. Because someone is counting on me, I am *accountable for* my actions before another. The term "responsibility" unites both meanings: "counting on" and "being accountable for." It unites them, adding to them the idea of a *response* to the question "Where are you?" asked by another who needs me. This response is the following: "Here I am!" a response that is a statement of self-constancy.[32]

By constructing a polar opposition between self-constancy and character, I wanted to highlight the properly ethical dimension of selfhood, irrespective of the perpetuation of character. I was thus able to mark the gap between the two modalities of permanence in time, well expressed by the term "self-constancy," opposed to that of the perpetuation of the same. Where, finally, are we to locate narrative identity along this spectrum of variations extending from the pole of selfhood as sameness belonging to character to the pole of the pure selfhood of self-constancy?

The answer to this question would appear to have already been given: narrative identity stands between the two; in narrativizing character, the

---

then, the aim of the true life, which MacIntyre, echoing Aristotle, places at the summit of the hierarchy of the levels of praxis. Now if this aim is to become a vision, it cannot help but be depicted in the narratives through which we try out different courses of action by playing, in the strong sense of the word, with competing possibilities. This allows us to speak of an "ethical imagination," which feeds off of the narrative imagination. Cf. Peter Kemp, "Ethics and Narrativity," in *Aquinas* (Rome: Presses de l'Université du Latran, 1988), pp. 435–58, and *Éthique et Médecine* (Paris: Éd. Tierce-Médecine, 1987).

32. E. Lévinas, *Otherwise than Being,* trans. A. Lingis (The Hague: M. Nijhoff, 1974), p. 180.

narrative returns to it the movement abolished in acquired dispositions, in the sediment of identifications-with. In narrativizing the aim of the true life, narrative identity gives it the recognizable features of characters loved or respected. Narrative identity makes the two ends of the chain link up with one another: the permanence in time of character and that of self-constancy.

Where, then, is the difficulty? It lies in the unsettling cases with which we concluded the preceding section. These limiting cases seem to propose such an extreme problematization of narrative identity that, far from underpinning the ethical identity expressed in self-constancy, narrative identity seems instead to rob it of all support. As long as the dividing line ran between the troubling cases of literary fiction and the puzzling cases of science fiction, the former performed a sort of apologetic function to the benefit of selfhood and to the detriment of its confusion with sameness. Why, indeed, would we be interested in the drama of the dissolution of the identity of Musil's character, and why would it puzzle us, unless the nonsubject remained one figure of the subject, be it in the negative mode? A nonsubject is not nothing, as the semiotics of the subject of discourse or of action serves to remind us.[33] This plea for selfhood, documented by the troubling cases of literary fiction, begins to shift into its opposite when, as fiction returns to life, the readers in quest of identity find themselves confronting the hypothesis of their own loss of identity, confronting this *Ichlosigkeit* that was at once Musil's torment and the meaning effect unceasingly cultivated by his work. The self refigured here by the narrative is in reality confronted with the hypothesis of its own nothingness. To be sure, this nothingness is not the nothing of which there is nothing to say. Quite the contrary, there is much to say about this hypothesis, as is evident by the vast scope of a work like *Man without Qualities*. The sentence "I am nothing" must keep its paradoxical form: "nothing" would mean nothing at all if "nothing" were not in fact attributed to an "I." But who is *I* when the subject says that it is nothing? A self deprived of the help of sameness, I have repeatedly stated. So be it. In this regard, the hypothesis is not unsupported by existential verifications: it may well be that the most dramatic transformations of personal identity pass through the crucible of this nothingness of identity, a nothingness that would be the equivalent of the empty square in the transformations so dear to Lévi-Strauss. So many conversion narratives attest to such nights of personal identity. In these moments of extreme destitution, the empty response to the question

---

33. I am adopting here the vocabulary introduced by J. Coquet in *Le Discours et son sujet*, vol. 1, *Essai de grammaire modale;* vol. 2, *Pratique de la grammaire modale* (Paris: Klincksieck, 1984–85).

"Who am I?" refers not to nullity but to the nakedness of the question itself.

It is precisely the nakedness of the question "who?" that, confronted with the proud answer "Here I am!", reopens the debate. How can the *problematic* character of the *ipse* on the narrative level continue to be maintained, together with its *assertive* character on the level of moral commitment? One is tempted to say that the troubling cases of literary fiction lead back, paradoxically, to the neighborhood of the ethical conclusion that Parfit drew from the indecidability of his puzzling cases: namely, that personal identity is not what matters. Then are extinguished not only the identity of the same but also the identity of the self, which was believed to have been saved from the disaster that befell the former. In a sense, this is true: the narratives that recount the dissolution of the self can be considered interpretive narratives with respect to what might be called an apophantic apprehension of the self.[34] Self-apophasis consists in the fact that the passage from "Who am I?" to "What am I?" has lost all pertinence. Now the "what" of the "who," as we said above, is character — that is, the set of acquired dispositions and sedimented identifications-with. The absolute impossibility of recognizing a person by his or her lasting manner of thinking, feeling, acting, and so on is perhaps not demonstrable in practice, but it is at least thinkable in principle. What is practicable lies perhaps in acknowledging that all the attempts at identification, which form the substance of those narratives of interpretive value with respect to the retreat of the self, are doomed to failure.

How, then, are we to maintain on the ethical level a self which, on the narrative level, seems to be fading away? How can one say at one and the same time "Who am I?" and "Here I am!"? Is it not possible to make the gap separating narrative identity and moral identity work to the benefit of their living dialectic? This is how I see the opposition between them transformed into a fruitful tension.

On the one hand, there is no doubt that the "Here I am!" by which the person recognizes himself or herself as the subject of imputation marks a halt in the wandering that may well result from the self's confrontation with a multitude of models for action and life, some of which go so far as to paralyze the capacity for firm action. Between the imagination that says, "I can try anything" and the voice that says, "Everything is possible but not everything is beneficial (understanding here, to others and to yourself)," a muted discord is sounded. It is this discord that the act of prom-

---

34. On the category of interpretive narrative, cf. my article "Interpretive Narrative," in *The Book and the Text: The Bible and Literary Theory,* ed. Regina Schwartz (Oxford: Basil Blackwell, 1990), pp. 237–57.

ising transforms into a fragile concordance: "I can try anything," to be sure, but "Here is where I stand!"

On the other hand, the tormenting question "Who am I?" exposed by the troubling cases of literary fiction can, in a certain manner, be incorporated into the proud declaration "Here is where I stand!" The question becomes: "Who am I, so inconstant, that *notwithstanding* you count on me?" The gap between the question which engulfs the narrative imagination and the answer of the subject who has been made responsible by the expectation of the other becomes the secret break at the very heart of commitment. This secret break is what makes the modesty of self-constancy differ from the Stoic pride of rigid self-consistency. It is precisely at this point that the path followed here crosses Parfit's path. In a sense, the characterization of selfhood in terms of the relation of ownership (or belonging) between the person and his or her thoughts, actions, and passions — in short, "experiences" — is not without ambiguity on the ethical plane. Whereas this relation does not lend itself to any confusion on the grammatical plane of deictic adjectives and pronouns (my/mine, your/yours, etc.), it is equally true that it does remain suspect on the plane where Parfit wages his combat against the principle of "self-interest." In a philosophy of selfhood like my own, one must be able to say that ownership is not what matters. What is suggested by the limiting cases produced by the narrative imagination is a dialectic of ownership and of dispossession, of care and of carefreeness, of self-affirmation and of self-effacement. Thus the imagined nothingness of the self becomes the existential "crisis" of the self.[35]

The self, stripped bare in this way, has been evoked by thinkers as different as Jean Nabert, Gabriel Marcel, and Emmanuel Lévinas — a fact that should make it clear to us that the issue here is the ethical primacy of the other than the self over the self. Even recognizing this, it is still necessary that the irruption of the other, breaking through the enclosure of the same, meet with the complicity of this movement of effacement by which the self makes itself available to others. For the effect of the "crisis" of selfhood must not be the substitution of self-hatred for self-esteem.

35. On the category of crisis, cf. Paul Landsberg and Éric Weil, *Logique de la philosophie* (Paris: Vrin, 1950), chap. 12, "Personnalité," pp. 293–96.

SEVENTH STUDY

The Self and the Ethical Aim

Taken together, the three studies that follow add a new dimension to the linguistic, practical, and narrative dimensions of selfhood, a dimension at once ethical and moral (subject to the distinction I shall propose shortly between the two terms, often taken to be synonymous). This dimension does introduce something new, but it makes no methodological break with respect to the preceding ones.

As was stated in the Introduction, these studies, up to the tenth study, are composed of four subsets which correspond, in fact, to four ways of answering the question "who?": Who is speaking? Who is acting? Who is telling his or her story? Who is the moral subject of imputation? We never leave the problem of selfhood as long as we remain within the orbit of the question "who?" The fourth subset, which we enter into here, also follows the basic rule of the detour of reflection by way of analysis, as did the other three: thus, the predicates "good" and "obligatory" applied to action play the same role as the stated proposition in relation to the speaker who designated himself or herself in uttering it, or as action sentences in relation to the positing of an agent capable of acting, or, finally, as narrative structures in relation to the constitution of narrative identity. The ethical and moral determinations of action will be treated here as predicates of a new kind, and their relation to the subject of action as a new mediation along the return path toward the self.

Determining action by predicates such as "good" and "obligatory" marks a radical break with all that precedes only in the tradition of thought stemming from Hume, for which "ought" is opposed to "is." Prescribing, then, denotes something entirely different from describing. One can already find in the preceding studies numerous reasons for rejecting this dichotomy.

To begin with, the "beings" on which we have been meditating are quite peculiar: they are speaking and acting beings; and it is part of the very idea of action that it be accessible to *precepts* which, in the form of advice, recommendation, and instruction, teach how to succeed — hence, how to do well — in what one has undertaken. Precepts, to be sure, are not all moral ones — far from it: they can be technical, strategic, aesthetic, and so on. Moral rules, at least, are inscribed within the larger circle of precepts, which themselves are intimately related to the practices they help to define.

Next, by placing narrative theory at the crossroads of the theory of action and moral theory, we have made narration serve as a natural transition between description and prescription. In this way, the notion of narrative identity was able to function, in the final pages of the preceding study, as a guiding idea for an extension of the practical sphere beyond the simple actions described in the framework of the analytic theories of action. The actions refigured by narrative fictions are complex ones, rich in anticipations of an ethical nature. Telling a story, we observed, is deploying an imaginary space for thought experiments in which moral judgment operates in a hypothetical mode.

Now, what is there to say about the distinction proposed between ethics and morality? Nothing in their etymology or in the history of the use of the terms requires such a distinction. One comes from Greek, the other from Latin; both refer to the intuitive idea of *mores,* with the two-fold connotation, which I shall attempt to decompose, of that which *is considered to be good* and of that which *imposes itself as obligatory.* It is, therefore, by convention that I reserve the term "ethics" for the *aim* of an accomplished life and the term "morality" for the articulation of this aim in *norms* characterized at once by the claim to universality and by an effect of constraint (later I shall say what links these two features together). It is easy to recognize in the distinction between aim and norm the opposition between two heritages — an Aristotelian heritage, where ethics is characterized by its *teleological* perspective, and a Kantian heritage, where morality is defined by the obligation to respect the norm, hence by a *deontological* point of view. I propose to establish, without concerning myself about Aristotelian or Kantian orthodoxy, although not without paying close attention to the founding texts of these two traditions: (1) the primacy of ethics over morality, (2) the necessity for the ethical aim to pass through the sieve of the norm, and (3) the legitimacy of recourse by the norm to the aim whenever the norm leads to impasses in practice — impasses recalling at this new stage of our meditation the various aporetic situations which our reflection on selfhood has had to face. In other words, according to the working hypothesis I am proposing, morality is held to constitute only a limited, although legitimate and even indispensable, actualization of the ethical aim, and ethics in this sense would then encompass morality. There will thus be no attempt to substitute Kant for Aristotle, despite a respectable tradition to the contrary. Instead, between the two traditions, I shall establish a relation involving at once subordination and complementarity, which the final recourse of morality to ethics will ultimately come to reinforce.

In what way does this articulation of a very peculiar kind between the teleological aim and the deontological moment affect our examination of selfhood? The articulation between teleological aim and deontological moment, first perceived on the level of the predicates applied to action — the predicates "good" and "obligatory" — will at last find its counterpart on the level of self-designation: to the ethical aim will correspond what we shall henceforth call self-esteem, and to the deontological moment, self-respect. According to the thesis proposed here, it will be made apparent (1) that self-esteem is more fundamental than self-respect, (2) that self-respect is the aspect under which self-esteem appears in the domain of norms, and (3) that the aporias of duty create situations in which self-esteem appears not only as the source but as the recourse for respect, when no sure norm offers a guide for the exercise *hic et nunc* of respect. In this way, self-esteem and self-respect together will represent the most advanced stages of the growth of selfhood, which is at the same time its unfolding.

To conclude this brief introduction to the three studies that follow, let me say a word about the way in which the distinction between ethics and morality responds to the Humean objection that there is a logical abyss between prescribing and describing, between what ought to be and what is. One can expect that the teleological conception by which we shall characterize ethics will link up in a direct way with the theory of action and its extension in the theory of narrative. It is, as a matter of fact, in the immediate evaluations and estimations applied to action that the teleological viewpoint is expressed. In contrast, the deontological predicates belonging to a morality of duty appear to be imposed from outside of — or from above — the agent of action, in the various forms of constraint which, precisely, are termed moral ones, all of which lends weight to the thesis of the irreducible opposition between ought and is. However, if we are able to show that the deontological viewpoint is subordinate to the teleological perspective, then the gap between ought and is will appear less unbridgeable than in a direct confrontation between description and prescription, or in a related terminology, between judgments of value and judgments of fact.

1. Aiming at the "Good Life" . . .

The present study will be confined to establishing the primacy of ethics over morality — that is, of the aim over the norm. It will be the task of the following study to grant their rightful place to moral norms, without letting them have the final word.

Is our inquiry into the ethical aim, leaving aside the deontological moment, a renouncement of any meaningful discussion, allowing free reign to effusions of "good" sentiments? Not at all. The definition that follows, on the contrary, will, because of its articulated character, give rise to a labor of thinking that will occupy the remainder of this study. Let us define "ethical intention" as *aiming at the "good life" with and for others, in just institutions*. The three high points of this definition will be taken, each in turn, as the object of a separate analysis. The same three components will, in the two studies that follow, form the successive reference points for our reflection on the relation between the moral norm and the ethical aim.

The major advantage of entering into the ethical problematic by way of the notion of the "good life" is that it does not refer directly to selfhood in the figure of self-esteem. If self-esteem does indeed drawn its initial meaning from the reflexive movement through which the evaluation of certain actions judged to be good are carried back to the author of these actions, this meaning remains abstract as long as it lacks the dialogic structure which is introduced by the reference to others. This dialogic structure, in its turn, remains incomplete outside of the reference to just institutions. In this sense, self-esteem assumes its complete sense only at the end of the itinerary of meaning traced out by the three components of the ethical aim.

The first component of the ethical aim is what Aristotle called "living well," or the "good life" — "true life," one could say in the wake of Marcel Proust. The "good life" is what should be mentioned first because it is the very object of the ethical aim. Whatever the image that each of us has of a full life, this apex is the ultimate end of our action. This is the moment to recall the distinction Aristotle makes between the good that people aim at and Platonic Good. In Aristotelian ethics, it can only be a question of the good for us. This relativity with respect to us does not prevent the fact that the good is not contained in any particular thing. The good is rather that which is lacking in all things. This ethics in its entirety presupposes this nonsaturable use of the predicate "good."

Is the discussion threatened, once again, by vagueness? Not at all. The first great lesson we receive from Aristotle is to seek the fundamental basis for the aim of the "good life" in praxis.[1] The second is to attempt to set

---

1. The opening lines of the *Nichomachean Ethics* set us on the path: "Every art [*tekhnē*] and every inquiry [*methodos*], and similarly every action [*praxis*] and pursuit [*proairesis*, preferential choice] is thought to aim at some good; and for this reason the good has rightly been declared to be that at which all things aim" (1.1.1094a1–3). Let us leave aside the equation between happiness and the good. Let us linger instead on the roughly hewn enumeration of the activities teleologically oriented in this way. *Tekhnē* is the first term mentioned; it is paired with *methodos,* the practical in general being coordinated with the

up the teleology internal to praxis as the structuring principle for the aim of the "good life." In this regard, it is not certain that Aristotle resolved the apparent paradox in which praxis, at least the right praxis, would itself be its own end, all the while aiming at an ulterior end. The paradox would be resolved if one were to find a hierarchical principle that would allow finalities to be included, as it were, one within another, the higher being the excess of the lower. But the books that follow in the *Nichomachean Ethics* do not seem to offer a coherent analysis of this hierarchy of actions and their corresponding ends. Numerous commentators have seen a discordance between book 3 and book 6. Some hold it to be unsurmountable, others do not. The discordance consists in this: in book 3, as we recalled in the fourth study, everything rests on the tie between preferential choice and deliberation. Now the same book proposes a model of deliberation that seems to exclude deliberation about ends. This limitation of deliberation to means is repeated three times: "We deliberate not about ends [note the plural] but about means [i.e., about the means to reach the ends [*peri tōn pros ta telē*]" (3.3.1112b12). To be sure, we understand that everything that escapes our power is eliminated from the field of deliberation: on the one hand, eternal entities; on the other, all the events that cannot be produced by us. But from there to reduce the things that depend upon us to means requires a step that is taken in the examples that follow: the doctor does not ask himself whether he should heal, nor the orator whether he should persuade, nor the politician whether he should establish good laws. Once each has posited an end, he then examines how and by what means he will realize it, deliberation concerning the choice of the most appropriate means. Restricting the domain of deliberation even further, Aristotle hastens to compare this choice of means to the construction of a geometric figure, where the figure to be constructed takes the place of the end in relation to all the intermediary operations.

Of course, Aristotle's predilection for this model is understandable: if deliberation is to concern things that depend on us, the means to arrive at our ends are indeed that which is most in our power; aiming at certain ends must then be placed on the side of the wish (*boulēsis*), which easily involves things outside our power. Furthermore, and this is perhaps the

---

theoretical in general. Next, *tekhnē* is simply juxtaposed with *praxis* and *proairesis* without implying any hierarchy among these terms. Furthermore, *praxis* is not yet opposed to *poiēsis*. Only in book 6 is *praxis*, more precisely "practical science," opposed to "poetic science": we then learn that *praxis* is an activity that produces no work distinct from the agent, an activity that has no end other than action itself, "eupraxis," "for good action itself is its end," while *poiēsis* (and the poetic science corresponding to it) "has an end other than itself" (6.5.1140b6).

strongest argument, "If we are to be always deliberating, we shall have to go on to infinity" (*E.N.* 3.3.1113a2). But has it not been said that "we must stop somewhere [*anankē stēnai*]" and that happiness can be seen as that which sets an end to desire's headlong rush? And yet the argument still leaves us puzzled: could Aristotle have failed to consider that a person may be placed in the situation of choosing whether to become a doctor rather than an orator or a politician? Is not the choice among several courses of action a choice about ends, that is, about whether they conform more or less closely to an ideal in life — conform, that is, to what each person considers his or her aim of happiness, his or her conception of the "good life"? This puzzlement, which later will supply us with food for thought, forces us to admit that the ends-means model does not cover the entire field of action but only that of *tekhnē,* to the extent that it is not the object of any fundamental reflection until the appearance of *phronēsis* in book 6. What is worse, the means-end model seems even to lead us along the wrong path, inasmuch as it invites us to construct all the relations between subordinate ends and an ultimate end on the basis of a relation which remains essentially instrumental.[2]

Book 6, we must remember, treats the dianoetic virtues and is no longer concerned with the virtues of character discussed in books 2–5 (courage, temperance, generosity, justice). It offers, however, a more complex model of deliberation. Here, deliberation is the path followed by *phronēsis,* practical wisdom (translated in Latin by *prudentia*),[3] and, more precisely, the path that the man of *phronēsis* — the *phronimos* — follows to guide his

---

2. Certain commentators have tried to lessen the difficulty by questioning the classical translation of the Greek *pros to telos* by "means"; now the Greek expression, which, according to them, is to be rendered as "things relative to the end," leaves open a number of possible interpretations. According to D. Wiggins ("Deliberation and Practical Reason," in *Essays on Aristotle's Ethics,* ed. A. O. Rorty [Berkeley: University of California Press, 1980], pp. 222–25), those things relative to an end include not only the instruments of action but the elements constitutive of the end itself. What is wrong with the examples given by Aristotle is that they limit *pros to telos* to a typical case, that in which the end is already established, the singular being taken in the distributive sense, the end of the doctor, that of the orator, that of the statesman. In sum, the doctor is already a doctor and does not ask himself every day if he was right to choose to become one or to remain one, which would be to deliberate about the end and, Aristotle fears, deliberate endlessly. A doctor, an architect, or a statesman transformed into Hamlet would, in Aristotle's eyes, no longer be a good doctor, a good architect, or a good statesman. It remains that these typical cases do not exhaust the sense of *pros to telos* and leave the door open for the sort of deliberation involving the following issues: what is going to count for me as an adequate description of the end of my life? If this is indeed the ultimate question, deliberation takes on an entirely different role than that of a choice between means; it consists instead in specifying, in making more determined in practice, in crystalizing the nebulous sense of what we call the "good life."

3. Pierre Aubenque, *La Prudence chez Aristote* (Paris: PUF, 1963).

life.[4] The question posed here would seem to be the following: What counts as the specification best suited to the ultimate ends pursued? In this regard, the greatest lesson of book 6 concerns the close tie established by Aristotle between *phronēsis* and *phronimos,* a tie that becomes meaningful only if the man of wise judgment determines at the same time the rule and the case, by grasping the situation in its singularity. We shall return to this usage of the term *phronēsis* in the ninth study, when we follow the return movement from the moral norm to the ethical aim in unusual singular situations.[5]

Accompanied by these perplexities and these rough sketches of solutions, we are going to look in the revision of the concept of action proposed in the preceding study for the means, if not of resolving the difficulties of Aristotle's text (in an archaeological and philological sense), at least of responding to them with the resources of contemporary thought.

We recall in what way, under the pressure of narrative theory, we were led not only to broaden but to hierarchize the concept of action in such a way as to carry it to the level of the concept of praxis: in this way, we have placed at different heights on the scale of praxis practices and life plans, put together by the anticipation of the narrative unity of life. We then emphasized the unifying principle proper to each of these practical entities. Once again we are now going to look over the same hierarchy of praxis, but this time from the viewpoint of its ethical integration under the idea of the "good life."

---

4. "Regarding practical wisdom we shall get at the truth by considering who are the persons we credit with it. Now it is thought to be the mark of a man of practical wisdom to be able to deliberate well about what is good and expedient for himself, not in some particular respect, e.g., about what sorts of thing conduce to health or strength, but about what sorts of thing conduce to the good life in general. This is shown by the fact that we credit men with practical wisdom in some particular respect when they have calculated well with a view to some good end which is one of those that are not the object of any art [*tekhnē*]. It follows that in the general sense also the man who is capable of deliberating has practical wisdom" (*E.N.* 6.5.1140a24–28). Note furthermore: "Practical wisdom . . . is concerned with things human and things about which it is possible to deliberate; for we say this is above all the work of the man of practical wisdom, to deliberate well, but no one deliberates about things invariable, nor about things which have not an end, and that a good can be brought about by action. The man who is without qualification good at deliberating is the man who is capable of aiming in accordance with calculation at the best for man of things attainable by action" (6.7.1141b8–14).

5. In 6.8.1142a22–31, Aristotle does not hesitate to compare the singular nature of choice in accordance with *phronēsis* to perception (*aisthēsis*) in the theoretical dimension. The argument formed in this way will not fail to astonish us: "for in that direction as well . . . there will be a limit" (ibid.) Practical wisdom thus seems to have two limits: an upper limit, happiness, and a lower limit, singular decision.

The unifying principle of a *practice* (profession, game, art) does not reside only in the logical relations of coordination — even in those of subordination or nesting[6] — nor in the role of constitutive rules in the sense of game theory and speech-act theory, which, we recall, are ethically neutral. The dimension of meaning contributed by the notion of constitutive rule, however, opens the sphere of meaning in which appraisals of an evaluative (and subsequently normative) nature are attached to precepts of doing (something) well. The properly ethical character of these precepts is ensured by what MacIntyre calls "standards of excellence," which allow us to characterize as good a doctor, an architect, a painter, or a chess player.[7] These standards of excellence are rules of comparison applied to different accomplishments, in relation to ideals of perfection shared by a given community of practitioners and internalized by the masters and virtuosi of the practice considered. We see how precious this recourse to the standards of excellence of practice will be in helping to refute later any solipsistic interpretation of self-esteem, within whose scope we shall be placing practices. Practices, we observe following MacIntyre, are cooperative activities whose constitutive rules are established socially; the standards of excellence that correspond to them on the level of this or that practice originate much further back than the solitary practitioner. This cooperative and traditional character of practices does not exclude controversy but instead provokes it, mainly with respect to the definition of standards of excellence, which also have their own history. It remains true, nonetheless, that competition between practitioners and the controversy over standards of excellence would not occur if the practitioners did not share a common culture that contained a rather lasting agreement on the criteria defining levels of success and degrees of excellence.

In what way do these standards of excellence relate to the ethical aim of living well? In two ways. On the one hand, before characterizing a practitioner as good at something, standards of excellence allow us to give a sense to the idea of *internal goods* immanent to a practice. These internal goods constitute the teleology immanent to the action, as is expressed on

---

6. This tie between coordination and subordination in the logical connection of a practice authorizes a prudent reinterpretation of the relation between *poïēsis* and *praxis* in Aristotle. From the viewpoint of linear coordination, the tie is more like Aristotelian *poïēsis*, in which action has a result outside the agent in the sense that the result is external to the segment considered, to which the agent entrusts his or her power of acting; from the viewpoint of subordination, the tie is closer to Aristotelian *praxis*, in the sense that tilling the soil is done *pros to telos*, in view of the end, while practicing the profession of farming is an action done "for itself," as long as the farmer does not question his choice of profession. If our analysis is correct, no action is only *poïēsis* or only *praxis*. Are not the epic, which recounts the action of heroes, and tragedy, which puts it on stage, forms of *poïēsis*?

7. MacIntyre, *After Virtue*.

the phenomenological plane by the notions of interest and satisfaction, which must not be confused with those of pleasure. This concept of internal good, dear to MacIntyre, thus provides an initial support for the reflexive moment of self-esteem, to the extent that it is in appraising our actions that we appraise ourselves as being their author. On the other hand, the concept of internal goods will be held in reserve for subsequent reconsideration within the properly normative conception of morality, when we shall have to provide a content for the empty form of the categorical imperative. In this sense, the idea of internal goods occupies a twofold strategic position in our undertaking.

The integration of partial actions in the broader unity of life plans gives a parallel extension to this notion of goods internal to practice. We recall how narrative theory brought us to take into consideration this higher degree of integration of actions in global projects, including, for example, professional life, family life, leisure time, and community and political life. A second look at this notion brings us back to one of the difficulties encountered in the *Nichomachean Ethics* concerning the validity of the means-ends relation. According to this model, the doctor is already a doctor; he does not ask whether he wishes to remain one; his choices are strictly of an instrumental nature: medication or surgery, purge or operate. But what of the choice of the vocation of medicine? Here, the means-end model no longer suffices. Instead, it is a matter of making specific vague ideals about what is considered to be a "good life" for the person as a whole, while making use of that *phronēsis* which we showed above escapes the means-ends model. The action-configurations that we are calling life plans stem, then, from our moving back and forth between far-off ideals, which have to be made more precise, and the weighing of the advantages and disadvantages of the choice of a given life plan on the level of practice. It is in this sense that Gadamer interprets Aristotelian *phronēsis*.[8]

One additional remark concerning the expression "life plan": The appearance of the word "life" merits reflection. It is not taken in a strictly biologic sense but in the ethicocultural sense, familiar to the Greeks and their comparison of the respective merits of the *bioi* offered to the most radical of choices: the life of pleasure, the active life in the political sense, or the contemplative life. The word "life" designates the person as a whole, in opposition to fragmented practices. Thus Aristotle (him again!) asked whether there is an *ergon* — a function, a task — for man as such, as there is a task for the musician, the doctor, and the architect. Taken as a singular term, the word "life" receives the appreciative, evaluative dimension of

8. Hans-Georg Gadamer, *Truth and Method* (New York: Crossroad, 1986). Cf. pt. 2, chap. 2, sec. 2(b), "The Hermeneutic Relevance of Aristotle," pp. 278–89.

ergon which is used to qualify man as such. This *ergon* is to life, taken in its entirety, as the standard of excellence is to a particular practice.

This tie between the *ergon* of man — what we are calling the "life plan" — and the standards of excellence specified by each practice allows us to reply to the difficulty in the *Nichomachean Ethics* mentioned above: how, we asked, can one maintain at the same time that each praxis has an "end in itself" and that all action tends toward an "ultimate end"? In the relation between practices and life plan the secret of the nesting of finalities, one inside the other, is to be found. Once it is chosen, a vocation confers upon the deeds that set it in motion this very character of an "end in itself"; and yet we never stop rectifying our initial choices. Sometimes we change them entirely, when the confrontation shifts from the level of the execution of practices that have already been chosen to the question of the adequation between the choice of a practice and our life's ideals, however vague these may be, and yet at times even overriding the rules of a profession we have considered up to that moment to be invariable. Here, *phronēsis* gives rise to an exceedingly complex deliberation, in which the *phronimos* is no less at issue than the *phronēsis*.

I shall not return here to the place assigned by MacIntyre to the "narrative unity of a life" between practices and life plans and what Aristotle designated by the phrase "living well." The term "life" that figures three times in the expressions "life plan," "narrative unity of a life," and "good life" denotes both the biologic rootedness of life and the unity of the person as a whole, as that person casts upon himself or herself the gaze of appraisal. From the same perspective Socrates said that an unexamined life is not worth living. As for the term "narrative unity," the aspect we are emphasizing here is less the function of assembling-together, performed by the narrative at the summit of the scale of praxis, than the connection the narrative makes between estimations applied to actions and the evaluation of persons themselves. The idea of the narrative unity of a life therefore serves to assure us that the subject of ethics is none other than the one to whom the narrative assigns a narrative identity. Moreover, while the notion of life plan places an accent on the voluntary, even willful, side of what Sartre termed the existential project, the notion of narrative unity places its accent on the organization of intention, causes, and chance that we find in all stories. The person appears here from the outset as suffering as well as acting, subject to those whims of life which have prompted the fine Hellenist and philosopher Martha Nussbaum to speak of the "fragility of goodness," the fragility of the goodness of human action, that is.[9]

---

9. Martha C. Nussbaum, *The Fragility of Goodness: Luck and Ethics in Greek Tragedy and Philosophy* (Cambridge: Cambridge University Press, 1986).

The series of intermediaries we have just traced have, if not a completion, at least a horizon (or, of one prefers, a limiting idea) in the notion,
already mentioned several times, of "good life." We must not, however,
be misled about the content and the status of this notion in the theory of
praxis.

With respect to its content, the "good life" is, for each of us, the nebu-
lus of ideals and dreams of achievements with regard to which a life is held
to be more or less fulfilled or unfulfilled. It is the plane of "time lost" and
of "time regained." In this sense, the "good life" is "that in view of which"
all these actions are directed, actions which were nevertheless said to have
their ends in themselves. This finality within finality, however, does not
destroy the self-sufficiency of practices as long as their end has been posited and continues to be so. This opening, which fractures practices otherwise held to be closed in upon themselves when doubts arise about the
direction of our life, maintains a tension, most often a discrete and tacit
one, between the closed and the open within the global structure of praxis.
What we are summoned to think here is the idea of a higher finality which
would never cease to be internal to human action.

The epistemological status of this horizon or limiting idea turns on the
tie mentioned above between *phronēsis* and *phronimos*. In more modern
terms, we would say that it is in unending work of interpretation applied
to action and to oneself that we pursue the search for adequation between
what seems to us to be best with regard to our life as a whole and the
preferential choices that govern our practices. There are several ways of
introducing the hermeneutical point of view at this final stage. First, between our aim of a "good life" and our particular choices a sort of hermeneutical circle is traced by virtue of the back-and-forth motion between
the idea of the "good life" and the most important decisions of our existence (career, loves, leisure, etc.). This can be likened to a text in which
the whole and the part are to be understood each in terms of the other.
Next, the idea of interpretation adds to the simple idea of meaning that of
a meaning for someone. For the agent, interpreting the text of an action
is interpreting himself or herself. Here, I link up with one of Charles Taylor's major themes in his *Philosophical Papers:* man, he says, is a self-
interpreting animal.[10] By the same token, our concept of the self is greatly
enriched by this relation between interpretation of the text of action and
self-interpretation. On the ethical plane, self-interpretation becomes self-
esteem. In return, self-esteem follows the fate of interpretation. Like the
latter, it provokes controversy, dispute, rivalry — in short, the conflict of

10. Charles Taylor, *Philosophical Papers,* 2 vols. (Cambridge: Cambridge University Press,
1985), vol. 1, *Human Agency and Language,* chap. 2, p. 45.

interpretations — in the exercise of practical judgment. This means that the search for adequation between our life ideals and our decisions, themselves vital ones, is not open to the sort of verification expected in the sciences of observation. The adequation of interpretation involves an exercise of judgment which, at best, can aspire to plausibility in the eyes of others, even if, in the eyes of the agent, his or her own conviction borders on the sort of experiential evidence which, at the end of book 6 of the *Nichomachean Ethics,* made *phronēsis* comparable to *aisthēsis.* This experiential evidence is the new figure in which *attestation* appears, when the certainty of being the author of one's own discourse and of one's own acts becomes the conviction of judging well and acting well in a momentary and provisional approximation of living well.

2. . . . with and for Others . . .

At the beginning of this study, in a single stroke and without any apparent continuity in our solution, we proposed a definition of the ethical perspective: *aiming at the good life with and for others in just institutions.* At the second stage of our meditation, the question that arises is the following: how does the second component of the ethical aim, which we designate by the beautiful name of *solicitude,* link up with the first one? The question takes on a paradoxical twist calling for discussion when the reflexive aspect of this aim is characterized by self-esteem. Reflexivity seems indeed to carry with it the danger of turning in upon oneself, of closing up, and moving in the opposite direction from openness, from the *horizon* of the "good life." Despite this certain danger, my thesis is that solicitude is not something added on to self-esteem from outside but that it unfolds the dialogic dimension of self-esteem, which up to now has been passed over in silence. By unfolding, as has already been stated in another context, I mean, of course, a break in life and in discourse that creates the conditions for a second-order continuity, such that self-esteem and solicitude cannot be experienced or reflected upon one without the other.

That the solution to the paradox as it is sketched out here is *not unthinkable,* is all that can be asserted at the end of the present analysis.

Let us first observe that it is not by chance that we have continually been speaking of esteem of the self and not esteem of myself. *To say self is not to say myself.* To be sure, mineness is implied in a certain manner in selfhood, but the passage from selfhood to mineness is marked by the clause "in each case" (in German, *je*) which Heidegger is careful to add to the positing of mineness. The self, he says, is in each case mine.[11] Upon

11. Heidegger, *Being and Time,* §25.

what are we to base this "in each case" if not upon the unexpressed reference to others? On the basis of this "in each case" my own possession of my experiences is distributed, as it were, to all the other grammatical persons. But under what condition is this other not just a reduplication of myself — another myself, an alter ego — but genuinely an other, other than myself? In this regard, the reflexivity from which self-esteem proceeds remains abstract, in the sense that it does not mark the difference between me and you.

Another preliminary observation: if one asks by what right the self is declared to be worthy of esteem, it must be answered that it is not principally by reason of its accomplishments but fundamentally by reason of its capacities. To understand the term "capacity" correctly, we must return to Merleau-Ponty's "I can" and extend it from the physical to the ethical level. I am that being who can evaluate his actions and, in assessing the goals of some of them to be good, is capable of evaluating himself and of judging himself to be good. The discourse of "I can" is, to be sure, a discourse in *I*. But the main emphasis is to be placed on the verb, on being-able-to-do, to which corresponds on the ethical plane, being-able-to-judge. The question is then whether the mediation of the other is not required along the route from capacity to realization.

The question is in no way rhetorical. On it, as Charles Taylor has maintained, depends the fate of political theory. In this way, many philosophies of natural law presuppose a subject, complete and already fully endowed with rights before entering into society. It results that this subject's participation in community life is in principle contingent and revocable, and that the individual — since this is how the person has to be called under this hypothesis — is correct in expecting from the state the protection of rights constituted outside of him or her, without bearing any intrinsic obligation to participate in the burdens related to perfecting the social bond. This hypothesis of a subject of law, constituted prior to any societal bond, can be refuted only by striking at its roots. Now the root is the failure to recognize the *mediating* role of others between capacities and realization.

It is indeed just this mediating role that is celebrated by Aristotle in his treatise on friendship (*philia* in the *Nichomachean Ethics* 8–9).[12] It does not displease me to travel along this road with Aristotle for a moment, in a study whose tone is Aristotelian from start to finish. But the reasons for this choice are more topical. First of all, in Aristotle himself, friendship

12. On the place of the Aristotelian philosophy of friendship in ancient philosophy, cf. J.-C. Fraisse, *Philia, La notion d'amitié dans la philosophie antique* (Paris: Vrin, 1984), pp. 189–286.

serves as a transition between the aim of the "good life," which we have seen reflected in self-esteem, apparently a solitary virtue, and justice, the virtue of human plurality belonging to the political sphere. Next, friendship belongs not primarily to a psychology of feelings of affection and attachment to others (which, in many respects, the Aristotelian treatise is as well) but rather to an ethics: friendship is a virtue — an excellence — at work in deliberative choices and capable of being elevated to the rank of *habitus*, without ceasing to require actual exercise, without which it would no longer be an activity. Finally, and most especially, the treatise, which for much of its length appears to praise what could well be taken to be a refined form of egotism, under the title of *philautia*, ends up, quite unexpectedly, propounding the idea that the happy man or woman needs friends (*E.N.* 9.9). Otherness, therefore, repossesses the rights that *philautia* appeared to eclipse. It is in connection with the notions of capacity and realization — that is, finally of *power* and *act*[13] — that a place is made for *lack* and, through the mediation of lack, for *others*. The famous aporia, consisting in determining whether one must love oneself in order to love someone else, must not blind us. In fact, this aporia leads directly to the heart of the problematic of the self and the other than self.[14] However, we shall not directly attack this disputed question, provoked as much by popular sayings and by literary memories (e.g., Homer, Thucydides, and the tragic poets) as by the academic quarrels, beginning with Plato's *Lysis* and envenomed by the latter's successors at the head of the Academy. Two theses must first be presented.

We must begin by drawing solid support from the definition Aristotle proposes in order to distinguish himself, precisely on the ethical plane, from his predecessors and competitors: friendship, Aristotle declares straightaway, is not of one kind only; it is an essentially equivocal notion that one can clarify only by asking about the sort of things that give rise to it — its "object," in this sense — the *philēta*. Thus, we must distinguish three types of friendship: for the sake of the "good," of "utility," or of "pleasure." One cannot too strongly emphasize, in the perspective of the famous aporia of "egotism," this distinction between the three objects/ motives. The "objective" side of self-love is the reason why *philautia* — which makes each person his or her own friend — will never be the un-

13. One will see in *E.N.* 9.9 the analysis of friendship run up against the difficult problem of power and act, of activity (*energeia*) and of act in the strong sense (*entelekheia*), which we shall take the risk of confronting directly in the tenth study, sec. 2.

14. We shall be particularly attentive in this respect to the subtle and perfectly well-controlled play between the pronoun *autos* (him) and its reflexive form *heauton, heautou, heautō* (oneself, of oneself, to oneself), always declined.

mediated predilection of oneself but desire oriented by its reference to the good.

Second preliminary thesis: regardless of the place of *philautia* in the genesis of friendship, the latter presents itself from the outset as a *mutual* relationship. Reciprocity is part of its most basic definition and so encompasses the disputed question of the primacy of *philautia*. The latter will never be anything but an aspect belonging to the genesis of sense rather than to the chronology of the feelings of reciprocity. This reciprocity, as we shall see, extends all the way to the commonality of "living together" (*suzēn*) — in sum, all the way to intimacy.

This second feature is as important as the first for our own investigation: not only does friendship actually belong to ethics, as being the first unfolding of the wish to live well; but, more than this, it brings to the forefront the problematic of reciprocity, authorizing us to reserve for a second-order dialectic, inherited from the Platonic dialectic of the "great kinds" — the Same and the Other — the question of otherness as such.[15] The idea of mutuality indeed has its own requirements which are not eclipsed by either a genesis based on the Same, as in Husserl, or a genesis based on the Other, as in Lévinas. According to the idea of mutuality, each loves the other *as being the man he is* (8.3.1156a18–19). This is precisely not the case in a friendship based on utility, where one loves the other for the sake of some expected advantage, and even less so in the case of friendship for pleasure. We therefore see reciprocity imposing itself already on the ethical plane, which reciprocity, on the plane of morality, at the time of violence, will be required by the Golden Rule and the categorical imperative of respect.[16] This "as being" (as being what the other is) averts any subsequent egoistic leanings: it is constitutive of mutuality. The latter, in turn, cannot be conceived of in absence of the relation to the good, in the self, in the friend, in friendship, so that the reflexivity of oneself is not abolished but is, as it were, split into two by mutuality,

15. The provisional definition that we saw in *E.N.* 8.2.1156a2–5 clearly indicates the combination of the two features of friendship on the ethical level: the primacy of virtuous friendship over useful and pleasurable friendship, the mutual nature of feelings of goodwill (to which Aristotle adds nonignorance, which we shall find again later in connection with the technical conception of conscience): "How could one call them friends when they do not know their mutual feelings? To be friends, then, they must be mutually recognized as bearing goodwill and wishing well to each other for one of the aforesaid reasons."

16. It is noteworthy in this respect that the first use of the reflexive pronoun is tied to mutuality mediated by the good: "Now those who love each other for their utility do not love each other for themselves [*kath' hautous*] but in virtue of some good which they get from each other [*autois par' allēllōn*]" (8.3.1156a10–12). This play between the nonreflexive term (*autos*) and the reflexive forms (*heauton* etc.) runs throughout books 8 and 9.

under the control of the predicate "good," applied to agents as well as to actions.[17]

Let us add that through mutuality, friendship borders on justice; the old adage "equals among friends" denotes exactly the zone of intersection: each of two friends rendering to the other a portion equal to what he or she receives. Friendship, however, is not justice, to the extent that the latter governs institutions and the former interpersonal relationships. This is why justice encompasses many citizens, whereas friendship tolerates only a small number of partners. Moreover, in justice equality is essentially proportional equality, taking into account the inequality of contributions, while friendship exists only between those of equal rank. In this sense, equality is presupposed by friendship, whereas in the cities it remains an aim to be attained. This is why friendship alone can aim at the familiarity — *sunētheia* (8.6.1158a15) — of a shared life (*suzēn*).

We therefore see the long-term preparation of a nuanced response to the question in dispute, whether one must be one's own friend in order to be someone else's friend. The treatment of this difficulty inherited from the tradition is entirely subordinated to the reference to the good in the wishes that friends formulate with respect to one another. For the oneself that one loves is what is best in one, called several times thought or intellect (*nous*), or even soul, namely that which in oneself is the most lasting, the most stable, the least vulnerable to changes in humors or desires as well as to the accidents of fortune. Well before reaching (in 9.4 and 9.8) the famous question in dispute, Aristotle declares that the greatest good that a friend desires for his friend is to stay just as he is, and not, for example, to be a god; to which he adds: "But perhaps not *all* the greatest goods [will he wish his friend]; for it is for himself [*hautō*] most of all that each man wishes what is good" (8.7.1159a11–12). The love of a good man for himself fails too to contradict the disinterest proposed by Plato in the *Lysis* for the reason that what one loves in oneself is not the desiring part that motivates friendship for the sake of utility or pleasure but the best part of oneself.[18]

17. "Perfect friendship is the friendship of men who are good, and alike in virtue; for these wish well alike to each other *qua* good, and they are good in themselves [*kath' hautous*]" (8.3.1156b7–9); and later: "And in loving a friend men love what is good for themselves [*hautois*]; for the good man in becoming a friend becomes a good to his friend" (8.5.1157b33–34).

18. I shall leave aside the casuistry in the discussion of friendship that cuts through both of the treatises devoted to friendship in the *Nichomachean Ethics*. The philosopher continually plays on the boundaries, whether in the case of friendships among equals or unequals, or in that of borderline situations at the crossroads of disinterest, interest, and pleasure. My own interest lies solely in the dialectic of the self and the other in the treatment of *concepts* that structure friendship between people of goodwill.

This solidity of the reasonable being, sheltering the self even from regret and from penitence, may seem to us to be far removed from the fragility and vulnerability that were emphasized in our reflection on personal identity. Later we shall see the limits of this claim, when we examine the need, hence lack, that drives the self toward the other. However, it is to the stability of the best part of oneself that we owe the beautiful expression that holds the friend to be "another self [*allos autos*]" (9.4.1166a32).[19] It then becomes a simple academic matter, which Aristotle adds to other disputed questions, whether one has to love oneself rather than another. His verdict is clear: the adversaries of *philautia* are right if the latter belongs to the sphere of utility or of pleasure in matters of friendship; but they are wrong if they pretend to ignore that what is lovable in each of us is the best of the self, the thinking part, the intellect. What Aristotle is suggesting here, but does not seem to question, is that reflexivity clings to the reasonable, if it is true that "reason in each of its possessors chooses what is best for itself [*heautō*]" (9.8.1169a18). The argument requires simply that this reflexivity be shared equally by oneself and others. In this way, it does not prevent friendship from being disinterested, even to the point of sacrifice (9.8), for disinterestedness is already rooted in the relationship of self to self, by virtue of the original bond between intellect, excellence, and reflexivity. One may simply regret that Aristotle leaves in suspension the question whether there can be friendship between the self and itself; this, Aristotle says, "is a question we may dismiss for the present" (9.4.1166a32). The true response is to be sought instead in the inquiry into a question more fundamental than all the preceding ones, namely "whether the happy man will need friends or not" (9.9.1169b3).

The question posed here is so far from secondary that Aristotle deploys the most impressive battery of arguments to be found in the entire double treatise on friendship.[20] With need and lack, the otherness of the "other self [*heteros autos*]" (9.9.1169b6–7 and 1170b6) moves to the forefront. The friend, inasmuch as he is that other self, has the role of providing what one is incapable of procuring by oneself (*di' hautou*) (9.9.1169b6–7). "Friends," we are surprised to read, "are thought the greatest of external

19. One will note again here the subtle play between the nonreflexive *autos* and the reflexive *heauton* encountered in the expression: the good man should be a lover of self (*dei philauton einai*) (9.8.1169a12).

20. In their translations Tricot (pp. 464–65) and Gauthier-Jolif (vol. 2, *Commentaires*, pt. 2, pp. 757–59) count no less than a dozen "protosyllogisms" and "arguments" — or "reasonings" (Gauthier-Jolif) — in the part of the chapter where Aristotle says that he will grasp "even tighter the very nature of things [*phusikōteron*]" (Tricot's rendering; Gauthier-Jolif translates the passage: "to get to the bottom of our nature"; Ross has "to look deeper into the nature of things").

goods" (1169b10). It is remarkable that, in order to resolve this difficulty, Aristotle is forced to play the best cards of his metaphysics, namely to rely on the distinction between *act* and *power,* to which the notion of possession at issue here belongs.

If the good and happy man needs friends, it is because friendship is an "activity" (*energeia*), which is obviously a "becoming" and hence simply the incomplete actualization of a power. It is therefore lacking with respect to the act, in the strong sense of *entelekheia.* The door is therefore open for a rectification of the intellectualist conception of friendship developed up to now. Under the aegis of need, a link is made between activity and life and, finally, between happiness and pleasure. Friendship, therefore, works toward establishing the conditions for the realization of life, considered in its *intrinsic goodness and its basic pleasure.* We must go even further: to the notions of life and activity, we must add that of *consciousness.*[21] Consciousness is not only the consciousness of perception and activity but consciousness of life as well. So, to the extent to which the consciousness of life is pleasant, one can say that the profound meaning of *philautia* is *desire:* the good man's own being is desirable to him; given this, the being of his friend is then equally desirable to him. Having thus joined together activity and life, the desirable and the pleasant, the consciousness of existing and the joy of the consciousness of existing, Aristotle can then posit, as a partial conclusion to his complicated reasoning: "If all this be true, as his own being is desirable for each man, so, or almost so, is that of his friend" (9.9.1170b7–8). And the argument can spring back: "Now his being was seen to be desirable because he perceived his own goodness, and such perception is pleasant in itself. He needs, therefore, to be conscious of the existence of his friend as well" (1170b9–11). And this can be realized only in "living together [*suzēn*]" (1170b11).

In what way does this tortuous reasoning reply to the question posed, that is, in what sense can a man be his own friend? The answer, at least in part, lies in the affirmation made above: for the good man, his own existence is desirable for him. This *désirable propre* — the desirableness of what is one's own — so to speak, is not foreign to the need for friends experienced by the happy man. This need has to do not only with what is active and incomplete in living together but also with the sort of shortage or lack belonging to the very relation of the self to its own existence. By the same token, the assurance of stability upon which friendship rests, when it is understood as a purely intellectual sharing of opinions and thoughts, is seen to be secretly threatened by this reference to the desirable and the

---

21. The verb *sunaisthesthai* used here (9.9.1170b4) prefigures most exactly the Latin *conscientia.*

pleasant, to being and the consciousness of being, supported by living together. *In this way lack dwells at the heart of the most solid friendship.*

One will readily grant that there is no place for a straightforward concept of otherness in Aristotle. Will Christian *agapē* be sufficient to do justice to it? Or will we have to wait until the idea of *struggle* spills over from the field of politics to the field of interpersonal relations, transforming, as in Hegel's *Phenomenology of Spirit,* the contemporary conflict of the splitting of consciousness into two self-consciousnesses? Or is it only in our own day that a thinker like Lévinas dares to reverse the statement "no other-than-self without a self," substituting for it the inverse statement "no self without another who summons it to responsibility"? Only in the tenth study, when we bring our ethicomoral inquiry to a close, shall we possess the means to carry the debate to the level of what I shall call, in memory of Plato, the "great kinds" of the Same and the Other.

From Aristotle, I should like to retain only the ethics of reciprocity, of sharing, of living together. This theme of intimacy, with which his analysis in book 9.12 concludes, holds in suspension the two opposing interpretations that we shall contrast when the time comes. As for the idea that only a self can have an other than self,[22] it seems to me to be consis-

---

22. Here I concur with some of the analyses of Rémi Brague in *Aristote et la question du monde* (Paris: PUF, 1988), a book to which I shall return at length in the tenth study. In his concern with bringing to light what is unexpressed in Aristotelian ontology under the guidance of a Heideggerian approach, the author accords to the self the function of openness in relation to the englobing structure of being-in-the-world. *Everything* is the business of the self. Brague finds this central character of the self in numerous texts of Aristotle outside of those commented on here; at the same time he deplores the confusion between the *self,* a phenomenological theme, and *man,* an anthropological theme. When the time comes, I shall state why I do not follow Brague in this dichotomy, contrary to the mediating role I grant to all objectivities (discursive, practical, narrative, and prescriptive predicates) in the reflexive process of the self. Having said this, I want to pay homage to the precise analyses and superb translations that he gives, among others, of the fragments in which the self is put on stage (pp. 132, 137, 142, 171, 173, 183, 187). Prefacing his analysis, he quotes Xenophon's "I know myself" (*autos oida*) (p. 11), where the nonreflexive term *autos* means "in person" or "personally," as in the German *Selbstgegebenheit,* "self-givenness." For there to be a world, I must be there in person, without the self being enumerated among the things that furnish the world. In this sense the reflexive *hauton* comes to emphasize this nontotalization of the self and the things in the world. In this regard, the treatise on friendship can be compared to the treatise on *phronēsis* (*E.N.* 6). Within this framework we encounter the expression "knowing what is good for oneself" (6.8.1141b33). *Phronēsis* is just such a "knowledge belonging to the self [*to hautō eidenai*]" (1141b34), which allows the interpretation "knowing that it is up to oneself to. . . ." This is why Brague does not seem in any way shocked that friendship in Aristotle is built upon this self-interest, perfectly compatible with disinterest in the moral sense of the term. The other, finally, is other than the self only because he or she is another self, that is, like us, a self: "We want what is good to be ours because we are, definitively and irrevocably, a self — 'ourselves'" (Brague, *Aristote,* p. 141). And why is this so? Because it is

tent with all our earlier studies; it finds its best source of legitimation in the idea that self-esteem is the primordial reflexive moment of the aim of the good life. To self-esteem, friendship makes a contribution without taking anything away. What it adds is the idea of reciprocity in the exchange between human beings who each esteem themselves. As for the corollary of reciprocity, namely equality, it places friendship on the path of justice, where the life together shared by a few people gives way to the distribution of shares in a plurality on the scale of a historical, political community.

At the end of this route in company with Aristotle, the question arises concerning the features we are attributing to solicitude which have not already been described under the heading of friendship.

I shall not linger on those characters of ancient *philia* that have more to do with the history of *mentalités* than with conceptual analysis, such as the tie between friendship and leisure — related to the condition of the free citizen, from which are excluded slaves, metics, women, and children — and the narrowing of living together to thinking together, itself oriented toward the sage's contemplative life, as described in the final book of the *Nicomachean Ethics*. I shall start with the relation between *autos* and *heauton* to develop an inclusive concept of solicitude, based principally on the exchange between *giving* and *receiving*.[23] Friendship, even when it is released from the sociocultural limitations of *philia*, appears to me to constitute a fragile balance in which giving and receiving are equal, hypothetically. In truth, it is this equality that Aristotle has in mind when he defines the *mutual* character of friendship. Now this balance can be considered as the midpoint of a spectrum, in which the end points are marked by inverse disparities between giving and receiving, depending on whether the pole of the self or that of the other predominates in the initiative of exchange.

To begin with, let us assume the first hypothesis. E. Lévinas's entire philosophy rests on the initiative of the other in the intersubjective relation. In reality, this initiative establishes no relation at all, to the extent that the other represents absolute exteriority with respect to an ego de-

---

impossible for us to be the other and to fail to recognize this basic fact. "'I am other' is an impossible statement for Aristotle" (p. 134). I grant to Brague that Aristotle does not provide the means of understanding in what sense "the intellect is the *ipse*, even the *ipsissimum* of man" (p. 173), or, what is even more serious, of saying that man is himself closest to himself, to the point of being his own friend. For my part, I believed that I found a partial answer to this difficulty in the idea that the self is structured by the desire for its own existence. And if Aristotle has no complete answer to these questions, is this truly because the anthropological concept of man has stifled the phenomenological concept of self, a concept that only an ontology of care would enable us to constitute?

23. Kemp, *Éthique et Médecine.*

fined by the condition of separation. The other, in this sense, absolves himself of any relation. This irrelation defines exteriority as such.[24]

By virtue of this irrelation, the "appearing" of the Other in the *face* of the Other eludes vision, seeing forms, and even eludes hearing, apprehending voices. In truth, the face does not appear; it is not a phenomenon; it is an epiphany. But whose face is it? I do not think I am unduly limiting the scope of the admirable analyses of Lévinas's *Totality and Infinity,* to say nothing here of his *Otherwise than Being,* by saying that this face is that of a master of justice, of a master who *instructs* and who does so only in the ethical mode: this face forbids murder and commands justice. What is there to say about the relation between this instruction, this injunction, and friendship? What strikes one immediately is the contrast between the reciprocity of friendship and the dissymmetry of the injunction. To be sure, the self is "summoned to responsibility" by the other. But as the initiative of the injunction comes from the other, it is in the *accusative* mode alone that the self is enjoined. And the summons to responsibility has opposite it simply the passivity of an "I" who has been called upon. The question is then whether, to be heard and received, the injunction must not call for a response that compensates for the dissymmetry of the face-to-face encounter. Taken literally, a dissymmetry left uncompensated would break off the exchange of giving and receiving and would exclude any instruction by the face within the field of solicitude. But how could this sort of instruction be inscribed within the dialectic of giving and receiving, if a capacity for giving in return were not freed by the other's very initiative? Now what resources might these be if not the resources of *goodness* which could spring forth only from a being who does not detest itself to the point of being unable to hear the injunction coming from the other? I am speaking here of goodness: it is, in fact, noteworthy that in many languages goodness is at one and the same time the ethical quality of the aims of action and the orientation of the person toward others, as though an action could not be held to be good unless it were done on behalf of others, out of *regard* for others. It is this notion of regard that must now attract our attention.

In order to grasp it, we have to return to the working hypothesis that governs this study and the next one, namely the primacy of the ethical over the moral. From this point of view, the vocabulary of summons and injunction is perhaps already too "moral" and, having admitted this, rightly

24. I shall express here only a small part of my debt to Lévinas, saving for the tenth study the discussion of the vast theme of otherness, which belongs, as I suggested above, to an investigation of the "great kinds" proper to philosophical discourse, at the crossroads of ethics and ontology.

haunted by War, by Evil.[25] This is why the Other, in the figure of the master of justice, and even in that of the persecutor, passing to the forefront in *Otherwise than Being,* has to storm the defenses of a separate "I." But we are already in the sphere of the imperative, of the norm. Our wager is that it is possible to dig down under the level of obligation and to discover an ethical sense not so completely buried under norms that it cannot be invoked when these norms themselves are silent, in the case of undecidable matters of conscience. This is why it is so important to us to give solicitude a more fundamental status than obedience to duty.[26] Its status is that of *benevolent spontaneity,* intimately related to self-esteem within the framework of the aim of the "good" life. On the basis of this benevolent spontaneity, receiving is on an equal footing with the summons to responsibility, in the guise of the self's recognition of the superiority of the authority enjoining it to act in accordance with justice.[27] This equality, to be sure, is not that of friendship, in which giving and receiving are hypothetically balanced. Instead, it compensates for the initial dissymmetry resulting from the primacy of the other in the situation of instruction, through the reverse movement of recognition.

At the other end of the spectrum from solicitude, what then is the inverse situation from that of the instruction by the other in the figure of the master of justice? And what new inequality is to be compensated for here? The situation that is the reverse of injunction is *suffering.* The other is now a suffering being, that being whose empty place has continually been indicated in our philosophy of action, whenever we depicted men and women as acting *and* suffering. Suffering is not defined solely by physical pain, nor even by mental pain, but by the reduction, even the destruction, of the capacity for acting, of being-able-to-act, experienced as a violation of self-integrity. Here initiative, precisely in terms of being-able-to-act, seems to belong exclusively to the self who *gives* his sympathy, his compassion, these terms being taken in the strong sense of the wish to share someone else's pain. Confronting this charity, this benevolence, the other appears to be reduced to the sole condition of *receiving.* In a sense, this is actually the case. And it is in this manner that suffering-with gives itself, in a first approximation, as the opposite of the assignment of responsibility by the voice of the other. And, in another way than in the

25. The word "War" appears on the very first page of the Preface to *Totality and Infinity.*
26. In the following study we shall interpret the Golden Rule as the transitional structure between solicitude and the categorical imperative, by which I must treat humanity in my own person and in that of others as an end in itself and not simply as a means.
27. Concerning this relation between authority and the recognition of superiority, cf. Gadamer, *Truth and Method,* pp. 245ff.

preceding case, a sort of equalizing occurs, originating in the suffering other, thanks to which sympathy is kept distinct from simple pity, in which the self is secretly pleased to know it has been spared. In true sympathy, the self, whose power of acting is at the start greater than that of its other, finds itself affected by all that the suffering other offers to it in return. For from the suffering other there comes a giving that is no longer drawn from the power of acting and existing but precisely from weakness itself. This is perhaps the supreme test of solicitude, when unequal power finds compensation in an authentic reciprocity in exchange, which, in the hour of agony, finds refuge in the shared whisper of voices or the feeble embrace of clasped hands. It is perhaps here that Aristotle, too preoccupied with the distinction between virtuous friendship and the pair friendship of utility and friendship of pleasure — a distinction inseparable from the almost exclusive attention he pays to intellectual friendship devoted to the search for wisdom — fails to notice another dissymmetry, different from that upon which Lévinas constructs his ethics, the dissymmetry opposing suffering to enjoyment. Sharing the pain of suffering is not symmetrically opposite to sharing pleasure.[28] In this regard, philosophy must continue to allow itself to be instructed by tragedy. The trilogy "purification" (*katharsis*), "terror" (*phobos*), and "pity" (*eleos*) cannot be classified under the subcategory of friendship for the sake of pleasure. The obverse of the "fragility of goodness" — to borrow again Martha Nussbaum's happy expression, to which we shall return later — works to correct, if not to belie, the claim of *philautia* to stability, to endurance. A self reminded of the vulnerability of the condition of mortality can receive from the friend's weakness more than he or she can give in return by drawing from his or her own reserves of strength. Here magnanimity — another Greek virtue, one celebrated by Descartes as well — must lower its flag. We shall have the opportunity in the tenth study to return to the category of being-affected and its relation with the "great kind," the Other. On the phenomenological level, where we are now situated, feelings are to be considered as affects incorporated into the course of motivation on the level designated by Aristotle with the term "disposition," a term that will return under another guise — *Gesinnung* — in Kant himself. Let us confine ourselves here to emphasizing the role played by *feelings* — which, in the last analysis, are affects — in solicitude. For it is indeed feelings that are revealed in the self by the other's suffering, as well as by the moral injunction coming from

---

28. Aristotle, it is true, includes as part of living together the sharing of joys and pains (*E.N.* 9.9). He even writes that friendship "seems to lie in loving rather than in being loved" (8.8.1159a27).

the other, feelings spontaneously directed toward others.[29] This intimate union between the ethical aim of solicitude and the affective flesh of feelings seems to me to justify the choice of the term "solicitude."

Let us attempt, in conclusion, to take an overview of the entire range of attitudes deployed between the two extremes of the summons to responsibility, where the initiative comes from the other, and of sympathy for the suffering other, where the initiative comes from the loving self, friendship appearing as a midpoint where the self and the other share equally the same wish to live together. While equality is presupposed in friendship, in the case of the injunction coming from the other, equality is reestablished only through the recognition by the self of the superiority of the other's authority; in the case of sympathy that comes from the self and extends to the other, equality is reestablished only through the shared admission of fragility and, finally, of mortality.[30]

It is this search for equality in the midst of inequality, whether the latter results from from particular cultural and political conditions, as in friendship between unequals, or whether it is constitutive of the initial positions of the self and the other in the dynamics of solicitude, as this defines the place of solicitude along the trajectory of ethics. To self-esteem, understood as a reflexive moment of the wish for the "good life," solicitude adds essentially the dimension of *lack,* the fact that we *need* friends; as a reaction to the effect of solicitude on self-esteem, the self perceives itself as another among others. This is the sense of Aristotle's "each other" (*allēlous*), which makes friendship *mutual.* This apperception can be analyzed into several elements: reversibility, nonsubstitutibility, similitude. We find an initial model of *reversibility* in language in the context of interlocution. The exchange of personal pronouns is exemplary in this respect: when I say

29. In this regard, feelings of pity, compassion, and sympathy, formerly exalted by English-language philosophy, deserve to be rehabilitated. In this perspective, Max Scheler's analyses devoted to sympathy, hate, and love remain unequaled, in particular with respect to the major distinction between sympathy and fusion or affective confusion, as well as concerning the play of distance and proximity in love (Max Scheler, *The Nature of Sympathy,* trans. Peter Heath [Hamden, Conn.: Shoe String Press, 1970]). Allow me to express in passing the regret that, except for Stephan Strasser in his fine work *Phenomenology of Feeling* (trans. Robert E. Wood [Pittsburgh: Duquesne University Press, 1977]), phenomenologists have too often avoided any description of feelings, as if for fear of slipping into some affective fallacy. This is to forget that feelings have been just as powerfully shaped by language, and carried just as high as thoughts in literary worth.

30. Werner Marx, *Ethos und Lebenswelt. Mitleidenkönnen als Mass* (Hamburg: Felix Meiner Verlag, 1986). It has also been said that it is only in the theater that this superior justice can operate, a justice that grants each of the protagonists his or her share of the truth and, in this, assigns to each his or her share of esteem. Cf. G. Fessard, *Théâtre et Mystère,* Preface to Gabriel Marcel, *La Soif* (Paris: Desclée de Brouwer, 1938).

"you" to someone else, that person understands "I" for himself or herself. When another addresses me in the second person, I feel I am implicated in the first person; reversibility concerns simultaneously the roles of speaker and listener, as well as the capacity of self-designation presumed to be equal in the sender of the discourse and in its receiver. But these are simply roles that are reversible.

Alone the idea of *nonsubstitutibility* takes into account the persons who play these roles. In a sense, nonsubstitutibility is equally presupposed in the practice of discourse but in another way than in interlocution, namely in relation to the anchoring of the "I" in use.[31] Because of this anchoring I do not leave my place and I do not eliminate the distinction between here and there, even when I place myself in the place of the other in imagination and in sympathy. What language teaches, precisely as practice, is verified by all practices. The agents and patients of an action are caught up in relationships of exchange which, like language, join together the reversibility of roles and the nonsubstitutibility of persons. Solicitude adds the dimension of value, whereby each person is *irreplaceable* in our affection and our esteem. In this respect, it is in experiencing the irreparable loss of the loved other that we learn, through the transfer of the other onto ourselves, the irreplaceable character of our own life. It is first for the other that I am irreplaceable. In this sense, solicitude replies to the other's esteem for me. But if this response were not in a certain manner spontaneous, how could solicitude not be reduced to dreary duty?

Finally, above the ideas of the reversibility of roles and the nonsubstitutibility of persons (this latter idea raised to the level of irreplaceability), I shall place *similitude,* which is not just the natural accompaniment of friendship but, in the manner we have stated, of all the initially unequal forms of the bond between oneself and the other. Similitude is the fruit of the exchange between esteem for oneself and solicitude for others. This exchange authorizes us to say that I cannot myself have self-esteem unless I esteem others *as* myself. "As myself" means that you too are capable of starting something in the world, of acting for a reason, of hierarchizing your priorities, of evaluating the ends of your actions, and, having done this, of holding yourself in esteem as I hold myself in esteem. The equivalence between the "you too" and the "as myself" rests on a trust that can be held to be an extension of the attestation by reason of which I believe that I can (do something) and that I have worth. All the ethical feelings mentioned above belong to this phenomenology of "you too" and of "as myself." For they well express the paradox contained in this equivalence, the paradox of the exchange at the very place of the irreplaceable. Becom-

31. Cf. below, second study, sec. 2.

ing in this way fundamentally equivalent are the esteem of the *other as a oneself* and the esteem of *oneself as an other*.[32]

3. . . . in Just Institutions

The fact that the aim of living well in a way encompasses the sense of justice is implied in the very notion of the other. The other is also other than the "you." Correlatively, justice extends further than face-to-face encounters.

Two assertions are involved here: according to the first, living well is not limited to interpersonal relations but extends to the life of *institutions*. Following the second, justice presents ethical features that are not contained in solicitude, essentially a requirement of *equality*. The institution as the point of application of justice and equality as the ethical content of the sense of justice are the two issues of the investigation into the third component of the ethical aim. From this twofold inquiry will result a new determination of the self, that of "each": to each, his or her rights.

By "institution," we are to understand here the structure of *living together* as this belongs to a historical community — people, nation, region, and so forth — a structure irreducible to interpersonal relations and yet bound up with these in a remarkable sense which the notion of distribution will permit us later to clarify. What fundamentally characterizes the idea of institution is the bond of common mores and not that of constraining rules. In this, we are carried back to the *ēthos* from which ethics takes its name. A felicitous manner of emphasizing the ethical primacy of living together over constraints related to judicial systems and to political organization is to mark, following Hannah Arendt, the gap separating *power in common* and *domination*. We recall that Max Weber, in his presentation of the major concepts of sociology at the beginning of *Economy and Society,* distinguished the political institution from all other institutions by the relation of domination, separating the governing from the governed.[33] This relation marks at one and the same time a split *in connection with power-in-common* and a reference to *violence,* both of which belong to the

32. Is this the secret of the commandment "Love thy neighbor as thyself"? This commandment would seem to belong to ethics more than to morality, if one could, following Franz Rosenzweig in *The Star of Redemption* (trans. William W. Hallo [Boston: Beacon Press, 1972; Notre Dame, Ind.: University of Notre Dame Press, 1985]), maintain that the commandment "Love me" addressed by the lover to the loved one in the spirit of the Song of Songs is earlier and superior to all laws.

33. Weber, *Economy and Society,* chap. 1, §16, *Macht, Herrschaft* (Power, authority, and imperative control).

THE SELF AND THE ETHICAL AIM

moral plane, the object of the next study.[34] More fundamental than the relation of domination is that of power-in-common. According to Arendt, power stems directly from the category of action as irreducible to those of labor and work: this category has a political significance, in the broad sense of the word, irreducible to the state, if one stresses, on the one hand, the condition of *plurality*[35] and, on the other, *action in concert*.[36]

The idea of plurality suggests the extension of interhuman relations to all those who are left outside of the face-to-face encounter of an "I" and a "you" and remain third parties. The third party, however, is straightaway, and no pun intended, the *inclusive middle term* (*tiers inclus*) within the plurality that constitutes power. In this way there is a limit imposed on every effort to reconstruct the social bond on the sole basis of a strictly diadic dialogic relation. The plurality includes third parties who will never be faces. A plea for the anonymous in the literal sense of the term is therefore included in the fullest aim of the true life.[37] Including the third party, in turn, must not be limited to the *instantaneous* aspect of wanting to act together but must be spread out over a *span of time*. It is from the institution, precisely, that power receives this temporal dimension. The temporal

34. In "The Profession and Vocation of the Politician," a lecture delivered to young German pacifists drawn to nonviolence after the disastrous outcome of World War I, Max Weber defined the state as a relation of domination (*Herrschaft*) of man over man on the basis of the means of legitimate violence (that is, upon violence that is considered to be legitimate) (in *Gesammelte politische Schriften* [Tübingen, 1958], pp. 533–48; English trans. by E. Matthews, "Politics as a Vocation," in *Max Weber: Selections in Translation* [Cambridge: Cambridge University Press, 1978], pp. 212–25).

35. "Action, the only activity that goes on directly between men without the intermediary of things or matter, corresponds to the human condition of plurality" (Arendt, *Human Condition*, p. 7).

36. "*Power* corresponds to the human ability not just to act but to act in concert. Power is never the property of an individual; it belongs to a group and remains in existence only so long as the group keeps together" (Hannah Arendt, *Crisis of the Republic* [New York: Harcourt Brace Jovanovich, 1972], p. 143). She mentions in what follows Pericles' *isonomie*, Roman *civitas*, and also the experiment of the Soviets, the workers' councils, the Budapest insurrection, the "Prague spring," and the many examples of resistance to foreign occupation. There is thus nothing nostalgic about this rehabilitation of the power of all, not only in the face of violence, but even against the relation of domination. What alone is important is the nonhierarchical and noninstrumental nature of the power relation: "It is the people's support that binds power to the institutions of a country, and this support is but the continuation of the consent that brought the laws into existence to begin with" (p. 140).

37. This inclusion of the distant in the ethical project could have been anticipated on the basis of what was said earlier about practices (professions, games, art); these are, we said, rule-governed interactions — in this sense, institutions. The standards of excellence that situate these practices along the scale of praxis and hence along the trajectory of living well contain from the outset a "corporate" dimension, inseparable from the dimension of traditionality correlative to that of innovation.

dimension does not simply have to do with the past, with tradition and its more or less mythical origin — all of which Hannah Arendt places under the heading of Authority, in memory of the Roman *auctoritas: potesta in populo, autoritas in senatu;* it has even more to do with the future, the ambition to last — that is, not to pass but to remain. This was already Machiavelli's purpose: how to rescue the republics from the ephemeral? This is still Arendt's concern.[38] How does the *vita activa* reply to the harsh temporal condition of being mortal? Action, in its political dimension, constitutes the highest attempt to confer immortality, if not eternity, on perishable things. To be sure, power has its own fragility, since it exists only as long as people act together and vanishes when they disperse. In this sense, power is the model of an activity in common that leaves no work behind it and, like Aristotle's *praxis,* exhausts its meaning in its own exercise. Nevertheless, the fragility of power is not the raw and naked vulnerability of mortals as such but the second-order fragility of institutions and of all the human affairs gravitating around them.

The idea of *action in concert* is more difficult to determine, if one does not wish to enter too quickly into the details of institutional structures proper to different spheres of activity in common, as we shall do prudently and sparingly at the end of the next study. Hannah Arendt confines herself to speaking of public action as a web of human relations within which each human life unfolds its brief history. The idea of public space and the related notion of publicness are familiar to us since the period of the Enlightenment. These are the notions included by Arendt under the title of "public space of appearance," within which the activities we have termed practices come to light. However, publicness taken in this sense is, as we well know, more a task to be accomplished than something already given. Along with Hannah Arendt herself, we must admit that this stratum of power characterized by plurality and action in concert is ordinarily *invis-*

---

38. In a preface I wrote to the French translation of *The Human Condition* in 1983, I proposed an interpretation of the passage from Arendt's first great work, *The Origins of Totalitarianism,* to *The Human Condition,* based upon the thesis that totalitarianism rests on the myth that "everything is permitted, everything is possible" — according to which the master can manufacture a new man. The task is then to conceive of the conditions for a nontotalitarian universe: "The criterion best suited for the new inquiry can then consist in an evaluation of the different human activities from the temporal viewpoint of their durability" (Preface, p. 15). This approach concerns not only politics, but all the categories examined in the book, including the triad labor, work, action. The consumable nature of the products of labor points up its precariousness. The function of artifice summed up in the work is to offer to mortals a means of lasting that is more enduring and more stable than they themselves are (cf. *Human Condition,* pp. 167–68). In this sense, the time of labor is passage, the time of the work is duration. Action finally finds its stability in the coherence of a story told that recounts the "who" of action.

ible, because it is so extensively covered over by relations of domination, and that it is brought to light only when it is about to be destroyed, leaving the field open for violence, as occurs in great historical debacles. This is why it is perhaps reasonable to give to this common initiative, this desire to live together, the status of something *forgotten.*[39] This is why this constitutive element can be discerned only in its discontinuous irruptions onto the public stage when history is its most tumultuous. This is also why in ordinary times we remember only the augmentation constituted by authority, which we can speak of today perhaps only in the past tense.[40]

However illusive power may be in its fundamental structure, however weak it may be without the help of an authority that articulates it on ever more ancient foundations, it is power, as wanting to live and act together, that brings to the ethical aim the point of application of its indispensable third dimension: *justice.*

Does the sense of justice still belong to the ethical and teleological, and not the moral and deontological, plane? Is not the work of John Rawls, which we shall discuss in the next study, from start to finish the verification that it is in a Kantian, hence fundamentally deontological, framework and in opposition to *one* teleological tradition, incarnated by utilitarianism, that the idea of justice is to be rethought? The fact that Rawls's reconstruction of the idea of justice belongs to an antiteleological perspective is not contestable. However, the idea of justice is related to a different teleology from that of English-language utilitarians. This teleology is opportunely enjoined to recall the use of the term "virtue" in the opening declaration of the *Theory of Justice:* "Justice is the first virtue of social institutions, as truth is of systems of thought."[41]

The *just,* it seems to me, faces in two directions: toward the *good,* with respect to which it marks the extension of interpersonal relationships to institutions; and toward the *legal,* the judicial system conferring upon the law coherence and the right of constraint.[42] In this study we shall remain exclusively on the first side of the issue.

Two reasons authorize this enterprise. On the one hand, the quasi-

39. Paul Ricoeur, "Pouvoir et violence," in *Ontologie et Politique. Hannah Arendt* (Paris: Tierce, 1989), pp. 141–59.

40. In *Between Past and Future* (New York: Viking Press, 1961, 1968), her essay dealing with the concept of authority, Hannah Arendt recalls that this concept refers to a few, more or less mythicized, founding events. But in truth we know of hardly any societies that do not refer to such founding events. Thus, even today *auctoritas* constitutes the augmentation (*augere*) that power draws from the energy transmitted from these beginnings.

41. John Rawls, *A Theory of Justice* (Cambridge: Harvard University Press, 1971), p. 3.

42. The word *droit* in French includes both uses; we speak of *un homme droit* (a righteous man) and of his *droiture* (rectitude) in a nonlegal sense, but we also speak of *le droit* and *loi* (law school; the discipline of law).

immemorial origin of the idea of justice — its emergence out of the mythical mold in Greek tragedy and the perpetuation of its divine connotations
in secular societies — shows that the sense of justice is not limited to the
construction of legal systems, which, nevertheless it never ceases to bring
about. On the other hand, the idea of justice is better named *sense* of
justice on the fundamental level where we remain here. Sense of justice
and of injustice, it would be better to say here, for what we are first aware
of is injustice: "Unjust! What injustice!" we cry. And indeed it is in the
mode of complaint that we penetrate the field of the just and the unjust.
And even on the plane of justice as an institution, before courts of justice,
we continue to behave as "plaintiffs" and to "lodge a complaint against
someone." The sense of injustice is not simply more poignant but more
perspicacious than the sense of justice, for justice more often is lacking and
injustice prevails. And people have a clearer vision of what is missing in
human relations than of the right way to organize them. This is why, even
for philosophers, it is injustice that first sets thought in motion. To wit,
Plato's *Dialogues* and Aristotelian ethics, and their equal concern with
naming together the just and the unjust.

Aristotle! The objection may perhaps be raised to our effort to enroll
him in our cause that, if he did place justice in the field of virtues, and
hence of ethics in the teleological sense we are attaching to this term, it
was because he applied to the direct transactions between individuals its
initial definition — its sketch, as he called it — taken from common sense
and received ideas (*endoxa*): "We see that all men mean by justice that kind
of state of character [*hexis*] which makes people disposed to do [*praktikoi*]
what is just and makes them act justly and wish for what is just" (*E.N.*
5.1.1129a6–9). And to better anchor justice on the plane of virtue, he
seeks the "median" — the just measure, the middle term — the *mesotēs*
between two extremes that assigns to justice a place among the virtues
from the perspective of philosophical reflection. Now the *mesotēs* is the
reasonable trait common to the virtues, whether they are private or interpersonal ones.

However, it must be replied that it is those traits proper to the *mesotēs*
by which the just is distinguished from the unjust that make us pass without any transition from the interpersonal to the institutional plane. The
most important methodological decision taken by Aristotle, at the beginning of his chapter on justice, is in fact his foray into the vast polysemy of
the just and the unjust.[43]

43. "Now 'justice' and 'injustice' seem to be ambiguous but because their different meanings approach near to one another the ambiguity escapes notice and is not so obvious as it
is, comparatively, when the meanings are far apart" (*E.N.* 5.1.1129a26–27). The ambiguity

The intersection of the private and the public aspect of distributive justice can be recognized at every stage of the analysis.

To begin with, Aristotle holds the domain he circumscribes as a "part" (*meros*) of the "whole" (*holos*) field of actions prescribed by laws (*nomima*). At this globalizing level, the institutional extension is not in doubt inasmuch as it is positive law that defines legality. Here, ethics and politics overlap.[44] The "partial" virtue to which Aristotle confines himself can, as a result, be no less ethicopolitical than the complete virtue that encompasses it.

There is another reason for holding institutional mediation to be indispensable: it is always in relation to external and precarious goods, in the context of prosperity and adversity, that the vice of always wanting to have more — *pleonexia* — and inequality are determined. Now these evils and these adverse goods are, precisely, goods to be shared, burdens to be shared. And this sharing cannot help but pass through the institution. In fact, the first kind of particular justice is very exactly defined by a *distributive* operation that implies the political community, whether it is a matter of distributing "honor or money or the other things that fall to be divided among those who have a share in the [political community]" (*E.N.* 5.2.1130b30–33).[45]

Are we to reproach Aristotle for having limited the field of justice too narrowly by defining it as distributive justice? In my opinion, at this stage

---

of "injustice" is taken as a guide first: "Both the lawless man and the grasping and unfair man are thought to be unjust" (1129a32). However, when we pass from the unjust man to the just man, we find simply the qualities of being law-abiding and fair. Passing then to the agent of action, it is said: "The just, then, is the lawful and the fair, the unjust the unlawful and the unfair" (1129a35–b1). Taking more than one's share and not being fair have a common feature — the *anisotēs* (inequality) of the *pleonektēs* (the greedy, the grasping man). The greedy man, like the grasping man, is said to be "unfair; for this [unfairness] contains and is common to both" (1129b10). What remains, then, is the ambiguity of the law-abiding and the fair.

44. "Now the laws in their enactments on all subjects aim at the common advantage . . . ; so that in one sense we call those acts just that tend to produce and preserve happiness and its components for the political society" (*E.N.* 5.1.1129b14–18). It is also noteworthy that Aristotle calls justice "complete virtue"; it is conformity to the law in the sense that the law commands us also to do the acts corresponding to all the other virtues; justice thus becomes the *pros heteron*, the relation to others, in respect of all the virtues (1129b20–26).

45. We shall say nothing here of corrective justice, which, Aristotle holds, concerns private transactions, whether these are voluntary (purchases, sales, loans) or involuntary (wrongs of all sorts and acts of vengeance). Institutional mediation is not absent but indirect, whether it is the law that determines the wrong or courts that arbitrate conflicts. In this way the *relation to others* is the strong tie that remains, despite the ambiguity of the terms "just" and "unjust" (*E.N.* 5.2.1130b1).

of the analysis we have to maintain the greatest flexibility for the term
"distributive," namely its contribution of the element of distinction lacking in the notion of wanting to act together.[46] This aspect of distinction
moves to the forefront with the concept of *distribution,* which, from Aristotle to the medieval philosophers and to John Rawls, is closely tied to
that of justice. This concept must not be limited to the economic plane, as
a complement to the concept of production. It denotes a feature fundamental to all institutions, to the extent that they govern the apportionment
of roles, tasks, and advantages or disadvantages between the members of
society. The very term "apportionment" deserves our attention: it expresses the other side of the idea of sharing, the first being the fact of being
part of an institution; the second side is held to be that of the distinction
of shares assigned to each individual in the system of distribution. Being
part is one thing; receiving a share is something else again. And the two
things go together. For it is to the extent that the shares distributed are
coordinated among themselves that those who have them can be said to
participate in the society considered, to use Rawls's expression, as a cooperative enterprise. In my opinion it was necessary to introduce the concept of distribution at this stage of our analysis in order to assure the
transition from the interpersonal level to the societal level within the ethical aim. The importance of the concept of distribution lies in the fact that
it rejects both sides of a false debate over the relation between the individual and society. In line with the sociology of a Durkheim, society is
always more than the sum of its members; from the individual to society,
there is no continuum. Inversely, in line with a methodological individualism, the key concepts of sociology denote nothing more than the probability that individuals will conduct themselves in a certain way.[47] Through
the idea of probability one avoids any reification, and finally any ontology,
of social entities. The conception of society as a system of distribution
transcends the terms of the opposition. The institution as the regulation
of the distribution of roles, hence as a system, is indeed something more
and something other than the individuals who play these roles. In other
words, the relation is not reduced to the terms of the relation. But at the
same time, a relation does not constitute a supplementary entity. An institution considered a rule of distribution exists only to the extent that individuals take part in it. And this participation, in the sense of taking part,

46. We already encountered this danger of giving in to the tendency toward fusion in
the relation with others when we contrasted on the interpersonal level the idea of sympathy
to that of emotional fusion, following Max Weber.
47. Note Max Weber's definition of domination centered on the state (see n. 34 above).
It is inscribed within a series of definitions where the idea of probability relieves us in each
case from having to introduce entities other than individuals.

lends itself to probabilistic analyses that have no point of application other than individual comportments. It is not the object of the present study to advance any further in epistemological discussion. This brief incursion in a domain that is not my own has been aimed solely at finding solace for the one idea that matters to this inquiry, namely that a consideration of the institution is part of the ethical aim taken in its full scope. It was necessary that there be no wall between the individual and society, preventing the transition from the interpersonal to the societal plane. A distributive interpretation of the institution contributes to tearing down this wall and assures the cohesion between the three components — individual, interpersonal, and societal — of our concept of ethical aim.

The ethicojudicial framework of the analysis having been made more precise, a name can be given to the ethical core common to distributive justice and to reparative justice. This common core is *equality* (*isotēs*). Correlatively, the unjust, often cited before the just, is synonymous with the *unequal*. It is the unequal that we deplore and condemn. Aristotle thus is the prolongation of a great Greek tradition, more precisely an Athenian tradition, marked by Solon and Pericles. But the stroke of genius — in truth, a double stroke — is to have given a philosophical content to the idea received from the tradition. On the one hand, Aristotle finds in the equal the character of intermediateness between two extremes, which he carries from virtue to virtue. In fact, where there is sharing, there may be too much or not enough. The unjust man is one who takes too much in terms of advantages (and this again is *pleonexia,* wanting to have more) or not enough in terms of burdens.[48] On the other hand, he carefully marks out the type of intermediateness, namely *proportional equality,* that defines distributive justice. Arithmetic equality is not suitable, he holds, because of the nature of the persons and of the things shared. For one thing, in a society of antiquity, persons have unequal shares, related to unequal merits, which, moreover, different constitutions define in different ways; for another thing, the shares are themselves unequal outside of justice — one might say, susceptible to brute division, as in war or pillage. Distributive justice then consists in equalizing two relations between, in each case, a person and a merit. It therefore rests on a proportional relation with four terms: two persons and two shares.[49]

48. The intermediate "is the equal; for in any kind of action in which there is a more and a less there is also what is equal. If, then, the unjust is unequal, the just is equal, as all men suppose it to be, even apart from argument" (*E.N.* 5.3.1131a12–13). The recourse to common opinion remains a constant in Aristotle. It will have no less importance in Kant, as we shall state in the following study. This is why we speak of the sense of justice.
49. "The just, then, . . . is equality of ratios, and involves four terms at least" (*E.N.* 5.3.1131a30–33).

Aristotle thus posed the formidable problem, which Rawls will take up again, of justifying a certain idea of equality without crediting egalitarianism. Our problem is not to know whether or not equality can always be defined in terms of the intermediate, and whether the idea of proportional equality is not a nest of inextricable difficulties; it is rather to gather together the convincing and lasting strength of the connection between justice and equality. The intermediate and proportional equalities are, in this respect, no more than secondary procedures for "saving" equality, philosophically and ethically. *Equality,* however it is modulated, *is to life in institutions what solicitude is to interpersonal relations.* Solicitude provides to the self another who is a face, in the strong sense that Emmanuel Lévinas has taught us to recognize. Equality provides to the self another who is an *each.* In this, the distributive character of "each" passes from the grammatical plane, where we encountered it in the Introduction, to the ethical plane. Because of this, the sense of justice takes nothing away from solicitude; the sense of justice presupposes it, to the extent that it holds persons to be irreplaceable. Justice in turn adds to solicitude, to the extent that the field of application of equality is all of humanity.

There is no doubt that a certain ambiguity, already evident in the introduction to the idea of distribution, profoundly affects the idea of justice. The idea of fair shares refers back, on the one hand, to the idea of a belonging that extends all the way to that of an infinite *mutual indebtedness,* which is not without recalling Lévinas's theme of the hostage; on the other hand, the idea of just shares leads, in the best hypothesis, to the idea that we find in Rawls of a mutual disinterest for the interest of others: at worst, it leads back to the idea — another of Lévinas's themes — of separation.

EIGHTH STUDY

The Self and the Moral Norm

Only the first of the three propositions composing the thesis presented at the beginning of the preceding study has been developed to any extent, namely the assertion that ethics has primacy over morality. On the basis of the single predicate "good," we then constructed three phases of a discourse extending from the aim of the good life to the sense of justice, passing by way of solicitude. To this tripartite structure of the predicate "good" applied to actions, there was seen to correspond, in reflexive terms, the homologous structure of *self-esteem*. To the present study falls the task of justifying the second proposition, namely that it is necessary to subject the ethical aim to the test of the norm. It will then remain to show in what way the conflicts provoked by formalism, itself closely tied to the deontological moment, lead us back from morality to ethics, but to an ethics enriched by the passage through the norm and exercising moral judgment in a given situation. The present study will focus on this tie between *obligation* and *formalism,* not in order to denounce hastily the weaknesses of the morality of duty but in order to express its grandeur, as far as we can be carried by a discourse whose tripartite structure will exactly parallel that of the ethical aim.

In the first stage of our new course, the aim of the "good life" will be subjected to the test of the norm without any consideration of the dialogic structure of the norm itself. This structure will be at the center of the second stage, echoing solicitude, which denoted the primordial relation of the self to the self's other on the ethical level. In the course of the third stage we shall continue our investigation into the sense of justice, at the moment when the latter becomes the rule of justice, under the aegis of moral formalism extended from interpersonal relations to social relations and to the institutions that underlie them. It results from this that self-respect, which on the moral plane answers to self-esteem on the ethical plane, will reach its full meaning only at the end of the third stage, when respect for the norm will have blossomed into respect for others and for "oneself as another," and when respect will be extended to anyone who has the right to expect his or her just share in an equitable distribution. Self-respect has the same complex structure as self-esteem. Self-respect is self-esteem under the reign of moral law. This is why its triadic structure is homologous to that of self-esteem.

1. The Aim of the "Good" Life and Obligation

The fact that we are putting off for now an examination of the dialogic moment of the norm does not mean that we are placing some sort of moral solipsism before the reciprocity of persons. Should there be any need to recall this, the self is not the "I." It is instead a matter of isolating the moment of *universality* in which, as an ambition or as a claim (this will be discussed in the next study), the norm puts the wish to live well to the test. Correlatively, this will be the same universality by which the self will draw its authority on the reflexive plane. There are good reasons for objecting to the abstract character of a search for the norm that does not take persons into account: it is precisely this abstraction that will push us from the first to the second configuration of the norm. There is no way, however, to make this abstraction fit neatly into any *egological* viewpoint. At this stage, the universal is, properly speaking, neither you nor me.

Without by any means denying the break made by Kantian formalism with respect to the great teleological and eudaemonic tradition, it is not inappropriate to indicate, on the one hand, the features by which this tradition points toward formalism and, on the other hand, the features by which the deontological conception of morality remains attached to the teleological conception of ethics.

In the matter of anticipations of universalism implicit in the teleological perspective, is it not possible to say that Aristotle's establishing a criterion common to all the virtues — namely *mesotēs*, the middle term, the intermediate — acquires retrospectively the sense of a beginning of universality? And when we ourselves, following once again in the wake of Aristotle, posit as the object of self-esteem capacities such as the initiative of acting, choice on the basis of reasons, estimating and evaluating the goals of action, did we not implicitly give a universal sense to these capacities, as being that *by virtue of which* we hold them to be worthy of esteem, and ourselves as well?[1] Similarly, when, following Heidegger, we recog-

---

1. Alan Gewirth's moral theory in *Reason and Morality* (Chicago: University of Chicago Press, 1978) rests on making explicit the universal dimension attached to the acknowledgment that each of us possesses these capacities. If he speaks here of "generic" features, this is not with respect to a classification into genera and species but in order to show the universal character of the capacities *by reason of which* we recognize ourselves to be members of the human genus — or human species — in a unique sense of the terms "genus" and "species."

nized in mineness a character assigned "in each case" to the self, does not this "in each case" denote the feature that can be said to be universal, by reason of which one can write: *das Dasein, das Selbst?* It is, however, incontestable that the universal aspect of what we nevertheless call existentialia does not call into question the distinction between two identities, that of *ipse* and that of *idem:* because these existentialia are universals, we can say precisely in what way *ipse* is distinguished from *idem* or, equivalently, in what way the "who?" is worthy of esteem.

Now if ethics points toward universalism through the features we have just recalled, moral obligation is itself not without some connection to the aim of the "good life." The anchoring of the deontological moment in the teleological aim is made evident by the place occupied in Kant by the concept of good will at the threshold of the *Groundwork of the Metaphysics of Morals:* "It is impossible to conceive anything at all in the world, or even out of it, which can be taken as good without qualification [*ohne Einschränkung*], except a *good will*."[2]

This introductory declaration contains two assertions, both of which preserve a certain continuity between the deontological point of view and the teleological perspective, despite the significant break that we shall discuss later. It is first understood that "morally good" means "good without qualification," that is, without regard to the internal conditions and the external circumstances of action; while the predicate "good" conserves its teleological imprint, the reservation "without qualification" announces that anything that might lift the moral mark from the use of the predicate "good" has been set out of bounds.[3] The second assertion: that which

2. Kant, *Groundwork of the Metaphysics of Morals,* trans. H. J. Paton (New York: Harper & Row, 1964) 4.393, p. 61. One will note the frequent occurrences of the terms "esteem" and "estimable" in the first section of the *Groundwork,* always in connection with good will. These terms do not express simply an anchoring in the teleological tradition but an anchoring in ordinary moral experience. As in Aristotle, moral philosophy in Kant does not begin from nothing; the task is not to invent morality but to extract the *sense* of the *fact* of morality, as Éric Weil says of Kantian philosophy as a whole; cf. his *Problèmes kantiens* (Paris: Vrin, 1970), "Sens et fait," pp. 56–107.

3. Otfried Höffe in his *Introduction à la philosophie pratique de Kant (la morale, le droit, la religion),* trans. F. Rüegg and S. Gillioz (Fribourg, Albeuve, Switz.: Éd. Castella, 1985), defines as "metaethics" this first assertion that makes the concept of the good without restriction "the necessary and sufficient condition for determining definitively the question of the good" (p. 59). I shall term this introductory declaration simply ethical, in order to emphasize the tie with the ethical aim. In addition, Höffe is right to stress the fact that the normative idea of the good without restriction is of such vast scope that it covers two areas in juxtaposition, that of personal praxis, to which the *Groundwork* and the *Critique of Practical Reason* are confined, and that of public praxis, treated only in the part of the *Metaphysics of Morals* devoted to the *Metaphysical Elements of Justice.* We shall return to this in the section on justice later in this study.

receives the predicate "good" is henceforth the *will*. Here, too, a certain continuity with the ethical perspective is preserved: one can pair the Kantian concept of will with the power of positing a beginning in the course of things, of determining oneself through reasons, a power which, as we stated, is the object of self-esteem. The will, however, takes the place in Kantian morality that rational desire occupied in Aristotelian ethics; desire is recognized through its aim, will through its relation to the law.[4] It is the place of the question "What ought I to do?" In a vocabulary closer to our own, one could say that will is expressed in the speech acts belonging to the family of *imperatives,* whereas the verbal expressions of desire — including happiness — are speech acts in the *optative* mode.

We have entered the Kantian problematic through the royal gate of universality. This problematic by itself, however, is not enough to characterize a morality of obligation. Inextricably tied to the idea of universality is the idea of *constraint,* characteristic of the idea of *duty;* and this is so by reason of the limitations that characterize a finite will. Indeed, by its fundamental constitution, the will is nothing but practical reason, common in principle to all rational beings; by its finite constitution, it is empirically determined by sensible inclinations. It results that the tie between the notion of good will — the access to the deontological problematic — and the notion of an action done out of duty is so close that the two expressions become substitutes for one another.[5] A good will without qualification is, in the first instance, a will that is constitutionally subject to limitations. For it, the good without qualification has the form of duty,

4. Kant's definition of the will, in its most general sense, bears the mark of this reference to the norm; unlike natural phenomena that exemplify laws, the will is the faculty whereby one acts *"in accordance with his idea* of laws" (*Groundwork* 4.412, p. 80). The definition is characteristic of the legislative style that permeates Kant's entire work, as Simone Goyard-Fabre has observed at the beginning of her work *Kant et le problème du droit* (Paris: Vrin, 1975).

5. In order to elucidate "the concept of a will estimable in itself and good apart from any further end," one has to "take up the concept of *duty,* which includes that of a good will, exposed, however, to certain subjective limitations and obstacles. These, so far from hiding a good will or disguising it, rather bring it out by contrast and make it shine forth more brightly" (*Groundwork* 4.397, pp. 64–65). It is here that the break between the critique and ordinary moral sense occurs: "Yet in this Idea of the absolute value of a mere will, all useful results being left out of account in its assessment, there is something so strange that, in spite of all the agreement it receives even from ordinary reason, there must arise the suspicion that perhaps its secret basis is merely some high-flown fantasticality, and that we may have misunderstood the purpose of nature in attaching reason to our will as its governor. We will therefore submit our Idea to an examination [*Prüfung*] from this point of view" (4.394–95, p. 62). This idea of examination, or testing, will be the guideline for our reconstruction of obligation-based morality.

the imperative, moral constraint. The entire critical process aims at moving back from this finite condition of the will to practical reason, conceived as self-legislation, as *autonomy*. Only at this stage will the self find the first support for its moral status, without any influence from the dialogic structure which, while not being added on from outside, unfolds its meaning in the interpersonal dimension.

Beneath this summit, moral reflection is a patient *examination* of the candidates for the title of good without qualification and, by implication, by reason of the status of finite will, for the title of categorically imperative. The style of a morality of obligation can then be characterized by the progressive strategy of placing at a distance, of purifying, of excluding, at the end of which the will that is good without qualification will equal the self-legislating will, in accordance with the supreme principle of autonomy.

If we approach this strategy from the viewpoint of what is set aside in this way, several stages have to be distinguished. At the first stage, inclination, the sign of finiteness, is set aside only by reason of its purely epistemic inadequacy with respect to the criterion of universality. It is important for the subsequent discussion that the *empirical* impurity in inclination be separated from recalcitrance, and hence from virtual disobedience, which take into account the constraining character of the moral imperative. The two problematics, that of universality and that of constraint, are doubtless difficult to distinguish because of the finite constitution of the will. However, one can at least *conceive* of a mode of subjective determination that would not bear the mark of the antagonism between reason and desire. There would then be no reprobation attached to putting inclination out of the picture: its empirical status would alone disqualify it. This stage can definitely be isolated in the Kantian program. It corresponds to the step of submitting the maxims of action to the *rule of universalization*.[6] It is indeed solely by means of these maxims — that is, of "propositions which contain a general determination of the will, having under it several practical rules"[7] — that inclinations can be tested. For how could I know whether, in the course of an action, the esteem of a thing is adequate to the absolute esteem of good will, if not by asking the question: Is the maxim of my action universalizable? The mediation provided here by the maxim presupposes that, when the will posits a project of some

6. According to O. Höffe's apt expression, in his remarkable analysis of the maxim as an "object of universalization" (*Introduction*, pp. 82–102), maxims are regularities the agent himself constitutes by making them his own.

7. Kant, *Critique of Practical Reason*, trans. Lewis White Beck (New York: Liberal Arts Press, 1956), p. 17, hereafter referred to as *C.Pr.R.*

amplitude, there be potentially included a *claim to universality*, the very matter the rule of universalization comes to test.[8] One has to admit that, characterized in this way, the notion of maxim is unprecedented in the teleological tradition, despite the traces of universalism noted above. It is not actually the claim to universality but internal teleology which, in Aristotle, first characterized the notion of "rational desire," and then, in our own analyses of praxis, the notions of practices, of life plans, and of the narrative unity of life. This last notion can, of course, be retranscribed in the vocabulary of maxims, thanks to their kinship with the character of generality displayed by the maxim on the level of a phenomenology of praxis; but it is the *test of universalization* that gives the maxim its specific meaning, at the same time that this test defines formalism for the first time, as witnessed by the most general formulation of the categorical imperative: "Act only on that maxim through which you can at the same time will that it should become a universal law" (*Groundwork*, p. 88). At this stage, there is no consideration of any recalcitrance of inclination; alone the criterion of universalization manifests the inadequation of the *claim* to universality attached to the maxim, with respect to the *requirement* of universality inscribed within practical reason.[9]

With the second and third degrees of separation a morality of obligation possesses the features that set it in the most radical opposition to an ethics based on the aim of the "good life." In the preceding analysis, we isolated the universal aspect from the constraining aspect of duty, despite their close connection in the structure of a finite will, that is, an empirically determined will. The constraining aspect deserves a distinct examination in its turn, inasmuch as this aspect determines the form of the *imperative* in which the rule of universalization appears. Considered from the viewpoint of the theory of speech acts, the imperative poses a specific problem: in addition to the conditions for success (was an order actually given in accordance with the conventions authorizing it?), speech acts are also subject to conditions on their satisfaction (was this order followed by obedience or not?).[10] This relation between commanding and obeying marks a new difference between the moral norm and the ethical aim. It is worth

8. Concerning the Kantian notion of maxim, cf. in addition to O. Höffe, B. Carnois, trans. David Booth, *The Coherence of Kant's Doctrine of Freedom* (Chicago: University of Chicago Press, 1987).

9. In the next study we shall question this privilege granted by Kant to the rule of universalization and the narrow version that he gives of it exclusively in terms of non-contradiction.

10. On the distinction between conditions for success and conditions of satisfaction, cf. Daniel Vanderveken, *Les Actes du discours* (Liège, Brussels: Mariaga, 1988).

noting that, in ordinary language, this type of speech act requires a speaker and a listener who are distinct from one another: one orders, and the other is compelled to obey by virtue of the condition for satisfying the imperative. This is the situation that Kant internalized by placing in the same subject the power of ordering and that of obeying or disobeying. Inclination is then defined by its power of disobedience. This power is assimilated by Kant to the passivity inherent in inclination, which makes him call desire "pathological."[11]

It is difficult at this point not to take up again the classical accusation of rigorism, whereby Kant is said to have considered desire to be intrinsically hostile to rationality.[12] One can counter this accusation up to a certain point by situating the dividing line, as Kant does, within the family of imperatives and distinguishing, as he is known to have done, between the categorical imperative and imperatives that are simply hypothetical, involving skill and prudence. This distinction proves to be the exact counterpart, in the order of constraint, to the one introduced by the criterion of universalization. If one admits that the imperative form is required by the structure of a finite will, then the categorical imperative is the imperative that successfully passes the test of universalization.

The novelty introduced by the constraining character of obligation is made fully explicit only in the first theorem and in the two problems of the "Analytic of Pure Practical Reason." What is theorized here is precisely what the categorical imperative excludes, namely the motivation proper to the other imperatives.[13] We thereby cross a second threshold of formalism: mediation by maxims is not forgotten, but subjective maxims are carried

11. "In the will of a rational being affected [pathologically] by feeling, there can be a conflict [*Widerstreit*] of maxims with the practical laws recognized by this being" (*C.Pr.R.*, p. 17).

12. Kant, in fact, seems close to Plato, distinguishing between the part of the soul that commands because it is rational and the part that, because it is irrational, is capable of rebelling. Even Platonic *thumos,* placed in the middle, is not without its parallel in the Kantian analysis of the voluntary act, which itself is divided between the will determined by law (*Wille*) and the will capable of hesitating between the law and desire and, as such, placed in the position of arbitrator between the two: this is precisely the meaning of *arbitrium,* which in Kant has become *Willkür,* and which is to be translated simply as "arbitrator."

13. Theorem 1 states that a principle that is based only on the capacity of feeling pleasure or pain may serve as a maxim but not as a law. The role of possible disobedience — of "conflict" — is rigorously defined by the terminal state of what up to now has been called inclination, namely pleasure and pain set up as determining principles of arbitration. Theorem 2 aligns with pleasure and pain affects as different, phenomenologically speaking, as pleasantness, satisfaction, contentment, felicity (the vocabulary of affects is, in this respect, unbelievably rich). The faculty of desiring is thus unified by reason of its antagonistic position, self-love and personal happiness falling under the same heading.

back en masse to their single source, the "faculty of desiring" and the objective maxims to the simple (*blosse*) form of legislation.[14]

The split is finalized with the idea of self-legislation, or *autonomy*.[15] It is no longer simply a matter of the will but of freedom. Or rather, freedom denotes will (*Wille*) in its fundamental structure and no longer in terms of its finite condition (*Willkür*). The "Dialectic" of the *Critique of Pure Reason* was able to establish only that this freedom was conceivable. Here freedom is justified practically: first in negative terms, by its total independence with respect to "all determining grounds of events in nature according to the law of causality" (*C.Pr.R.*, Problem 1, p. 28); and then positively, as the self-givenness of the law (Theorem 4). With *autonomy*, the split whose development we have been following step-by-step reaches its most radical expression: to autonomy is opposed the *heteronomy* of the arbitrator, in virtue of which the will gives itself only "directions for a reasonable obedience to pathological laws" (Theorem 4, p. 34). With this opposition — this *Widerstreit* — between autonomy and heteronomy, formalism reaches its apex; Kant can then proclaim that morality resides where "the mere legislative form of maxims is the sole sufficient ground of a will" (p. 28). To be sure, we have not left the vocabulary of the imperative, but we have in a sense sublimated it: when autonomy substitutes for obedience to another obedience to oneself, obedience has lost all character of dependence and submission. True obedience, one could say, is autonomy.

The reconstruction preceding from the Kantian concept of morality has been reduced to the elements that suffice to characterize the deontological viewpoint in contrast to the teleological concept of ethics: good will as determining the good without qualification, the criterion of universalization, legislation by form alone, and, finally, autonomy. The antagonisms

14. "All material practical rules place the ground of the determination of the will in the lower faculty of desire, and if there were no purely formal laws of the will adequate to determine it, we could not admit [the existence of] any higher faculty of desire" (*C.Pr.R.*, §3, Theorem 2, Corollary, p. 21).

15. Höffe rightly characterizes autonomy as a "metacriterion," to distinguish it from the rule of universalization, the sole criterion of the "good without restriction" (*Introduction*, p. 127). He notes the origin of the idea of self-legislation in Rousseau: "Obedience to a law one prescribes to oneself is freedom" (*The Social Contract*, bk. 1, chap. 8, quoted in Höffe, *Introduction*, p. 128). Autonomy thus becomes the equivalent of a contract made with oneself: "A will to which only the legislative form of the maxim can serve as a law is a free will" (*C.Pr.R.*, Problem 1, p. 28). This link between moral formalism and the contractualist tradition is all the more interesting to us, as the latter will again appear when we consider the formal rule of justice. Concerning the place of autonomy in the "genealogical tree" of the various concepts of freedom in Kant, cf. Carnois, *Coherence*.

characteristic of the Kantian foundation have been placed in the progressive order of a logic of exclusion. The opposition between autonomy and heteronomy has thus appeared as constitutive of moral selfhood. In the spirit of Kantianism, the positing of a legislating self must not be confused with an egological thesis. As was stated above in general terms, the abstract character of this first moment of the triadic structure of morality is proportional to the degree of universality obtained by moral judgment in general. Consequently, the principle of autonomy is held to escape the alternatives of monologue and dialogue. Following Kant's statement in the *Groundwork*, one will observe a progression of a very peculiar kind when one moves from the general formulation of the categorical imperative to the second and third formulations, and this will serve as our guide in the second and third stages of our own itinerary. The progression, Kant says, is from the "*form*, which consists in their universality," to "*matter*," in which persons are apprehended as ends in themselves, and from there to the "*complete determination* of all maxims" following the notion of the kingdom of ends.[16] "A progression," Kant adds, "may be said to take place through the categories of *unity* of the form of the will (its universality); of the *multiplicity* of its matter (its objects, that is, its ends); and of the *totality* or completeness of its system of ends" (*Groundwork* 4.436, p. 104).[17] Unity, multiplicity, and totality are, of course, categories of quantity. But it is only "in a way" (*en quelque sorte*) that the *unity* of the form is distinguished from the *plurality* of matter. This unity is not that of a solitary ego. It is that of the universality of willing, grasped in the abstract moment when it is no longer divided among the plurality of persons. This purely pedagogical or psychogogic progression will be the object of a detailed discussion once we have completed the entire circuit of all the formulations of morality.

Before moving from the autonomy of the self, in its universal dimension, to the order of plurality that will characterize the second stage of our investigation, let us indicate three "places" that, prior to any critique di-

16. *Groundwork*, pp. 103–4. Kant strongly emphasizes that each formula "by itself contain[s] a combination of the other two"; he adds: "There is nevertheless a difference between them, which, however, is subjectively rather than objectively practical: that is to say, its purpose is to bring an Idea of reason nearer to intuition (in accordance with a certain analogy) and so nearer to feeling" (4.436, p. 103).

17. "It is, however, better if in moral *judgement* we proceed always in accordance with the strict method and take as our basis the universal formula of the categorical imperative: '*Act on the maxim which can at the same time be made a universal law*'. If, however, we wish also to secure acceptance for the moral law, it is very useful to bring one and the same action under the above-mentioned three concepts and so, as far as we can, to bring the universal formula nearer to intuition" (ibid. 4.436–37, p. 104).

rected from outside against Kantian morality, are highlighted by the Kantian text itself as places of potential aporia.[18]

The first of these "places" has to do with the nature of the "deduction" that Kant states he has made on the basis of the principle of autonomy.

If, as one should, one understands by deduction, in the legal sense of *quaestio juris,* the process of returning to ultimate presuppositions, then one has to admit that, in the case of autonomy, this process stops with the attestation of a fact, the famous *Factum der Vernunft* — the "fact of reason" — which has given rise to so many commentaries. To be sure, Kant speaks of a fact only with respect to the consciousness (*Bewusstsein*) that we have of the self-legislating capacity of the moral subject (*C.Pr.R.*, pp. 31ff.). This consciousness, however, is the sole access we have to the sort of synthetic relation that autonomy establishes between freedom and the law. In this sense, the fact of reason is nothing other than the consciousness we have of this primordial connection. For my part, I willingly recognize in this consciousness the specific form taken by the attestation of "who?" in the moral dimension; in other words, it bears witness to the practical status of free will.[19] Kant's vocabulary confirms this: in this *factum,* he says, "pure reason shows itself [*sich beweist*] actually to be practical" (p. 43). It is in this sense very peculiar that autonomy is itself termed

18. I deliberately have not presented a full picture of the original contribution of the "Dialectic of Pure Practical Reason" in this reconstruction, concerned as I am here with precisely situating the moment of the greatest gap between the deontological point of view and the teleological perspective. This dialectic opens, so to speak, a new workplace with its theme of the highest good. Under this heading Kant interrogates what is appropriately called "the unconditioned totality of the object of pure practical reason" (ibid. 5.109, p. 112). It might be said that this new interrogation carries Kant back into the waters of Aristotelian teleology. Expressions such as the following — "the entire and perfect good as the object of the faculty of desire of rational finite beings" (5.110, p. 114) — give some credit to this interpretation. However, except for the fact that the conjunction (not analytic but synthetic) between virtue and happiness itself poses a specific problem, which in turn ends in the more considerable problem of the postulates of practical reason, it is important to repeat, after Kant, that the "Dialectic" does not undo what the "Analytic" has constructed: it is only for an autonomous will that the career is opened for this new problematic of the highest good and of happiness. It is striking, too, that in focusing on the nature of the bond between virtue and happiness, whether or not they are "absolutely identical," Kant had no reason to cross Aristotle on his path; among his predecessors, he encounters only the Epicurean and the Stoic (5.112ff., pp. 115ff.). The formalism of morality prevented him from posing the problem of the sovereign good in terms of dynamism and aim, despite the expressions quoted above, in appearance so close to Aristotle.

19. My interpretation resembles that of O. Höffe: "With the term 'fact of practical reason,' Kant wants to indicate that morality actually exists" (*Introduction,* p. 136). Further on: "Kant speaks of a fact [*factum*] because he considers the consciousness of the moral law to be a reality, like something real and not fictive, something simply accepted" (p. 137).

a fact "apodictically certain" (p. 48).[20] The relation between model and
copy, archetype and ectype, the world of pure understanding and the sensible world, justifies the analogical use of nature in the first secondary
formulation of the categorical imperative: "as through our will a natural
order must arise" (p. 45).[21] At the end of this testing and sifting of the
competitors of duty, the trust initially placed in common moral experience
is renewed. But can this self-attestation be assimilated to self-positing? Is
there not instead, concealed beneath the pride of the assertion of autonomy, the avowal of a certain receptivity, to the extent that the law, in
determining freedom, *affects* it?

This suspicion finds some confirmation in the treatment that the *Critique of Practical Reason* reserves for *respect*. In a sense it may seem premature to speak of respect before having developed it in accordance with the
threefold composition of morality, following the distinction that has just
been made between unity (or universality), plurality, and totality. Respect,
which we have made the emblematic title of the entire doctrine of morality, will receive its full significance only after its triadic structure has
been assured. Nevertheless, it is on the level of the principle of autonomy,
in the nakedness of the relation of freedom to law, when persons have not
yet been taken into account as ends in themselves, that respect reveals its
strange nature.[22] This nature has to do with the place of respect, as feeling,

---

20. We read the first occurrence of the term "fact of reason" here: "In order to regard
this law without any misinterpretation as given, one must note that it is not an empirical fact
but the sole fact of pure reason, which by it proclaims itself as originating law (*sic volo, sic
iubeo*)" (*C.Pr.R.*, p. 31). One will also note other expressions: "credential [*Creditiv*] for the
moral law" (p. 49), "the certitude [*Sicherung*] of its problematical concept of freedom"
(p. 50). It is also stated that the "significance" of this fact is "exclusively practical" (p. 51)
and that it is "inexplicable from any data of the world of sense" (p. 44). Kant appears to
identify this practical observation with a genuine breakthrough in the noumenal order all the
way to "the supersensuous nature of [rational] beings" (ibid.). However, the reservation that
follows should not be omitted: this supersensuous nature which is known only by laws of a
practical nature "is nothing else than nature under the autonomy of the pure practical reason"
(ibid.).

21. On these difficult texts, cf. D. Henrich, "Der Begriff der sittlichen Einsicht und
Kants Lehre von Factum der Vernunft," in *Kant*, ed. G. P. Prauss (Cologne: Kieperheuer
und Witsch, 1973), pp. 223–24; cf. also Carnois, *Coherence*, 56–72.

22. We find confirmation of the fact that respect can be considered either from the perspective of the general formula of the categorical imperative, which is nothing but the rule
of universalization set up as a principle, or from that of the second formulation of this principle, in which the plurality of persons has been taken into account, in the juxtaposition of
texts in which it is the moral law that is the object of respect and those in which persons are
the object of respect. Thus we read, "Respect always applies to persons only, never to things"
(*C.Pr.R.*, p. 79), while the expression "respect for the moral law" is the one that appears

among the "motives of pure practical reason" ("Analytic," chap. 3). Respect is a motive in that it inclines us, in the manner of an affect passively received, "to make this law itself a maxim" (p. 79).[23]

Now it is noteworthy that Kant did not raise the problem of the relation between the quasi-positing character of the self by itself in autonomy and the virtual nature of affection by the other implied by the status of respect as a motive. He thought that the difficulty could somehow be resolved, before being formulated in these terms, by *splitting* affectivity itself in two and by devoting all his efforts to this split. The idea of a feeling imprinted in the human heart by reason alone is supposed to put out the flame before it has been kindled. After this, everything rests on the division, within the domain of affects, between those that continue to belong to the pathology of desire and those that can be held to constitute the very mark of reason in feeling: namely, in the negative mode, the humiliation of self-love and, in the positive mode, the veneration for the power of reason in us.

This split, which breaks affectivity in two, cannot help but concern our investigation into the tie — never severed, in my opinion — between the moral norm and the ethical aim. If self-esteem is indeed, as we have admitted, the reflexive expression of the aim of the "good life," it seems to fall under the Kantian knife, which casts it over onto the other side of the dividing line.[24] The question for us has never been, however, making the Kantian tone harmonize with the Aristotelian tone. Actually, the real question is not that at all. For it is perfectly legitimate to see in Kantian respect the variant of self-esteem that has successfully passed the test of the crite-

---

most often. This apparent oscillation is explained by the fact that what is really at stake here is not the *object* of respect but its status as *feeling*, hence as affect, in relation to the principle of autonomy.

23. Our emphasis, following O. Höffe, on the notion of maxim finds additional justification here. The equating of maxim and motive is almost complete in this statement: "It is also a subjective determining principle, that is, a motive to this action, inasmuch as it has influence on the morality of the subject and produces a feeling conducive to the influence of the law on the will" (ibid. 5.75, p. 79).

24. The moral condemnation of self-love (*Selbstliebe*) is leveled at the latter under the double form of amour-propre (*Eigenliebe*), in the sense of excessive benevolence toward oneself, and of presumption (*Eigendünkel*), or self-conceit (*Wohlgefallen*). The most explicit text on this matter is the following: "This propensity to make the subjective determining grounds of one's choice [*Willkür*] into an objective determining ground of the will [*Wille*] in general can be called self-love; when it makes itself legislative and an unconditional practical principle, it can be called self-conceit" (ibid., p. 77). What we have called self-esteem does not appear to escape this condemnation: "All claims of self-esteem [*Selbstschätzung*] which precede conformity to the moral law are null and void" (p. 76).

rion of universalization. Anticipating what we shall say later concerning the place of evil in our deontological conception of morality, we can state that what is "knocked down" and "humiliated" is the variant of self-esteem that Kant calls *Selbstliebe* and that constitutes the always possible and, in fact, most ordinary perversion of self-esteem.[25] In this sense, placing "love of self" out of bounds plays a critical function with regard to self-esteem and a purgative function with regard to evil. Self-love, I shall venture to say, is self-esteem perverted by what we shall later call the penchant for evil.[26] Respect is self-esteem that has passed through the sieve of the universal and constraining norm — in short, self-esteem under the reign of the law. Having said this, the most formidable problem posed by respect as a motive is the introduction of a factor of *passivity* at the very heart of the principle of autonomy. This conjunction within respect between self-positing and self-affection authorizes us to question, in the following study, the independence of the principle of autonomy — the flower of the teleological conception of morality — in relation to the teleological perspective, in other words, to doubt the autonomy of autonomy.

The third "place" of virtual aporia, in relation to the eminent place conferred upon autonomy in the "Analytic," is to be sought in the opening essay on radical evil in *Religion within the Limits of Reason Alone*. Everything in this essay that tends to exonerate desire — inclination — tends at the same time to make (free) choice the source of all the splits we observed above: the inadequation of inclination, insofar as it is empirical, to meet the test of the rule of universalization, the opposition of pathological desire to the categorical imperative, the resistance of the penchant toward

25. One of Kant's expressions makes this interpretation plausible: evoking the feeling of elevation (*Erhebung*), the positive and inverse side of the feeling of coercion (*Zwang*) in the contrasting composition of respect, he suggests that "the subjective effect on feeling [with respect to this elevating aspect] . . . can also be called self-approbation [*Selbstbilligung*]" (ibid., p. 83). One reason to think that the critique of *Selbstliebe* does not break every possible bond with a positive evaluation of the self as autonomous is provided by the numerous considerations of ends, ever present in the *Critique of Judgment*, referring to the full exercise of the inclinations constitutive of human nature. The personality is placed at the summit of the hierarchy of these inclinations, as will be recalled later in his *Essay on Radical Evil*. In the chapter of the *Critique of Practical Reason* devoted to motives, we read that what elevates man above himself "is nothing else than personality, i.e., the freedom and independence from the mechanism of nature regarded as a capacity of a being which is subject to special laws (pure practical laws given by its own reason), so that the person as belonging to the world of sense is subject to his own personality so far as he belongs to the intelligible world" (p. 89).

26. Note that Kant speaks here, as in the essay entitled "Radical Evil in Human Nature," of self-love as a penchant, a propensity (*Hang*), to make inclinations the supreme practical condition.

heteronomy to the principle of autonomy. If desire is innocent,[27] then evil must be situated on the level of the *formulation of the maxims,* before one can ask — doubtless in vain — about its origin and declare it to be inscrutable. Evil is, in the literal sense of the word, perversion, that is, a reversal of the order that requires respect for the law to be placed above inclination. It is a matter here of a misuse of (free) choice and not of the maleficence of desire (nor, moreover, is it a matter of the corruption of practical reason itself, which would make humankind diabolical and not simply — if we may say so — bad).[28]

Once again, everything occurs on the level of maxims. But this time it is a matter of making room for a bad maxim which will be the subjective grounding for all the bad maxims. In this primordial maxim consists the propensity (*Hang*) for evil. To be sure, Kant is careful to distinguish this propensity for evil from the predisposition (*Anlage*) to good, which he holds to be inherent in the condition of a finite will and, consequently, to affirm the contingency of this propensity on the scale of human history. It nevertheless remains that the propensity for evil *affects* the use of freedom, the capacity for acting out of duty — in short, the capacity for actually being autonomous. This is the true problem for us. For this affection of freedom, even if it does not strike the principle of morality, which continues to be autonomy, does put into question the exercise, the realization of freedom. This uncommon situation opens, moreover, a place for religion that is distinct from that of morality — religion, according to Kant, possessing no theme other than the *regeneration* of freedom, that is, restoring to freedom the control over it of the good principle. In addition, this consideration of the capacity — lost and to be recovered — of freedom brings back to the forefront the problem of good and evil, which a strictly deontological version of morality had relegated to a subsidiary level (*C.Pr.R.,* "Analytic," chap. 2). In other words, the question of good and

27. The principle of evil cannot be placed in sensuous nature and in the inclinations that follow from it because "these [are] not directly related to evil" (*Religion within the Limits of Reason Alone,* trans. Theodore M. Greene and Hoyt H. Hudson [New York: Harper & Row, 1960], p. 30).

28. "Hence the distinction between a good man and one who is evil cannot lie in the difference between the incentives which they adopt into their maxim (not in the content of the maxim), but rather must depend upon *subordination* (the form of the maxim)" (*Religion,* p. 31). It is noteworthy that Kant does not linger over the litany of complaints concerning human wickedness but goes straight to the most subtle figure of evil, that in which self-love becomes the motive for an entirely external conformity to the moral law, which is the precise definition of *legality* in opposition to morality. When evil is lodged in the malice of a human heart that fools itself about the true nature of its intentions, it appears more devious than if it were simply identified with sensuous nature as such.

evil returns with the question of "the subjective ground of the use of freedom." [29]

This problem directly concerns the status of autonomy, by reason of the sort of affection that appears to be coextensive with its actualization. Two ideas should be kept in mind here. The first is the idea, so heavily underscored by Nabert, that evil, in reference to the formation of maxims, is to be thought in terms of a *real opposition,* in the sense of the attempt to introduce into philosophy the concept of negative magnitude.[30] On the plane where the moral law is itself a motive, the penchant for evil rises up as "real repugnance," to borrow Nabert's expression, namely as an incentive contrary to the moral law and influencing choice (*Religion,* p. 20). We thus have to admit that the penchant for evil affects free choice on the very level where respect is itself the specific affection that has been stated, the affection of freedom by the law. And it is as such that evil is radical (and not original): "This evil is *radical,* because it corrupts the ground of all maxims; it is, moreover, as a natural propensity, *inextirpable* by human powers" (p. 32).[31]

29. In carrying the question of evil to the level of "predispositions" (*Gesinnungen*), Kant links up with the teleology of the *Critique of Judgment.* He reviews the degrees of this teleology applied to human nature at the start of the essay on radical evil: the disposition to *animality,* to *humanity,* to *personality* (*Religion,* p. 21). To the extent that the concept of predisposition belongs to teleology, the vocabulary of good and evil returns in the present context, in an entirely different sense, it is true, than the one rejected in the *Critique,* in chapter 2 of the "Analytic." It is, in fact, on the level of the third predisposition that the propensity for evil is exercised, a predisposition defined here as ˙the capacity for respect for the moral law as *in itself a sufficient incentive of the will*" (pp. 22–23). We are reminded that "all of these predispositions are not only *good* in negative fashion (in that they do not contradict the moral law); they are also predispositions *toward good* (they enjoin the observance of the law). They are *original,* for they are bound up with the possibility of human nature" (p. 23). It is on this predispositional terrain — steeped in finality! — that the notion of *propensity* to evil takes its place: "By propensity (*propensio*) I understand the subjective ground of the possibility of an inclination . . . so far as mankind in general is liable to it" (pp. 23–24). The propensity to evil is therefore inscribed in the most general theory of predispositions, as a sort of second-order predisposition, a predisposition deeply rooted in the formation of maxims that deviate from those of the moral law. This is why one can speak of them only in terms of *subjective ground.*

30. Jean Nabert, "Note sur l'idée du mal chez Kant," in *Essai sur le mal* (Paris: PUF, 1955), pp. 159–65. Nabert is commenting here on the note by Kant in *Religion,* pp. 18–19.

31. I am not considering here that which in the essay on "radical evil" invol·es the "historical" or "rational" origin of this penchant. This question carries Kant back to the shores of an ancient discussion, and the sides taken by Augustine and Pelagius. We, in fact, see that Kant is careful to preserve something of the Augustinian tradition — by making the penchant for evil a quasi nature, to the point of declaring the penchant for evil to be *innate* — all the while assuming a deliberately Pelagian stance. Evil, in a certain sense, begins anew with

The second important idea is that, in radicalizing evil, in introducing the difficult idea of a bad maxim of all maxims, Kant also radicalized the very idea of (free) choice by the sole fact of having made it the seat of a real opposition at the very source of the formation of maxims. In this, evil reveals something about the ultimate nature of (free) choice. Human (free) choice appears to carry with it an original wound that affects its capacity for determining itself for or against the law; the enigma of the origin of evil is reflected in the enigma that affects the actual exercise of freedom. The fact that this penchant is always already present in every opportunity to choose but that it is at the same time a maxim of (free) choice is no less inscrutable than the origin of evil.

From the union of these two ideas there results the supposition that will henceforth govern the entire series of moments of the deontological conception of morality: does it not follow from evil and from the inscrutable constitution of (free) will that there is, consequently, a *necessity* for ethics to assume the features of morality? Because there is evil, the aim of the "good life" has to be submitted to the test of moral obligation, which might be described in the following terms: "Act solely in accordance with the maxim by which you can wish at the same time that what *ought not to be*, namely evil, will indeed *not exist*."

2. Solicitude and the Norm

Just as solicitude is not an external addition to self-esteem, so the respect owed to persons does not constitute a heterogeneous moral principle in relation to the autonomy of the self but develops its implicit dialogic structure on the plane of obligation, of rules.

This thesis will be justified in two stages: first, we shall show the tie by which the norm of respect owed to persons is connected to the dialogic structure of the ethical aim, that is, precisely to solicitude. We shall then verify that the respect owed to persons is, on the moral plane, in the same relation to autonomy as solicitude is to the aim of the good life on the ethical plane. This indirect procedure will make more comprehensible to us the abrupt transition in Kant from the general formulation of the cate-

---

each evil act, although, in another sense, it is always already there. This emphasis on the question of the origin is responsible for the generally hostile reception of the essay and has prevented readers from recognizing its true greatness, so magnificently made apparent to us by Nabert ("Note") and Karl Jaspers ("Le mal radical chez Kant," in *Bilan et perspectives*, trans. H. Naef and J. Hirsch [Paris: Desclée de Brouwer, 1956], pp. 189–215; originally published as "Das radikal Böse bei Kant," in *Rechenschaft und Ausblick. Reden und Aufsätz* [Munich: Piper, 1951]).

gorical imperative to the notion of the person as an end in himself or herself, in the second subsidiary formulation of the imperative.

Just as the appraisal of good will as unconditionally good seemed to us to assure the transition between the aim of the good life and its moral transposition in the principle of obligation, it is the *Golden Rule* that seems to us to constitute the appropriate transitional formula between solicitude and the second Kantian imperative. As was the case for the esteem in which we hold good will, the Golden Rule appears to be part of the *endoxa* acclaimed by Aristotle's ethics, one of those received notions that the philosopher does not have to invent, but to clarify and justify. Now what does the Golden Rule say? We can read it in Hillel, the Jewish master of Saint Paul (Babylonian Talmud, *Sabbath,* 31a): "Do not do unto your neighbor what you would hate him to do to you. This is the entire law; the rest is commentary." We read the same thing in the Gospels: "Treat others as you would like them to treat you" (Luke 6:31).[32] The respective merits of the negative formula (do not . . .) and the positive formula (do such and such) balance one another; the interdiction leaves open the range of things that are not forbidden and in this way makes room for moral invention in the order of what is permitted; on its part, the positive commandment designates more clearly the motive of benevolence that prompts us to do something on behalf of our neighbor. In this regard, the positive formula can be likened to the commandment we read in Leviticus 19:18, which is repeated in Matthew 22:39: "Love your neighbor as yourself." This last expression marks perhaps better than the preceding ones the connection between solicitude and the norm. Hillel's formula and its equivalent in the Gospels, however, better express the structure common to all these statements, namely the enunciation of a *norm of reciprocity.*

The most remarkable thing, however, in the formulation of this rule is that the reciprocity demanded stands out against the background of the presupposition of an initial dissymmetry between the protagonists of the action — a dissymmetry that places one in the position of agent and the other in that of patient. This absence of symmetry has its grammatical projection in the opposition between the active form of doing and the passive form of being done, hence of suffering or submission. The passage from solicitude to the norm is of a piece with this basic dissymmetry, to the extent that it is upon this dissymmetry that all the maleficent offshoots of interaction, beginning with influence and culminating in murder, will be grafted. At the end point of this deviance, the norm of reciprocity appears to separate itself from the movement of solicitude and to be con-

---

32. And in Matthew as well: "Always treat others as you would like them to treat you: that is the Law and the Prophets" (7:12).

centrated on the prohibition of murder, "You shall not kill." The tie between this prohibition and the Golden Rule seems even to have been
entirely obliterated here. This is why it is not useless to reconstruct the
intermediary forms of the dissymmetry in the action presupposed by the
Golden Rule, inasmuch as the itinerary from solicitude to the prohibition
of murder repeats that of violence by way of the figures of nonreciprocity
in interaction.

The occasion of violence, not to mention the turn toward violence,
resides in the *power* exerted *over* one will by another will. It is difficult to
imagine situations of interaction in which one individual does not exert a
power over another by the very fact of acting. Let us underscore the expression "power-over." Given the extreme ambiguity of the term "power,"
it is important to distinguish the expression "power-over" from two other
uses of the term "power" which we have employed in the earlier studies.
We termed *power-to-do,* or power to act, the capacity possessed by an agent
to constitute himself or herself as the author of action, with all the related
difficulties and aporias. We also termed *power-in-common* the capacity of
the members of a historical community to exercise in an indivisible manner
their desire to live together, and we have been careful to distinguish this
power-in-common from the relation of domination in which political violence resides, the violence of those who govern as well as that of the governed. The power-over, grafted onto the initial dissymmetry between what
one does and what is done to another — in other words, what the other
suffers — can be held to be the occasion par excellence of the evil of violence. The descending slope is easy to mark off, from influence, the gentle
form of holding power-over, all the way to torture, the extreme form of
abuse. Even in the domain of physical violence, considered the abusive use
of force against others, the figures of evil are innumerable, from the simple
use of threats, passing through all the degrees of constraint, and ending in
murder. In all these diverse forms, violence is equivalent to the diminish-
ment or the destruction of the power-to-do of others. But there is something even worse: in torture, what the tormentor seeks to reach and
sometimes — alas! — succeeds in destroying is the victim's self-esteem, esteem which our passage by way of the norm has elevated to the level of
self-respect. What is called humiliation — a horrible caricature of hu-
mility — is nothing else than the destruction of self-respect, beyond the
destruction of the power-to-act. Here we seem to have reached the depths
of evil. But violence can also be concealed in language as an act of discourse, hence as action; this anticipates the analysis that we shall undertake
of promising: it is not by chance that Kant counts false promises among
the major examples of maxims unamenable both to the rule of universalization and to the respect of the difference between persons as ends in

THE SELF AND THE MORAL NORM 221

themselves and things that are means to an end. The betrayal of friendship, the inverse figure of faithfulness, without being equivalent to the horror of torture, tells us a lot about the malice of the human heart. By taking a broad view of language, Éric Weil, at the start of his great work *Logique de la philosophie,* makes a global opposition between violence and discourse. A similar opposition could easily be found in the ethics of communication in J. Habermas or in K. O. Apel, in the figure of what could be called the rejection of the best argument. In a different sense, the category of having designates a vast domain in which the wrong done to others wears innumerable disguises. In the *Metaphysics of Morals,* Kant has sketched a configuration of wrong on the basis of the distinction between *mine* and *yours;* this insistence may be peculiar to an epoch in which the right of property occupies an excessive place in the judicial apparatus and especially one in which the violation of this right sets off such an exaggerated reaction, as echoed in the scale of punishments. However, we do not know of any political or social order where the distinction between mine and yours would disappear, even if it were to remain only on the level of habeas corpus. In this sense, the category of having remains an indispensable point of reference in a typology of wrong. A remarkable combination between betrayal on the verbal plane and wrong on the plane of having can be found in the ruse, the depraved form of both irony and skillfulness. Here, another's trust is abused twice over. And what more is there to say about the stubborn persistence of forms of sexual violence, from harassment to rape, and including the suffering of women battered and children abused? In this body-to-body intimacy all forms of torture can slip in.

This sinister — though not exhaustive — enumeration of the figures of evil in the intersubjective dimension established by solicitude has its counterpart in the series of prescriptions and prohibitions stemming from the Golden Rule in accordance with the various compartments of interaction: you shall not lie, you shall not steal, you shall not kill, you shall not torture. In each case, morality replies to violence. And if the commandment cannot do otherwise than to take the form of a prohibition, this is precisely because of evil: to all the figures of evil responds the *no* of morality. Here, doubtless, resides the ultimate reason for which the negative form of prohibition is inexpungible. Moral philosophy will all the more readily admit to this fact as, in the course of this descent into hell, it does not lose sight of the primacy of the ethical over the moral. On the level of the ethical aim, however, solicitude, as the mutual exchange of self-esteems, is affirmative through and through. This affirmation, which can well be termed original, is the hidden soul of the prohibition. It is what, ultimately, arms our indignation, that is, our rejection of *indignities* inflicted on others.

Let us now undertake the second phase of our argument, namely the fact that the respect owed to persons, posited in the second formulation of the Kantian imperative,[33] is, on the moral plane, in the same relation to autonomy as solicitude was to the aim of the "good life" on the ethical plane. Now the latter tie had a peculiar characteristic, namely that the continuity between the first and the second moment of the ethical aim was at the price of a genuine leap, otherness coming to break what Lévinas calls the "separation" of the ego; only at this price was solicitude able to appear *after the fact* as the unfolding of the aim of the "good life." In Kant, things appear to be quite different: the second formulation of the categorical imperative is explicitly treated as a development of the general form of the imperative "Act in such a way that the maxim of your will can always hold at the same time as a principle of universal law." [34] In light of the intimate dialectic of solicitude, the second Kantian imperative reveals itself as the seat of a tension between the two key terms: that of humanity and that of the person as an end in himself or herself. The idea of humanity as a singular term is introduced in the context of an abstract universality that governs the principle of autonomy, without the consideration of persons. The idea of persons as ends in themselves, however, demands that one take into account the plurality of persons, without allowing one to take this idea as far as the conception of otherness. Everything in Kant's explicit argumentation aims at giving priority to the continuity, assured by the idea of humanity, with the principle of autonomy, at the expense of the unavowed discontinuity that marks the sudden introduction of the idea of an end in itself and of persons as ends in themselves.

In order to bring out the tension hidden in the Kantian statement, it seems opportune to base our discussion on the Golden Rule, as it represents the simplest formula that can serve as a transition between solicitude and the second Kantian imperative. By placing the Golden Rule in this intermediary position, we allow ourselves the possibility of treating the Kantian imperative as the formalization of the Golden Rule.

It is, indeed, the Golden Rule that imposes from the start the new ground upon which formalism will attempt to impose itself. What Kant termed *matter* or *plurality* is quite precisely this field of interaction where one will exerts a power over another and where the rule of reciprocity replies to the initial dissymmetry between agent and patient. Applied to

33. The Kantian formulation reads: "Act in such as way that you always treat humanity, whether in your own person or in the person of any other, never simply as a means, but always at the same time as an end" (*Groundwork* 4.429, p. 96).

34. We mentioned earlier the texts in the *Groundwork* in which the explanation followed the line of the categories: "This progression may be said to take place through the categories of the *unity* of the form of will (its universality), of the *multiplicity* of its matter (its objects — that is, its ends), and of the *totality* or completeness of its system of ends" (ibid. 4.436, p. 104).

this rule of reciprocity which makes patient and agent equivalent, the process of formalization tends to repeat, in this new field of plurality, the test of the rule of universalization that had assured the triumph of the principle of autonomy. It is here that the notion of *humanity,* superimposed on the polarity of agent and patient, comes into play. In this regard, the notion of humanity can be considered the plural expression of the requirement of universality that presided over the deduction of autonomy, hence taken as the plural unfolding of the very principle of autonomy. Introduced as the mediating term between the diversity of persons, the notion of humanity has the effect of lessening, to the point of eliminating, the otherness that is at the root of this diversity, otherness which is dramatized in the dissymmetrical relation of the power one will holds over another, opposed by the Golden Rule.

This formalizing intention, expressed by the mediating idea of humanity, appears clearly when one measures the distance that Kant takes with respect to the Golden Rule (which, moreover, is rarely cited by him and only disdainfully when he does refer to it). This distrust is explained by the imperfectly formal character of the rule. It can no doubt be held to be partially formal, in that it does not say what others would like or dislike to have done to them. It is imperfectly formal, however, to the extent that it refers to liking and disliking; it thereby introduces something on the order of inclinations. The test of universalization is in full operation here: it eliminates every candidate that does not pass its test. All the degrees of the process of purification conducted above on behalf of the principle of autonomy are found again here. Love and hate are the subjective principles of maxims which, as empirical, are not adequate to the requirement of universality. Moreover, love and loathing are, potentially, desires hostile to the rule, and so enter into the conflict between the subjective principle and the objective principle. In addition, if one takes into account the corruption in actual fact of these affections, then one has to admit that the rule of reciprocity lacks a discriminatory criterion that would allow a decision to be made in the thick of these affections, establishing a distinction between a demand that is legitimate and one that is not. It results from this critique that no direct tie between the self and the other than self can be established without naming what, in my person and in the person of others, is worthy of respect. Now humanity, taken not in the extensive or enumerative sense of the sum of human beings but in the comprehensive or fundamental sense of that by reason of which one is made worthy of respect, is nothing other than universality considered from the viewpoint of the *multiplicity* of persons: what Kant termed "object" or "matter."[35]

35. This shift from unity to plurality finds a basis in the teleology of the *Critique of Judgment,* as we recalled earlier at the time of the discussion of radical evil, which placed the

In this respect, the Kantian intention is not in doubt: to anyone who might object that the idea of humanity acts as a screen in the direct confrontation between oneself and another, the answer would have to be, in the Kantian spirit: if you admit that the rule of universalization is a necessary condition for the passage from the ethical aim to the moral norm on the level of its first component, then you have to find for its second component the equivalent of the universal required for the first. This equivalent is nothing other than the idea of humanity; the latter presents the same dialogic structure as solicitude but eliminates from it all radical otherness, limiting itself to guiding the principle of autonomy from unity, which does not take persons into account, to plurality. In so doing, this pluralization, internal to the universal, retrospectively confirms that the self, reflexively implied by the formal imperative, was not monologic in nature but simply indifferent to the distinction of persons and, in this sense, capable of being inscribed in the field of the plurality of persons. It is precisely this inscription that poses a problem. If it were sufficient by itself, the argument in favor of the primacy of the categorical imperative in its general formulation would result, in relation to the second formulation of the imperative, in robbing the respect owed to persons in their diversity of any original significance.

It is here that the notion of *person* as an end in itself comes to balance that of *humanity,* to the extent that it introduces in the very formulation of the imperative the distinction between "your person" and "the person of anyone else." With the person alone comes plurality. This subtle tension within a formula that appears to be homogeneous remains hidden by reason of the fact that the test of universalization, essential in affirming autonomy, continues with the elimination of the opposite maxim: never treat humanity *simply as a means.* Was not the principle of utility the first candidate for the job of "good without qualification," the one eliminated in the first pages of the *Groundwork?* The parallel of the argument, however, masks the secret discontinuity introduced by the very idea of persons as ends in themselves. Something new is said when the notions of "matter,"

---

predisposition to personality, considered as a reasonable and responsible being, above the predisposition of man as a living being to animal nature (*Religion,* p. 21). This teleology, based upon the notion of original predisposition to the good in human nature, is not easy to dissociate entirely from the Aristotelian-style teleology that remains rooted in an anthropology of desire. In this respect, the Kantian break is perhaps not as radical as Kant had wanted and believed it to be. Our critique of the Critique finds one of its points of application here. It will be one of the effects of the crisis provoked by moral formalism to reintroduce, on the level of the conditions of the actualization of freedom and of the moral principles that govern it, something like "generic goods" and "social goods." Without this addition of plainly teleological concepts, one does not see what the "material" idea of humanity contributes to the "formal" idea of universality.

of "object," and of "duty" are identified with those of end-in-itself. What is said here that is new is precisely what the Golden Rule states on the level of popular wisdom, before it is sifted through the critique. For it is indeed the deepest intention of this rule that now emerges clarified and purified. What indeed is it to treat humanity in my person and in the person of others as a *means* if not to exert *upon* the will of others that power which, full of restraint in the case of influence, is unleashed in all the forms that violence takes, culminating in torture? And what is the occasion for this progressive violence of power exerted by one will upon another if not the initial dissymmetry between what one does and what is done to others? The Golden Rule and the imperative of the respect owed to persons do not simply have the same field of exercise, they also have the same aim: to establish reciprocity wherever there is a lack of reciprocity. And in the background of the Golden Rule there reappears the intuition, inherent in solicitude, of genuine otherness at the root of the plurality of persons. At this price, the unifying and unitary idea of humanity ceases to appear as a copy of the universality at work in the principle of autonomy, and the second formulation of the categorical imperative assumes once more its entirely original character.

Having said this, have we done violence to the Kantian text? The original character that we claim for the idea of persons as ends in themselves is ratified by the texts of *Groundwork of the Metaphysics of Morals,* which give an independent "demonstration" of the correlation between person and end-in-itself: "Suppose, however, there were something *whose existence* has *in itself* an absolute worth, something which as *an end in itself* could be a ground of determinate laws; then, in it, and in it alone, would there be the ground of a possible categorical imperative — that is, of a practical law. Now I say that man, and in general every rational being, *exists* as an end in himself, *not merely as a means* for arbitrary use by this or that will: he must in all his actions, whether they are directed to himself or to other rational beings, always be viewed *at the same time as an end*" (4.428, p. 95). A strange parallel is thus created between the principle of autonomy and that of respect of persons, no longer on the level of contents but on the level of the "demonstration." Autonomy and the notion of the person as an end in himself are *confirmed* directly in exactly the same way. Consciousness of autonomy, we observed above, is called a "fact of reason," namely the fact that morality exists. It is now stated that morality exists because the person himself exists (*existiert*) as an end in himself.[36] In other words, we have always known the difference between persons and

---

36. Kant returns to this point and stresses it: "The ground of this principle is: *Rational nature exists as an end in itself.* This is the way in which a man necessarily conceives his own existence [*sein eignes Dasein*]" (*Groundwork* 4.429, p. 96).

things: we can obtain things, exchange them, use them; the manner of
existing of persons consists precisely in the fact that they cannot be obtained, utilized, or exchanged.[37] Existence here possesses a character at
once practical and ontological: practical in the sense that it is in the manner of acting, of *treating* others, that the difference between modes of
being is confirmed; ontological in the sense that the proposition "rational
nature exists as an end in itself" is an existentiell proposition. If it does
not state being, it states being-thus. This proposition, which can be said
to be ethicopractical in nature, imposes itself without intermediary. It will
be objected that this proposition is found in the second section of the
Groundwork, hence before the connection made in the third section between the noumenal world and practical freedom; this is why Kant observes in a note: "This proposition I put forward here as a postulate. The
grounds for it will be found in the final chapter" (4.429, p. 96). But since
the belonging of reasonable beings to the intelligible world is itself not the
object of any knowledge, it adds nothing to the connection postulated
here between the status of the person and existence as an end in itself: "By
thinking itself into the intelligible world, practical reason does not overstep
its limits in the least: it would do so only if it sought to *intuit or feel itself*
into that world" (4.458, p. 126).

Everything considered, has Kant succeeded in distinguishing, on the
ontological plane where he situates himself, the respect owed to persons
from autonomy? Yes and no. Yes, inasmuch as the notion of *existing as an
end in itself* remains distinct from that of *giving oneself a law;* as a result,
plurality, which was lacking in the idea of autonomy, is introduced directly
together with that of person as an end in himself. No, inasmuch as in
expressions like "man," "every rational being," and "rational nature," otherness is prevented from deploying itself by the universality that encircles
it, by the viewpoint of the idea of humanity.[38]

In order to make this subtle discordance within the Kantian imperative
evident, was it not legitimate to see in this imperative the formalization of
the Golden Rule, which obliquely designates the initial dissymmetry out

37. "Rational beings . . . are called *persons* because their nature already marks them out
as ends in themselves — that is, as something which ought not to be used merely as a means"
(ibid. 4.428, p. 96).

38. One will note the alternation of singular and plural in the Kantian formulas. Singular: "Rational nature exists as an end in itself." Plural: "Rational beings . . . are called persons
because their nature already marks them out as ends in themselves." To this second order
belongs the idea of the *irreplaceability* of persons, directly derived from the opposition between end and means: persons "are *objective ends* — that is, things whose existence is in itself
an end, and indeed an end such that in its place we can put no other end to which they
should serve merely as means" (ibid.).

of which flows the process of victimization in opposition to which the Golden Rule sets forth its demand for reciprocity? And were we no less justified in allowing the voice of solicitude to be heard, behind the Golden Rule, the voice which asked that the plurality of persons and their otherness not be obliterated by the globalizing idea of humanity?

3. From the Sense of Justice to the "Principles of Justice"

It should not be surprising that the rule of justice expresses on the level of institutions the same normative requirement, the same deontological formulation, as autonomy on the predialogic level and as the respect for persons on the dialogic and interpersonal levels — not surprising, in any event, when one considers to what extent *legality* appears to sum up the moral vision of the world. The development of a deontological conception of justice, however — what we, following Charles Perelman, will call *rule of justice* — on the basis of a sense of justice still belonging to the ethical aim requires separate justification. This development has to be forcefully argued, if we are to be able to understand later what sort of recourse can be found in the sense of justice, when deontology becomes entangled in the conflicts it provokes.

Let us recall what was established in the pages dealing with the sense of justice in the preceding chapter. It is to institutions, we said, that the virtue of justice is first applied. By institutions, we meant the diverse structures of wanting to live together, which, to this end, secure duration, cohesion, and distinction. From this resulted the theme of distribution, which we found to be implied in the *Nichomachean Ethics* in the form of distributive justice. We shall now show that this concept of distribution is placed at the point of intersection of the ethical aim and the deontological perspective. The ideas of just division and of just share still belong to the ethical aim, under the aegis of the idea of equality. But if the idea of just share is the legacy that ethics bequeaths to morality, this legacy is burdened with heavy ambiguities which the deontological perspective will have the task of clarifying, in preparation for turning them over later to a situational judgment, once they have been sharpened. The first ambiguity concerns the very idea of just share, depending on whether the accent is placed on the *separation* between what belongs to one to the exclusion of the other or on the tie of *cooperation* established or reinforced by the division. We concluded our reflections on the sense of justice by saying that it tended both toward the sense of mutual indebtedness and toward that of disinterested interest. We shall see that the normative viewpoint gives precedence to the second sense, which leans toward individualism, over the first sense, which can be said to be more openly communitarian. Another ambiguity: if equality is the ethical mainspring of justice, how can one justify the fact that justice is split in half following two uses of equality: simple or arithmetic equality, where all the shares are equal, and proportional equality, where equality is an equality of relations supposing four terms and not an equality of shares? But a relation between what and what? What can we say today to justify certain inequalities in fact in the name of a complex sense of equality? Here again, the norm can decide, but at what cost? Will this not be, once again, to the benefit of a prudent calculation and at the expense of the sense of belonging? But the principal legacy of ethics to morality lies in the very idea of the *just*, which henceforth looks both ways: in the direction of the "good" as the extension of solicitude to "each one" of the faceless members of society; in the direction of the "legal," to such a degree does the prestige of justice appear to dissolve into that of positive law. It is the concern with bringing this major ambiguity to light that motivates the efforts to remove every teleological basis from the idea of justice and to assign to it a strictly deontological status. And it is in terms of a formalization very similar to the one we have seen applied in the preceding section to the Golden Rule that a purely deontological interpretation of justice has been proposed. In the pages that follow we shall be concerned exclusively with this formalization.

In anticipation of our final argument, we can state that it is in a strictly *procedural* conception of justice that a formalization such as this reaches its goal. The question will then be whether this reduction to procedure does not leave a residue that requires a certain return to a teleological point of view, not at the price of repudiating the formalization procedures, but in the name of a demand to which these very procedures lend a voice, in the manner we shall state when the time comes. But we must win the right to make this critique by accompanying as far as possible the process of formalization of the idea of justice from which the deontological perspective receives its glory.

The deontological approach was able to gain a foothold in the institutional domain, where the idea of justice applies only by joining with the contractualist tradition, more precisely with the *fiction* of a social contract through which a certain collection of individuals were able to overcome a supposedly primitive state of nature in order to accede to a state of law. This encounter between a deliberately deontological perspective in moral matters and the contractualist current is not the result of a contingency. The aim and the function of the fiction of a contract is to separate the *just* from the *good*, by substituting the procedure of an imaginary deliberation for any prior commitment to an alleged common good. According to this hypothesis, it is the contractual procedure that is assumed to engender the principle or principles of justice.

If this is the main issue, the subsequent question will be whether a contractualist theory is capable of substituting a procedural approach for any foundation of the idea of justice, for any conviction whatever concerning the common good of all, of *politeia*, of the republic or the commonwealth. On the plane of institutions the contract can be said to occupy the place occupied by autonomy on the fundamental plane of morality. It goes this way: a freedom sufficiently disengaged from the gangue of inclinations provides a law for itself which is the very law of freedom. However, while autonomy can be said to be a fact of reason, that is, the fact that morality exists, the contract can only be a fiction — a founding fiction, to be sure, as we shall say, but a fiction nonetheless — because the republic is not a fact, as is the consciousness born of the confused yet firm knowledge that a good will is alone unconditionally good, a consciousness which has always understood and accepted the Golden Rule that makes the agent and the patient of action equal. But do peoples who have been enslaved for millennia know, with a knowledge akin to attestation, that they are sovereign? Or is the fact instead that the republic has not yet been founded, that it has yet to be founded, or perhaps that it will never really exist? What remains, then, is the fiction of the contract in order to make a deontological conception of justice measure up to the moral principle of autonomy and of the person as end in himself.

The unresolved enigma of the foundation of the republic is apparent in the formulation of the contract in Rousseau[39] as well as in Kant.[40] In the former, recourse is made to a lawmaker in order to find a way out of the labyrinth of politics. In the second, the tie is presupposed, but not justified, between autonomy or self-legislation and the social contract through which each member of an aggregate gives up his or her primitive freedom in view of recovering it in the form of civil liberties as a member of a republic.

One of the most forceful efforts of the contemporary period has been

39. Jean-Jacques Rousseau, *The Social Contract*, bk. 2, chap. 7.

40. In §46 of *The Metaphysical Elements of Justice*, vol. 1 of the *Metaphysics of Morals*, trans. John Ladd (Indianapolis: Bobbs-Merrill, 1965), we read: "The legislative authority can be attributed only to the united Will of the people. Because all right and justice is supposed to proceed from this authority, it can do absolutely no injustice to anyone" (6.313, p. 78). And later in §47: "The act by means of which the people constitute themselves a state is the original contract. More properly, it is the Idea of that act that alone enables us to conceive of the legitimacy of the state. According to the original contract, all (*omnes et singuli*) the people give up their external freedom in order to take it back again immediately as members of a commonwealth, that is, the people regarded as the state (*universi*). Accordingly, we cannot say that a man has sacrificed in the state a part of his inborn external freedom for some particular purpose; rather, we must say that he has completely abandoned his wild, lawless freedom in order to find his whole freedom again undiminished in a lawful dependency, that is, in a juridical state of society, since this dependency comes from his own legislative Will" (6.315–16, pp. 80–81).

John Rawls's attempt to provide a solution to this unresolved problem.[41] He proposes the term "fairness" as the key to the concept of justice because fairness characterizes the original situation of the contract from which the justice of basic institutions is held to derive. Rawls therefore fully assumes for his own purposes the idea of an original contract between free and rational persons, concerned with promoting their individual interests. Contractualism and individualism thus move forward hand-in-hand. If the attempt were to succeed, a purely procedural conception of justice not only would shake off all presuppositions concerning the good but would definitively free justice from the tutelage of the good, first on the level of institutions, then by extension from that of individuals and of nation-states considered as great individuals. To take an accurate measure of the antiteleological orientation of Rawls's theory of justice, one has to say that his theory is explicitly directed only against one particular teleological version of justice, namely utilitarianism, which has predominated for the past two centuries in the English-language world and which finds its most eloquent advocates in John Stuart Mill and in Henry Sidgwick. Plato and Aristotle are accorded only a couple of footnotes. Utilitarianism is, indeed, a teleological doctrine, to the extent that it defines justice in terms of maximizing good for the greatest number. As for this good, applied to institutions, it is only the extrapolation of a principle of choice constructed on the level of the individual, according to which a simple pleasure, an immediate satisfaction, ought to be *sacrificed* to the benefit of a greater, although more distant, pleasure or satisfaction.

The first idea that comes to mind is that there is a great gap between the teleological conception of utilitarianism and the deontological conception in general: by extrapolating from the individual to the social whole as utilitarianism does, the notion of sacrifice takes on a formidable tone: what is sacrificed is no longer a private pleasure but an entire social stratum. Utilitarianism, as Jean-Pierre Dupuy,[42] a French disciple of René Girard, maintains, tacitly implies a sacrificial principle which amounts to legitimizing the strategy of the scapegoat. The Kantian reply to this would be that the least well off in an unequal division of advantages should not be sacrificed because this is a person, which is a way of saying that, in line with a sacrificial principle, the potential victim of the distribution would be treated as a means and not as an end. In a sense, this is also Rawls's conviction, as I shall attempt to show later. But if it is his conviction, it is not his argument. Now it is the argument that counts. The entire book is

---

41. Rawls, *Theory of Justice*.

42. Jean-Pierre Dupuy, "Les Paradoxes de *Theory of Justice* (John Rawls)," *Esprit,* no. 134 (1988): 72ff.

an attempt to shift the question of foundation to the question of mutual consent, which is the very theme of every contractualist theory of justice. The Rawlsian theory of justice is without a doubt a deontological theory, in that it is opposed to the teleological approach of utilitarianism, but it is a deontology without a transcendental foundation. Why? Because it is the function of the social contract to derive the contents of the principles of justice from a fair procedure without any commitment with respect to allegedly objective criteria of the just — under pain, according to Rawls, of ultimately reintroducing some presuppositions concerning the good. To provide a procedural solution to the question of the just is the declared aim of *A Theory of Justice*. A fair procedure in view of a just arrangement of institutions is exactly what is meant by the title of chapter 1, "Justice as Fairness."

Having completed these preliminary considerations, let us now consider the answers Rawls offers to the following three questions: What would guarantee the fairness of the situation of deliberation from which an agreement could result concerning a just arrangement of institutions? What principles would be chosen in this fictive situation of deliberation? What argument could convince the deliberating parties to choose unanimously the Rawlsian principles of justice rather than, let us say, some variant of utilitarianism?

To the first question corresponds the assumption of the *original position* and the well-known allegory that accompanies it, the *veil of ignorance*. One cannot stress too heavily the nonhistorical, but hypothetical, character of this position.[43] A great amount of speculation is dispensed by Rawls concerning the conditions under which the original situation can be said to be fair in every respect. The fable of the veil of ignorance is intended to draw up a list of these constraints.[44] The parallel but also the lack of similitude indicated above between the Kantian foundation of autonomy and the social contract explain the complexity of the responses Rawls pro-

43. In fact, the original position is substituted for the state of nature inasmuch as it is a position of equality. We recall that in Hobbes the state of nature was characterized by the war of all against all and, as Leo Strauss stresses, as a state in which everyone is motivated by the fear of violent death. What is at issue in Hobbes is therefore not justice but safety. Rousseau and Kant, without sharing Hobbes's pessimistic anthropology, describe the state of nature as lawless, that is, without any power of arbitration between opposing claims. The principles of justice, however, can become the object of a common choice if and only if the original position is fair — that is, equal. Now it can be fair only in a hypothetical situation.

44. The idea is this: "Among the essential features of this situation is that no one knows his place in society, his class position or social status, nor does anyone know his fortune in the distribution of natural assets and liabilities, his intelligence, strength, and the like. I shall even assume that the parties do not know their conceptions of the good or their special psychological propensities" (Rawls, *Theory of Justice*, p. 12).

vides to the question concerning what individuals should know behind the veil of ignorance in order that upon their choice depends a system of distribution of advantages and disadvantages in a real society, where, behind rights, interests are at stake. From this results the first constraint: every party must have a sufficient knowledge of the general psychology of human nature with respect to fundamental passions and motivations.[45] Second constraint: the parties must know what every reasonable being is presumed to wish to possess, namely primary social goods without which the exercise of freedom would be an empty demand. In this regard, it is important to note that self-respect belongs to this list of primary goods.[46] Third constraint: since the choice is between several conceptions of justice, the parties must have suitable knowledge about the principles of justice in competition. They have to know the utilitarian arguments and, of course, the Rawlsian principles of justice, since the choice is not between particular laws but between global conceptions of justice.[47] Deliberation consists, quite precisely, in giving a *rank* to alternative theories of justice. Another constraint: all the parties must be equal with respect to information; this is why the presentation of alternatives and of arguments has to be public.[48] Yet another constraint: this refers to what Rawls calls the stability of the contract, that is, the expectation that it will be constraining in real life, regardless of the prevailing circumstances.

The fact that he takes so many precautions attests to the difficulty of the problem to be resolved, namely "to set up a fair procedure so that any principles agreed to will be just. The aim is to use the notion of pure procedural justice as a basis of theory" (*Theory of Justice*, p. 136). What the initial situation must annihilate, more than anything else, are the effects of contingency, due to nature as much as to social circumstances, so-called merit being placed by Rawls among these effects of contingency.

---

45. Rawls frankly admits that his philosophical anthropology is very close to that of Hume in the *Treatise of Human Nature*, bk. 3, as regards needs, interests, ends, and conflicting demands, including "the interests of a self that regards its conception of the good as worthy of recognition and that advances claims in its behalf as deserving satisfaction" (Rawls, *Theory of Justice*, p. 127). Rawls calls these constraints the "circumstances of justice" (p. 126).

46. In this sense, teleological considerations are taken into account but from the viewpoint of the parties entering into deliberation, not as clauses of the contract itself; cf. §15, "Primary Social Goods as the Basis of Expectations." We shall return to this notion of expectation in the studies that follow.

47. This is one of the reasons why, in *A Theory of Justice*, the principles of justice are described and interpreted *before* the systematic treatment of the original position.

48. Rawls speaks in this regard of the "formal constraints of the concept of right" (ibid., §23) to designate the constraints that hold for the choice of every moral principle and not simply for the principles of justice.

The expectations of the theorist are then immense: "Since the differences among the parties are unknown to them, and everyone is equally rational and similarly situated, each is convinced by the same arguments" (§24, p. 139).[49]

The second question now arises: What principles will be chosen from behind the veil of ignorance? The answer to this question is found in the description of the two principles of justice and in their correct placement. These principles, it must be stated before presenting them, are principles of distribution. The preceding study has familiarized us with the notion of distribution and its epistemological implications concerning the false alternative between the transcendence of society and methodological individualism: the notion of social partner satisfies both requirements, to the extent that the rule of distribution defines the institution as system and that this rule exists only inasmuch as those holding shares, taken together, make the institution a cooperative venture. Rawls not only assumes this presupposition, he extends it by diversifying it. Justice as distributive is in fact extended to all the kinds of advantages capable of being treated as shares to be distributed: rights and duties, on the one hand, benefits and burdens, on the other. It is clear that, for Rawls, the accent is not to be placed on the particular significance of the things to be divided up, on their *evaluation as distinct goods,* under pain of reintroducing a teleological principle and, following this, of opening the door to the idea of a diversity of goods, even to that of irreducible conflicts among goods. The effect of the formalist nature of the contract is to neutralize the diversity of goods to the benefit of the rule of distribution. This primacy of procedure brings to mind the bracketing of inclinations in the Kantian determination of the principle of universalization. Once again, we are brought back to the difference between the problematic of autonomy and that of the contract. If the former can be authorized by a fact of reason — regardless of its sense — this is not so for the latter, to the very extent that it is the basis for the allocation of shares. Inasmuch as society presents itself as a system of distribution, every division into shares is problematic and open to equally reasonable alternatives. Since there are several plausible manners of dividing up advantages and disadvantages, society is through and through a consensual-conflictual phenomenon. On the one hand, every allocation of shares can be challenged — especially, as we are going to see, in the context of unequal distribution. On the other hand, to be stable, distribution requires a consensus about the procedures for arbitrating

---

49. And again: "If anyone after due reflection prefers a conception of justice to another, then they all do, and a unanimous agreement can be reached" (ibid., p. 139).

among competing demands. The principles we are now going to consider bear precisely upon this problematic situation engendered by the requirement of a fair and stable distribution.

Rawls is indeed confronted, as was Aristotle, with the central paradox introduced by the equation between justice and equality. It is remarkable in this respect that, in Rawls as well as in Aristotle and probably in all moralists, it is the scandal of inequality that sets thought in motion. Rawls first thinks of the inequalities affecting the initial chances at the very beginning of life, what can be called the starting places.[50] He is thinking here also, of course, of the inequalities related to the diversity of contributions made by individuals to the functioning of society, to differences of qualification, of competence, of efficiency in the exercise of responsibility, and so on: inequalities which no known society has been able to or has wanted to eliminate. The problem is, then, as it was in Aristotle, to define equality in such a way as to reduce these inequalities to their unavoidable minimum. But here again, just as the unique procedure of deliberation in the original situation shifted to the background the diversity of goods attached to the things shared, the equality of the contracting parties in the fictive situation confers in advance to the inequalities consented to by the terms of the contract the seal of fairness characteristic of the original condition.

This heading of fairness does not change the fact that the idea of justice has to generate two principles of justice and that the second itself contains two moments. The first ensures the equal freedoms of citizenship (freedom of expression and assembly, freedom to vote and to be eligible to hold public office). The second principle applies to the unavoidable conditions of equality mentioned above; in its first part, it sets out the conditions under which certain inequalities are to be considered preferable both to greater inequalities and, at the same time, to an egalitarian distribution; in its second part, it equalizes as far as possible inequalities related to differences of authority and responsibility: whence the name "principle of difference."[51] Just as important as the content of these principles is the

---

50. It is not without importance to note that, from the start, merit or desert is set aside, either as a variety of initial luck or as an improper justification for the inequalities affecting the starting positions.

51. The first statement of the two principles reads as follows: "First: each person is to have an equal right to the most extensive basic liberty compatible with a similar liberty for others. Second: social and economic inequalities are to be arranged so that they are both (*a*) reasonably expected to be to everyone's advantage, and (*b*) attached to positions and offices open to all" (Rawls, *Theory of Justice*, p. 60). Furthermore, "The second principle applies, in the first approximation, to the distribution of income and wealth and to the design of organizations that make use of differences in authority and responsibility, or chains of

rule of priority that ties them together. Rawls speaks here of a serial or lexical order, attacking Marxism as well as utilitarianism head-on.[52] Applied to the principles of justice, the serial or lexical order signifies that "a departure from the institutions of equal liberty required by the first principle cannot be justified by, or compensated for, by greater social and economic advantages" (*Theory of Justice*, p. 61). Moreover, the lexical order is imposed between the two parts of the second principle: the least advantaged in economic terms must have a lexical priority with respect to all the other parties. This is what J.-P. Dupuy has designated in his article "Les Paradoxes de *Theory of Justice* (John Rawls)" as the antisacrificial implication of Rawls's principle: whoever could be the victim must not be sacrificed even for the benefit of the common good. The principle of difference, in this way, selects the most equal situation compatible with the rule of unanimity.[53]

This last assertion leads to the third question: *For what reasons* do the parties placed behind the veil of ignorance prefer these principles in their lexical order rather than any version of utilitarianism? The argument, occupying a considerable place in *A Theory of Justice*, is borrowed from de-

---

command. While the distribution of wealth and income need not be equal, it must be to everyone's advantage, and at the same time, positions of authority and offices of command must be accessible to all. One applies the second principle by holding positions open, and then, subject to this constraint, arranges social and economic inequalities so that everyone benefits" (p. 61). One may well ask oneself about the weight of considerations familiar to a market economy in the formulation of the second principle. On the economic level, let us admit, the amount to be shared is not fixed in advance but depends on the manner in which it is divided up. In addition, the differences in productivity result from the way in which distribution is organized. In a system of arithmetic equality, productivity could even be so low that even the most disadvantaged would be even more so. There is thus a threshold at which social transfers would become counterproductive. It is here that the principle of difference comes into play.

52. This lexical or lexicographic order is easy to comment on: the first letter of any word is *lexically* first, in the sense that no compensation on the level of succeeding letters would erase the negative effect that would result from substituting any other letter in place of the first; this impossible substitution gives the first letter an infinite weight. Nevertheless, the order that follows is not without weight, since the letters that come after make the difference between two words having the same beginning. The lexical order gives a specific weight to all the components without making them mutually substitutable.

53. As a result of this distinction between two principles of justice, Rawls has found himself caught between two groups of adversaries. On his right, he is accused of egalitarianism (giving priority to the most disadvantaged); on his left, he is accused of legitimizing inequality. To the first group, he replies: in a situation of arbitrary inequality the advantages of the most favored would be threatened by the resistance of the poor or simply by the lack of cooperation on their part; to the second group: a more egalitarian solution would be rejected unanimously because everyone would lose out.

cision theory in the context of uncertainty. It is designated by the term "maximin" — the parties are supposed to choose the arrangement that maximizes the minimum share. The argument is most powerful in the original situation behind the veil of ignorance. No one knows what his or her place in actual society will be. Each one reasons, therefore, on the basis of mere possibilities. Now the contracting parties are committed to one another in virtue of a contract whose terms have been publicly defined and unanimously accepted. If two conceptions of justice are in conflict and if one of them makes possible a situation that someone would find unacceptable, whereas the other would exclude this possibility, then the second conception would prevail. The question therefore arises of deciding to what extent an "ahistorical" pact can *be binding on* a "historical" society. The sole fact that this question arises confirms to what degree the presumed social contract, by which a society is held to provide itself with its fundamental institutions, differs from autonomy, in which a personal freedom is held to provide itself with its own law. Here there is no fact of reason to assume, but the laborious recourse to decision theory under uncertainty. The difficulties tied to this unparalleled situation in moral theory give rise to the question of principle — better termed the crucial question, the question of confidence — that of determining whether the deontological theory of justice does not in a certain way call upon the ethical sense of justice. In other words: does a purely procedural conception of justice succeed in breaking all ties to a sense of justice that precedes it and accompanies it all along?

My thesis is that this conception provides at best the formalization of a sense of justice that it never ceases to presuppose.[54] Rawls himself admits that the argument upon which the procedural conception is based does

---

54. In an article entitled "Cercle de la démonstration dans *Theory of Justice* (John Rawls)" (*Esprit,* no. 2 [1988]: 78), I note that the work as a whole does not obey the lexical order prescribed in its statement of principles but follows a circular order. In this way, the principles of justice are defined and even developed (§§11–12) before the examination of the circumstances of choice (§§20–25), consequently, before the thematic treatment of the veil of ignorance (§24) and, even more significantly, before the demonstration that these principles are the only rational ones (§§26, 30). In fact, it is announced very early on (§3) that the principles of justice are those that "free and rational persons concerned to further their own interests would accept in an initial position of equality as defining the fundamental terms of their association" (p. 11). What is anticipated here is not only the criterion of the original situation but its main characteristics, namely the idea that the parties have interests but do not know what they are, and in addition that they do not take an interest in one another's interests (p. 13). In this way, the theory is posited as a whole, independently of any interlinking serial order, as we attempted to reconstruct, starting from the original position, the formulation of the principles to be examined, and finally the rational argument in support of them.

not allow us to construct an independent theory but rests upon a pre-understanding of what is meant by the unjust and the just, permitting us to define and interpret these two principles of justice before being able to prove — if ever we manage to do so — that these are indeed the principles that would be chosen in the original situation behind the veil of ignorance. In truth, Rawls never repudiates his ambition to give an independent proof of the truth of his principles of justice but, in a more complex way, demands for his theory what he calls a *reflective equilibrium* between the theory and our "considered convictions."[55] These convictions have to be well considered, for if, in certain cases of flagrant injustice (religious intolerance, racial discrimination), ordinary moral judgment seems a sure guide, we have less assurance when it comes to the fair distribution of wealth and authority. We must seek, Rawls says, a means of shedding our doubts. Theoretical arguments then play the same role of examination that Kant assigned to the rule of universalization of maxims.[56] The whole system of argumentation can therefore be seen as a progressive rationalization of these convictions, when they are affected by prejudices or weakened by doubts. This rationalization consists in a complex process of mutual adjustment between conviction and theory.[57]

At the end of this course, two conclusions stand out. On the one hand, one can show in what sense an attempt to provide a strictly procedural foundation for justice applied to the basic institutions of society carries to

55. "There is, however, another side to justifying a particular description of the original position. This is to see if the principles which would be chosen match our considered convictions of justice or extend them in an acceptable way" (Rawls, *Theory of Justice,* p. 19).

56. "We can check an interpretation of the initial situation, then, by the capacity of its principles to accommodate our firmest convictions and to provide guidance where guidance is needed" (ibid., p. 20).

57. "By going back and forth, sometimes altering the conditions of the contractual circumstances, at others withdrawing our judgments and conforming them to principle, I assume that eventually we shall find a description of the initial situation that both expresses reasonable conditions and yields principles which match our considered judgments duly pruned and adjusted. This state of affairs I refer to as reflective equilibrium" (ibid.). The entire book can be considered the search for this reflective equilibrium. Our critique will begin just where *A Theory of Justice* appears to find its own equilibrium. Let us situate straightaway the site of this debate: the sort of circularity that the search for reflective equilibrium seems to presuppose appears to be threatened by centrifugal forces exerted by the hypothesis to which the deontological approach has bound its fate. Already with the hypothesis of the veil of ignorance, the entire course of the argument obeys an artificialist and constructivist tendency that is reinforced by the demand for the autonomy of the theoretical argument. Is it possible to reconcile the complete autonomy of the argument with the initial wish to preserve the fitness between theory and conviction? This may be the cumbersome burden of any contractualist theory in its effort to be derived from an accepted procedure by means of the very principle of justice which, paradoxically, already motivates the search for a rationally independent argument.

its heights the ambition to free the deontological viewpoint of morality from the teleological perspective of ethics. On the other hand, it appears that this attempt also best illustrates the limits of this ambition.

Freeing the deontological viewpoint from all teleological tutelage has its origin in Kant's positing a criterion of morality defined as a requirement of universality. In this sense, the Kantian imperative, in its most radical form ("Act solely in accordance with the maxim which you would want to become a universal law") does not concern only the constitution of a rational, personal will, nor even the positing of the person as an end in himself or herself, but the rule of justice in its procedural formulation.

In the three moments of the analysis, the universalist ambition of the rule has as its first corollary the formalism of the principle; this means that no empirical content successfully passes the test of the criterion of universalization. Formalism therefore amounts to setting (something) aside, as this will be expressed in each of the three spheres of formalism: setting aside inclination in the sphere of rational will, excluding the treatment of others simply as means in the dialogic sphere, and, finally, eliminating utilitarianism in the sphere of institutions. In this regard, one cannot emphasize too strongly that the exclusion of utilitarianism in the original situation has the same signification as the other two exclusions we have just mentioned and is in a sense constructed on the base of these two prior exclusions. Finally, the deontological viewpoint is founded thrice over on a principle that provides its own legitimation: autonomy in the first sphere, the positing of the person as an end in himself in the second, and the social contract in the third. Here again, it must be strongly asserted that autonomy governs the three spheres; the idea of the person as end in himself is held to be the dialogic expression of autonomy, and the contract is its equivalent on the plane of institutions.

As for the inherent limits of an enterprise such as this, one attempting to free the deontological perspective, these can be read in the increasing difficulties encountered by the sort of self-foundation presupposed by this liberation. These difficulties appear to me to reach a remarkably critical point with the contractualist version of justice. Let us return to the starting point: the principle of autonomy. This principle draws its legitimacy solely from itself, whence the difficult status, in the *Critique of Practical Reason,* of the famous "fact of reason." If we admit, along with certain commentators, that this fact of reason means simply that morality exists, that it enjoys the same authority in the practical order as experience in the theoretical order, then one would have to say that this existence can only be attested to, that this attestation refers back to the opening declaration of the *Groundwork,* namely: "It is impossible to conceive anything at all in the world, or even out of it, which can be taken as good without qualification, except a *good will*" (4.393, p. 61). Now this statement roots the deontological viewpoint once more in the teleological perspective. We find the same problem and the same difficulty with the statement that the person exists as an end in himself, that this mode of being belongs to the nature of reasonable beings. We have always known that we cannot make use of a person in the same way as a thing, that things have a price and persons, worth. This practical preunderstanding is the exact parallel to the attestation of the fact of reason on the dialogic plane of practical reason. It is here that the comparison of the contractualist hypothesis, from which the theory of justice draws its legitimacy, with the two preceding modalities of attestation proves instructive. The contract is found to occupy on the plane of institutions the place that autonomy claims on the fundamental plane of morality. But whereas autonomy can be said to be a "fact of reason," the social contract appears to be capable only of drawing its legitimacy from a fiction — a founding fiction, to be sure, but a fiction nonetheless. Why is this so? Is this because the self-foundation of the political body lacks the basic attestation from which good will and the person as end in himself draw their legitimacy? Is it because peoples, enslaved for millennia to a principle of domination transcending their will to live together, do not know that they are sovereign, not by reason of an imaginary contract, but by virtue of the will to live together that they have *forgotten*? Once this has been forgotten, only this fiction can make the contract the equivalent of the principle of autonomy and of the person as an end in himself. If now, by moving backward, we carry this doubt affecting the fiction of the contract back to the principle of autonomy, does not the latter also risk finding itself a fiction intended to compensate for forgetting the foundation of deontology in *the desire to live well with and for others in just institutions?*

The Self and Practical Wisdom

Conviction

Here we consider the third volet of the thesis that governs the studies devoted to the ethical dimension of the self: a morality of obligation, we stated, produces conflictual situations where practical wisdom has no recourse, in our opinion, other than to return to the initial intuition of ethics, in the framework of moral judgment in situation; that is, to the vision or aim of the "good life" with and for others in just institutions. Having said this, two misconceptions are to be avoided.

First, it is not a matter of adding a third agency to the ethical perspective and to the moment of duty, that corresponding to Hegelian *Sittlichkeit*. This is true, despite the fact that we shall borrow on occasion from the Hegelian analyses concerning, in particular, the concrete actualization of meaningful action. Indeed, the recourse to an agency such as this, one declared superior to morality, involves a concept of mind—*Geist*—which, in spite of the force with which it combines a superior conceptuality and a heightened sense of actuality, seems to be superfluous in an investigation centered on selfhood. The passage from general maxims of action to moral judgment in situation requires, in our opinion, simply the reawakening of the resources of singularity inherent in the aim of the true life. If moral judgment develops the dialectic that we shall discuss, conviction remains the only available way out, without ever constituting a third agency that would have to be added to what we have called up to now the ethical aim and the moral norm.

The second misconception to set aside: this manner of referring morality back to ethics is not to be taken to mean that the morality of obligation has been disavowed. In addition to the fact that this morality continues to appear to us to be the means of testing our illusions about ourselves and about the meaning of our inclinations that hide the aim of the good life, the very conflicts that are produced by the rigorousness of formalism give moral judgment in situation its true seriousness. If we did not pass through conflicts that shake a practice guided by the principles of morality, we would succumb to the seductions of a moral situationism that would cast us, defenseless, into the realm of the arbitrary. There is no shorter path than this one to reach that point at which moral judgment in situation and the conviction that dwells in it are worthy of the name of *practical wisdom*.

INTERLUDE
Tragic Action
for Olivier again

In order to restore to conflict the place that all the analyses up to now have avoided granting to it, it seemed to me appropriate to make a voice heard other than the voice of philosophy—even moral or practical philosophy—one of the voices of nonphilosophy: that of Greek tragedy. From this untimely irruption, we await the shock capable of awakening our mistrust with respect not only to the illusions of the heart but also to the illusions born of the hubris of practical reason itself. In a moment we shall say why, like Hegel, we have chosen *Antigone* rather than, say, *Oedipus Rex,* to guide this uncommon instruction of ethics by tragedy.[1]

The irruption of tragedy, at this point in our meditation, owes its untimely character to its nonphilosophical dimension. This cannot be concealed by what has just been termed the instruction by tragedy. Quite the opposite, failing to produce a direct and univocal teaching, tragic wisdom carries practical wisdom back to the test of moral judgment in situation alone.

The fact that tragedy resists a complete "repetition" in the discourse of ethics or morality is a feature that must be recalled briefly, but firmly, for fear that philosophy be tempted to treat tragedy as a quarry to be mined, from which it would cut its most beautiful blocks, shaping them later to its own sovereign designs. To be sure, tragedy does have action as its theme, as Hegel will later be heard to stress. It is therefore the work of those who act and of their individuality. But as witnessed by Sophocles' *Antigone,* those who act are in the service of spiritual powers that not only surpass them but, in turn, open the way for archaic and mythical energies that are also, from time immemorial, sources of misfortune. In this way, the obligation that forces Antigone to give her brother a sepulcher in accordance with custom, even though he has become an enemy of the city, does more than express the rights of the family in opposition to those of

1. Sophocles, *Antigone,* trans. Elizabeth Wyckoff, in *Greek Tragedies,* vol. 1, ed. David Grene and Richmond Lattimore (Chicago: University of Chicago Press, 1960).

the city. The bond between sister and brother, which knows nothing of
the political distinction between friend and enemy, is inseparable from the
service of divinities of the underworld and transforms the family bond into
a sinister pact with death. As for the city, to whose defense Creon subor-
dinates his own family bonds by forbidding the burial of the friend now
become an enemy, it too receives from its mythical foundation, and from
its lasting religious structure, a significance that is more than political. To
consider simply a symptom of tragedy, evident on the surface of the text
and of the action itself, the totally discordant way in which the two protagonists draw the line between friend and enemy, between *philos* and
ekhthros, is so overdetermined with meaning that this practical determination cannot be reduced to a simple modality of choice and deliberation,
along the lines described by Aristotle and by Kant. And the passion that
pushes each of the two protagonists to extremes is buried in the mysterious depths of motivations that no analysis of moral intention can plumb:
a speculatively unavowable theology of divine blindness is inextricably
mixed with the unambiguous claim that each makes to be the sole responsible author of his or her acts.[2] As a result, the finality of the tragic spectacle infinitely exceeds every directly didactic intention. *Catharsis,* as we
know, without failing to clarify, to enlighten, to be legitimately related
to the understanding of the plot, never ceases to be a purification in pro-
portion to the depth behind the actions themselves, a depth we have
just attempted, if only briefly, to plumb; catharsis, therefore, cannot be
stripped of its framework of ritual, under the protection of Dionysios,
who is invoked by the chorus in one of its final lyric odes. This is why, if
tragedy can address itself indirectly to our power of deliberation, this is
inasmuch as catharsis addresses itself directly to the passions, not only in
provoking them but in purifying them as well. This metaphorization of
phobos and *eleos*—of terror and pity—is the condition for all properly ethical instruction.

These, then, are the features of the nonphilosophical character of
tragedy: adverse mythical powers echoing the identifiable conflicts of the
roles; an unanalyzable mixture of constraints of fate and deliberate choices;
the purgative effect of the spectacle itself at the center of the passions it
produces.[3]

2. "O crimes [*hamartēmata*] of my wicked heart" (l. 1261), Creon cries, too late. "This
is my guilt, all mine. I killed you, I say it clear" (ll. 1317–18). Concerning this theology,
which can only be shown, cf. the analysis of tragedy in my early work *The Symbolism of Evil,*
trans. Emerson Buchanan (Boston: Beacon Press, 1969).
3. The strangeness of tragedy, which cannot be repeated on the level of rationality, is
forcefully recalled by J.-P. Vernant in "Tensions et ambiguites dans la tragedie grecque," in
J.-P. Vernant and P. Vidal-Naquet, *Mythe et tragédie en Grèce ancienne* (Paris: La Découverte,

And yet tragedy teaches us. Indeed, I have chosen *Antigone* because this tragedy says something unique about the unavoidable nature of conflict in moral life and, in addition, outlines a wisdom—the tragic wisdom of which Karl Jaspers spoke[4]—capable of directing us in conflicts of an entirely different nature, conflicts we shall consider later in the wake of formalism in morality.

If the tragedy of *Antigone* can teach us something, it is because the very content of the conflict—despite the lost and unrepeatable character of the mythical ground from which it emerges and of the festive environment surrounding the celebration of the spectacle—has maintained an ineffaceable permanence.[5] The tragedy of *Antigone* touches what, following Steiner, we can call the agonistic ground of human experience, where we witness the interminable confrontation of man and woman, old age and youth, society and the individual, the living and the dead, humans and gods. Self-recognition is at the price of a difficult apprenticeship acquired over the course of a long voyage through these persistent conflicts, whose universality is inseparable from their particular localization, which is, in every instance, unsurpassable.

Is the instruction of ethics by tragedy limited to the admission, in the form of an observation, that these conflicts are intractable and not open to negotiation? There is a middle path to be traced between a direct piece of advice, which will prove most disappointing, and resignation to insoluble opposition. Tragedy is comparable in this respect to the aporia-producing limit experiences, which none of our preceding studies has been able to avoid. So let us try again here.

What *Antigone* teaches about the tragic wellspring of action was indeed perceived by Hegel in the *Phenomenology of Spirit* and in the *Aesthetics,* namely the narrowness of the angle of commitment of each of the characters. Perhaps we must, with Martha Nussbaum,[6] go even further in a direction which, as we shall see, is not as anti-Hegelian as she may think, and discern in the two main protagonists a strategy of avoidance with regard to the conflicts internal to their respective causes. On this second

---

1986), 1:21–40, and by George Steiner, at the start of and throughout his great work *Antigones* (Oxford: Clarendon Press, 1984).

4. Karl Jaspers, *Von der Wahrheit* (Munich: Piper Verlag, 1947), pp. 915–60. Pierre Aubenque, in *La Prudence chez Aristote* (pp. 155–77) is attentive to the "tragic source" of *phronēsis* in Aristotle, which recalls *phronein* in *Antigone*.

5. This contrast produces astonishment in George Steiner, who devotes a great deal of reflection to the reappropriations of *Antigone,* in particular in the nineteenth century, before Freud gave his preference to *Oedipus Rex*. Simone Fraisse had earlier produced a comparable work on French literature in *Le Mythe d'Antigone* (Paris: Colin, 1973).

6. Nussbaum, *Fragility of Goodness*.

point, even more than on the first, we can graft the tragic wisdom capable of directing a practical wisdom.

Creon's conception of his duties with respect to the city not only does not exhaust the wealth of meaning of the Greek polis but does not take into account the variety and perhaps the heterogeneity of the tasks belonging to the city. For Creon, as we have already mentioned, the opposition friend-enemy is confined to a narrow political category and admits of no nuance, no exception. This narrowness of viewpoint is reflected in his estimation of the virtues. Alone is "good" that which serves the city, "bad" that which is harmful to it; the good citizen alone is "just," and "justice" commands only the art of governing and being governed. "Piety," an important virtue, is reduced to the civic bond, and the gods are called upon to honor only those citizens who have died for their country. It is this impoverished and simplified vision of his own city that leads Creon to his downfall. His belated change of heart makes him the hero who learns only too late.[7]

We must grant to Hegel that Antigone's vision of the world is no less restrictive and subject to internal contradictions than that of Creon. Her manner of distinguishing between *philos* and *ekhthros* is no less rigid than Creon's; for her, the only thing that counts is the family bond, so magnificently concentrated in "sisterhood." This bond[8] is stripped of the *eros* found in Haemon and celebrated by the chorus in one of its most beautiful lyric odes (ll. 781–801). Ultimately, only the dead relative is *philos*. Antigone is placed at this limit point. The laws of the city have lost their sacred cast: "For me it was not Zeus who made that order. Nor did that Justice who lives with the gods below mark out such laws to hold among mankind" (ll. 450ff.) Now there is another Justice, another *Dikē*, no less mysterious, that is celebrated by the chorus: "You went to the furthest verge of daring, but there you found the high foundation of justice, and fell. Perhaps you are paying your father's pain" (ll. 854–56). These are indeed two partial and unilateral visions of justice that are set in opposition by the protagonists. The strategy of simplification, as Nussbaum calls it, sealed by the allegiance to the dead alone—"O tomb, O marriage-chamber" (l. 892)—does not make Antigone any less inhuman than Creon. Finally, the company of the dead will leave her without any fellow citizens, robbed of the help of the gods of the city, without husband and

7. The chorus says, "You have learned justice [*tēn dikēn*], though it comes too late" (l. 1270). We shall return later to the meaning of a lesson that cannot cure anything, or even alleviate suffering.

8. One will note in this regard the strange tie between *eros* and the laws (*thesmōn*) of the world, which introduces the conflict at the very heart of the divine ("For there is the goddess at play with whom no man can fight" [ll. 799–800]).

without offspring, and even without friends to mourn her (ll. 880–82). The figure that walks away into the distance is not simply a person who suffers but Suffering itself (ll. 892–928).

Why, nevertheless, does our preference go to Antigone? Is it the woman's vulnerability in her that moves us? Is it because, as an extreme figure of nonviolence in the face of power, she alone has done no violence to anyone? Is it because her "sisterhood" reveals a quality of *philia* that is not altered by *eros*? Is it because the ritual of burial attests to a bond between the living and the dead, which reveals the limit of politics—more precisely, the limit of the relation of domination which, itself, does not exhaust the political tie? This last suggestion finds support in the verses that have left the strongest mark on tradition, verses that Hegel quotes twice in the *Phenomenology:* "Nor did I think your orders were so strong that you, a mortal man, could over-run the gods' unwritten and unfailing laws. Not now, nor yesterday's, they always live, and no one knows their origin in time" (ll. 452–55). In a sense, Antigone herself narrowed these unwritten laws down to funereal demands. But in invoking them to found her intimate conviction, she posited the limit that points up the human, all too human, character of every institution.

The instruction of ethics by tragedy comes out of the recognition of this limit. But poetry does not proceed conceptually. It is mainly through the series of lyric odes recited by the chorus (as well as the words given to Haemon and Teiresias) that something, not a teaching in the most didactic sense of the word, but more closely resembling a conversion of the manner of looking, is sketched out, which ethics will work to extend in its own discourse. The celebration of the sun in the first ode likens it to an eye—"O golden day's eye"—one less partial than human eyes.[9] A little later, in the gnomic mode, we find the famous declaration that begins the ode on man: "Many the wonders [*deina*] but nothing walks stranger [*deinon*] than man" (ll. 332–33). How is *deinon* to be translated? "strange"? "marvelous"? In fact, *deinon,* used many times in the play, has the sense the expression "formidable" sometimes has: oscillating between the admirable and the monstrous.[10] In this ambiguous sense of the word, the

9. Nussbaum underscores an expression that the chorus applies to Polyneices and that is rendered in English as "dubious quarrel"; the Greek, however, in a stricter reading, suggests the idea of a "twosided argument" (*amphilogos,* l. 111). It is for an unhuman eye that Polyneices's quarrel contains this amphibology (Nussbaum, *Fragility of Goodness,* p. 71).

10. Nussbaum, to whom I owe this suggestion, observes to what large extent human praise is finally ambiguous: "Clever beyond all dreams the inventive craft that he has which may drive him one time or another to well or ill. When he honors the laws of the land and the gods' sworn right [*dikan*], high indeed is his city" (ll. 365–69). Other occurrences of the term *deinon* will also be noted: "Fate has terrible *deina* power" (l. 951). To wit, the ordeal of

tragic hero is more *deinon* than any man. Even later, when the fate of the protagonists is sealed, the chorus, now out of advice to give, can only lament: "For those whose house is shaken by the gods escape no kind of doom. It extends to all the kin" (ll. 584–85). And again: "Near time, far future, and the past, one law controls them all: any greatness in human life brings doom" (ll. 612–13). Here tragedy reveals itself, as we have said, in the nonphilosophical dimension. Confronting disaster, the elders of the chorus will simply oscillate from one side to the other, tending somewhat to the side of Haemon and Teiresias. Addressing Creon: "Lord, if your son has spoken to the point you should take his lesson. He should do the same. Both sides [*diplē*] have spoken well" (ll. 724–726). Alone the praise of Eros gives the lamentation an elevated viewpoint comparable to the hymn to the sun. But those who know themselves to be mortal, "born to death" (l. 835), cannot maintain themselves at this height. It is only the memory of immemorial defeats that the chorus will sing: Danae, Lycurgis, the nameless young girl, all paralyzed, immobilized, petrified, thrown outside of praxis (ll. 944–87). The only advice that can still be given will be, echoing Teiresias's objurgation: "Yield to the dead. Why goad him where he lies?" (l. 1029). The coryphaeus will yet have a word to say, which will serve as our key; to Creon, who has exclaimed, "To yield is dreadful. But to stand against him. Dreadful to strike my spirit to destruction," he will recommend "prudence [*euboulias*]" (l. 1098). And after an invocation to Bacchus, in the tone of the ode to the sun and of the ode to Eros, preserving the elevation of the sacred in the poverty of the counsel, the chorus will be reduced to deploring vainly: "You have learned justice [*tēn dikēn*], though it comes too late" (l. 1270). The chorus's final word is of distressing modesty: "Our happiness depends on wisdom [*to phronein*] all the way. The gods must have their due. Great words by men of pride bring greater blows upon them. so wisdom [*to phronein*] comes [is taught, *edidaxan*] to the old" (ll. 1347–53).

What is the lesson, then? This final appeal to *to phronein* provides a thread that deserves to be followed.[11] An appeal to "deliberate well" (*euboulia*) stubbornly winds through the play, as though "thinking justly"

Lycurgis, bearing the "yoke" of necessity: "As the terror [*deinon*] of madness went" (l. 959). Vanquished, Creon confesses: "to yield is dreadful [*deinon*]. But to stand against him. Dreadful [*deinon*] to strike my spirit to destruction" (ll. 1096–97).

11. Relying on Ellendt's *Lexicon Sophocleum,* Martha C. Nussbaum counts, in the play of *Antigone* alone, 50 occurrences (out of 180 in Sophocles' seven plays) of terms referring to deliberation based on the roots *boul, phren/phron.* To this should be added *manthanein,* "to learn," connected to *phronein* in ll. 1031–32.

were the answer sought to "suffering this terror [*pathein to deinon*]" (l. 96).[12]

In what way does moral philosophy answer this appeal to "think correctly," to "deliberate well"? If one expected from the instruction of tragedy the equivalent of a moral teaching, one would be entirely mistaken. The fiction forged by the poet is one of conflicts which Steiner rightly considers intractable, nonnegotiable. Taken as such, tragedy produces an ethicopractical aporia that is added onto those that have appeared throughout our quest for selfhood; it repeats, in particular, the aporias of narrative identity that were identified in the preceding study. In this respect, one of the functions of tragedy in relation to ethics is to create a gap between tragic wisdom and practical wisdom. By refusing to contribute a "solution" to the conflicts made insoluble by fiction, tragedy, after having disoriented the gaze, condemns the person of praxis to reorient action, at his or her own risk, in the sense of a practical wisdom in situation that best *responds* to tragic wisdom. This response, deferred by the festive contemplation of the spectacle, makes conviction the haven beyond catharsis.

We have yet to say how tragic catharsis, despite the failure of direct counsel, opens the path to the moment of conviction.

This transition from catharsis to conviction consists essentially in a meditation on the inevitable place of conflict in moral life. It is on this path that our meditation crosses Hegel's. One thing should be said straightaway: if one must, at some point, "renounce Hegel," his treatment of tragedy is not the place to do so; if Hegel is reproached with having imposed a "synthesis" upon all the divisions that his philosophy displays the genius for discovering or inventing, this synthesis is certainly not drawn from tragedy. And if some fragile reconciliation is announced, it finds its meaning solely in the genuine reconciliations that the *Phenomenology of Spirit* will encounter only at a much more advanced stage of the dialectic. We cannot fail to note, in this connection, that tragedy is mentioned only at the start of the vast itinerary that occupies all of chapter 6, entitled "Geist" (indicating that this chapter is homologous with the work as a whole): the genuine reconciliation occurs only at the very end of this

---

12. Creon does not want to be instructed in *phronein* by a young man like Haemon (l. 727), who dares to tell him that he has lost the sense of *eu phronein* (l. 755). Creon believes himself, precisely, to be the master of thinking justly (*euphronein*). To Teiresias, who has just asked, "How better than all wealth is wisdom [*euboulia*]?" Creon replies: "And so is imprudence [*mē phronein*] worse than anything" (l. 1051). Too late, Creon admits his folly (*dusbouliais*) (l. 1269). The chorus then declares: "Our happiness depends on wisdom [*to phronein*] all the way," but it is to the broken, old man that the blows of fortune have taught the "wisdom [*to phronein*]" that "comes to the old" (l. 1353). The cycle of *phronein* is now complete.

itinerary, at the outcome of the conflict between judging consciousness and acting man; this reconciliation rests on an actual renunciation by each party of his partiality and has the value of a pardon in which each is truly recognized by the other. Now it is precisely this reconciliation through renouncement, this pardon through recognition, that tragedy—at least the tragedy *Antigone*—is incapable of producing. If the ethical powers served by the protagonists are to continue to subsist together, the *disappearance* of their particular existence is the full price to be paid. In this way, the hero-victims of the drama[13] do not benefit from the "certainty of self" that is the horizon of the educational process in which consciousness is engaged.

The treatment of tragedy in the *Aesthetics* confirms and reinforces this diagnosis. Here, tragedy is not placed on the trajectory that, in the *Phenomenology,* leads to "spirit certain of itself"; it is simply opposed to comedy on the level of poetic genres. Now as one of the genres of poetic drama, tragedy is distinguished from comedy by the fact that, in the former, the individuals that incarnate spiritual powers (*die geistige Mächte*) and that are brought into inevitable collision by virtue of their one-sidedness have to disappear in death; in comedy, man remains, through laughter, the lucid witness to the nonessentiality of goals that are mutually destructive.[14] If we have to take another path, the point of divergence from Hegel is not where it has too often been situated, as if Hegel had imposed a *theoretical* solution to the conflict, and as though the conflict were to be hailed as a subversive factor with respect to the tyranny of totalitarian

13. In the *Phenomenology of Spirit,* tragedy is that moment of mind when the harmonious unity of the beautiful city is disrupted by an action (*Handlung*), the action of particular individualities, from which the conflict between the characters stems. The effect of this *Entzweiung*—this dividing in two—is to split the ethical powers that dominate them: the divine against the human, the city against the family, man against woman. Here, the finest pages are those that assign to the sister—the woman who is not daughter, mother, or spouse—the responsibility of guarding the family bond that links the living and the dead. By giving her brother a tomb, Antigone elevates death above natural contingency. But if there is a sense to all this, it is not "for them" but "for us." "For them," disappearance in death; "for us," the indirect lesson of this disaster. The calm reconciliation sung by the chorus cannot take the place of pardon. The one-sidedness of each of the characters, including Antigone, excludes any such mutual recognition. This is why Hegel moves from *Antigone* to *Oedipus Rex,* in which he sees the tragedy of ignorance and of self-recognition concentrated in the same tragic individual. Self-consciousness takes another step forward here, without reaching the sort of reconciliation proposed at the end of chapter 6. One must first cross through the conflict tied to culture (*Bildung*), which is that of "spirit alienated from itself" (*der sich entfremdete Geist*), in order to apprehend this outcome. This is why Hegel could not expect from tragedy the capacity to draw from itself the solution to the conflicts it produces.

14. Hegel, *Aesthetics,* trans. T. M. Knox (Oxford: Clarendon Press, 1975).

reason.[15] For us, after beginning with an Aristotelian-style ethics and then assuming the rigors of a Kantian-style morality, the question is to identify the conflicts that morality produces on the very level of the spiritual powers that Hegel seems to take to be uncontaminated by the conflict, the one-sidedness of the characters being the sole source of conflict. Tragedy, on the level our investigation has reached, is not to be sought only at the dawn of ethical life but, on the contrary, at the advanced stage of morality, in the conflicts that arise along the path leading from the rule to moral judgment in situation. This path is non-Hegelian in the sense that it takes the risk of depriving itself of the resources of a philosophy of *Geist*. I have discussed above the reasons for this reticence. They have to do with the mistrust of *Sittlichkeit,* which a philosophy of *Geist* requires placing above morality, and with respect to his political philosophy—more specifically, to the theory of the state to which all these developments lead. My wager is that the dialectic of ethics and morality, in the sense defined in the preceding studies, develops and resolves itself in moral judgment in situation, without the addition, as a third agency, of *Sittlichkeit,* the flower of a philosophy of *Geist* in the practical dimension.

Two questions thus are posed, at the pivotal point between tragic catharsis and moral conviction: What makes ethical conflicts inevitable? And what solution is action capable of bringing to these conflicts? To the first question, the response proposed will be this: the source of conflict lies not only in the one-sidedness of the characters but also in the one-sidedness of the moral *principles* which themselves are confronted with the complexity of life. To the second question, the response we shall sketch out is this: in the conflicts to which morality gives rise, only a recourse to the ethical ground against which morality stands out can give rise to the wisdom of judgment in situation. From tragic *phronein* to practical *phronēsis:* this will be the maxim that can shelter moral conviction from the ruinous alternatives of univocity or arbitrariness.

1. Institution and Conflict

The tragedy of action, forever illustrated by Sophocles's *Antigone,* carries moral formalism back into the thick of ethics. In each case, conflict is the goad that sends us to this court of appeal in the three areas we have already

---

15. M. Gellrich, *Tragedy and Theory: The Problem of Conflict since Aristotle* (Princeton: Princeton University Press, 1988).

crossed through twice: the universal self, the plurality of persons, and the institutional environment.

Several reasons have prompted me to repeat this crossing in the opposite direction. First reason: by carrying the sword of conflict first to the plane of institutions, we are immediately confronted by the Hegelian plea in favor of *Sittlichkeit,* the actual and concrete morality that is held to take over from *Moralität,* from abstract morality, and which has its center of gravity in the sphere of institutions and, crowning all others, in the state. If we were to succeed in showing that the tragedy of action deploys some of its exemplary figures in this sphere, we could thereby remove the Hegelian hypothesis concerning practical wisdom instructed by conflict. *Sittlichkeit* would then no longer denote a third agency, higher than ethics and morality, but would designate one of the places in which practical wisdom is exercised, namely the hierarchy of institutional mediations through which practical wisdom must pass if justice is truly to deserve the name of fairness. A second reason has guided our choice of the order followed here. Since our problem is not to add a political philosophy to moral philosophy but to determine the new features of selfhood corresponding to *political practice,* the conflicts belonging to this practice have served as a backdrop to the conflicts produced by formalism itself on the interpersonal plane between the norm and the most singularizing solicitude. Only when we have crossed through these two zones of conflict shall we be able to confront the idea of autonomy that, in the last analysis, remains the cornerstone of Kantian morality; it is here that the most deeply concealed conflicts designate the turning point between morality and a practical wisdom that does not forget its passage through duty.

Let us now take up the rule of justice where we left it at the end of the last study. The possibility of conflict seemed to us to be already inscribed in the equivocal structure of the idea of just distribution. Does it aim at separating out the interests of mutually disinterested individuals or at reinforcing the bond of cooperation? The expressions "share" and "sharing" appeared to us to betray this equivocalness already on the level of language. Far from resolving this equivocalness, Rawls's formalism confirms it and even risks strengthening it. The gap between the two versions of the idea of just distribution seemed to us to be simply covered over by the idea of a reflective equilibrium between the theory that gives the book its title and our considered convictions.[16] Indeed, according to the theory, the individuals placed in the original position are rational individuals independent from one another and careful to promote their respective interests without taking the interests of others into consideration. The

---

16. Cf. above, eighth study, sec. 8.

maximin principle, considered by itself, could therefore be reduced to a refined form of utilitarian calculation. This would be the case if it were not precisely balanced by considered convictions, in which the viewpoint of the most disadvantaged is taken as a term of reference. Now this consideration rests in the last analysis on the rule of reciprocity, close to the Golden Rule, the aim of which is to redress the initial dissymmetry related to the power an agent exercises over the patient of his action, a dissymmetry that violence transforms into exploitation.

This fine internal tear within the rule of justice does not yet indicate anything more than the possible place of conflict. A genuinely conflictual situation appears when, digging under the pure rule of procedure, one unearths the diversity among the goods that are distributed which the formulation of the two principles of justice tends to obliterate. As we have said, the diversity of the things to be shared disappears in the procedure of distribution. The qualitative difference between the things to be distributed is lost from sight in an enumeration that lists, one after the other, revenues and patrimony, social advantages and corresponding burdens, positions of responsibility and of authority, honors and blames, and so on. In short, the diversity of the individual or collective *contributions* occasions a problem of distribution. Aristotle encountered this problem in his definition of proportional justice, in which equality is not a matter of shares but of the relation of the share of one person to his contribution and the relation of another person to his different contribution. Now, estimating the respective value of these contributions is considered by Aristotle to vary depending on the political system.[17] If the accent is shifted from the distribution procedure to the difference between the things to be distributed, two sorts of problems are raised which, in the literature following Rawls's great book, have most often been discussed together, but which it is important to distinguish. The first marks the return in full force of the teleological concepts that once again connect the just and the good, through the idea of *primary social goods*. Rawls sees nothing wrong in this and appears comfortable with the idea, which he connects without any apparent reservation to the expectations of representative persons.[18] But if we ask what qualifies these social goods as good, we open up a space of conflict whenever these goods appear relative to heterogeneous significations or estimations. A second problem is posed, not, this time, by the diversity of the goods to be shared, but by the historically and culturally determined character of the estimation of these goods. The conflict here is

17. Cf. Tricot's note on the Aristotelian notion of *axia* in his translation *Ethique à Nichomaque*, p. 228 n. 1, on 1131a24.
18. Rawls, *Theory of Justice*, p. 62.

between the universalist claim and the contextualist limits of the rule of
justice. I am keeping the second problem for the final section of this study,
inasmuch as the conflict between universalism and contextualism affects
all the spheres of morality to the same extent. In the discussion that follows, then, we shall consider only the question of the real diversity of the
goods to be shared.

In an author like Michael Walzer,[19] when this real diversity of goods is
taken into account, based upon the estimations or evaluations that determine the things to be shared as goods, the result is the veritable dismem-
berment of the unitary principle of justice to the benefit of the idea of
"spheres of justice." Constituting a separate sphere are, for example, the
rules that govern membership in society and that concern the conditions
of acquiring or losing this membership, the rights of foreign residents,
emigrants, political exiles, and so on. So many current debates, even in
advanced democracies, attest to the fact that problems continually arise
which ultimately refer to positions of an ethical nature, whose political
nature we shall return to later. Another sphere is that of security and wel-
fare, answering to what are judged to be needs in our societies and which
call, by law, for protection and for the assistance of public powers. Another sphere is that of money and merchandise, defined by the question of
what, as a good, can be bought and sold. It is therefore not enough to
make the broad distinction between persons who have worth and things
that have a price; the category of merchandise has its own requirements
and limits. Yet another sphere is that of offices whose distribution rests
not on heredity or fortune but on qualifications duly evaluated by public
procedures (here we find the question of equal opportunity and of the
possibility of acceding to all offices or positions, in accordance with
Rawls's second principle of justice).

Our problem here is not to propose an exhaustive list of these spheres
of justice, nor even to clarify the fate of the idea of equality in each of
them. Instead, we are concerned with the arbitration required by the competition among these spheres of justice and by the threat of one being
trampled by another, which gives the notion of social conflict its real
meaning.[20]

19. Michael Walzer, *Spheres of Justice: A Defense of Pluralism and Equality* (New York: Basic Books, 1983).

20. Walzer's theory of goods can be summed up in the following statements: "All the goods with which distributive justice is concerned are social goods" (ibid., p. 7). "Men and women take on concrete identities because of the way they conceive and create, and then possess and employ social goods" (p. 8). "There is no single set of primary or basic goods conceivable across all moral and material worlds" (p. 8). "But it is the meaning of goods that determines their movement" (p. 8). "Social meanings are historical in character; and so dis-

It is here that one might be tempted by a Hegelian outcome of the conflict, to the very extent that the questions of delimiting and establishing the priority of spheres of justice depends upon a chance system of arbitrage that is the equivalent on the institutional plane to the practical wisdom that Aristotle called *phronēsis*. Is not the solution to carry back to the political sphere, and in particular to the state, the analysis of conflicts posed up to now in terms of justice? The arbitration of the conflict between the spheres of justice will then have to be placed under the Hegelian category of *Sittlichkeit* rather than under the Aristotelian category of *phronēsis*.

As I have stated, my problem is not to propose here a political philosophy of the stature of that of Éric Weil, Cornelius Castoriadis, or Claude Lefort. I am simply interested in determining whether *political praxis* calls upon the resources of a concrete morality that can be exercised only in the framework of a self-knowledge that the state as such would contain. This is precisely what Hegel teaches in the *Philosophy of Right*.

Let us first recall that the Hegelian concept of right, which encompasses the whole enterprise, surpasses the concept of justice on every side: "The system of right," it is stated in the introduction, "is the realm of freedom made actual, the world of mind brought forth out of itself like a second nature" (§4, p. 20). And again: "An existent of any sort embodying the free will, this is what right is. Right therefore is by definition freedom as Idea" (§29, p. 33). This problematic of realization, of the actualization of freedom, is ours as well in this study. But does it require the drastic restriction of the domain of justice which we shall describe, and in particular, does it demand the elevation of the public domain well beyond the sphere where the idea of justice is valid? The limitation of the field in which justice is exercised coincides with that of *abstract right,* whose primary function is to raise taking-possession to the level of legal property in a triangular relation between a will, a thing, and another will: the relationship constituting the legal contract. The field of this contract is reduced accordingly, so that, in the encounter with the contractualist tradition to which Rawls belongs, the whole ensemble of institutions is made to issue from a fictive contract. As a result, the concept of justice undergoes an identical contraction. It is noteworthy, indeed, that all forms of fraud,

---

tributions, and just and unjust distributions, change over time" (p. 9). "When meanings are distinct, distributions must be autonomous" (p. 10). It results that a standard is valid only for each social good, in each sphere of distribution in each particular society; and, since standards are often violated, goods taken, and spheres invaded by men and women in power, these unavoidable phenomena of usurpation and monopolization make the system of distribution the predominant place of conflict.

perjury, violence, and crime are introduced under the negative title of injustice (§§82–103); in return, abstract right amounts to counterviolence, responding to violence (*Zwang*) in the domain in which freedom is externalized in the things possessed: "Abstract right is a right to coerce, because the wrong which transgresses it is an external thing" (§94, p. 67).[21] What is fundamentally lacking in abstract right, as well as in the contract and the idea of justice bound up with it, is the capacity to bind men and women together organically; right, as Kant admitted, is limited to separating what is mine from what is yours.[22] The idea of justice suffers from essentially the same juridical atomism. In this sense, the split we have just mentioned which affects society as a whole as a system of distribution—a split presupposed by Rawls's original position—becomes, in Hegel, an insurmountable weakness. The juridical person remains as abstract as the law that defines it.

It is precisely as the opposite extreme from this external contractual bond between rational independent individuals, and beyond merely subjective morality, that *Sittlichkeit* is defined as the place of the figures of the "objective mind," to use the vocabulary of the *Encyclopedia*. And it is because civil society, the site of the interests in competition, also does not create any organic bonds between concrete persons that political society appears as the sole recourse against fragmentation into isolated individuals.

The reasons to "renounce Hegel" on the plane of political philosophy are not comparable to those imposed upon the ego on the plane of the philosophy of history.[23] Hegel's philosophical project in the *Philosophy of Right* remains very close to my own views, to the extent that it reinforces the claims directed against political atomism in the seventh study. We then admitted that it was only in a specific institutional milieu that the capacities and predispositions that distinguish human action can blossom; the individual, we said then, becomes human only under the condition of certain institutions; and we added: if this is so, the obligation to serve these institutions is itself a condition for the human agent to continue to de-

21. The category of court of law reappears in the framework of "ethical life" (*Sittlichkeit*) but now within the limits of *civil society;* the section entitled "Administration of Justice" (*Philosophy of Right*, §§209–29) is thus framed by the theory of civil society as a "system of needs" and by that of "the police and the corporation."

22. The *Metaphysical Elements of Justice*, which constitutes the first volume of the *Metaphysics of Morals*, constructs private law on the distinction between "mine and yours in general": "An object is mine *de jure* (*meun juris*) if I am so bound to it that anyone else who uses it without my consent thereby injures me. The subjective condition of the possibility of the use of an external object is [called] *possession* [*Besitz*]" (6.245, p. 51).

23. *Time and Narrative* 3; 2, chap. 6.

velop. These are all reasons to feel indebted to Hegel's work of hierarchizing the modalities of the actualization of freedom in the *Philosophy of Right*. To this extent, and to this extent alone, the notion of *Sittlichkeit*—understood, on the one hand, in the sense of the system of collective agencies of mediation interpolated between the abstract idea of freedom and its realization as "second nature" and, on the other, as the gradual triumph of the organic bond between men and women over the exteriority of the juridical relation (an exteriority aggravated by that of the economic relation)—has never ceased to instruct us. Might I add that I am interpreting the Hegelian theory of the state, following Éric Weil, as a theory of the liberal state, to the extent that its centerpiece is the idea of a constitution? In this sense, Hegel's political project has not been superseded by history and, for the most part, has not yet been realized. The question for us is instead this: is the obligation to serve the institutions of a constitutional state of another, even of a higher, nature than moral obligation? More precisely, has it a ground other than the idea of justice, the final segment of the trajectory of the "good life"? Has it a different normative-deontological structure than the rule of justice?

The opposition between *Sittlichkeit* and *Moralität* loses its force and becomes useless—if not even destructive, as I shall say later—if, on the one hand, one gives to the rule of justice, through the intermediary of that of distribution, a field of application more extensive than that assigned to it by the Kantian doctrine of private right and the Hegelian doctrine of abstract right and if, on the other hand, one dissociates, as far as possible, the admirable analyses of *Sittlichkeit* from the ontology of *Geist*—of mind/spirit—that transforms the institutional mediation of the state into an agency capable of thinking of itself by itself.[24] Separated from the ontology of *Geist*, the phenomenology of *Sittlichkeit* ceases to legitimatize an agency of judgment superior to moral consciousness in its triadic structure: autonomy, respect for persons, rule of justice.[25] What gives *Sittlichkeit* the appearance of transcendence in relation to formal morality is its tie to institutions, which, we admitted above, present an irreducible character in relation to individuals. Only, it is one thing to admit that institutions do

---

24. "The state is the actuality of the ethical Idea. It is ethical mind *qua* the substantial will manifest and revealed to itself, knowing and thinking itself, accomplishing what it knows and insofar as it knows it. The state exists immediately in custom, mediately in individual self-consciousness, knowledge, and activity, while self-consciousness in virtue of its sentiment towards the state finds in the state, as its essence and the end and product of its activity, its substantive freedom" (*Philosophy of Right*, §257, p. 155).

25. This is what Hegel does in §258 of the *Philosophy of Right*: "This final end [*Endzweck*] has the supreme right against the individual, whose supreme duty is to be a member of the state" (p. 156).

not derive from individuals but always from other previously existing institutions, and it is another thing entirely to confer upon them a spirituality distinct from that of individuals. What, finally, is inadmissable in Hegel is the thesis of the objective mind and its corollary, the thesis of the state erected as a superior agency endowed with self-knowledge. Most impressive, certainly, is the requisitory that Hegel addresses against moral consciousness when it sets itself up as a supreme tribunal in superb ignorance of the *Sittlichkeit* in which the spirit of a people is embodied. For us, who have crossed through the monstrous events of the twentieth century tied to the phenomenon of totalitarianism, we have reasons to listen to the opposite verdict, devastating in another way, pronounced by history itself through the mouths of its victims. When the spirit of a people is perverted to the point of feeding a deadly *Sittlichkeit*, it is finally in the moral consciousness of a small number of individuals, inaccessible to fear and to corruption, that the spirit takes refuge, once it has fled the now-criminal institutions.[26] Who would still dare to chide the beautiful soul, when it alone remains to bear witness against the hero of action? To be sure, the painful conflict between moral consciousness and the spirit of a people is not always so disastrous, but it always stands as a reminder and a warning. It attests in a paroxysmic manner to the unsurpassable tragedy of action, to which Hegel himself did justice in his fine pages on *Antigone*.

The best way of demystifying the Hegelian state and, in so doing, of freeing its inexhaustible resources on the level of political philosophy is to question *political practice* itself and to examine the specific forms that the tragedy of action takes there.

Now why would political practice be the place of specific conflicts? And in what way do these conflicts relate to the ethical sense of justice?

We must start here with the difference between *power* and *domination,* which we emphasized so strongly in the third section of the seventh study. Power, we admitted, following Hannah Arendt, exists only to the extent that—and only so long as—the desire to live and act together subsists in a historical community. This power is the highest expression of Aristotelian praxis, which produces nothing outside of itself but has as its end its own maintenance, its stability, and its long-lastingness. But as we also admitted, this power is forgotten as the origin of the political agency and is covered over by the hierarchical structures of domination between the governing and the governed. In this respect, nothing is more serious than the confusion between power and domination or, in Spinoza's vocabulary

26. Vaclav Havel, "The Power of the Powerless," trans. P. Wilson, in *Living in Truth,* ed. Jan Vladislov (London: Faber and Faber, 1986), pp. 36–122.

in his *Political Treatise,* between *potentia* and *potestas.*[27] The virtue of justice, in the sense of *isotēs* in Pericles and in Aristotle, aims precisely at
balancing this relation, that is, at placing domination under the control of
the power-in-common. Now this task, which perhaps defines democracy,
is an endless task, each new agency of domination proceeding from an
earlier one of the same nature, at least in Western societies.[28]

This gap between domination and power is marked, within the structure of the state itself, by the dialectic I once summed up under the name
political paradox, in which form and force continue to confront one another within the same agency.[29] Whereas form finds its expression in the
constitution's approximation of the relation of mutual recognition between individuals and between the latter and the higher agency, force finds
its mark in all the scars left by the violent birth of all states, since become
states of law; force and form are conjoined in the legitimate use of violence, which is considered by Max Weber to be a criterion in the definition
of politics.[30]

On the basis of this gap between domination and power, constitutive
of the political as such, we can define *the political* as the set of organized
practices relating to the distribution of political power, better termed
domination. These practices concern the vertical relation between the governing and the governed as well as the horizontal relation between rival
groups in the distribution of political power. The conflicts proper to these
spheres of praxis can be divided into three levels of radicality.

At the first level, that of everyday *discussion* in a state of law in which
the rules of the game have been largely agreed upon, conflict is in order
in the activities of deliberation involving the priorities to be established
among the primary goods, given short shrift in the Rawlsian theory of
justice and which his libertarian or communitarian adversaries have placed
at the very center of their reflection. The threat of monopoly usurpation
tied to the plurality of spheres of justice determines the first level, where
the object of political deliberation is the provisional establishment, always
open to revision, of an *order of priority* among the competing demands of
these spheres of justice. Deliberating and taking a position on these ordinary conflicts constitutes the first opportunity offered to us to shift He-

27. M. Revault d'Allonnes, "Amor Mundi: La persévérance du politique," in *Ontologie
et Politique, Hannah Arendt.*

28. One would have to consider in this connection sociological studies on the existence
of a political bond without a state, found in certain societies still in existence.

29. "Le Paradoxe politique," *Espirit,* May 1957; reprinted in *History and Truth,* trans.
Charles A. Kelbley (Evanston, Ill.: Northwestern University Press, 1965).

30. Weber, "Politics as a Vocation."

gelian *Sittlichkeit* in the direction of Aristotelian *phronēsis*. In a state of law, the Aristotelian notion of deliberation coincides with public discussion, with the "public status" (*Öffentlichkeit*), demanded with such fervor by the thinkers of the Enlightenment; Aristotelian *phronēsis*, in its turn, has as its equivalent the judgment in situation, which, in Western democracies, proceeds from free elections. In this regard, it is useless—when it is not actually dangerous—to count on a consensus that would put an end to the conflicts. Democracy is not a political system without conflicts but a system in which conflicts are open and negotiable in accordance with recognized rules of arbitration. In a society that is ever more complex, conflicts will not diminish in number and in seriousness but will multiply and deepen. For the same reason, the free access of the pluralism of opinions to public expression is neither an accident nor an illness nor a misfortune; it is the expression of the fact that the public good cannot be decided in a scientific or dogmatic manner. There is no place from which this good can be viewed and determined in a manner so absolute that discussion can be held to be closed. Political discussion is without conclusion, although it is not without decision. But every decision can be revoked in accordance with accepted procedures, themselves considered indisputable, at least at the level of deliberation where we are now situated. Numerous claims confront one another which manifest an initial degree of indetermination in the public space of discussion. These claims are ultimately relative to the priority to be granted, in a determined culture and historical situation, to this or that primary good defining the spheres of justice and, finally, to the preferences presiding over the interrelations between these spheres of justice in the absence of a lexical order as imperative as that of the formal principles of justice. In this judgment in situation, which the advanced democracies identify essentially with majority vote, the sole equivalent of *euboulia*—good deliberation—recommended by the chorus in the lyric odes of *Antigone*, is the enlightened judgment one can expect from public debate.

At a second level of judgment, the debate concerns what can be called the *ends of "good" government*. This is a longer-term discussion; the empirical or positivist political thinkers have a tendency to consider this debate as the privileged terrain of ideology, in the pejorative sense of the word.[31] Quite the opposite, the debate over "good" government is an integral part of the political mediation through which we aspire to a full life, to the "good life." This is why we encounter this debate along the return

31. For a more nuanced evaluation of the polysemy and polyvalence of the concept of ideology, cf. my essays on the subject in *From Text to Action*, pt. 3, and in my lectures published under the title *Lectures on Ideology and Utopia*, ed. G. H. Taylor (New York: Columbia University Press, 1986).

path from morality to ethics within the framework of political judgment in situation.

The controversy involves key words, such as "security," "prosperity," "liberty," "equality," "solidarity," and so forth. These are emblematic terms that dominate political discussion from above. Their function is to justify, not the obligation to live in a state in general, but the preference for a certain form of state. The debate takes place, therefore, halfway between the rules of deliberation within a previously agreed upon constitutional form and the principles of legitimation, which we shall discuss later. The fact that these grand words have an emotional charge far beyond their tenor of meaning and are therefore at the mercy of manipulation and propaganda is a situation that makes their clarification all the more necessary, and this is the task of political philosophy. And these grand words do have a respectable history in the greatest of political philosophers: Plato, Aristotle, Machiavelli, Hobbes, Locke, Rousseau, Kant, Hegel, Marx, Tocqueville, Mill. Set within their conceptual history, these expressions resist the arbitrariness of the propagandists that would like to make them say just anything at all. To cast them purely and simply on the side of emotional evaluations useless for analysis is actually to consent to their ideological misuse in the worse sense of the word. The task, on the contrary, is to capture the core of meaning they possess as evaluative terms in relation to the ends of good government. What may have led us to believe that these concepts could not be rescued is that two major phenomena have not been taken into account, phenomena which a hermeneutical-style philosophy of action is prepared to recognize; first, each of these terms has an insurmountable plurality of sense; second, the plurality of ends of "good" government is perhaps irreducible; in other words, the question of *the* end of "good" government is perhaps undecidable.[32] The irreducible plurality of the ends of "good" government implies that the historical realization of one set of values can be obtained only at the expense of another set; in short, this implies that one cannot serve all values at once. The necessity once again arises of bending Hegelian *Sittlichkeit* to the side of Aristotle's *phronēsis,* elevated here to the level of the search for the "good" constitution, just when the accidents of history create a constitutional void. It is

32. A remarkable exercise of clarification of the term "liberty" can be found in Isaiah Berlin's *Four Essays on Liberty* (London: Oxford University Press, 1969). Moreover, the polysemy characteristic of what I am calling the grand words of politics is recognized by Aristotle in reference to justice itself, in the first lines of the *Nichomachean Ethics* 5. If the polysemy of the emblematic terms of politics is as fundamental as Aristotle says in reference to justice, there is nothing surprising in the fact that a particular meaning of the term "liberty" may coincide with an aspect of the meaning of "equality," whereas another may differ entirely from another partial meaning of the latter term.

in a contingent (geographic, historical, social, cultural) situation, and for motives that are not transparent to the political actors of the moment, that they can claim to offer to their people a "good" constitution. This choice is a new example of political judgment in situation, where *euboulia* has no support other than the conviction of the constituting parties and, finally, their sense of justice—the virtue of institutions—in the moment of "historical" choice.

An even more formidable indecision than that resulting from the ambiguity of the grand words of political practice strikes a third level, one involving choices even more fundamental than those of the democratic constitution. It concerns the very process of *legitimation* of democracy under its various guises. People are right to speak of a *legitimation crisis* to denote the lack of any basis that appears to affect the very choice of a government of the people, by the people, and for the people. Our reflections on the distinction between domination and power take on their full significance here. If power is the forgotten source of domination, how is domination to be derived *visibly* from the desire to live together? It is here that the fiction of the social contract, carried to a higher level of refinement by the Rawlsian fable of an original position characterized by fairness, is revealed to fill a void, namely, as suggested above, the absence for the social contract of the sort of attestation by virtue of which autonomy is, for the individual, a "fact of reason" and the respect of persons, the implication of their "rational nature." There is an obvious absence of any parallel between moral autonomy and the self-legislation of a people, whom domination would simply awaken out of their forgetfulness to the desire to live together and to act together as a people. I join here, by another path, an analysis Claude Lefort makes of democracy in contrast to totalitarianism. It was precisely the error—or rather, the crime—of totalitarianism to want to impose a univocal conception of what it believed to be a new man and to thereby avoid the historical gropings of modern man in the attempt to reach self-understanding. The thinker of democracy begins by confessing a "fundamental indeterminacy as to the basis of power, law, and knowledge, and as to the basis of relations between *self* and *other*, at every level of social life."[33] According to Lefort, democracy is born out of a revolution at the heart of the most fundamental symbolism from which all the forms of society stem; it is the system that accepts its contradictions to the point of institutionalizing conflict.[34] This "fundamental indetermi-

33. Claude Lefort, *Democracy and Political Theory,* trans. David Macey (Minneapolis: University of Minnesota Press, 1988), p. 19.

34. "Democracy thus proves to be the historical society *par excellence,* a society which, in its very form, welcomes and preserves indeterminacy and which provides a remarkable con-

nacy" cannot be the last word: for men and women have *reasons* to prefer to totalitarianism a system as uncertain as this one regarding the foundation of its legitimacy. These are the very reasons that are constitutive of wanting to live together, and one of the ways of becoming aware of them is through projecting the fiction of an ahistorical social contract. These reasons mix together claims to universality and the historical contingencies in what Rawls terms, in an essay written fifteen years after the *Theory of Justice,* "overlapping consensus." [35] This intersects with several cultural traditions: in addition to the project of the Enlightenment, which Habermas rightly judges to be "incomplete," [36] it encounters the reinterpreted forms of Jewish, Greek, and Christian traditions that have successfully undergone the critical test of *Aufklärung.* There is nothing better to offer, in reply to the legitimation crisis (which, in my opinion, affects the idea of domination more than that of power, as a people's desire to live and act together), than the memory and the intersection in the public space of the appearance of the traditions that make room for tolerance and pluralism, not out of concessions to external pressures, but out of inner conviction, even if this is late in coming. It is by calling to mind all the beginnings and all the rebeginnings, and all the traditions that have been sedimented upon them, that "good counsel" can take up the challenge of the legitimation crisis. If, and to the extent that, this "good counsel" does prevail, Hegelian *Sittlichkeit*—which itself is also rooted in *Sitten,* in "mores"—proves to be the equivalent of Aristotle's *phronēsis:* a plural, or rather public, *phronēsis* resembling the debate itself.

Might this not be the place to recall the distinction Aristotle makes at the end of his study of the virtue of justice between justice and equity: "On examination, they [equity and justice] appear to be neither absolutely the same nor generically different . . . for the equitable [*epieikēs*], though it is better than one kind of justice, yet is just, and it is not as being a different class of thing that it is better than the just" (*E.N.* 5.10). Aristotle himself suggests that the difference that makes equity superior in relation to justice has to do with the singularizing function of *phronēsis:* "The reason is that all law is universal but about some things it is not possible to make a universal statement which shall be correct" (5.10.1137b12–14).

trast with totalitarianism which, because it is constructed under the slogan of creating a new man, claims to understand the law of its organization and development, and which, in the modern world, secretly designates itself as a *society without a history*" (ibid., p. 16).

35. John Rawls, "Un consensus par recoupement," *Revue de métaphysique et de morale,* no. 1 (1988): 3–32.

36. J. Habermas, "La Modernité: Un projet inachevé," *Critique* 37, no. 413 (October 1981): 950–67.

Equity remedies justice "where the legislator fails us and has erred by over-simplicity" (1137b21–22). In correcting the omission, the public decision maker says "what the legislator himself would have said had he been present, and would have put into his law if he had known" (1137b22–24). Aristotle concludes, "And this is the nature of the equitable, a correction of law where it is defective owing to its universality."[37] When we reread these lines today, we tend to think that public debate and the decision making that results from it constitute the only agency qualified to "correct the omission" that today we call the "legitimation crisis." Equity, we shall conclude, is another name for the *sense* of justice, when the latter traverses the hardships and conflicts resulting from the application of the *rule* of justice.

2. Respect and Conflict

A second region of conflict is marked out by the applications of the second Kantian imperative: treat humanity in one's own person and in the person of others as an end in itself and not simply as a means. Our critique will be guided by the idea coming from the suggestion made in the preceding study that a fine dividing line tends to separate the universalist version of the imperative, represented by the idea of humanity, from what can be called the pluralist version, represented by the idea of persons as ends in themselves. According to Kant, there is no opposition here, to the extent that humanity designates the dignity *by reason of which* persons deserve respect, despite—so to speak—their plurality. The possibility of conflict arises, however, as soon as the otherness of persons, inherent in the very idea of *human* plurality, proves to be, in certain remarkable circumstances, incompatible with the universality of the rules that underlie the idea of humanity. Respect then tends to split up into respect for the law and respect for persons. Under these conditions, practical wisdom may consist in giving priority to the respect for persons, in the name of the solicitude that is addressed to persons in their irreplaceable singularity.

Before entering into the thick of the argument, it is important to distinguish it from the objection too often raised against formalism of vacuity, by definition as it were. On the contrary, it is because the categorical imperative generates a multiplicity of rules that the presumed universalism of these rules can collide with the demands of otherness, inherent in solicitude.

---

37. Cf. *E.N.* 5.10. 1137b19–27; 1137b31–1138a3. It is noteworthy that Gauthier-Jolif in the commentary on the *Nichomachean Ethics* (2: 431–34) considers this chapter as the conclusion to book 5.

The falseness of the equation between formalism and vacuity has to do with a misconception about the role of maxims in Kant.[38] Two points should be recalled here: first, the rule of universalization is applied to the *multiple* maxims which are already behavioral regularities; without them, the rule of universalization would, so to speak, have no "grist to grind," nothing to test. Next, and this remark is more novel, there are maxims that successfully pass the test of universalization; these are the very ones that Kant calls duties (in the plural).[39] These duties are not deduced in the logical sense of the term but are derived, to the extent that what could be called the *propositions of meaning* arising from everyday life—bearing insult without seeking vengeance, resisting the temptation to commit suicide out of disgust with life, not giving in to the attractions of false promises, developing one's talents rather than giving in to laziness, giving aid to others, and so on—meet the test of universalization. The plurality of duties results from the fact that it is to the plurality of maxims, themselves responding to a diversity of situations, that the formal rule is applied. A certain productivity of moral judgment is brought to light here.

It is precisely on the path of this productivity that conflict may appear. Kant accords no place to it, because he considers only a single route to be possible in the test of the maxim: the ascending route, subsuming the maxim under a rule. It is along a second route, that of the application to a concrete situation, where the otherness of persons demands to be recognized, that conflict can appear.

On the first path, the moral character of maxims is verified in a two-step test: first the maxim is stated in terms such that one can later ask whether, formulated in this way, it successfully passes the test of universalization. As for the second stage, that of the actual testing, it is strictly limited to the test of contradiction internal to the maxim itself. In the final section of this study, we shall return to this limited use of the Kantian notion of universality.

Let us verify this using the example of false promises, which, in the

---

38. It is, in part, from the perspective of this discussion that I have placed such emphasis, following Bernard Carnois and Otfried Höffe, on the role of maxims in Kantian morality.

39. If this were not so, it would be inconceivable that Kant could write in the *Groundwork:* "We will now enumerate a few duties, following their customary division into duties towards self and duties towards others and into perfect and imperfect duties" (4.421, p. 89). These duties are not "examples" in the precise sense of the term (despite the note in which Kant announces a more complete and better argued discussion in a future *Metaphysics of Morals* [ibid.]). The idea of a morality based on examples was discarded by Kant earlier, if by that we mean, as in popular morality, a direct instruction doing without "pure" principles. In connection with these "examples," Kant speaks a bit later of "deduction" (4.424, pp. 1–92), if indeed *Abteilung*, which we find in the Academy edition, is to be corrected to *Ableitung*).

class of strict duties, illustrates the subclass of duties toward others and so places us at the heart of our problem of the relations between respect and solicitude. Let us follow Kant's argument closely; it consists in a thought experiment in which we imagine the agent reasoning in the following way: "Can the maxim of my action really become a universal law of nature?" (*Groundwork* 4.422, p. 89). The knife falls: a maxim such as this could never "subsist as a system of nature" but would "contradict itself."[40] The contradiction appears, we see, only if the agent has accepted the proposed thought experiment. A contradiction that one could class among the performative contradictions precedes this final test: it consists in the freedom the agent accords himself to make an exception on his own behalf, hence in the refusal really to wish that his maxim would become a universal law (*Groundwork* 4.424, p. 91). In short, the contradiction is that of a will not subject to the test of universalization. It insinuates itself, so to speak, between the rule and the exception and consists in the fact that a rule that admits of exceptions is no longer a rule. One will, however, have noted that in all the examples considered by Kant first in the *Groundwork* and later in the two volumes of the *Metaphysics of Morals,* the sole exception taken into account is that claimed on behalf of the agent by reason of self-love. What about the exception made on behalf of others?

This new question arises only along the second path, the one that Kant did not consider, the path of application to singular situations, where others stand in their irreplaceable singularity. Along this second path the suggestion made in the preceding study can now take on substance, namely that in considering persons as ends in themselves, a new factor is introduced, one that is potentially discordant in relation to the idea of humanity, which is limited to extending universality in plurality to the detriment of otherness.

40. If we follow Kant in his argument, it is difficult to admit that noncontradiction is the sole issue of the refutation: "Everyone in need can make any promises he pleases with the intention not to keep it [which] would make promising, and the very purpose of promising, itself impossible, since no one would believe he was promising anything, but would laugh at utterances of this kind as empty shams" (ibid. 4.422, p. 90). Does the fact of defiance provoked by the promise constitute only an *external* confirmation, involving the consequences of the false promise, with respect to the *internal* contradiction contained in the idea of a promise one has decided not to keep? Noncontradiction is even more difficult to demonstrate in the two "examples" that follow: the duty to become cultivated and the duty to give aid to others; in what way does laziness as a way of life logically contradict the will, assumed to be common to all reasonable beings, to develop their own talents? As for the help owed to one's neighbor in times of difficulty, Kant readily agrees that humankind is not threatened to disappear if one more unfortunate soul is not helped. But then in what way does the maxim enter into contradiction with itself? In truth, the contradiction is apparent only if the agent has made the hypothesis that his maxim were to become a universal law, which he precisely does not do.

Let us return to the argument that condemns false promises: are others really taken into consideration here? This is doubtful. It is striking that the condemnation of suicide and that of false promising, although belonging to two different classes of duties toward others, tend to be confused to the extent that it is humanity that is treated merely as a means, first in ones own person and a second time in the person of others.[41] Perhaps one should go even further: is it not actually personal integrity that is at stake in the so-called duties toward others? Is it not oneself that one despises in giving a false oath?[42] The wrong done to others as other than myself could perhaps not appear along the first path moving from action to maxims and from maxims to the criterion that tests their moral tenor. It could only be visible along the second path, the complement of the first, along the descending path of concretization, of application in the strong sense of the word.[43]

On this second path, the rule is submitted to another sort of test, that of circumstances and consequences. And another sort of exception from the one mentioned above—an exception to the rule in favor of oneself—is proposed; the exception here takes on a different countenance, or rather it becomes a countenance, a face, inasmuch as the genuine otherness of persons makes each one an exception.

The promise then ceases to be connected to the sole concern for personal integrity and enters the space of application of the rule of reciprocity and, more precisely, of the Golden Rule, since the latter takes into account the initial dissymmetry of agent and patient, with all the effects of violence that result from this dissymmetry. Treating others simply as means is al-

41. Based upon this suspicion, one can observe that the case of suicide and that of false promising are treated twice in the *Groundwork:* once under the heading of the first secondary formulation of the categorical imperative, where the analogical idea of *nature* serves as the pivotal point of the argument, and a second time in the wake of the second formulation, where the emphasis is placed on *humanity* as an end in itself. Does not this doublet suggest that the consideration of others as ends in themselves is not essential to the argument? Basically, the idea of humanity, like that of nature, tends to attenuate, if not to annihilate, the otherness of the other.

42. This assertion is central to the response that Kant gives to Benjamin Constant in his brief essay "On an Alleged Right to Lie out of Altruism" (1797), translated by Beck in the 1949 edition of *Kant's Critique of Practical Reason.*

43. One can legitimately wonder whether Kant had not been prevented from considering this second problematic by the fact that it transposes to the practical domain a problematic proper to the theoretical domain, that of the transcendental deduction, and whether the process of purification, separating the a priori from the empirical, does not tend to break the springs of action. In this sense, the question posed by Hegel concerning the actualization of freedom better respects the unity of human action (cf. Charles Taylor, "Hegel's Concept of Action as Unity of Poiesis and Praxis," in *Hegel's Philosophy of Action,* ed. L. S. Stepelvich and D. Lamb [Atlantic Highlands, N.J.: Humanities Press, 1983]).

ready starting to do violence to them. In this regard, the false promise is a figure of the evil of violence in the use of language, on the plane of inter-locution (or of communication). This tie between the promise and the Golden Rule, or the rule of reciprocity, is misconstrued, if one is not care-ful to distinguish the rule holding that one must keep ones promises from the constitutive rule whereby promising is distinguished from other speech acts. The constitutive rule of promising simply says: "*A* places himself under the obligation of doing *X* on behalf of *B* in circumstances *Y*." In saying this, *A* certainly does do something: he commits himself; but keep-ing the promise depends simply on the conditions of *satisfying* the prom-ise, not on the condition of *success*, otherwise the promise would not exist as a determinate speech act. Now by characterizing promises in this way as speech acts, we have not yet posed the moral problem, namely the rea-son why one must keep one's promises. Promising is one thing. Being obligated to keep one's promises is something else again. Let us call the obligation to keep one's promises the principle of fidelity. It is now im-portant to show the dialogic structure of this principle in order to be able to graft upon it the conflicts of duty that we shall mention. This dialogic structure, moreover, is to be analyzed into a dyadic, or dual, structure, involving two persons—the one who promises and the one to whom the former makes the commitment—and a plural structure, involving, pos-sibly, a witness before whom a commitment is made and, then, behind this witness, the institution of language which one pledges to safeguard, even the reference to some social pact in whose name a kind of mutual trust may reign among members of a community prior to any promise. Through this plural structure, the principle of fidelity is indistinguishable from the rule of justice discussed above.[44] This is why we shall confine ourselves here to the dyadic structure where two persons are involved.

It is easy to overlook this dyadic structure of promising; it may be that Kant contributed to this by his treatment of the false promise as an inner contradiction to a maxim in which a person involves only himself or her-self. A truncated phenomenology of commitment tends in the same di-rection.[45] Does not a commitment have all the characteristics of a firm

---

44. We know to what extent unjust institutions can pervert interpersonal relations. When fear and lies are institutionalized, even trust in a friend's word can be subverted. One has to have experienced this series of perversions to discover, through its lack, how mutual trust on the most intimate interpersonal level depends on what Saint Thomas called the "tranquility of order."

45. M. H. Robins, in a carefully argued work—*Promising, Intending, and Moral Au-tonomy* (Cambridge: Cambridge University Press, 1984)—attempts to derive the constrain-ing force of the obligation to keep one's promises from the monologic structure of intention. This structure is seen to cross through three stages, marking the progressive reinforcement

intention? Have we not ourselves made self-constancy through time the highest expression of the identity of *ipse* in contrast to that of *idem,* that is, in opposition to the mere permanence or perseverance of things (a permanence that is found on the plane of selfhood only in character)? There is nothing to repudiate in these analyses. What must be shown, however, is the dialogic-dyadic structure of self-constancy, once it contains a moral significance. The obligation to maintain one's self in keeping one's promises is in danger of solidifying into the Stoic rigidity of simple constancy, if it is not permeated by the desire to respond to an expectation, even to a request coming from another. It is, in truth, at the very first stage, that of firm intention, that the other is implied: a commitment that did not involve doing something that the other could choose or prefer would be no more than a silly wager. And if I nourish the firm purpose of placing self-constancy above the intermittent nature of my desires, disdainful of external obstacles and difficulties, this, as it were, monologic constancy risks confronting the alternative that Gabriel Marcel described in his admirable analysis of availability: "In a sense," he wrote in *Being and Having,*[46] "I cannot be faithful except to my own commitment, that is, it would seem, to myself" (p. 42). But here arises the alternative: "At the moment of my commitment, I either (1) arbitrarily assume a constancy in my feelings which it is not really in my power to establish, or (2) I accept in advance that I shall have to carry out, at a given moment, an action which will in no way reflect my state of mind when I do carry it out. In the first case I am lying to myself, in the second I consent in advance to lie to someone else" (p. 50). How is one to escape this double bind of self-constancy? We know Gabriel Marcel's response: "All commitment is a

---

of the intention. At the lowest level, the firm *intention* to do something can be held to be a virtual promise, in that it posits the identity between two "I" s—the one who promises and the one who will act. An embryo of obligation is therefore contained in self-subsistence through time. To pass to the next stage, it is enough that this self-subsistence become the content aimed at by the intention, so that the moment of obligation stands out. This intention of holding firm, which Robins calls the exclusivity clause, can be termed a *vow:* I place my commitment above external and internal vicissitudes. In doing this, I bind myself, which is already to obligate myself. We then pass to the third stage, that of *obligation* in the strong sense, when the content of the thing to be done governs self-subsistence, despite not only external and internal vicissitudes but also eventual changes of intention. A dialectical relation is then established between the requirement that comes from the thing to be done and the intention that subscribes to it; on the one hand, the requirement seems to be separated off from the intention and to govern it in an extrinsic manner as a mandate, and on the other, this mandate obligates me only to the extent that I make it my concern, my "cause." The tie that binds *me* is the same as that by which *I* bind myself.
46. Gabriel Marcel, *Being and Having: An Existentialist Diary* (Gloucester, Mass.: Peter Smith, 1976).

response" (p. 46). It is to the other that I wish to be faithful. To this fidelity, Gabriel Marcel gives the beautiful name of *disponibilité* (availability,
disposability).[47]

The conceptual network to which the notion of availability belongs
is very far reaching. Through its opposite, unavailability, it approaches
the dialectic of being and having. Availability is the key that opens self-
constancy to the dialogic structure established by the Golden Rule. The
latter, as a rule of reciprocity posited in an initially dissymmetric situation,
establishes the other in the position of someone to whom an obligation is
owed, someone who is counting on me and making self-constancy a response to this expectation. To a large extent, it is not to disappoint or
betray this expectation that I make maintaining my first intention the
theme of a redoubled intention: the intention not to change my intention.
In the forms of promising sanctioned by law—oaths, contracts, and so
on—the expectation of others who count on me becomes, for its part, a
right to require something of me. We have then entered the field of legal
norms, in which the relation between the norm and solicitude is, as it
were, obliterated, erased. One must move back from these forms of promises sanctioned by the courts to those where the tie between the normative
moment and the ethical intention is still perceptible: "From you," says the
other, "I expect that you will keep your word"; to you, I reply: "You can
count on me." This *counting on* connects self-constancy, in its moral tenor,
to the principle of reciprocity founded in solicitude. The principle of being
faithful to one's word as it is given is thus no more than the application of
the rule of reciprocity to the class of actions in which language itself is
involved as the institution governing all the forms of community. Not
keeping one's promise is betraying both the other's expectation and the
institution that mediates the mutual trust of speaking subjects.

This summary analysis of promising emphasizes the caesura so carefully
concealed by Kant between respect for the rule and respect for persons.
This caesura, which will become a gaping tear in the case of the conflicts
we shall mention, was probably not able to appear along the path where
we subsumed actions under maxims and maxims under rules. The tear
cannot help but attract attention, however, once we take the return path
from the maxim, sanctioned by rules, to concrete situations. The possibility of these conflicts is indeed inscribed in the structure of reciprocity belonging to the promise. If fidelity consists in responding to the expectation
of the other who is counting on me, I must take this expectation as the
measure for applying the rule. Another sort of exception is beginning

---

47. Paul Ricoeur, "Entre éthique et ontologie, la disponibilité," in *Actes du Colloque Gabriel Marcel (1988)* (Paris: Bibliothèque Nationale, 1989).

to take shape, one differing from the exception in my favor, namely the exception on behalf of others. Practical wisdom consists in inventing conduct that will best satisfy the exception required by solicitude, by betraying the rule to the smallest extent possible. We shall take two examples, one concerning the "end of life," the other the "beginning of life." The first example is well known under the title of telling the truth to the dying. A breach, indeed, appears to open between two extreme attitudes. Either that of telling the truth without taking into account the capacity of the dying to receive it, out of sheer respect for the law, assumed to abide no exceptions; or that of knowingly lying, out of fear, one believes, of weakening the forces in the patient struggling against death and of transforming the agony of a loved one into torture. Practical wisdom consists here in inventing just behavior suited to the singular nature of the case. But it is not, for all that, simply arbitrary. What practical wisdom most requires in these ambiguous cases is a meditation on the relation between happiness and suffering. "There is no ethics without the idea of a happy life," Peter Kemp aptly recalls in *Éthique et Médecine*. "It remains, however, to situate the role of happiness in ethics" (p. 63). Now Kant, by including in the *Critique of Practical Reason* (Theorem 3), under the single heading of the lower faculty of desiring, all forms of affectivity, shut the door on an investigation admitting differences, one that would decompose the equivocal term "happiness" into the enjoyment of material goods and what Peter Kemp denotes as "a common practice of giving and receiving between free persons" (p. 64). Considered in this way, happiness "no longer comes into absolute contradiction with suffering" (p. 67).[48] It is false to say of this meditation on the relation between suffering and happiness that the concern, at any price, not to "make patients suffer" at the end of their life leads to establishing as a rule the duty to lie to the dying. Never can practical wisdom consent to transforming into a rule the exception to the rule. Even less should one legislate in an area where the responsibility for difficult choices cannot be made easier by laws. In such cases, one must have compassion for those who are morally or physically too weak to hear the truth. In certain other cases, one must know how to communicate this truth: it is one thing to name an illness, it is another to reveal the degree of seriousness and the slight chance of survival, and yet another to wield the clinical truth as a death sentence. But there are also situations, more numerous than is thought, where telling the truth may

48. One also reads in Kemp's book: "happiness, suffering, and anguish before death" (*Éthique et médecine*, pp. 63ff.). One learns that one's own apprenticeship of aging, as well as the respect for the aging of others, is not unrelated to this proper use of solicitude, when it moves in the narrow space where it remains true that there is no ethics without happiness, but where it is false that happiness excludes suffering.

become the opportunity for the exchange of giving and receiving under the sign of death accepted.[49]

In a similar spirit we can approach the problem of the respect for persons at the "beginning of life." The problem, it is true, presents an additional degree of complexity by reason of the ontological considerations posed by the beginning of life that do not arise with the end of life. Considering the embryo and then the human fetus, it is difficult not to ask what sort of beings they are, whether they are neither things nor persons. In a sense, the Kantian position on persons was not without ontological implications, as the celebrated formula reminded us earlier: rational nature exists as an end in itself. In contrast, things, as manipulable, received a different mode of existence, defined precisely by the aptitude to be manipulated. In addition—and this remark will take on its full force later—in this bipolar opposition between persons and things, the distinction between mode of beings remained inseparable from practice, that is, from the manner of treating persons and things. The new question posed by the beginning of life lies elsewhere: what the embryo and the human fetus place in question is the dichotomous character of these ethico-ontological considerations. To complicate matters, it is not only the human embryo in the maternal uterus but the separated embryo, conceived in a test tube, placed in a freezer, available for scientific research that poses the most troublesome questions. As Anne Fagot has written: "There is conflict between the principle of respect due to the human being and the instrumentalization of this being at the embryonic or fetal stages—unless a human embryo is not a human *person?*"[50]

It is necessary to listen to the spokespersons of the opposing theses in order best to determine the point of insertion of practical wisdom. According to the partisans of a biological criterion for the presence or absence of a human person, person and life are indissociable, inasmuch as the latter supports the former: according to this argument, the genetic or genomic heredity that signs biologic individuality is constituted from the moment of conception.[51] In the most moderate form of the so-called bio-

49. The question of aggressive therapy and that of passive—or even active—euthanasia should be dealt with in the same spirit.

50. Anne Fagot and Geneviève Delaisi, "Les Droits de l'embryon," *Revue de métaphysique et de morale,* no. 3 (1987): 361–87.

51. In fact, in the contemporary discussion, the biologic argument serves as a scientific guarantee for a substantialist-type ontological conception, itself bound up with theological considerations regarding the status of the human being as creature. These considerations result, for the most part, from the old debate over the moment when the spiritual soul is infused in the human being. Add to this the fear that the mastery over the phenomena of death and life will establish an all-powerful relation over the human, by which technology

logic thesis, the ethical consequence is the following: the embryo's "right to life" is a right to a "chance to live": when in doubt, one must not risk homicide. This notion of risk, let us admit, makes the "biologic" argument enter into the region of practical wisdom, as we shall state later. And as such it deserves to be heard, when it concludes that any practice that does not serve the presumed ends of the embryo and the fetus, which are to live and to develop, is to be prohibited. One may nevertheless wonder whether practical wisdom, without entirely losing this biologic criterion from sight, must not take into account the phenomena of thresholds and stages that put into question the simple alternative between person and thing. Alone the substantialist ontology that goes along with the biologic argument prevents the formulation of an ontology of development capable of situating prudent judgment in a typically "intermediary" domain. The distinction that we have been proposing throughout these essays between identity as sameness and identity as selfhood should authorize us, if not to ignore the biologic argument, at least to dissociate it from the underlying substantialist ontology.

The opposing thesis calls for comparable remarks: if one attaches the idea of dignity only to fully developed capacities, such as autonomy of willing, only adult, cultivated, "enlightened" individuals are persons. Strictly speaking, "with regard to beings that are below the capacity of 'minimal' autonomy, the community of persons can decide to protect them (as one protects nature), not to respect them (as one respects the autonomy of persons)" (Fagot and Delaisi, "Droits," p. 372). One does not see, then, how respect can be understood in the present debate, if it is not accompanied by a minimum ontology of development that adds to the idea of capacity, belonging to a logic of all or nothing, that of aptitude which admits of degrees of actualization.[52]

---

would transgress its legitimate field of mastery. The same argument, Fagot notes, also has a theological form: God alone is the master of life. In this sense, the biologic criterion rarely operates alone. We are isolating it only for the particular needs of our own investigation: "Behind the rigidity of the principles posited, there is thus a tragic vision of moral life: when man substitutes his decisions for those of nature, he can only do evil" (ibid., p. 370).

52. In reference to the pragmatic (in particular, British) viewpoint, according to which the question of knowing how the embryo is to be treated is itself to be free of any ontological criteria, Fagot observes: "We believe that what is currently sought under the cover of pragmatism is an ethics based on a *progressive* ontology, in accord with the simple and common intuition that the embryonic being is a being in development and that with regard to a living cell, then a five month old fetus, and then a five year old child, our moral obligations cannot be the same" (ibid., p. 377). Here we link up with the notion of "*potential* human person" invoked by the consulting committee on ethics in France and by other commissions of experts elsewhere in the world.

I shall permit myself the suggestion that the hoped-for progressive ontology is perhaps not any more autonomous with respect to ethics than
the criteria of persons and things in Kant. To be sure, the identification of
thresholds and degrees marking the appearance of properties of personal
being is dependent on science alone. But the ontological tenor assigned to
the predicate "potential" in the expression "potential human person" is
perhaps not separable from the manner of "treating" beings corresponding
to these various stages. Manner of being and manner of treating would
seem to be mutually determined in the formation of prudential judgments
occasioned by each advance in the power that technology confers today
on humankind over life in its beginnings. Once again, if science is alone
competent to describe the thresholds of development, the appreciation of
rights and duties relative to each of them belongs to a genuine moral invention that will establish, following a progression comparable to that of
the biologic thresholds, qualitatively different rights: the right not to suffer, the right to protection (this notion itself presenting several degrees of
"force" or "emphasis"), the right to respect, once something like an exchange, even asymmetrical, of preverbal signs is begun between the fetus
and its mother. It is this give-and-take between the description of thresholds and the appraisal of rights and duties, in the intermediary zone between things and persons, that justifies classifying bioethics in the zone
of prudential judgment. Indeed, the differentiated and progressive appreciation of the rights of the embryo, then of the fetus, informed by the
science of development and eventually rooted in an ontology of development, cannot fail to incorporate estimations marked by the same style of
traditionality as cultural heritages, torn out of their dogmatic slumber and
open to innovation. In this complex play between science and wisdom, the
weighing of risks run with regard to future generations cannot help but
temper the audacity encouraged by technological wonders. The fear of the
worst, as Hans Jonas forcefully asserts in his "imperative of responsibility,"[53] is a necessary component of all the forms of long-term responsibility demanded by the technological age. In this sense, reticence, for
example, in the matter of the manipulation of surplus embryos, is not
necessarily solely the concern of unconditional "right-to-lifers" with regard to human embryos. It is part of that practical wisdom required by
conflictual situations resulting from respect itself in an area in which the
dichotomy between persons and things is akimbo.

The kinship between the part of practical wisdom incorporated in bioethics and that we have more easily identified in the sphere of promising
and in the cases of conscience posed at the end of life is evident in the

53. Hans Jonas, *The Imperative of Responsibility: In Search of an Ethics for the Technological
Age* (Chicago: University of Chicago Press, 1984).

presence of the same three features in the various cases considered. First, it is prudent to be sure that the adverse positions call upon the same principle of respect and differ only in the amplitude of the field of application, in particular in the intermediary zone between things and morally developed persons. Second, the search for the "just mean"—Aristotelian *mesotēs*—seems to be good advice, without having the value of a universal principle; in this way, the determination of the period of gestation during which abortion is not a crime demands a highly developed moral sense. Here, it is good to recall that the "just mean" can be something other than a cowardly compromise, that is it may itself be an "extreme."[54] Generally, the most serious moral decisions consist in drawing the dividing line between what is permitted and what is forbidden in zones which themselves are "median" and resistant to familiar dichotomies. The third feature of practical wisdom common to all our examples: moral judgment in situation is all the less arbitrary as the decision maker—whether or not in the position of legislator—has taken the counsel of men and women reputed to be the most competent and the wisest. The conviction that seals decision then benefits from the plural character of the debate. The *phronimos* is not necessarily one individual alone.[55]

In conclusion, one can say that it is to solicitude, concerned with the otherness of persons, including "potential persons," that respect refers, in those cases where it is itself the source of conflicts, in particular in novel situations produced by the powers that technology gives humans over the phenomena of life. But this is not the somewhat "naive" solicitude of the seventh study but a "critical" solicitude that has passed through the double test of the moral conditions of respect and the conflicts generated by the latter. This *critical solicitude* is the form that practical wisdom takes in the region of interpersonal relations.

3. Autonomy and Conflict

Our return route has carried us back to the bastion of morality in the Kantian sense of the term: the affirmation of autonomy, of self-legislation, as the metacritique of morality. Our thesis that it is morality itself which, through the conflicts it generates on the basis of its own presuppositions,

54. "Hence in respect of its substance and the definition which states its essence virtue is a mean, with regard to what is best and right an extreme" (*E.N.* 2.6.1107a6–7). This remarkable text by Aristotle is recalled by Peter Kemp at the end of his lecture "Éthique et technique: bio-éthique," delivered at the Palais de l'Europe in Strasbourg on November 4, 1988.

55. Let us cite Aristotle once more: "Virtue, then, is a state of character concerned with choice, lying in a mean, i.e. the mean relative to us, this being determined by a rational principle, and by that principle by which the man of practical wisdom [*phronimos*] would determine it" (*E.N.* 2.6.1106b36ff.).

refers back to the most original ethical affirmation, finds its final point of application here. It is based upon the specific arguments that have been approached or even anticipated several times in the preceding two sections and that it is now important to make explicit. In various guises, these arguments converge toward a confrontation between the *universalist claim* attached to the rules claiming to belong to the principle of morality and the recognition of positive values belonging to the *historical and communitarian contexts* of the realization of these same rules. My thesis is here that there would be no room for a tragedy of action unless the universalist claim and the contextualist claim had to be maintained each in a place yet to be determined, and unless the practical mediation capable of surmounting the antinomy were entrusted to the practical wisdom of moral judgment in situation.

In order to give the argument its full strength, one must, in my opinion, completely revise Kantian formalism, with the intention not to refute it but to bare the universalist claim that forms its hard core and, in this way, to unleash the full force of the antagonism with which our investigation of moral selfhood will conclude.

This revision will be made in three stages. In the first stage, we must question the order of priority granted by Kant to the principle of autonomy in relation to respect applied to the plurality of persons and to the principle of justice relevant to the plane of institutions. In the preceding study, I took as a working hypothesis the unexpressed presupposition according to which the self of autonomy can and must be preserved from contamination by any sort of egological thesis. Now the entire discussion that precedes—and this is perhaps the major advantage of working backward as we have done in the present study—tends to suggest that the nonegological, nonmonologic, and, if one may say so, predialogic status of the autonomous self can be saved only at the end of a regressive path starting from the idea of justice, crossing through the principle of respect owed to persons in their plurality and in their otherness, in order to reach in fine the principle that states in what way the category of the most disadvantaged has to be taken as the term of reference for all just distribution and in what way the one who receives my action—its potential victim—has to be respected as an equal of the agent I am. There is no doubt that reading backward, which places autonomy at the end and not at the beginning of moral reflection, reverses the order of method conceived in the *Groundwork:* from "form" (unity) to "matter" (multiplicity) and to "complete determination" (totality).[56] Now it is the very sense of

56. The use of the term "method" here is that of Kant in the second section of the *Groundwork* (4.436, p. 104).

autonomy that is affected by this reversal of order that places it at the end of the route. An approach to autonomy through the rule of justice on the plane of institutions and the rule of reciprocity on the interpersonal plane indeed allows the aporias left in suspension at the end of our presentation of the Kantian principle of morality to bear fruit. Three aporetic "places" were carved out, as it were, by the proud affirmation of the principle of autonomy. This was, first, at the time of the discussion of the "fact of reason," the recognition of a certain receptiveness by virtue of which liberty is affected by the very law it gives itself, as though self-positing could not be thought without self-affection. Next, this was the affection by the other tied to respect, understood as motive, by virtue of which the reason of a finite being, in affecting its own sensibility, makes itself an affected reason, in accordance with the opposing modes of humiliation and exaltation. Finally, this was the *radical* affection, radical in the same way as radical evil, following which the will is always already subject to the "propensity" to evil, which, without destroying our predisposition toward the good, affects our capacity to act out of duty.

In what way does the backward approach to autonomy that we are practicing here allow us to reconcile the idea of autonomy with these marks of receptiveness, passivity, and even powerlessness? By showing that an autonomy that is of a piece with the rule of justice and the rule of reciprocity can no longer be a *self-sufficient* autonomy. Dependency as "externality," related to the dialogic condition of autonomy, in a sense takes over from dependency as "interiority" revealed by these three aporias.

From this reinterpretation of the principle of authority results the necessity to rework the opposition between autonomy and heteronomy. Two different ideas are henceforth to be distinguished. The first, the one Kant had in mind in speaking of heteronomy, is indistinguishable from the state of "tutelage" denounced by the pamphlet *What Is the Enlightenment?* This state of tutelage consists in allowing oneself to be under the guidance of others in such a way that one's own judgment depends on the judgment of others; in contrast to this state, autonomy assumes its strong sense, namely the responsibility for one's own judgment. Now Kant did not take into account the fact that this assumption of responsibility goes hand-in-hand with the rule of reciprocity of justice, which places it in precisely the same space of plurality where the state of tutelage reigns (by reason of which autonomy is as much a political principle as a moral principle; it is a political principle moralized by Kant). Autonomy therefore appears to be dependent on heteronomy, but in another sense of "other": the other of freedom in the figure of the law, which freedom nevertheless gives itself; the other of feeling in the figure of respect; the other of evil in the figure of the penchant toward evil. In its turn, this threefold otherness within the self joins the properly dialogic otherness that makes autonomy part and parcel of, and dependent on, the rule of justice and the rule of reciprocity. The very idea of others bifurcates into two opposing directions, corresponding to two figures of the master: one, the dominator, facing the slave; the other, the master of justice, facing the disciple. It is the "heteronomy" of the latter that has to be integrated into autonomy, not to weaken it, but to reinforce Kant's exhortation in *What Is the Enlightenment?: Sapere aude!* Dare to learn, taste, savor for yourself!

At a second stage, one must question the restrictive use Kant makes of the *criterion of universalization,* in relation to which the principle of autonomy plays the role of metacriterion (to borrow Otfried Höffe's vocabulary). This use is restrictive in the sense that, in the thought experiment proposed at the time of the famous "examples," a maxim is declared to be nonmoral if, raised by hypothesis to the level of a universal rule, it proves to be the source of an *internal* contradiction. The maxim, Kant states, then destroys itself.

Reducing the test of universalization in this way to noncontradiction gives us an extraordinarily poor idea of the coherence to which a system of morality can aspire; when one attempts to derive from the highest principle of morality—let us say, from the second categorical imperative—a plurality of duties, the question is no longer whether a maxim considered in isolation does or does not contradict itself but whether the derivation expresses a certain productivity of thought, while preserving the coherence of the whole set of rules. The question we are raising here does not lead us into a purely academic quarrel, for the most significant conflicts that are brought about by morality's claim to universality arise over the duties said to be derived from it while at the same time remaining caught up in the contextual gangue of a historical culture. It is therefore necessary to be clear about the scope and the limit of the coherence of systems of morality.[57]

57. The problem arises within Kantianism itself as soon as one is no longer confined to the analysis of isolated "examples" but looks instead at their mode of derivation. This is sketched out as early as the *Groundwork* and treated explicitly in the *Metaphysics of Morals.* In fact, scant attention has been paid to the model of coherence set out in the *The Metaphysical Principles of Virtue;* instead commentators have dismissed it as tiresome, banal, or old-fashioned. It is true that the double partitioning into strict duties and broad duties, and into duties toward oneself and duties toward others, represents a classification rather than a derivation, which considerably limits the interest of the treatise. Nevertheless, one must give attention to the authentic derivation resulting from the conjunction between end and duty. Everything in the *The Metaphysical Principles of Virtue* rests on the idea of an end that is a duty: "Only an end which is at the same time a duty can be called a *duty of virtue*" (*The Metaphysics of Morals,* pt. 2, *The Metaphysical Principles of Virtue,* trans. James Ellington [New York: Bobbs-Merrill, 1964], p. 40; 6.383). The plurality of duties therefore stems from the

A more constructive conception of coherence is proposed by *judicial reasoning*. In English-language authors, whether they be philosophers of law or of morality, the flexibility and inventiveness afforded by common law are always present.[58]

Let us take the case in which a complaint—for example, a demand for damages based on the legal right to privacy—has not been the object of any previous judicial decision. In this case and in all similar hard cases, the judge will examine the precedents that appear in one way or another to be most relevant; without seeing in this the exemplification of moral institutions comparable to factual evidence, he will treat them as specific instances of a principle that remains to be constructed and which will include precedents as well as new cases, in the name of the responsibility of the judge with respect to the coherence that has prevailed up to then. We can already see dawning the idea of a conflict between the reasonable conviction invested, on one hand, in the precedents and, on the other, in the new case. The judge may, for example, think that it is unjust to punish a murder attempt as harshly as a murder actually committed and yet may still experience some difficulty in making this position agree with his no less well-reasoned feeling that the guilt of the accused resides in the intention rather than in the action considered as something that simply happens. The presupposition is that every conception of justice requires a coherence that is not merely to be preserved but to be constructed. The kinship between this presupposition and the Kantian criterion of universalization is not in doubt, but the "constructive" character of its implementation is very different from canonical Kantian usage: a judicial concept is first derived from a group of related cases, then it is applied to new cases, until an intractable case appears, breaking with the earlier ones, and requiring the construction of a new concept.[59]

---

plurality of ends capable of being derived from the person as an end in himself: These ends are "one's own perfection and the happiness of others" (6.385, p. 43). Here, the moral concept of end in itself, applicable to the person alone, is articulated on teleological concepts, mentioned above, received from the *Critique of Judgment*. From the plurality of these teleological concepts results that of duties: "Therefore, there are many duties of virtue, but only one obligation of virtue. This is so because there are many objects that are ends for us, and it is at the same time our duty to have these ends" (6.410, p. 70). One therefore cannot say that formalism leaves morality empty. The question is whether the multiplicity of duties forms a system: it is here that the modern discussion of the coherence of a moral system commences.

58. Cf. R. Dworkin, *Taking Rights Seriously* (Cambridge: Harvard University Press, 1977), chap. 4, 6, 7.

59. Alan Donagan in *The Theory of Morality* (Chicago: University of Chicago Press, 1977) develops an argument similar to Dworkin's, based in its turn on the works of the great

But can the coherence of a moral system be that of a legal system? The differences are important ones. First of all, the notion of precedent has a very precise sense in the judicial system, where it is a matter of verdicts handed down by the courts of law, verdicts that have the force of law as long as they have not been amended or overturned. Next, these are public agencies that have authority to construct the new coherence required by new cases. Finally, and most especially, the responsibility of the judge with respect to coherence expresses the conviction, shared in the society considered, that coherence matters in the governing of human affairs. From these features proper to judicial systems, it results that they never cover anything more than the region of interactions in which conflicts are open to settlement by the verdict of the courts. The whole question is therefore whether a moral system, which does not have the support of the judicial institution, is capable of establishing its own coherence. Then, too, the coherence of judicial systems refers back to that of the moral system, to the extent that one can ask if the "public viewpoint" which is that of the judge, according to Dworkin, itself has a moral grounding.

The most remarkable effort in this regard is that of Alan Donagan in *The Theory of Morality*. He has undertaken to rework the Kantian enterprise of deriving a plurality of duties from the imperative of respect owed to persons as rational beings, by taking into account the constructivist resources of the judicial model, but by subordinating, like Kant, legality to morality. From Donagan's reconstruction, I shall retain the role he assigns to "additional" or "specificatory" premises, because of the roles they will play in the discussion of the objections posed by *contextualism* to moral universalism. The function of these premises is first to delimit, then to correct, or even to extend the class of actions to which the formal imperative applies. According to Donagan, if the derivation has been performed correctly, one should be able to say: "No action of the kind K, as such, fails to respect any human being as a rational creature" (p. 67). The task of moral philosophy is here to redefine the classes of action in such a way that the content of the rule is adequate to the form of the principle. A rather incontestable example is provided by the case of self-defense: the rule according to which killing is permitted if one is oneself in danger of death, or if there is no other means to protect a third party who is in danger of death, limits the field of application of the prohibition of killing to the class of murder and assassination. The apparent exception to the

---

jurist Edward H. Levi, who characterized as *circular motion* the shuttling back-and-forth between the level where concepts are constructed and the level where new and unforeseen cases are situated (cited in Donagan, *Theory of Morality*, p. 68).

imperative "Thou shall not kill" is then placed under the rule made more precise by the specificatory premise.

It can be conceded to Donagan that it is a legitimate task of moral philosophy to develop as far as possible the reconstruction of the moral system most worthy to make a claim to universality.[60] The coherence of a system such as this denotes three things: first, that formalism does not imply vacuity: one can derive a plurality of duties on the basis of the single imperative that commands that we respect all persons as rational beings.[61] Next, it denotes that these duties, although they cannot be derived from one another, do not generate situations such that in order to obey one, one must disobey another—for example, lying in order not to kill, or killing in order not to lie.[62] Finally, it denotes that the rules of derivation must be such that the contents be in agreement with the immediately superior rule.[63]

It is here that the difference between a moral system and a legal system is confirmed. Instead of precedents already endowed with a legal status, we most often are dealing on the moral plane with unexpressed—and frequently restrictive—"specificatory premises" that mark the intermingling

60. For centuries this was the job of casuistry, which can be held to parallel on the moral plane jurisprudence on the legal plane.

61. Kant, we saw, does this on the basis of the plurality of ends justified by reflective judgment in the spirit of the *Critique of Judgment*.

62. In this precise sense, a conflict of duties is inconceivable *if* the rule considered is truly a duty, that is, if it is correctly derived from the principle. Donagan (*Theory of Morality*, pp. 143ff.) recalls that Saint Thomas denied the possibility of perplexity *simpliciter* (which would correspond to the case where, in order to escape a bad action, it would be necessary to commit another one, equally bad) and admitted only perplexity *secundum quid*, related to meritorious actions having as their condition a prior misdeed. Kant says nothing different: "A conflict of duties (*collisio officiorum s. obligationum*) would be that relationship between duties by virtue of which one would (wholly or partially) cancel the other. Because, however, duty and obligation are in general concepts that express the objective practical necessity of certain actions and because two mutually opposing rules cannot be necessary at the same time, then, if it is a duty to act according to one of them, it is not only a duty but contrary to duty to act according to the other. It follows, therefore, that a conflict of duties and obligations is inconceivable (*obligationes non colliduntur*)" (*Metaphysics of Morals*, vol. 1, *Metaphysical Elements of Justice*, Introduction, 6.224, p. 25). As we see, the argument in Kant is as much logical as moral: "two mutually opposing rules cannot be necessary at the same time."

63. The expression "unformalized analytical reasoning," used by Donagan (*Theory of Morality*, p. 72) to safeguard the relation between moral reasoning and legal reasoning, while it does emphasize the specificity of the former, it designates a problem to be solved as much as an absolutely convincing solution. The author grants that it cannot be a matter here of formal proof, when a system of duties cannot attain the rigor of an axiomatic system. This is why the impossibility of contradiction between multiple duties excluding exceptions cannot be proved formally; one can simply state that all the counterexamples are refutable when the moral system has been rigorously constructed and competently formulated.

of relations of domination and violence, themselves institutionalized, at the heart of moral convictions held to be closest to the Golden Rule. Consequently, besides the procedures of constructive interpretation similar to legal reasoning, moral philosophy has to incorporate a sharp critique of prejudices and ideological residues in its enterprise of reconstructing the specificatory premises capable of assuring the fragile coherence of the moral system. It is here that rationalism unexpectedly crosses paths with tragic wisdom: is it not true that the narrowing affecting the vision of "spiritual greatness" that the two protagonists of Sophocles' *Antigone* are held to serve has as its equivalent, on the plane of moral theory, a perverse use of the "specificatory premises" that have to be unmasked by a critique of ideologies?[64]

It remains that it is the plea for *universality* that gives full weight to the problems tied to the *historicity* of concrete morality.

A third reinterpretation of the Kantian heritage provides us a new occasion to make tragic action appear in the wake of the requirement of universality, identified, in the final analysis, with the moment of morality. I am referring to the reconstruction of formalism by Karl-Otto Apel and Jürgen Habermas on the basis of a morality of communication.[65] My thesis is that this undertaking becomes fully authorized if it is kept along the regressive path of *justification,* thereby leaving uncovered the conflictual zone situated along the progressive path of *actualization.*[66] The paradox is that the concern with justifying the norms of communicative action tends to conceal the conflicts that lead morality back toward a practical wisdom whose place is that of moral judgment in situation. This paradox, in my opinion, explains the heatedness of the controversy provoked by the morality of communication: the advocates of a contextualist and communitarian ethics[67] simply exalt, through overcompensation, the conflicts that are in a certain sense hidden by the morality of communication. I do main-

---

64. It is here that the earlier analyses by Habermas in *Knowledge and Human Interests,* trans. Jeremy J. Shapiro (Boston: Beacon Press, 1971) take on their full force: between discourse, power (in the sense of domination), and possession, the ties are so inextricable that a social therapeutics of the systematic distortions of language has to be added to a simple hermeneutic incapable of curing by its discourse alone the misunderstanding in discourse.

65. K.-O. Apel, *Sur le problème d'une fondation rationnelle de l'éthique à l'âge de la science: L'a priori de la communauté communicationnelle et les fondements de l'éthique,* trans. R. Lellouche and I. Mittmann (Lille: Presses Universitaires de Lille, 1987); Jürgen Habermas, *Moral Consciousness and Communicative Action,* trans. Christian Lenhardt and Shierry Weber Nicholson (Cambridge: MIT Press, 1990); J.-M. Ferry, *Habermas. L'Éthique de la communication* (Paris: PUF, 1987), chap. 10, "Éthique et communauté."

66. On the distinction between the regressive path of justification and the progressive path of actualization, cf. sec. 2 above.

67. M. Walzer, M. Sandel, C. Taylor, and A. MacIntyre.

tain, however, that these conflictual situations would be stripped of their dramatic character if they did not stand out against the backdrop of a demand for universality which today finds its most adequate expression in the morality of communication.

The force of the morality of communication lies fundamentally in the fact that it has merged the three Kantian imperatives into a single problematic: the principle of autonomy following the category of unity, the principle of respect following the category of multiplicity, and the principle of the kingdom of ends following the category of totality. In other words, the self is founded in a single stroke in its dimension of universality and in its dialogic dimension, interpersonal as well as institutional. In the present study, which has no design other than to take into account the moral dimension of selfhood, we shall confine ourselves to those aspects of the ethics of discourse that have to do with this foundation. This is why we shall go straight to the central argument of *Moral Consciousness and Communicative Action,* in the third section of the work.[68] The fact that Habermas's argument is situated on the regressive path of justification and of grounding is amply attested by the order followed in the argument. It begins by establishing the tie between the foundational enterprise and the "claims to validity raised in norm-related (or regulative) speech acts" (p. 44). Next, it justifies the recourse to formal pragmatics in order to elicit the claims to validity. And finally the question is posed which Habermas holds to be fundamental, namely: "How can we justify the principle of universalization itself, which alone enables us to reach agreement through argumentation on practical questions?" (p. 44). It is this final question that is of interest to us. We hold as given, therefore, on the one hand, the recognition of a tie between normative expectations and communicative action,[69] and on the other hand, the recognition of the tie between normative expectations and validation by *reasons.* Having said this, the important thing for us resides in the transformation undergone by the requirement of coherence following its connection to a theory of *argumentation,* one reducible neither to deductive reasoning nor to empirical proof. The logic of practical discourse holds the place here that was held in the preceding pages by the analysis of the conditions of coherence in moral systems; whereas this analysis was conducted without any concern for the dialogic dimension of the principle of morality, in Apel and in Habermas the theory of argumentation unfolds entirely within the frame-

68. "Discourse Ethics [*Diskursethik*]: Notes on a Program of Philosophical Justification," *Moral Consciousness and Communicative Action,* pp. 43–115.

69. "I call interactions *communicative* when the participants coordinate their plans of action consentually, with the agreement reached at any point being evaluated in terms of the intersubjective recognition of validity claims" (p. 58).

work of communicative action.[70] Habermas by no means denies that the conflicts of daily life provoke the normative expectations contained in the logic of practical discourse.[71] This very concern with the arguments actually put forth by the various participants distances Habermas from the Rawlsian fiction of an original situation and from the fable of a hypothetical contract (p. 66). Practical discourse is a *real* discourse.[72] It is, therefore, not the historical conditions of the actualization of practical discourse that Habermas considers but the foundation in reason of the principle of universalization underlying discourse ethics. What pushes him, following Apel, in this direction are the objections that the skeptic opposes to the very idea of a moral agreement produced by means of argumentation. It is in connection with these objections that recourse is made to the pragmatic presuppositions of argumentation in general in order to ground in reason the argumentative rules of practical discourse. The effort intervenes precisely at the point where Kant stops when he states as a "fact of reason" the consciousness we have of the self-legislative character of freedom. In Karl-Otto Apel, this is nothing less than an "ultimate foundation" (*letze Begrundung*). The latter calls upon the idea, inaccessible to Kant, of *performative contradiction,* which enables us to save the self-referentiality proper to transcendental argumentation from the well-known accusation of infinite regress or an arbitrary interruption in the chain of discourse, or of circular reasoning. *Transcendental pragmatics* repeats, in the practical field, the Kantian transcendental deduction by showing how the principle of universalization, acting as a rule of argumentation, is implicit in the presuppositions of argumentation in general. The presupposition of an "unlimited community of communication" has no role other than to state, on the level of presuppositions, the perfect congruence between the autonomy of judgment of each person and the expectation of consensus of all the persons involved in practical discourse.

I shall not enter into the open discussion between Habermas and Apel concerning this claim of a final foundation, an ultimate stage along the regressive path, whose counterpart we shall turn to in a moment—the

---

70. Applied to moral norms, Hare's consistency postulate comes to this: every individual, before making a particular norm a basis for his moral judgment, should test whether he can advocate or 'will' the adoption of this norm by every other individual in a comparable situation" (ibid., p. 64).

71. "By entering into a process of moral argumentation, the participants continue their communicative action in a reflexive attitude with the aim of restoring a consensus that has been disrupted. Moral argumentation thus serves to settle conflicts of action by consental means" (ibid., p. 67).

72. "In the process one will cite to another the *reasons* he has for willing that an action be declared socially binding. Each member must be convinced that the proposed norm is equally good for all. And this process is what we call practical discourse" (ibid., p. 71).

progressive path leading from the norm to its actualization. Let us simply note that Apel's ambition extends further than does Habermas's, for whom the very idea of ultimate foundation puts back into question the shift of paradigm by which a philosophy of language has taken over from a philosophy of consciousness. The recourse to performative contradiction, for Habermas, denotes nothing more than an admission that there exists no principle of replacement within the framework of argumentative practice, without this transcendental presupposition standing as a final justification.[73] I shall confine myself to stating that it is precisely by renouncing the idea of an ultimate foundation (which hermeneutics will confirm by its insistence on the finiteness of justification) that we are invited to follow the inverse path from that of justification. If indeed we admit along with Habermas himself that "the *moral* intuitions of everyday life are not in need of clarification by the philosopher" and that the foundational enterprise has, in the final analysis, only a therapeutic function, in the sense of Wittgenstein, with regard to skeptical counterarguments set up as "professional ideologies" (p. 98)—then the ethics of discussion will not simply involve an attempt to found the requirement of universalization along a regressive path but will also involve an examination along a progressive path on the level of actual practice.[74]

∗

The sole ambition of the preceding pages was to carry the requirement of universality to its highest level of credibility and, in conjunction with this, to carry to an equivalent level the objections arising from the *contextual* character of the realizations of the ethics of discourse. As we have repeatedly affirmed, the conflicts that give weight to the contextualist theses are encountered along the path of actualization rather than along that of justification. It is important to be clear about this difference of site so as not to confuse the arguments that stress the historical character of choices to be made along the second path with the skeptical arguments that are ad-

73. "No harm is done," Habermas states, "if we deny that the transcendental-pragmatic justification constitutes an ultimate justification" (ibid., p. 98). This reticence explains why Habermas is prepared to seek a "maieutic method" (p. 97) conforming to the theory of the development of moral and legal conscience propounded by Lawrence Kohlberg. The support drawn from a developmental psychosociology will not fail to have an effect on the discussion that follows, inasmuch as the developmental model proposed by Kohlberg rests on the progress from the preconventional to the conventional, and finally to the postconventional, the final stage corresponding to Kantian autonomy. Later, I shall state some drawbacks attaching to this "control" method.

74. This reversal of perspective continues to be encouraged by the objection raised by Habermas to Rawls regarding the substitution of an argument conducted in an original hypothetical situation for the real arguments conducted among the persons involved.

dressed to the foundational enterprise. This remark is of the greatest importance for any discussion of the universalist thesis that we hold to be exemplary, namely that of Habermas's discourse ethics.

The arguments that we shall consider under the heading of contextualism are not new conflicts as to their content. These are the very ones we encountered in our discussion of the conditions for the actualization of the rule of justice, then those of the rule of reciprocity. But while we have stressed up to now the equivocalness, even the undecidability, of the situations that moral judgment must come to grips with, we must now take into account the historically and culturally determined character of the estimations among which historical judgment has to find its orientation.

Let me recall the first occurrence of this dilemma: it was at the time of the strictly procedural interpretation of the principles of justice in Rawls—an interpretation that justified casting any teleological consideration back to the private consciousness of the parties in the social contract. The concept of the just could in this way be entirely detached from that of the good. Now with the idea of primary social goods—an idea inseparable from that of distribution—teleological principles stormed back in force, to the point of shattering the unitary idea of justice into a plurality of spheres of justice, related to the diversity of the *estimations* that govern the meaning attached to the goods considered (citizenship, needs, merchandise, positions of responsibility or authority, and so on). We then postponed until now any consideration of the problem posed by the historical and communitary nature of these meanings and estimations in order to focus our attention on the problem posed by the real diversity of the goods concerned. This historical and communitarian character can now be brought to the forefront. This concerns not only the meaning that each of these needs, taken separately, may possess in a given culture but also the order of priority established in each case among the spheres of justice and the diverse and potentially rival goods that correspond to them. In this sense, every distribution, in the broad sense that we have attributed to this word, appears problematic: in fact, there is no system of distribution that is universally valid; all known systems express revocable, chance choices, bound up with the struggles that mark the violent history of societies.

It is therefore not surprising that the same historicity affects all the levels of political practice, inasmuch as the latter has at stake no less than the distribution of power on which depends the priority assigned in each case among the goods to be distributed. From one level of political practice to another—from that of institutionalized political debate in pluralist democracies to that of discussion about the ends of good government (security, prosperity, equality, solidarity, and so on), and finally to the level of the legitimation of democracy itself—a growing indetermination of the ends to be pursued has appeared. This is what now leads us to stress the historicity of the choices by which societies make decisions in the face of this accumulation of perplexities.[75]

Passing from the political sphere to that of interpersonal relations, new sources of conflict have appeared, stemming principally from the split between respect for the law and respect for persons. In this new framework, it was the real plurality of persons rather than that of goods that posed a problem, the otherness of persons opposing the unitary aspect of the concept of humanity. At that time we stressed several particularly painful matters of conscience, those touching the "end of life" and those concerned with the "beginning of life" in the age of technology. Now these same matters of conscience can be reformulated in terms of conflicts between the requirement of universality, tied to the principle of the respect owed to persons *as rational beings,* and the stumbling search for solutions—which can, in this sense, be termed historical—posed by the treatment of beings that no longer satisfy or do not yet satisfy the explicit criterion of humanity, upon which respect is founded.[76]

In this way, all the discussions conducted in the first and second sections of this study find an echo and the focal point of their reflection, as it were, in the conflict between universalism and contextualism. There is nothing unexpected in this connection, to the extent that the demand for universalization, related to the principle of autonomy that in the final analysis defines moral selfhood, finds its privileged field of manifestation in interpersonal relations governed by the principle of respect owed to persons and in institutions governed by the rule of justice.

By reformulating as a dilemma between universalism and contextualism the conflicts provoked by a procedural conception of justice and by an abstract conception of humanity common to all persons, we have paved the way for a discussion centered on the ethics of argumentation.

It can be maintained that all the problems mentioned can find a solution through an ethics of argumentation inasmuch as the latter belongs to a higher rank than that of the rule of justice and the rule of respect, the limits of their application having been made apparent by the conflicts de-

75. We recall here Claude Lefort's characterization of democracy as the "historical society *par excellence*" (see n. 34 above).

76. Although the discussion of these matters of conscience touches the very heart of person-to-person relations, it also overlaps with the preceding discussion concerning political practice, inasmuch as discussions on the interpersonal level often call for a juridical framework (concerning, for example, whether or not to decriminalize abortion), but also for a political one (even if this is only from the viewpoint of allocating public funds to institutions of research, social protection, or hospital services).

picted above. Does not the adjudication of shares—of whatever sort—result ultimately from the confrontation of arguments, not only those of the original situation of the Rawlsian fable, but those of real discussions, the upshot of which will be the just distribution of whatever is in question? We shall add: the more a conception of justice wants to be strictly procedural, the more it defers to an argumentative ethics to resolve the conflicts it engenders. Is not the situation identical for the matters of conscience produced by the principle of respect owed to persons as rational beings? For example, does not the recourse made to a developmental ontology to decide the question whether a fetus is a person, a thing, or an intermediary entity amount to the search for the best argument in the debate concerning the rights of the fetus? And does not this search retain a meaning outside of the presupposition of the universalist requisites that justify the ethics of argumentation?

I recognize the force of this thesis, and I am willing to adopt it up to a certain point, which I shall make clear in a moment, in opposition to a use, in my opinion disastrous, of the contextualist objections drawn from the observation of the way in which the conflicts in different historical communities are dealt with and resolved. In our days we see these objections attributed to the claim that "cultures" are ultimately multiple, and the term "culture" being taken in an ethnographic sense far removed from that of instruction in the ways of reason and liberty coming from the Enlightenment and strengthened by Hegel. One thus ends us with an apology of difference for the sake of difference, which, finally, makes all differences indifferent, to the extent that it makes all discussion useless.[77]

What I am criticizing in the ethics of argumentation is not the invitation to look for the best argument in all circumstances and in all discussions but the reconstruction under the title of a strategy of *purification*, taken from Kant, that makes impossible the contextual mediation without which the ethics of communication loses its actual hold on reality. Kant directed his strategy of purification against inclination, the search for pleasure or happiness (lumping all affective modalities together). Habermas directs his against everything that can be placed under the title of *convention*.[78] I attribute the rigorousness of the argumentation to an interpreta-

---

77. I am concurring here with the fears expressed by Alain Finkielkraut in *La Défaite de la pensée* (Paris: Gallimard, 1987).

78. In this regard, the recourse to L. Kohlberg's model of developmental psychosociology reinforces the antinomy between argumentation and convention, to the extent that the scale of development is marked by preconventional, conventional, and postconventional stages. Thus it is amusing to observe that, following this model, the Golden Rule, belongs to the conventional model and the rule of justice does not reach the higher level of the postconventional stage.

tion of modernity almost exclusively in terms of breaking with a past thought to be frozen in traditions subservient to the principle of authority and so, by principle, out of the reach of public discussion. This explains why, in an ethics of argumentation, convention comes to occupy the place held by inclination in Kant. In this manner, the ethics of argumentation contributes to the impasse of a sterile opposition between a universalism at least as procedural as that of Rawls and Dworkin and a "cultural" relativism that places itself outside the field of discussion.[79]

At the end of this long journey, I should like to suggest a reformulation of the ethics of argumentation that will allow it to integrate the objections of contextualism, while allowing the latter, at the same time, to take seriously the requirement of universalization in order to focus on the conditions for placing this requirement in context (it is for this last reason that I prefer to use the term "contextualism" rather than "historicism" of "communitarianism").

What has to be questioned is the antagonism between argumentation and convention, substituting for it a subtle dialectic between *argumentation* and *conviction,* which has no theoretical outcome but only the practical outcome of the arbitration of moral judgment in situation.

In order to enter into this difficult dialectic it is good to recall that argumentation, considered along the path of actualization, is a language game, which, hypostatized, ceases to correspond to any form of life, if not to the professionalization for which Habermas himself reproaches the advocates of the skeptical objections along the regressive path of the justification of the ethics of argumentation. In real discussions, argumentation in its codified, stylized, even institutionalized form is but an abstract segment in a language process that involves a great number of language

79. The same observation can be made about Habermas's continually pejorative use of the idea of tradition, following his long-standing confrontation with Gadamer. Elsewhere, I suggested distinguishing three uses of the word "tradition": the *style* of traditionality, innovation being one of its somewhat antagonistic components; the *traditions* of a people, a culture, a community, which can be living or dead; and the *Tradition,* as an anti-argumentative authority. It is only in the last sense that the antitraditionalist crusade of the ethics of argumentation is acceptable. We touch here, as in connection with the idea of convention, on a sensitive point of the ethics of argumentation, namely its tendency to overevaluate the break of modernity, to confirm secularization not only as a fact but as a value, to the point of excluding from the field of discussion, either tacitly or openly, anyone who does not accept as a prior given the Nietzschean profession of the "death of God." Only, one forgets that, under the heading of the Enlightenment, one can denote at times a style of traditionality that Koselleck has well described in terms of the categories of space of experience and horizon of expectation (cf. *Time and Narrative* 3: 208–16); at times a tradition or a group of traditions with their strongly marked cultural backdrops, as Hegel already deals with in chap. 6 of the *Phenomenology of Spirit;* and at others, an anti-Tradition, which the apology of the Enlightenment actually became after Nietzsche.

games, which themselves also have a relation to the ethical choices made
in perplexing cases. We turn, for example, to narratives, to life histories,
that produce, according to the case, admiration, even veneration, or disgust, even repulsion, or more simply curiosity for the thought experiments
in which novel types of life are explored in the mode of fiction.[80] These
language games constitute as many communicative practices in which humans learn what is meant by wanting to live together, on a level prior to
any argumentative formulation. To be sure, argumentation is not a language game like others, precisely by reason of its requirement of universalization. But this requirement becomes operative only if it assumes the
mediation of other language games that participate in the formation of
options that are the stakes of the debate. The intended goal is then to
extract from the positions in confrontation the best argument that can be
offered to the protagonists in the discussion. But this corrective action of
the ethics of argumentation presupposes that the discussion is about something, about the "things of life."[81]

And why must argumentation accept the mediation of other language
games and assume a corrective role with respect to their potential for argumentation? Precisely because argumentation is not simply posited as the
antagonist of tradition and convention, but as the critical agency operating
at the heart of convictions, argumentation assuming the task not of eliminating but of carrying them to the level of "considered convictions," in
what Rawls calls a *reflective equilibrium.*

It is just such a reflective equilibrium between the requirement of universality and the recognition of the contextual limitations affecting it that
is the final issue in the judgment in situation within the framework of the
conflicts mentioned above.

What makes conviction an inescapable party here is the fact that it expresses the positions from which result the meanings, interpretations, and
evaluations relating to the multiple goods that occupy the scale of praxis,
from practices and their immanent goods, passing by way of life plans, life
histories, and including the conceptions humans have, alone or together,
of what a complete life would be. For, finally, what do we discuss, even on
the level of political practice, where the goods concerned transcend the
goods immanent in various practices—for example, in the debate over the
ends of good government or the legitimacy of democracy—yes, what do
we discuss, if not the best way for each party in the great debate to aim,
beyond institutional mediations, at a complete life with and for others

---

80. On the relation between narrativity and ethics, cf. above sixth study, sec. 3.
81. Cf. Rüdiger Bubner, "Moralité et *Sittlichkeit*—sur l'origine d'une opposition," *Revue
internationale de philosophie*, no. 3, 1988, *Kant et la raison pratique*, pp. 341–60.

in just institutions? The articulations that we never cease to reinforce between deontology and teleology finds its highest—and most fragile—expression in *the reflective equilibrium between the ethics of argumentation and considered convictions.*[82]

An example of this subtle dialectic is provided by the current discussion of human rights. Basically, these rights, taken on the level of declarative and not properly legislative texts, can be held to be well-argued derivatives of the very ethics of argumentation. They have been ratified by just about every state; and yet the suspicion remains that they are simply the fruit of the cultural history belonging to the West, with its wars of religion, its laborious and unending apprenticeship of tolerance. It is as though universalism and contextualism overlapped imperfectly on a small number of fundamental values, such as those we read in the universal declaration of the rights of man and of the citizen. But what about the precise legislation that guarantees the exercise of these rights? This legislation is indeed the product of a singular history that is broadly that of Western democracies. And to the extent that the values produced in this history are not shared by other cultures, the accusation of ethnocentrism is shifted toward the declarative texts themselves, which have nevertheless been ratified by all the governments on this planet. One must, in my opinion, reject this drift and assume the following paradox: on the one hand, one must maintain the universal claim attached to a few values where the universal and the historical intersect, and on the other hand, one must submit this claim to discussion, not on a formal level, but on the level of the convictions incorporated in concrete forms of life. Nothing can result from this discussion unless every party recognizes that other potential universals are contained in so-called exotic cultures. The path of eventual consensus can emerge only from mutual recognition on the level of acceptability, that is, by admitting a possible truth, admitting proposals of meaning that are at first foreign to us.

This notion of universals in context or of potential or inchoate universals is, in my opinion, the notion that best accounts for the reflective equilibrium that we are seeking between universality and historicity.[83] Only a

82. I like to recall that, in German, conviction is rendered *Überzeugung*, a term related by its root to *Bezeugung*, which signifies "attestation"—the password for this entire book.
83. The term "value," one we have not used until now, corresponds in public discussion to those inchoate universals whose genuine moral tenor will be established only by the subsequent history of the dialogue between cultures. In this sense, I hold the quasiconcept of value to be a compromise term, at the point of intersection of the claim to universality and the admission of the historicity of certain derivative duties to which corresponds the right of others to make claims on us. In this sense, the notion of value is not a genuine moral concept but a compromise concept, justified by the cases in which universality and historicity provide

real discussion, in which convictions are permitted to be elevated above conventions, will be able to state, at the end of a long history yet to come, which alleged universals will become universals recognized by "all the persons concerned" (Habermas), that is, by the "representative persons" (Rawls) of all cultures. In this regard, one of the faces of practical wisdom that we are tracking throughout this study is the art of conversation, in which the ethics of argumentation is put to the test in the conflict of convictions.

✳

Our final word in this "little ethics" that covers the seventh, eighth and ninth studies will be to suggest that the practical wisdom we are seeking aims at reconciling Aristotle's *phronēsis,* by way of Kant's *Moralität,* with Hegel's *Sittlichkeit.* Of *phronēsis* we retain the fact that its horizon is the "good life," its mediation deliberation, its actor the *phronimos,* and its place of application singular situations.[84] But if at the end of these three studies the cycle appears to be complete, it is at another altitude, so to speak, that we now move, situated above our starting point: between the "naive" *phronēsis* of our first pages (seventh study) and the "critical" *phronēsis* of our final pages extends, first, the region of moral obligation, of duty (eighth study), wherein lies the demand that what ought not to be not be (namely, evil) and, more particularly, the demand that the suffering inflicted on humans by other human beings be abolished; and beyond this arid zone, extends the region of conflicts belonging to tragic action (ninth study). In this way, "critical" *phronēsis* tends, through these mediations, to be identified with *Sittlichkeit.* The latter, however, has been stripped of its pretention to mark the victory of Spirit over the contradictions that it itself provokes. Reduced to modesty, *Sittlichkeit* now joins *phronēsis* in moral judgment in situation. In return, because it has crossed through so many mediations and so many conflicts, the *phronēsis* of moral judgment in situation is saved from any temptation of anomie. It is through public debate, friendly discussion, and shared convictions that moral judgment

---

mutual comfort to one another, rather than separating off from one another: the condemnation of torture, of xenophobia, of racism, of the sexual exploitation of children or nonconsenting adults, etc. It was already in this partly transcendental, partly empirical—partly a priori, partly historical—sense that Jean Nabert used the term "value" in his *Elements for an Ethic,* trans. William J. Petrek (Evanston, Ill.: Northwestern University Press, 1969), chap. 7, "Ascesis through Goals," 100–114.

84. I should like to recall the great texts of book 6 of the *Nichomachean Ethics* quoted above in sec. 1 of the seventh study. At the apex of all these texts, I place the statement that identifies *phronēsis* with moral judgment in situation, by reason of its singularizing function, comparable to that of sensible intuition (*E.N.* 6.11.1143a25–b13).

in situation is formed. Concerning the practical wisdom suited to this judgment, one can say that *Sittlichkeit* "repeats" *phronēsis* here, to the extent that *Sittlichkeit* "mediates" *phronēsis*.

✳

At the end of the seventh, eighth and ninth studies it is important to designate the new determinations of the self that have been added to that of the self as the speaking, acting, character-narrator of its own history. Since, in addition, these studies complete the hermeneutical-phenomenological cycle formed by the nine studies that find their completion here, it seems appropriate to take as a guide the three fundamental problematics stated at the beginning of the Introduction: the detour of the reflection on "who?" by the analysis of "what? why? how?"; concordance and discordance between *idem*-identity and *ipse*-identity; the dialectic of the self and the other than self.

The first four studies gave priority to the first problematic, the following two to the second, and now our ethicomoral studies have placed their main emphasis on the third problematic. Nevertheless, a rereading of these studies authorizes us to state that they have allowed the three problematics to progress together. This is what I shall now show by selecting for each of them an emblematic term borrowed from ancient and modern moral philosophy, one which our investigations perhaps have enabled us to enrich and to clarify.

To the first problematic, in fact, belongs the entire detour through the determinations of the predicates "good" and "obligatory," whose articulations punctuate the course of these three studies. This detour corresponds to that by way of the structures of action and of the narrative in the earlier studies; the predicates "good" and "obligatory" are, in fact, first applied to *actions* as completed or to be done. We began the movement of returning to the self by making the estimation of the aims of action correspond to the esteem of a self capable of hierarchizing its preferences and of acting knowledgeably. There lacked, however, a term to mark the correlation between the ethical and moral evaluation of action and the increasingly complex forms of self-esteem in the course of the developments following the first section of the seventh study, where the notion of self-esteem was developed. The classical term of *imputability* appeared to me to respond to this request, at the price of a reactualization suggested by our investigations.[85] The advantage of choosing this term is that it allows us to return to the analysis of the notion of *ascription* just where we left it

---

85. We first encountered this notion in the framework of the discussion of the third cosmological antimony in the fourth study above, in the third part of sec 2.

at the end of the fourth study, which, as we recall, took an aporetic turn. Imputability, we shall say, is the ascription of action to its agent, *under the condition of ethical and moral predicates* which characterize the action as good, just, conforming to duty, done out of duty, and, finally, as being the wisest in the case of conflictual situations.

The fact that imputability is placed in the extension of ascription is what is presupposed in definitions like that of the *Vocabulaire technique et critique de la philosophie,* published in the past by A. Lalande: "*Imputable,* we read there, originally signifies: that which can be attributed to [put to the account of] a given person." What alone is held to characterize imputability is "the relation of the act to the agent, abstracting, on the one hand, from moral value and, on the other, from the rewards, punishments, profits or damages that may ensue." [86] In fact, this definition adds nothing to what we termed "ascription" and which concerned the specific causation of the agent of action. One understands, to be sure, the concern of the authors of this definition, namely not to confuse *imputing* and *incriminating*. [87] The opposite risk would be assumed by a definition of imputability based upon the distinction proposed by Alan Donagan between two sorts of moral precepts: [88] the precepts he terms first-order precepts, relating to human actions considered as deeds, and the second-order precepts, relating to the state of mind of the agents. Whereas the former are defined in relation to the opposition permissible-impermissible, the latter are defined in relation to the opposition culpable-inculpable. [89] Both, however, claim

---

86. A. Lalande, *Vocabulaire technique et critique de la philosophie* (Paris: PUF, 1960), p. 484.

87. I am leaving aside for the moment the notion of *compte* in the expression *porter au compte* (assign, attribute); I shall return to this in the context of the second problematic, that of selfhood and sameness.

88. Donagan, *Theory of Morality,* chap. 4.

89. The fact that these two sorts of precepts do not overlap is confirmed by the cases in which the impermissible does not involve culpability; this is the case in which excuses, previously defined and recognized, contribute to attenuating or canceling the judgment by which the agent is declared to be culpable. Inversely, the intention of an agent can be condemned as culpable when no actual violation of a rule has been committed, some obstacle having prevented the deliberate intention to commit a bad act from being realized. We catch a glimpse of the wealth of analyses that this distinction between first- and second-order precepts holds. Aristotle had opened the way for this most legitimate casuistry by introducing the clause of *ignorance* as capable of allowing us to hold as involuntary (or performed in spite of oneself) certain actions that, nevertheless, were chosen after due deliberation (*E.N.* 3.2). If this involves casuistry, it is because one has to distinguish between ignorance about facts (the son did not know that the man he struck was his father) and ignorance about right (he did not know it was wrong to dishonor his father). Now if ignorance of the right only with difficulty constitutes an excuse, ignorance of the facts is not always accepted as an excuse either: the agent perhaps did not want to know, or avoided informing himself, when he

universality. A definition of imputability can result from this distinction between "objective" and "subjective" precepts; its function would be to coordinate the categories of permissible-impermissible and of culpable-inculpable. Imputing would not only be placing an action under someone's responsibility but would moreover be placing an *action,* as that which can come under the category permissible-impermissible, under the responsibility of *someone* who can be deemed culpable-inculpable. This manner of inscribing in the definition of imputability the distinction between the two sorts of precepts, by stressing the subordination of second-order precepts to first-order ones, is reflected in more popular definitions that refer to blame and to praise [90]—expressions that combine (and in the eyes of the analyst, confuse) the two orders of precepts: permissible-impermissible for actions, culpable-inculpable for agents.

There is something correct, in my opinion, in the concern with dissociating imputability from incrimination—and also in the apparently opposite concern with referring to blame and to praise. The distinction I am making between the ethical plane and the moral plane opens the way for a definition that would allow for both concerns. Donagan's precepts belong, indeed, to a theory of morality that is unaware of the distinction that guides our three ethicomoral studies: thus the Golden Rule is reinterpreted there in terms of the Kantian imperative.

If our distinction is accepted, then the formative core of the concept of imputation must be assigned to the most profound ethical level. We are thus sent back to self-esteem, but as mediated by the entire course of determinations of the just, the good, the mandatory, procedural justice, and, finally, moral judgment in situation. To whom then is an action imputable? To the self, as capable of passing through the entire course of the ethicomoral determinations of action, a course at the end of which self-esteem becomes conviction. In conviction we encounter Donagan's first- and second-order precepts, that is, the ethicomoral objectivities of action and the subjectivity of the agent, which turns back upon the self starting from, and passing through, these objectivities. It is at this price that imputation can

---

could have, etc. The idea of culpable negligence is of great importance in this type of debate, as has been resoundingly echoed by the tragic events of World War II.

90. In the *Robert* dictionary, at the word *imputation,* we find: "1. Action, fact of imputing, of attributing to someone (a blameworthy action, a mistake . . .)" (p. 448). At the word *imputer,* it proposes: "I. *Imputer à:* place (something) under the responsibility of someone; 1. Attribute (to someone) something blameworthy; 2. Classical language: Generally: Attribute (to someone) something praiseworthy, favorable" (p. 449). Aristotle does not fail to refer to blame and to praise in an ethical perspective in which the evaluation of actions is governed by recognized "excellences" in the order of human action.

be held to be the ethicomoral expression of the ascription of an action to an agent, without having to make incrimination the canonical form of imputability. It is enough that action and its agent appear conjointly liable to praise and to blame. But in a certain way it is praise that wins out over blame in self-esteem.

Let us now place our ethicomoral considerations back into the perspective of the second problematic, in which the notion of the self is involved in the conflictual relation between selfhood and sameness. Here the concept of *responsibility*—more recent, it appears, than that of imputability (at least in moral philosophy)—will serve as our point of reference, while it too receives further enrichment and greater preciseness as a result of our analyses. Let us start from what was at stake in the study on narrative identity, namely that component of identity that has to do with time, under the guise of permanence in time. We saw two acceptations of this category confront one another on the plane of narrative, depending on whether self-constancy or empirical perseverance overlapped or were separate. It is the same dialectic that the notion of responsibility assumes and carries one step further.

To show this, let us set out the relations between responsibility and temporality in the three directions that temporality implies. It is in the third direction that the relation between selfhood and sameness reveals its extreme complexity.

From the angle of the *future,* our reflection most easily fits in with that of common sense. Following one of its commonplace meanings, responsibility implies that someone assumes the consequences of her actions, that is, holds certain events to come as delegates of herself, despite the fact that they have not been expressly foreseen and intended. These events are her work, in spite of herself. This meaning has taken shape, on the one hand, within the framework of civil law, with respect to the obligation to repair the damages that one has caused by one's fault (or in certain other cases determined by law: responsibility, for example, of the owner or keeper of an animal), and on the other hand, within the framework of penal law, with respect to the obligation to suffer punishment. This double priority of law in the use of the concept of responsibility does not prevent us from attaching a moral, and not simply legal, sense to the idea of accepting or suffering the consequences of one's own acts, to an extent that cannot be determined in advance. On this basis Hans Jonas attempted to reconstruct the "principle of responsibility"[91] by taking into consideration the long-term consequences of the decisions of public powers and of citizens in the age of technology. He thinks in this way he can cause a revolution in our

91. Jonas, *Imperative of Responsibility.*

concept of responsibility, by raising it to the rank of a new categorical imperative, that of acting in such a way that a future humanity will still exist after us, in the environment of a habitable earth. This is indeed a revolution, inasmuch as, by emphasizing the consequences of our actions, the moralist directs our gaze in the opposite direction from that of the search for the most deeply hidden intentions, as the notion of imputability prompts us to do. The consequence is paradoxical: with imputability, there can be guilt without realization, without actualization; with responsibility, there can be guilt without intention; the bearing of our acts, a concept we evoked above, extends beyond that of our projects.

The notion of responsibility, however, also has a side turned toward the *past,* inasmuch as it implies that we assume a past that affects us without its being entirely our own work but that we take on as ours. The idea of a debt, which held a large place in some of my reflections in *Time and Narrative* 3, belongs to this retrospective dimension of responsibility. It will be developed in the tenth study in the context of a reflection on passivity and otherness. Let us say now that recognizing one's own indebtedness with respect to that which has made one what one is, is to hold oneself responsible.

These two acceptations of responsibility, prospective and retrospective, join together and overlap in responsibility in the *present.* But this present is not the instant as a break, the point-instant of chronological time. It has the thickness that the dialectic of selfhood and sameness gives it, in connection with permanence in time. Holding oneself responsible is, in a manner that remains to be specified, accepting to be held to be the same today as the one who acted yesterday and who will act tomorrow. As in the case of narrative identity, upon which moral identity is based, the two meanings of identity enter into competition: on the one hand, a certain physical or psychological continuity, hence a certain sameness, with which we earlier identified character, underlies the recognition of moral identity, in particular in the cases of responsibility that concern civil law and penal law. On the other hand, there are limit cases, comparable to the puzzling cases of narrative identity, where identification in terms of the usual corporeal or psychological criteria becomes doubtful, to the point at which one says that the defendant in criminal law is no longer recognizable. In these limit cases, self-constancy, a synonym for *ipse*-identity, is assumed by a moral subject who demands to be considered the same as the other that he or she appears to have become. But this responsibility in the present assumes that the responsibility of the consequences to come and that of a past with respect to which the self recognizes its debt are integrated in this nonpointlike present and in a sense recapitulated in it.

This self-constancy, irreducible to any empirical persistence, perhaps contains the key to the phenomenon that we skirted above and then set aside, although it is incorporated in a common definition of imputation, namely that to impute is to place something *au compte de,* "on (some-one's) account." It is as though our acts were inscribed in a great book of accounts, registered there, preserved there. Perhaps this metaphor of in-scription and registration expresses the objectification of what we just called the recapitulation in the present of the responsibility for conse-quences and of the responsibility for indebtedness. Self-constancy, objec-tified in this way, in the image of an interlinking of all of our acts outside of us, has the appearance of a fate that makes the Self its own enemy.[92]

I shall be briefer concerning the contribution of the last three studies to the dialectic of the self and the other than self. In a certain way, this dialectic has been present explicitly in all the earlier developments. In ad-dition, it will be considered once again in the next study under the heading of the Same and the Other. If I nevertheless had to name a category that corresponded to the categories of imputability and responsibility on the level of the third problematic involved in the return to the self, I would choose the term *recognition,* so dear to Hegel in the Jena period and throughout the subsequent course of his work. Recognition is a structure of the self reflecting on the movement that carries self-esteem toward solicitude and solicitude toward justice. Recognition introduces the dyad and plurality in the very constitution of the self. Reciprocity in friendship and proportional equality in justice, when they are reflected in self-consciousness, make self-esteem a figure of recognition. What we shall say in the next study about conscience, in the sense of German *Gewissen,* is rooted in these conjunctions of the same and the other in the heart of hearts.

---

92. Here a confrontation with Eastern thought on the interconnection of acts in karma would be fruitful, as T. Hisashige has begun to show in his work *Phénoménologie de la con-science de culpabilité. Essai de pathologie éthique* (Tokyo: University of Senshu Press, 1983).

What Ontology in View?

This study, more than any of the others, is exploratory in nature. It aims at bringing to light the ontological implications of the earlier investigations, placed under the heading of a hermeneutics of the self. What mode of being, then, belongs to the self, what sort of being or entity is it? In order to divide the difficulty into more manageable portions, and to apply to these the fragmentary method we have continually practiced, let us return to the questions proposed in the Introduction. According to this schema, hermeneutics is the site of three interrelated problematics:

1. the indirect approach of reflection through the detour of analysis;
2. the first determination of selfhood by way of its contrast with sameness;
3. the second determination of selfhood by way of its dialectic with otherness.

We were able to give the name of hermeneutics to this series, by reason of the exact equivalence between self-interpretation and the unfolding of this triple mediation.

The hierarchization of these three problematics has not served as the guideline for our earlier studies, constructed instead upon a certain polysemy of the question "who?" (who speaks? who acts? who tells his or her story? who is responsible?). Nevertheless, the order followed up to now has not been entirely foreign to the train of these three mediations: the connection between reflection and analysis, indeed, was already apparent in the first study and has been continuously present in all the studies that followed; the dialectic of selfhood and sameness clearly came to the forefront in the fifth study; finally, the dialectic of selfhood and otherness has more completely dominated in the last three studies. These three problematics, these three mediations, will guide, in the order we have just outlined, the ontological sketch that follows. Their final intersection will make apparent the multiplicity of the meanings of being concealed behind the question posed initially: what sort of being is the self? In this regard, the entire study that follows is dominated by the polysemic conception of being received from Plato and Aristotle.

An initial question posed concerns the general ontological commitment of all our studies and can be formulated on the basis of the notion of *attestation*, with which the Introduction concluded. The second question concerns the ontological bearing of the distinction between selfhood and sameness; it procedes from the first one, inasmuch as attestation can be identified with the assurance that each person has of existing as the same in the sense of ipseity, of selfhood. The third question, by far the most complex and most inclusive, as it involves the very title of this work, concerns the specific dialectical structure of the relation between selfhood and otherness.

The dialectic in which these two terms oppose one another and are related to one another belongs to a second-order discourse, recalling that of Plato in the *Theatetus,* the *Sophist,* the *Philebus,* and the *Parmenides;* this discourse places on stage metacategories, the "great kinds" akin to the Platonic Same and Other, which transcend the first-order discourse to which belong the categories or existentials such as persons and things that appeared as early as our first study under the title of basic particulars, and to which predicates such as those of action are ultimately attributed. In this regard, our last three studies, in giving an ethical and no longer simply analytic-descriptive status to the distinction between person and thing, did not step outside the framework of this first-order discourse. A careful treatment of the metacategory of otherness, resulting from the third dialectic of our hermeneutics of the self, will force us to make a clear distinction between this second-order discourse and the more manifestly phenomenological aspects of the hermeneutics of the self.

However, it is the third dialectic that best allows the speculative dimension of an ontological investigation into the mode of being of the self to appear. A final reason to situate at this point the first ontological approaches within the perspective of the third dialectic is that neither selfhood nor otherness, in the sense in which we take these terms, can simply be reformulated in the frozen language of an ontology, ready for repetition, in the flattest sense of repetition. The other than self will never be a strict equivalent of Platonic Otherness, and our selfhood will never repeat Platonic Sameness. The ontology we are outlining here is faithful to the suggestion made in our Introduction, namely that an ontology remains possible today inasmuch as the philosophies of the past remain open to reinterpretations and reappropriations, thanks to a meaning potential left unexploited, even repressed, by the very process of systematization and of school formation to which we owe the great doctrinal corpora that we ordinarily identify under the name of their authors: Plato, Aristotle, Descartes, Spinoza, Leibniz, and so on. In truth, if one cannot reawaken and

liberate these resources that the great systems of the past tend to stifle and
to conceal, no innovation would be possible, and present thought would
only have the choice between repetition and aimless wandering. This position on principle concerning the relations between philosophy in the
making and the history of philosophy can be compared to what I stated
elsewhere—in *The Rule of Metaphor* and in *Time and Narrative*—concerning the relations between tradition and innovation. But putting this
maxim into practice is particularly perilous on the level of the "great kinds"
such as the Same and the Other, whose history is, at the very least, intimi-
dating. It will not take long for us to see that the ontological commitment
of attestation and the ontological bearing of selfhood as such do not make
our confrontation with tradition any easier.

1. The Ontological Commitment of Attestation

We begin our ontological investigation at the point where our Introduction stopped. The homage we paid then to attestation as *credence* and as
trust was intended to fit in both with the ambition of self-founding certainty stemming from the Cartesian cogito and with the humiliation of
the cogito reduced to sheer illusion following the Nietzschean critique. It
is therefore in relation to the quarrel of the cogito that our first approach
to attestation was situated. Now the studies that form the body of this
work have unfolded in a place that we have called *atopos* in relation to the
place where the cogito was posited and hence also in relation to the place
where it was deposed. This is why we can no longer confine ourselves to
the definition of attestation made at the beginning in terms of certainty;
or rather, by defining attestation from the viewpoint of *alētheia* (truth),
we have already engaged, without saying so, another discussion than that
which could be said to be purely epistemic, as if it were a matter of simply
situating attestation on a scale of knowledge. The alethic characterization
of attestation is not limited to a given epistemic determination. If we accept taking as our guide the polysemy of being, or rather of beings, which
Aristotle states in *Metaphysics* 6.2, *being-true* and *being-false* are original
significations of being, distinct from and, it seems, of the same rank as
being according to the categories, as being potentially and actually, and as
being by accident.[1] It is under the aegis of being as true that all our earlier

1. "But since the unqualified term 'being' has several meanings, of which one was seen
to be the accidental, and another the true ('non-being' being the false), while besides these
are the figures of predication [categories] (e.g. the 'what,' quality, quantity, place, time, and
any similar meanings which 'being' may have), and again besides all these there is that which
'is' potentially or actually" (Aristotle, *Metaphysics*, trans. W. D. Ross, in *The Basic Works of
Aristotle*, ed. McKeon, 6.2.1026a32–b2, hereafter referred to as *Meta.*).

remarks about attestation as credence and as trust can be assembled. Is this to say that the metacategories of being-true and being-false can be repeated in the terms in which Aristotle once formulated them? This is the first opportunity to test our working hypothesis concerning the tie between innovation and tradition in today's thought.

Attestation, in fact, first finds opposite it the articulation between reflection and analysis, in the strong sense that analytic philosophy gives to this notion. What is first attested to is the being-true of the *mediation* of reflection by analysis. This situation is, in a good many respects, without precedent. The main paradox consists in the fact that it is the passage through analysis, which other authors would have called objectification, in an expressly critical sense, that gives the entire process a *realist* twist. I want, in this regard, to do justice to analytic philosophy for the support I shall constantly draw from it in executing my ontological sketch. My first step, in Strawson's company, was encouraged by the *referential* requirement of Fregean semantics; thus the discourse concerning bodies and persons as basic particulars is from the outset a discourse *on;* the person is already that *about which* one is speaking. This realist tendency of analytic philosophy served from the very start seriously to counterbalance the tendencies, idealist and phenomenalist respectively, stemming from Descartes and Hume. Next, the realist emphasis Davidson placed on the notion of event, set on an equal footing with objective or substantialist entities, has been of great help to me, even if I cannot follow Davidson on the physicalism to which his event ontology finally leads. I would say the same thing about the search for the objective criteria of personal identity in Parfit. In its turn, the notion of narrative identity, as imbued with fiction as it is, owes to its relation (even if it is one of conflict) with the notion of personal identity coming from analytic philosophers a sharpened sense of the ontological bearing of affirmations about the self, strongly mediated by the analyses of Strawson, Davidson, and Parfit, to name only those with whom I have attempted most systematically to confront a hermeneutics of phenomenological origin.

However, the service rendered is mutual: the attestation that is indeed of the self has an effect, in turn, upon analysis itself and shields it from the accusation of being limited, because of its *linguistic* constitution, to the explicitation of idioms of this or that natural language, or—even worse— that of the false appearances of common sense. To be sure, we often were able to distinguish within ordinary language between contingent uses tied to the particular constitution of a given natural language and meanings that can be termed transcendental, in the sense that they represent the condition of the possibility for the use of the former. However, this thoroughly Kantian distinction between the transcendental and the empirical remains difficult to establish and to maintain, if one cannot affirm the dependence of the linguistic determinations of action upon the ontological constitution of action. In this sense, the help that attestation, in its turn, provides to linguistic analysis justifies the fact that the latter can, on the one hand, make use of the most relevant uses of ordinary language as a *thesaurus* of the most appropriate expressions—as Austin noted—and, on the other hand, can be authorized to criticize ordinary language as the depository of the prejudices of common sense, even of the expressions that a misleading grammar might take to lead in the direction of a mistaken ontology, as Russell suspected.

This is not the only service that the ontology implicit in hermeneutics renders to linguistic analysis. The latter can be accused of a more serious fault than its dependency on the contingent uses of a given natural language; paradoxically, the *linguistic turn,* despite the referential twist of philosophical semantics, has often signified a refusal to "go outside" of language and a mistrust equal to that of French structuralism with respect to any extralinguistic order. It is even important to emphasize that the implicit axiom that "everything is language" has often led to a closed semanticism, incapable of accounting for human action as actually *happening* in the world, as though linguistic analysis condemned us to jumping from one language game to another, without thought ever being able to meet up with *actual* action. In this regard, a phenomenology like Husserl's, according to which the stratum of language is "ineffectual" in relation to the life of intentional consciousness, has a corrective value, just because it proposes the opposite extreme.[2]

It is, finally, to the *chiasm* between reflection and analysis, on the very level of the mode of being of the self, that attestation bears witness.

I find again here the sort of *ontological vehemence* whose advocate I have been elsewhere in the name of the conviction that—even in the uses of language that appear to be the least referential, as is the case with metaphor and narrative fiction—language expresses being, even if this ontological aim is as though postponed, deferred by the prior denial of the literal referentiality of ordinary language.

2. In Jean-Luc Petit's *L' Action dans la philosophie analytique* we find a very critical appraisal of the closed semanticism he attributes to Wittgenstein, and from which the entire post-Wittgensteinian school is held to be unable to extricate itself, floating from sentence to sentence without ever reaching the terra firma of effective action. According to Petit, only a phenomenology of intentional consciousness, considered in its practical dimension, in relation to a world that is itself *practicable,* can rescue analysis from this closed semanticism.

However, if, by all these features, the alethic (veritative) dimension of attestation is indeed inscribed in the prolongation of Aristotelian being-true, attestation still retains something specific with respect to this dimension from the sole fact that the being-true it expresses has to do with the self. It does this through the objectifying mediations of language, action, narrative, and the ethical and moral predicates of action. This is why it is not possible purely and simply to repeat the Aristotelian distinction between being-true and being-false, since it remains to such an extent prisoner both to the presumed preeminence of assertive judgment, of *apophansis,* in the order of truth, and to a metaphysics for which reappropriation is, if not impossible, at least extremely difficult and risky. We shall say something about this later.

I should like to indicate the gap separating the being-true of attestation from the being-true of Aristotle's metaphysics by means of a single differential feature. Attestation, as was stated in our Introduction, has as its contrary suspicion. In this sense, suspicion occupies the place of being-false in the Aristotelian pair. However, if suspicion does belong to the same alethic level as attestation—hence to a plane that is at once epistemological and ontological—it is related to attestation in an entirely original manner. It is not simply the contrary of attestation, in a strictly disjunctive sense as being-false is in relation to being-true. Suspicion is also the path *toward* and the crossing *within* attestation. It haunts attestation, as false testimony haunts true testimony. This adherence, this inherence of suspicion with respect to attestation, has marked the entire course of these studies. In this way, suspicion insinuated itself at the time of the very first occurrence of the aporia of ascription; it took on renewed strength with the aporias of personal identity, and again with those of narrative identity; it took on an even more insidious form in the guise of hesitations punctuating conviction in moral judgment in situation, confronted by the conflict of duties. A kind of uneasy balance between attestation and suspicion was then imposed, whenever certainty of self had to take refuge in the inexpungible retreat of the question "who?"

It therefore seems difficult to make any more headway along the path of the ontological commitment of attestation until we clarify, without delay, that what is ultimately attested to is selfhood, at once in its difference with respect to *sameness* and in its dialectical relation with *otherness.*

2. Selfhood and Ontology

As has just been suggested, attestation is the assurance—the credence and the trust—of *existing* in the mode of selfhood. By presenting the ontological stakes of selfhood in this way, we are adding a new dimension to ontology, one that our hermeneutics of the self summons in its wake.

One path deserves to be explored, even if the difficulties here seem more intractable than those encountered in the preceding section: this path connects the investigation of the being of the self to the reappropriation of one of the four primordial acceptations of being, which Aristotle places under the distinction of *act* and of *power*.

All of our analyses prompt this exploration, inasmuch as they point in the direction of a certain unity of human action—setting aside for the moment the complementary theme of suffering to which we shall return in the following section. Does not this unity belong to the metacategory of being as act and as power? And does not the ontological significance of this metacategory preserve what we have already termed on several occasions the *analogical* unity of action, in order to mark the polysemic character of action and of the acting individual, which the fragmentary nature of these studies has underscored? Better yet: have we not, in the course of our investigations, often taken the term "act" (speech act!) to be synonymous with the terms "acting" and "action"? And have we not, in the same contexts, employed the term "power" to express either the power-to-act of an agent to whom an action is ascribed or imputed or the power-in-common of a historical community, which we hold to be more fundamental than the hierarchical relations of domination between governing and governed? In short, the language of act and of power has never ceased to underlie our hermeneutical phenomenology of acting man. Do these anticipations justify our joining the simply analogical unity of human action to an ontology of act and of power?

1. As much as the task itself appears to be justified in its principle by the plurality of acceptations of being that seem to open to the ideas of act and of power their own, autonomous career, to this same extent the realization of this task runs up against difficulties so formidable that they render extremely hazardous our effort to reactualize Aristotelian ontology as well as the efforts of our contemporaries, which I shall discuss when the time comes.

It is in the *Metaphysics* 5.12 and 9.1–10, where *dunamis* and *energeia* are explicitly discussed, that the resistances to a reappropriation in favor of an ontology of selfhood begin to accumulate. In 5.12, which deals with *dunamis* and related notions in the context of a book written in the form of a philosophical glossary, the reader meets straightaway the polysemy of a term which we expect to underlie the analogical unity of acting. There is indeed in this polysemy a dominant (sometimes called "simple") signification, namely "a source of movement or change, which is in another thing than the thing moved or in the same thing *qua* other" (*Meta.* 5.12.1019a15ff.).[3] But besides the fact that the relation between power and act is not taken into consideration, the place of human praxis in relation to change immediately poses a problem: the examples that are given—the art of building, the art of healing—lean to the side of *poiēsis*, while "doing well" (sense number three, which will return in book 9.2) is said more commonly of praxis.

If we move from this exercise in definitions to the systematic treatment of the pair *dunamis-energeia* in *Metaphysics* 9, it grows even more puzzling.

First, it does seem that the two terms are defined by one another, without our being able to establish the sense of one independently of the other, or risk that the polysemy recognized in 5.12 will result in their separate dissolution. But can one *define* notions that are preceded by nothing?[4]

Furthermore, Aristotle is less miserly with words when it is a matter of showing what these radical notions enable us to think. Another type of dispersion then prevails, that of fields of application. In this way, being as potentiality (beginning in 9.1–5) allows us to include change within being, contrary to Parmenides' prohibition, and , more precisely, to include local motion. Because potentiality is a genuine mode of being, change and motion are rightfully beings. But if we ask what sort of being motion is, we are referred back to the troubling definition of motion in the *Physics,* namely "the fulfilment [*entelekheia*] of what exists potentially, insofar as it exists potentially" (3.1.201a10–11). The intention is clear indeed: guar-

3. The other meanings of *dunamis* do not induce, it is true, such great gaps in the use of the term: whether it is a matter of the *active* power of producing change or movement, of the *passive* power of receiving or suffering them, or of the "capacity of performing this well or according to intention." In addition, the multiple meanings of "potent" or "capable" (*dunaton*) correspond rather well to those of *dunamis*. Only the impossible (whose contrary is necessarily true) and the possible (whose contrary is not necessarily false) lead to a neighboring but different area, at the frontier of the logically possible and of the ontologically possible.

4. Book 9 begins with the idea of potency in its relation to movement and introduces actuality only in chap. 6: "Actuality, then, is the existence of a thing not in the way which we express by 'potentially'; we say that potentially, for instance, a statue of Hermes is in the block of wood and the half-line is in the whole, because it might be separated out, and we call even the man who is not studying a man of science, if he is capable of studying; the thing that stands out in contrast to each of these exists actually" (*Meta.* 9.6.1048a30–35). To the apparent circularity is added, for lack of a direct definition, the recourse to induction and to analogy: "Our meaning can be seen in the particular cases by induction, and we must not seek a definition of everything but be content to grasp the analogy, that it is as that which is building is to that which is capable of building, and the waking to the sleeping, and that which is seeing as that which has its eyes shut but has sight, and that which has been shaped out of the matter to the matter, and that which has been wrought to the unwrought. Let actuality be defined by one member of this antithesis, and the potential by the other" (1048a35–b5).

antee to motion a full-fledged ontological status, but at the cost of what strangeness: the entelechy of potentiality! So much for the first field of application, that of being as potentiality.

If we now move to the other end of the chain of beings, the notion of act without potentiality is asked to characterize the ontological status of the heaven of fixed beings, at the cost of a daring assimilation, made in book 12, between a pure act such as this and the "thought of thought," which is also said to be an *energeia akinēsias*![5]

Even more serious: despite the lofty titles that the idea of potency draws from its so-to-speak transcendental function with respect to physics, this notion is conceived only on the basis of that of actuality: nothing can be said to be potential without reference to something said to be real, in the sense of actual, completed; in this sense the actual has priority over the potential "both in formula and in substantiality" (*Meta.* 9.8.1049b10) (to distinguish this priority from that of anteriority in time) and even over the relation to substance, which is not without importance for our discussion. In fact, the intersecting of these two primitive significations of being, that of being appropriate to the categories (*ousia*, which in Latin is translated by *substantia*) and that of being as actuality and potentiality, leads, it seems, to weakening the ever so precious conquest of the idea of potency and actuality.[6]

Does not the theory of substance, then, tend to lessen the benefit drawn from the distinction between the two primitive significations of being—the being belonging to the categories and being as potentiality and actuality? Without going this far, we may well admit that it would be of no avail to use the plurality of the acceptations of the notion of being as the basis for *opposing* an ontology of actuality to an ontology of substance, as we have continued to do. To be sure, what we attacked, at the time of the opposition of selfhood and sameness, was more the substantialism of the tradition (to which Kant continues to belong from the perspective of the first analogy of experience) than Aristotelian *ousia*, which cannot be reduced to the former. It nevertheless remains that, whatever the possibility may be of freeing Aristotelian *ousia* from the chains of the scholastic tradition stemming from its Latin translation as *substantia*, Aristotle appears to be more concerned with interconnecting than with dissociating the significations

5. *Metaphysics* 9 concurs on this point with *Physics* 3: "The word 'actuality', which we connect with 'complete reality', has, in the main, been extended from movements to other things; for actuality in the strict sense is thought to be identical with movement" (*Meta.* 9.3.1047a32).

6. "The actuality is the end, and it is for the sake of this that the potency is acquired. Further, matter exists in a potential state, just because it may come to its form; and when it exists actually, then it is in its form" (ibid. 9.8.1050a9, 15–16).

attached, respectively, to the pair *energeia-dunamis* and to the series of
acceptations opened by the notion of *ousia* (and to *ousia* itself, to which
the books of the *Metaphysics* preceding book 9 are devoted).[7]

To these three sources of difficulty—the circular determination of actuality and potentiality, the splitting up of their respective fields of application (the physics of motion, on the one hand, and the cosmotheology
of rest and of the "thought of thought," on the other), the primacy of
actuality over potentiality in connection with the theory of substance—is
now added a specific difficulty concerning the relation between this primitive acceptation of being and human action. It is at this point that our
entire undertaking is directly concerned. In a sense, one can in fact say that
the examples drawn from human operations—seeing, understanding, living well, making things, acting (in the sense in which praxis is taken in the
Ethics)—have a paradigmatic value.[8]

In another sense, the examples belonging to the human sphere of activity do not appear conducive to serving as models, for they risk defeat-
ing Aristotle's metaphysical enterprise, in the twofold aspect mentioned
above: on the one hand, securing for motion the ontological dignity re-
fused to it by the Parmenidians; on the other hand, taking as a basis

7. In this way some extremely subtle exchanges are established between the *morphē* of
substance and *energeia:* on the one hand, actuality is complete only in the finished form of
substance; on the other, *ousia* is confirmed in its dynamism by the application to it of the
signification *energeia;* in this sense, it would not be forcing Aristotle's text to say that substance is "having to be" (*à être*) what it is, following the analysis of F. Calvo in *Cercare l'uomo
Socrate. Platone. Aristotele* (Genoa: Ed. Marietti, 1989), who kindly asked me to write a
preface to his work. If this interpretation of *ousia* is not exaggerated, it is not surprising that
it is in man, in the discussion of his soul, that *ousia* is interpreted in terms of *energeia-
dunamis,* just as much as, if not even more than, the other way around. This exchange between distinct significations of being is obvious in the definition of the soul in *De anima:* the
soul is said here to be "substance [*ousia*] as the form [*eidos*] of a natural body possessing life
potentially." Rémi Brague, in *Aristote et la question du monde* (p. 333), shows how Aristotle
uses the term "entelechy" (Aristotle, *De anima* 2.1.412a21ff.) in his first definition of the
soul and substitutes that of *organikos* in his second definition, so that the soul is, finally, "the
first grade of actuality of a natural organized body" (412b5). I shall return to discuss at
greater length this impressive work by Brague, when I examine the attempts at a Heideggerian reinterpretation of Aristotle's philosophy.

8. As early as *Metaphysics* 9.1, *entelekheia* and *ergon* are paired (1045b33–34): 9.8 concludes the argument establishing the priority of actuality over potentiality by placing in a
series the three terms *energeia, entelekheia, ergon.* In the case in which action is truly praxis,
one can truly say: "For the action is the end, and the actuality is the action [*ergon*]. And
so even the *word* 'actuality' is derived from 'action', and points to the complete reality"
(9.8.1050a21). This is what authorizes Rémi Brague's translation of *energeia* by "être-en-
oeuvre" (*Aristote,* p. 335). And has not this proximity between *energeia* and *ergon* encouraged countless commentators to give a craftsmanship model to the entire series: *entelekheia,*

the notion of pure actuality to give ontological dignity to the entities of cosmotheology.[9]

There is, however, a fragment of 9.6 (1048b18–35) in which, despite its isolation (this fragment resembles a loose sheet of paper, and not all the medieval commentators were familiar with it), the notion of actuality is clearly dissociated from movement and made to fit action, in the sense of praxis. What makes this text remarkable is that the disjunction between action and movement is upheld by a grammatical criterion involving the use of verb tenses, namely the possibility of saying at the same time, "together" (*hama*): we are seeing and we have seen, we are living well and have lived well, are happy and have been happy.[10] One can, to be sure, make much of this astonishing text, but it is not apparent how it can, all by itself, clear up the mass of ambiguities that we have listed.

What remains is to transform the obstacle that these ambiguities pose to our progress into a means of support, whether this be the circular definition of potentiality and actuality, the extreme spread of the respective fields of application of these notions, or the uncertainty about the central-

---

energeia, ergon? As a result of this banalization, the entire effort to reappropriate the ontology of actuality-potentiality in favor of the being of the self is rendered more or less pointless.

9. The distinction introduced in 9.2 and 9.5 between "rational" (*meta logou*) and "non-rational" (*alogoi*) potentialities seems to circumscribe the field in which the examples drawn from human operations are pertinent; the distinction is even maintained by precise differential features: thus, the "rational" potentiality alone is a potentiality of contraries, namely realization or its privation (9.2); the passage from potentiality to act in production, however, takes place without encountering any obstacle, whereas in the natural order intermediaries are necessary; in this way, the seed is not potentially a man until it is deposited in another being and thereby undergoes a change (9.7).

10. Rémi Brague devotes a brilliant analysis to this fragment (*Aristote*, pp. 454–74). The argument based on tense grammar is the following: "The criterion permitting the separation of movement and action is to be sought on the side of the *telos* and its relation to the action, a relation of inhering in or of externality depending on whether one is dealing, respectively, with an *energeia* or a movement" (p. 467). The play of verb tenses articulated around this difference reveals a fundamental phenomenology that touches the temporality proper to human acting: "The fact that the present and the present perfect are 'together' implies that all that the perfect contains of the past is recapitulated in the present" (p. 473). Then, action survives its own end, and the word "action" substituted for *entelekheia* denotes "a liberation of activity returning to itself [rather than] its realized completion" (p. 471). Brague is not wrong to stress the place of *eu zēn*, of living well ("we have had and now have the good life," he prefers to translate), and its relation to happiness among the examples of actions that are not movements. Brague's major reservation—that Aristotle nevertheless only had in mind the content of happiness and its connection with contemplation, the higher form of life, and that he never thematized the action of being happy qua action, in its completion—is too tightly bound up with his overall interpretation of Aristotle's philosophy for us to say any more about it here.

ity of the examples taken from human action. I even propose to start with the equivocal character of the last difficulty noted in sketching out the reappropriation I am suggesting. Is it not essential, for a deepened ontological understanding of human action, that the examples taken from this final sphere appear by turns as *central* and as *decentered?* Let me explain this: if *energeia-dunamis* were simply another way of saying *praxis* (or, worse, of extrapolating in a metaphysical manner some craftsmanship model of action), the lesson of ontology would have no bearing; it is instead to the extent that *energeia-dunamis* irrigates fields of application other than human action that its fecundity becomes manifest. In Aristotle's text it matters little that sometimes *dunamis* is invoked on behalf of the physics of motion, and sometimes pure actuality on behalf of cosmotheology. What is essential is the *decentering* itself—both upward and downward in Aristotle—thanks to which *energeia-dunamis* points toward a ground of being, at once potentiality and actuality against which human action stands out. In other words, it appears equally important that human action be the place of readability par excellence of this acceptation of being as distinct from all the others (including those that substance carries in its wake) and that being as actuality and as potentiality have other fields of application than human action alone. The central character of action and its decentering in the direction of a *ground* of actuality and of potentiality are two features that equally and conjointly constitute an ontology of selfhood in terms of actuality and potentiality. This apparent paradox attests to the fact that, if there is a being of the self—in other words, if an ontology of selfhood is possible—this is in conjunction with a ground starting from which the self can be said to be *acting*.

2. Allow me to specify what I mean by a *ground of being, at once potentiality and actuality* by means of a comparison between my effort of reconstruction and the efforts of those who claim to follow the Heidegger of the gestation period of *Being and Time*. I shall first recall some of the themes of this great work with which my hermeneutics of selfhood is in agreement, before saying a few words about the reinterpretations of Aristotle that these themes have inspired and, finally, indicating the slight difference that remains between my attempt at reconstructing *energeia-dunamis* and the reconstructions inspired by Heidegger.

Without restricting myself to following the order of appearance of the themes in *Being and Time* with which I feel the greatest affinity, I should like to begin with the role assigned by Heidegger to *Gewissen*—a word generally translated "conscience" (or "moral conscience," to distinguish it more clearly from "consciousness," *Bewusstsein,* in the sense of Husserlian phenomenology). The way the notion is introduced is worth emphasizing; the question posed with such insistence is that of knowing whether

WHAT ONTOLOGY IN VIEW ?

the analyses conducted in the previous chapter, centered around being-toward-death, are indeed primordial, as they claim to be. The attestation of conscience—or better, conscience as attestation—is the sought-after gauge of the primordiality of this analysis and of all those that have preceded it. The idea that *Gewissen*, before designating the capacity for distinguishing good and evil on the moral plane and of responding to this capacity by the distinction between "good" and "bad" conscience, signifies attestation (*Bezeugung*) is of great help to me. It confirms my working hypothesis that the distinction between selfhood and sameness does not simply concern two constellations of meaning but involves two modes of being.

The equating of conscience and attestation makes a happy transition between the reflections of the preceding section of *Being and Time* and those that more properly belong to the ontology of selfhood. Heidegger inaugurates this ontology by establishing a relation of immediate dependence between selfhood—*Selbstheit*—and the mode of being that we are in each case, as that being whose being is an issue for it, namely *Dasein*. It is by reason of this dependence between a modality of self-apprehension and a mode of being in the world that selfhood can figure among the existentials. In this sense, it is to Dasein what the categories (in a rigorously Kantian sense) are to the beings that Heidegger classifies under the mode of being of *Vorhandenheit* (a term translated by Martineau as "être-sous-la-main" and Vezin as "être-là-devant" and in Macquarrie and Robinson's English translation as "presence-at-hand"). The ontological status of selfhood is therefore solidly based upon the distinction between two modes of being, Dasein and Verhandenheit. In this regard, the correlation between the category of sameness in my own analyses and the notion of Vorhandenheit in Heidegger is the same as that between selfhood and the mode of being of Dasein.[11]

The connection between selfhood and Dasein, in its turn, occurs in *Being and Time* through the mediation of the notion of care (*Sorge*), which is the most fundamental existential capable of ensuring the thematic unity of the work, at least until temporality appears on the stage in the second section. One can, in this regard, follow the thread in *Being and Time* that runs from the assertion of Dasein's character of being in each case *mine* (§§5, 9), passing through the existential question "who?" of Dasein

---

11. This kinship finds an important confirmation in the distinction Heidegger makes between two manners of enduring in time, one close to the permanence of substance (which Kant attaches to the first category of relation in the first analogy of experience), the other manifested by the phenomenon of self-constancy (*Selbständigkeit*), a term that Heidegger decomposes, as we mentioned above, into *Selbst-Ständigkeit*. Here, we are not far from the opposition resulting from our notion of narrative identity between character (ourselves as *idem*) and moral constancy illustrated by promising (ourselves as *ipse*).

(§25), then by equating the being of Dasein with care (§41), finally leading to the connection between care and selfhood (§64). *Care* then appears
as the ground of the philosophical anthropology of *Being and Time,* before
ontology is oriented beyond philosophical anthropology by the notion of
temporality. Now care cannot be captured by any psychologizing or soci-
ologizing interpretation, nor in general by an immediate phenomenology,
as would be the case for the subordinate notions of *Besorgen* (concern with
things) and *Fürsorge* (solicitude or concern with people). This eminent
place given to care cannot leave us indifferent. The question can legitimately be raised whether action does not occupy in our undertaking a
place comparable to that assigned to *Sorge* in *Being and Time,* to the extent
that, for us, no linguistic, praxic, narrative, or ethicomoral determination of
action exhausts the sense of acting. It is in this manner that I ventured, in
the Introduction, to speak of the *analogical unity of acting,* although, at
that time, it was to counter the ambition of the cogito to be an ultimate
foundation. We must now take a new look at this notion in light of the multiple determinations of action that the preceding studies have presented in
a fragmentary way. Might care, taken in its ontological dimension, be the
equivalent of what we have called the analogical unity of action?

We cannot reply directly to this question without first setting *Sorge*
itself back within the broader framework of being-in-the-world, which is
most certainly the final, inclusive notion of the analytic of Dasein. Everything turns, as we know, on the sense of the preposition "in," which has
no equivalent on the side of the relation among beings belonging to the
metacategory of Vorhandenheit. Only a being that is a self is *in* the world;
correlatively, the world in which this being is, is not the sum of beings
composing the universe of subsisting things or things ready-to-hand. The
being of the self presupposes the totality of a world that is the horizon of
its thinking, acting, feeling—in short, of its *care.*

What about the place of this concept of world or of an equivalent concept
in our hermeneutics of the self?[12] If the concept has not been thematized
as such, essentially because of its ontological status, which, at best, remained implicit, we can admit that it has been called for by this hermeneutics, to the extent that the detour by way of things has constituted our
unwavering strategy. Once the answer to the question "who?" can be
answered only through the detour of the question "what?" and the ques-

---

12. The concept of horizon, taken from Husserl, or that of world in the sense of Heidegger, has not been lacking in my past work. In *The Rule of Metaphor,* I plead for the idea
of metaphoric truth, which has as its horizon the world in which we have life, movement,
and being. In a similar spirit, *Time and Narrative* places face-to-face the world of the text and
the world of the reader.

tion "why?", then the being of the world is the necessary correlate to the being of the self. There is no world without a self who finds itself in it and acts in it; there is no self without a world that is practicable in some fashion.

It remains that the concept—if we can still speak in these terms—of being-in-the-world is expressed in numerous ways, and that it is together that oneself, care, and being-in-the-world are to be determined.

In an effort to articulate these three terms correctly, a certain reappropriation of Aristotle under the guidance of Heideggerian concepts can lead back in turn to a better apprehension of the leading concepts of *Being and Time*.[13]

I must confess that this reappropriation is, for me, fraught with pitfalls, for it is a matter of interpreting my own hermeneutics of the self ontologically, by using the Heideggerian reappropriation of Aristotle.[14] This convoluted path seems to me, in the present state of my research, the shortest one, given the futility of a scholastic repetition of Aristotle's ontology in general and, more to the point, of its distinction between being as actuality/potentiality and being in terms of categories related to substance.

The reappropriation of Aristotle through Heidegger is not without an important conceptual readjustment; this at times even goes so far as reconstructing something implicit but unstated that Aristotle's text is held to cover over. One could, it is true, confine oneself to comparing a limited group of Aristotelian concepts to their Heideggerian counterparts and interpret the former in relation to the latter. In this way, the comparison between *Sorge* in Heidegger and *praxis* in Aristotle could occasion a deeper understanding of both concepts. For my part, I am all the more attentive, as it has been the Aristotelian concept of *praxis* that helped me to widen the practical field beyond the narrow notion of action in terms of analytic philosophy; in turn, Heideggerian *Sorge* gives to Aristotelian *praxis* an ontological weight that does not seem to have been the major intention of Aristotle in his *Ethics*. In this way, Franco Volpi has been able to attribute to *Sorge* a global effect of ontologization with respect to

13. Today we know that in the decade preceding the publication of *Being and Time*, Heidegger worked at great length on Aristotle, to the point that Rémi Brague has stated that "Heidegger's major work is the substitute for a work on Aristotle that did not see the light of day" (*Aristote*, p. 55). "It is as though," he adds, the concepts developed by Heidegger in *Sein und Zeit* "had been carved to the measurements of Aristotle—to the measurements of an Aristotle in negative" (p. 56).

14. The most important text of Heidegger himself, in the present state of the publication of the *Gesamtausgabe*, is the interpretation of *Metaphysics* 9.1–3: *Aristoteles, Metaphysik Θ 1–3. Von Wesen und Wirklichkeit der Kraft*, GA 33 (Frankfurt: Vittorio Klostermann, 1981).

praxis.[15] This effort certainly helps us in securing the marker we are trying to put in place between selfhood and being as actuality/potentiality. Acting is elevated in this way to the level of a second-order concept in relation to the successive versions of action that we have presented in the preceding studies, or, yet again, in relation to our threefold series, more epistemological than ontological: description, narration, prescription.

Is it necessary, for all this, to give to Aristotelian *praxis* and to my own concept of power-to-act a unitary function for the entire field of human experience? If Volpi is right to carry back to temporality the unitary principle held, ultimately, to mark Aristotelian *praxis*, perhaps this concept should not be overburdened with a function it does not possess. In any event, the kind of plurality that Aristotle preserves by leaving *theōria*, *praxis*, and *poiēsis* side-by-side seems to me to agree better with the sort of philosophy I prefer, one that is not too quick to unify the field of human experience from on high, as is the case of the philosophies from which I distanced myself in the Introduction. Even if acting can be said to include theory within it, as theoretical activity, the hegemonic tendency thereby accorded to acting must be corrected by an admission of its

15. Franco Volpi, the author of *Heidegger e Aristotele* (Padua: Daphni, 1984), has published in the collective volume *Phaenomenologica* (Dordrecht: Kluwer Academic Publ., 1988) an article entitled "*Dasein* comme *praxis:* L'Assimilation et la radicalisation heideggérienne de la philosophie pratique d'Aristote." It is first demonstrated that Heidegger did indeed attempt in the 1920s to reconstruct Aristotle's practical philosophy from the perspective of other meanings of being in Aristotle and, more precisely, on the basis of the privilege accorded to being-true. The author does not hide the audacious character of the correlation he establishes between *Sorge* and *praxis*, at the cost of the ontologization of *praxis*, raised above the actions of the simply ontic level. In this way, *praxis* assumes a revelatory function capable of transcending the distinction between "theoretical" and "practical," and especially of raising *praxis* above the other terms of the triad *poiēsis-praxis-theōria*. This basic correlation between *praxis* and *Sorge* is held to govern an entire series of related correlations. Thus, to the teleology of the concept of *praxis* would correspond Dasein's to-be (*zu-sein*); to Aristotle's *phronēsis* would answer Heidegger's *Gewissen* (this correlation is confirmed by Gadamer in his recollections about Heidegger: *Heideggers Wege* [Tubingen: Mohr, 1983], pp. 31–32, and "Erinnerungen an Heideggers Anfange," *Itinerari* 25, nos. 1–2 [1986]: 10); to the passions (*pathé*) would correspond *Befindlichkeit;* to *nous praktikos*, *Verstehen;* to *orexis dianoētikē*, *Rede;* to *proairesis*, *Entschlossenheit*. Where, according to Volpi, is the decisive split between Heidegger and Aristotle to be situated? "Aristotle is held to have failed to see primordial temporality as the unitary ontological ground of the determinations of human life, even though he grasps it and describes it, because he remained within the horizon of a naturalist, chronological, and non-kairological understanding of time" ("*Dasein* comme *praxis*," p. 33). Unable to link *praxis* to primordial temporality, Aristotelian *praxis* is held to remain one of the fundamental attitudes alongside *theōria* and *poiēsis*, despite indications that suggest that *praxis* is the unitary determination from which the other two derive.

polysemy, which authorizes no more than the idea of an analogical unity of acting.[16]

Permit me to conclude this resume of some Heideggerian reinterpretations or reappropriations of Aristotle by that of Rémi Brague, from whom I have occasionally borrowed certain elements; his reinterpretation is complex indeed. He does not take what Aristotle says as his theme but instead that which, in what Aristotle says, remains unthought, that is, fundamentally, the interpretation of Aristotelian *energeia* in terms of Heideggerian being-in-the-world. What is unthought in Aristotle then has to be reconstructed, inasmuch as Aristotle's anthropology, cosmology, and theology are arranged in such a way that what is unthought cannot come into language. I want to say here up to what point I am prepared to follow Brague and precisely where my reservations begin.

The fact that the self and being-in-the-world are basic correlates seems indisputable to me. Oneself thus becomes the unsaid of the Aristotelian theory of the soul and, more generally, of the entire Aristotelian anthropology. But is it acceptable to say that the sharpness of the meaning of the term *autos* is dulled by the confusion between the *self,* a phenomenological concept, and *man,* an anthropological concept? The role we assign to analysis implies that the detour by way of objectification is the shortest path from the self to itself. In this sense, the anthropological concept of man seems to me to be justified. To be sure, despite the affirmation of life's

---

16. It is noteworthy that J. Taminiaux, who has also assumed the task of reappropriating the *Nichomachean Ethics* (in *Lectures de l'ontologie fondamentale. Essais sur Heidegger* [Grenoble: Jerome Millon, 1989], pp. 147–89), did not take as his guideline Heidegger's *Sorge* but the pair authenticity (*Eigentlichkeit*) and inauthenticity (*Uneigentlichkeit*), which he pairs with the Greek *poiēsis-praxis*. In this way, *poiēsis* becomes the model for the relation of man to the everyday world and, by extention, of *Vorhandenheit*, inasmuch as even things that are not immediately manipulable are susceptible to eventual manipulation. But he does not go as far as to make *praxis* the unitary principle, although he affirms the ethical and political superiority of *praxis* over *poiēsis*. In addition, the comparison between Heidegger and Aristotle is not without a rather sharp critique of Heidegger, who is reproached, on the one hand, with having lost the tie between *praxis* and a plurality of actors and an opinion (*doxa*), reversible and fragile—a tie that is, on the contrary, forcefully reaffirmed by Hannah Arendt—and, on the other hand, with assigning to philosophical *theōria* a preeminence even in the field of politics, forsaking Aristotelian modesty for haughty Platonic claims: "in fundamental ontology, everything occurs as though *bios theōrētikos* devoured and controlled all *praxis*" (p. 175). However, the recovery of *energeia* in the analytic of Dasein is looked upon favorably (p. 159, 163–64, 166). Finally, Taminiaux admits that during the period of the fundamental ontology of Dasein, Aristotelian *phusis* is not yet understood in terms of the dimension that will rescue it from the critique of *Vorhandenheit* and its inauthenticity, which will require a rehabilitation of *poiēsis*, the status of fallenness being reserved for modern technology alone (p. 171).

interiority in relation to itself, the self is essentially an opening onto the world, and its relation to the world is indeed, as Brague says, a relation of total concern: *everything* concerns me. And this concern indeed extends from being-alive to militant thinking, passing by way of praxis and living well. But how is one to do justice to this very opening, if one does not perceive in human initiative a specific coordination with the movements of the world and all the physical aspects of action? It is the detour of reflection *by way of* analysis that is at issue here. The revelatory function recognized in Dasein not only does not seem to me to be a substitute for this objectifying detour, it appears to presuppose it or to require it.

What poses the greatest problem to me, however, is the very notion of being-in-the-world, held to be what remains unthought in *energeia*. Not that I am contesting the distinction between the phenomenological concept of world and the cosmological concept of universe (a distinction that does not exclude even greater detours than those that connect the phenomenology of the self to the anthropology of man). My reticence is on a single, but essential, point. Must one make *presence* the fundamental nexus between being oneself and being-in-the-world? To be sure, presence must not be separated from concern, whose richness of sense I have just recalled. But if "concern" is not inclusive of presence, how can presence be held to be what is most plausibly left unthought in Aristotelian *energeia*?[17] The presence of being-self-in-the-world is finally pulled in the direction of Heideggerian *facticity*.[18] I doubt that facticity is the best key for reinterpreting Aristotle's *energeia* and *entelekheia*.[19] I do admit that *energeia*, which was translated in Latin by *actualitas,* denotes in a global manner what in which we actually exist. But by placing the main emphasis on the "always al-

17. Cf. the remarkable chapter that concludes Rémi Brague's work, "L'Être en acte" (*Aristote,* pp. 463–509). I stated above what I owe to the exegesis of the fragment of *Meta.* 9.6.1048b18–35, presented as an "Aristotelian aerolith" (*Aristote,* pp. 454ff.). This exegesis occupies a strategic position in the chapter, in that the examples upon which Aristotle bases the key distinction between actuality and movement lead back, through the *decisive* experience of happiness, to the *fundamental* experience of human life. This is held to include perception, itself understood on the basis of contact, of the state of awakenness, or better, of being awake. From this, one moves to the idea that perception is "left on its own" (p. 490) at the same time that it is delivered over to the world: "Life is for us a domain from which we cannot escape and into which we have not entered" (p. 491).

18. "Presence in the world is such that we find ourselves in an inside, whose threshold we have never crossed, an inside that has no outside. This is why this inside is defined by continuity, by the impossibility of reaching, starting from within, any sort of limit at all" (ibid., p. 492).

19. One will note that, despite the proximity between *energeia* and *ergon,* and between *entelekheia* and *telos,* it is finally the common prefix *en* (in) that attracts Brague's curiosity the most (ibid., pp. 492–93).

ready" and on the impossibility of getting away from this tie of presence—in short, on facticity—does one not diminish the dimension of *energeia* and of *dunamis* by virtue of which human *acting* and *suffering* are rooted in being? In order to account for this rootedness I proposed the notion of a *ground at once actual and in potentiality*. I stress both adjectives. A tension exists between potentiality and actuality that seems to me to be essential to the ontology of action but that appears erased in the equating of *energeia* and *facticity*. The difficult dialectic between the two Greek terms is in danger of disappearing in an apparently unilateral rehabilitation of *energeia*. Yet it is on this very difference between *energeia* and *dunamis*, as much as on the primacy of the first over the second, that the possibility ensues of interpreting human action and being together as both act and potentiality.

3. The relatively disappointing results of our careful attention to Heideggerian interpretations that attempt to reappropriate Aristotelian ontology invites us to look for another connection between the phenomenology of the acting and suffering self and the actual and potential ground against which selfhood stands out.

For me, this connection is Spinoza's *conatus*.

I have written very little on Spinoza, although he is always to be found in my meditation and my teaching. I share with Sylvain Zac the conviction that "all Spinozist themes can be centered around the notion of life."[20] But to say life is also to say power, as the *Ethics* confirms, through and through.[21] Power here does not mean potentiality but productivity, which is not to be opposed to act in the sense of actuality or realization. Both realities are degrees of the power of existing. From this result, on the one hand, the definition of the soul as the "idea of an individual actually existing thing" (*Ethics*, bk. 2, prop. 11)[22] and, on the other, the assertion that

---

20. Sylvain Zac, *L'Idée de vie dans la philosophie de Spinoza* (Paris: PUF, 1963), pp. 15–16.

21. I am not concerned with Spinoza's "theology": the accusation of pantheism or of atheism is irrelevant to the recovery of the notion of *conatus*, which alone matters here. A single formula, in appearance theological, suffices for my purposes: "It is impossible for us to conceive that God does not act as that God does not exist" (*Ethics*, bk. 2, prop. 3, scholium, p. 65, cited in Zac, *L'Idée*, p. 18). Thus, it is posited from the outset that the "properties" of God express the fundamental property of the latter as being an *essentia actuosa*. Concerning the meaning, in Spinoza, of the expression "God is Life," cf. pp. 24ff. For us, the essential point is that a God-craftsman, striving to realize a work conforming to a model, is replaced by an infinite power, an *acting energy*. It is at this point that Spinoza encounters Saint Paul affirming that in God we have being and movement (letter 73 to H. Oldenburg, quoted on p. 86).

22. Spinoza, *Ethics*, p. 68.

this power of animation "is of quite general application and applies to men no more than to other individuals" (prop. 13, scholium).[23]

It is against this overly hastily drawn backdrop that the idea of *conatus* stands out, as the effort to persevere in being, which forms the unity of man as of every individual. Here I like to quote proposition 4 of book 3: "Each thing, in so far as it is in itself, endeavors to persist in its own being"[24] (the demonstration is in the main a reference to book 1, where it is shown that "particular things are modes whereby the attributes of God are expressed in a definite and determinate way . . . , that is . . . , they are things which express in a definite and determinate way the power of God whereby he is and acts."[25]

I realize that this dynamism of living things excludes all initiative that would break with the determinism of nature and that persevering in being does not involve going beyond this being in the direction of something else, in accordance with some intention that could be held to be the end of that effort. This is excluded by the definition of *conatus* immediately following in proposition 7: that by which "each thing endeavors to persist in its own being is nothing but the actual essence of the thing itself" (*Ethics*, bk. 3, p. 109). The demonstration then evokes the idea of necessity that book 1 tied to that of expression, so that "the power or conatus by which it perseveres in its own being, is nothing but the given, or actual, essence of the thing" (p. 110). We should not, however, forget that the passage from inadequate ideas, which we form about ourselves and about things, to adequate ideas signifies for us the possibility of being truly *active*. In this sense, the power to act can be said to be increased by the retreat of passivity tied to inadequate ideas (cf. *Ethics*, bk. 3, prop. 1, proof and corollary). This conquest of activity under the aegis of adequate ideas makes the work as a whole an *ethics*. Thus there is a close connection between the internal dynamism worthy of the name of life and the power of the intelligence, which governs the passage from inadequate to adequate ideas. In this sense, we are powerful when we understand adequately our, as it were, horizontal and external dependence with respect to all things, and our vertical and immanent dependence with respect to the primordial power that Spinoza continues to name "God."

What finally matters to me more than any other idea is the idea toward which the preceding discussion of Aristotle's *energeia* was directed, namely, on the one hand, that it is in man that *conatus*, or the power of being of all things, is most clearly readable and, on the other hand, that

23. Ibid., p. 72.
24. Ibid., p. 109.
25. Ibid.

everything expresses to different degrees the power or life that Spinoza calls the life of God. Here, at the end of this all too rapid overview of Spinoza's *Ethics*, I concur with the idea that "self-consciousness, far from being, as it is in Descartes, the starting point for philosophical reflection, presupposes, on the contrary a long detour" (Zac, *L'Idée,* p. 137). It is precisely the priority of the *conatus* in relation to consciousness—which Spinoza terms the idea of the idea—that imposes on adequate self-consciousness this very long detour, which is concluded only in book 5 of the *Ethics.*

Welcome indeed the thinker who would be able to carry the "Spinozist" reappropriation of Aristotelian *energeia* to a level comparable to that now held by the "Heideggerian" reappropriations of Aristotelian ontology. For if Heidegger was able to join together the self and being-in-the-world, Spinoza—himself of Jewish more than Greek origin—is the only one to have been able to articulate the *conatus* against the backdrop of being, at once actual and powerful, which he calls *essentia actuosa.*

3. Selfhood and Otherness

It was stated at the beginning of this study that the dialectical tie between selfhood and otherness was more fundamental than the articulation between reflection and analysis—which, nonetheless, has been shown by attestation to have ontological stakes as well—and even more fundamental than the contrast between selfhood and sameness, the ontological dimension of which is marked by the notion of being as act and as potentiality.

The fact that otherness is not added on to selfhood from outside, as though to prevent its solipsistic drift, but that it belongs instead to the tenor of meaning and to the ontological constitution of selfhood is a feature that strongly distinguishes this third dialectic from that of selfhood and sameness, which maintains a preeminently disjunctive character.

In order to guide us in the final stage of this ontological investigation, we shall rely upon the remarks that were made above concerning the primacy of this dialectic. We first underscored its participation in the same second-order discourse as the dialectic of the Same and the Other begun by Plato in the "metaphysical" dialogues. The, so to speak, *speculative* character of the dialectic of selfhood and otherness announced itself first and was then projected retrospectively on the other two moments of the ontological investigation. It is here, then, that we surprise this character in its place of origin. In anticipation, we then announced the *polysemic* character of otherness, which, we said, implied that the Other was not reduced, as is too often taken for granted, to the otherness of another Person. This second point deserves explanation. It is the result of the change of orientation of the celebrated dialectic of the Same and the Other when it comes in contact with the hermeneutics of the self. In fact, it is the pole of the Same that is the first to lose its univocity, through the fragmentation that occurs when the identical is split by the dividing line that separates *ipse* from *idem*. The temporal criterion of this division, namely the twofold valence of permanence in time, depending on whether it designates the immutability of *idem* or the self-constancy of *ipse*, deserves to be recalled one last time. The polysemy of selfhood, the first to have been remarked, is revealing with respect to the polysemy of the Other, which stands opposite the Same, in the sense of oneself (*soi-même*).

How are we to account for the work of otherness at the heart of selfhood? It is here that the play between the two levels of discourse—phenomenological discourse and ontological discourse—proves to be most fruitful, by reason of the power of discovery that this play provokes at the same time on both planes. In order to determine our vocabulary here, let us posit that the *phenomenological* respondent to the metacategory of otherness is the variety of experiences of passivity, intertwined in multiple ways in human action. The term "otherness" is then reserved for speculative discourse, while passivity becomes *the* attestation of otherness.

The main virtue of such a dialectic is that it keeps the self from occupying the place of foundation. This prohibition is perfectly suited to the ultimate structure of a self that will neither be exalted, as in the philosophies of the cogito, nor be humiliated, as in the philosophies of the anticogito. In the Introduction I spoke of this work of the broken cogito in order to express this unusual ontological situation. I must now add that this situation is the object of an *attestation which itself is broken,* in the sense that the otherness joined to selfhood is attested to only in a wide range of dissimilar experiences, following a diversity of centers of otherness.

In this regard, I suggest as a working hypothesis what could be called the *triad of passivity and, hence, of otherness.* First, there is the passivity represented by the experience of one's own body—or better, as we shall say later, of the *flesh*—as the mediator between the self and a world which is itself taken in accordance with its variable degrees of practicability and so of foreignness. Next, we find the passivity implied by the relation of the self to the *foreign,* in the precise sense of the other (than) self, and so the otherness inherent in the relation of intersubjectivity. Finally, we have the most deeply hidden passivity, that of the relation of the self to itself, which is *conscience* in the sense of *Gewissen* rather than of *Bewusstsein*. By placing conscience in third place in relation to the passivity-otherness of one's own body and to that of other people, we are underscoring the extraordinary complexity and the relational density of the metacategory of otherness. In return, conscience projects after the fact its force of attestation on all the experiences of passivity placed before it, inasmuch as conscience is also, through and through, attestation.

One last remark before sketching out the investigations called for by each of the three fields of gravitation: it is a matter here not of adding one, two, or three levels to those that have already been reviewed—linguistics, praxis, narrative, ethics—but instead of eliciting the degree of lived passivity proper to these various levels of experience and, hence, of identifying the kind of otherness that corresponds to each on the speculative plane.

a. One's Own Body, or the Flesh

This first figure of passivity-otherness most easily puts into play the referral of phenomenology to ontology. The enigmatic nature of the phenomenon of one's own body has been perceived on at least three separate occasions in the course of our earlier studies.

This occurred first at the time of Strawson's analysis of the basic particular that is the person: how, we asked, can mental and physical predicates be ascribed to one and the same entity, if the human body is not at once a body among others and my body? We confined ourselves at that time to the assertion that persons are also bodies out of linguistic constraint when we speak of things as we do. We did not fail to remark that, if persons are also bodies, it is to the extent that each person is for himself his own body. Accounting for this presupposition requires that we base our language on the ontological constitution of these entities called persons.

The twofold adherence of one's own body to the domain of things and to that of the self also became apparent in our discussion with Davidson: how can human action constitute an event in the world, the latter taken as the sum of all that occurs, and at the same time designate its author in a self-referential manner, if the latter does not belong to the world in a mode in which the self is constitutive of the very sense of this belonging? One's own body is the very place—in the strong sense of the term—of this belonging, thanks to which the self can place its mark on those events that are its actions.

The question of personal identity, carried to its greatest degree of refinement by Parfit, finally took this very problematic of one's own body back to the drawing board, when it was necessary to tie the corporeal and mental criteria of identity—continuity of development, permanence of character, *habitus,* roles, and identifications—to the constancy of a self that finds its anchor in its own body.

However, the phenomenology of passivity does not go beyond the implicit stage we have evoked several times, until, in this global phenomenon of anchoring, we underscore one important feature which our earlier analyses have not sufficiently taken into account, namely *suffering*. Undergoing and enduring are, in a sense, revealed in their complete passive dimension when they become suffering. We have even counted several times on this original correlation between acting and suffering. In this way, in our treatment of narrative identity, we observed that it is the virtue of the narrative to join together agents and patients in the entangling of multiple life histories. But we must go further and take into account more deeply concealed forms of suffering: the incapacity to tell a story, the refusal to recount, the insistence of the untellable—phenomena that go far beyond mishaps and adventures, which can always be made meaningful through the strategy of emplotment. Discussing the place of the Golden Rule in ethics in an earlier study, we measured the basic dissymmetry, inherent in interaction, resulting from the fact that an agent, by exerting a power over another, treats the latter as the patient of his or her action. But here again, we must go further to the very forms of disesteem of self and hatred of others, in which suffering exceeds physical pain. With the decrease of the power of *acting,* experienced as a decrease of the effort of *existing,* the reign of suffering, properly speaking, commences. Most of these sufferings are inflicted on humans by humans. The result is that most of the evil in the world comes from violence among human beings. Here, the passivity belonging to the metacategory of one's own body overlaps with the passivity belonging to the category of other people; the passivity of the suffering self becomes indistinguishable from the passivity of being the victim of the other (than) self. Victimization appears then as passivity's underside, casting a gloom over the "glory" of action.

To articulate speculatively the modality of *otherness* that corresponds to this passivity, we have to grant to the metacategory of one's own body a fullness comparable to that suffering gives to undergoing or enduring. In a sharp-edged dialectic between praxis and pathos, one's own body becomes the emblematic title of a vast inquiry which, beyond the simple mineness of one's own body, denotes the entire sphere of *intimate* passivity, and hence of otherness, for which it forms the center of gravity. In this perspective, one would have to review the conceptual labor that has been done from the classic treatises on the passions, passing by way of Maine de Biran, up to the meditations of Gabriel Marcel, of Merleau-Ponty, and of Michel Henry on embodiment, the flesh, affectivity, and self-affection. I shall not do this here but shall confine myself to hammering out a few points of reference.

I should like, at the start of this brief overview, to give proper credit to the one who opened up this field of investigation of the lived body, namely Maine de Biran: he truly gave an appropriate ontological dimension to his phenomenological discovery, by dissociating the notion of existence from that of substance, and by relating the former to the notion of act. To say "I am" is to say "I want, I move, I do."[26] Now apprehension, distinct from all objectivizing representation, includes within the same certainty the acting self and its contrary, which is also its complement, corporeal passivity. Maine de Biran is therefore the first philosopher to have introduced one's own body into the region of nonrepresentative certainty. This inclusion of one's own body presents increasing degrees of passivity. On the first level, the body denotes resistance that gives way to effort. This is for Maine de Biran the paradigmatic example, effort occupying here the place of impression and sensation in Hume and Condillac. The relational structure of the self itself is wholly contained here, effort and resistance forming an indivisible unity. The body receives here the indelible significance of being my body with its intimate diversity, its extension irreducible to any imagined or represented extension, its mass, and its gravity. This is the experience *priceps,* that of the "active body" illustrated by the happiness and grace of the dancing body, submissive to the music alone. A second degree of passivity is represented by the coming and going of capricious humors—impressions of content or discontent, the movements of which are anxiously noted by Maine de Biran in his *Journal:* passivity, here, becomes foreign and hostile.[27] A third degree of passivity is marked by the resis-

---

26. G. Romeyer-Dherbey, in *Maine de Biran ou le Penseur de l'immanence radicale* (Paris: Seghers, 1974), presents a synthetic view of the revolution in thought made by Maine de Biran. The shift in ontological problematic that results from it is indeed even greater than may at first appear. The old identification between being and substance, which Descartes in no way questioned, rests on an exclusive privilege accorded to quasi-visual representation, which transforms things into a spectacle, into images grasped at a distance. Descartes's doubt is a doubt about the spectacle of things. And if Descartes can doubt that he has a body, it is because he has given himself an image of it that doubt easily reduces to a dream. This is no longer the case if self-apperception is taken as the apperception of an act and not the deduction of a substance. If such an apperception is indubitable, it is to the extent that it is not a form of vision simply turned inside, an intro-spection, which, however close its object may be, contains the minimal distance of reduplication. The intimate sense, it must be said, has no object. An opposition such as this between (immanent) apperception and (transcendent) representation is not without a parallel in post-Wittgensteinian analytic philosophy: E. Anscombe terms a knowledge without observation the knowledge of what we can do, of the position of our body, and so forth. Likewise, the notion of basic action, in Danto and von Wright, rests on this sort of nonobjectivizing apprehension of oneself. What is proper to Maine de Biran is to have perceived the strong tie that exists between being as act, and this apprehension without distance.

27. Commentators have noted that, in Maine de Biran himself, the experience of passive impressions is poorly coordinated with that of the resistance that gives way. Michel Henry, in *Philosophy and Phenomenology of the Body,* trans. Girard Etzkorn (The Hague: Nijhoff,

tance of external things; it is through active touch, in which our effort is extended, that things attest to their existence as indubitably as our own. Here, existing is resisting. It is therefore the same sense that gives the greatest certainty of one's own existence and the greatest certainty of external existence. With the variety of these degrees of passivity, one's own body is revealed to be the mediator between the intimacy of the self and the externality of the world.[28]

The second point of reference, and the most important one along the path that leads from Maine de Biran's philosophy of effort to the three great philosophies of one's own body that I named earlier and to which I shall simply refer the reader, is incontestably to be found in the phenomenology of Husserl. In a sense, his contribution to what has to be termed an ontology of the flesh is more important than that of Heidegger. This affirmation is at first sight paradoxical. This is so in two ways: first, the decisive distinction between *Leib* and *Körper*, "flesh" and "body," occupies a strategic position in the *Cartesian Meditations*, where it represents simply one step in the constitution of a shared nature, that is, of an intersubjectively founded nature. In this way, the notion of flesh is developed only to make possible the pairing (*Paarung*) of one flesh with another flesh, on the basis of which a common nature can be constituted. Finally, with respect to its fundamental *intention*, this problematic remains the constitution of all reality in and through consciousness, a constitution of a piece with the philosophies of the cogito with which we parted ways as early as the Introduction to this work. One might then think that the philosophy of being-in-the-world of *Being and Time* offers a more suitable framework for an ontology of the flesh, by the very reason of its break with the problematic of constitution based on the intentionality of consciousness. But here lies the second side of the paradox; for reasons we shall state, *Being and Time* did not allow an ontology of the flesh to unfold, and it is instead in Husserl, in the work most openly devoted to the renewal of transcendental idealism, that we find the most promising sketch of the ontology of the flesh that would mark the inscription of hermeneutical phenomenology in an ontology of otherness.

The flesh/body polarity owes the radical nature of its opposition pre-

---

1975), has sought the key to the relation between what Maine de Biran calls the active body and the passive body in the Husserlian theory of "passive syntheses." The Biranian theory of habit lends plausibility to this solution.

28. Later we shall ask whether this externality of material things is complete without the testimony of others in addition to myself, which has the effect of decentering the world and removing it from the sphere of mineness by which the sense of touch annexes things themselves to my effort.

cisely to its strategic position in the argumentation of the *Cartesian Meditations*.[29] Here we are in a self-proclaimed egology and not in a philosophy of the self. And it is precisely the difficulties of an egology such as this that will make all the more urgent the distinction between flesh and body. I must add that it is not in connection with some "I can" or "I move" that this theme imposes itself, although this dimension is not absent, but on the level of perception. In the *Cartesian Meditations* the theme of the flesh remains within the pale of *leibhaft selbst* (being given in itself, in the flesh) of the earlier writings. If movement is taken into account, it is to the extent that I can change my perspective of perception and in this way move *myself.*

I am not discussing here the question of whether or not the notion of the *other,* what Husserl calls "the intrinsically first other," namely the other ego, animates the search for an ownness that the ultimate reduction performed in the fourth "Meditation" claims to have isolated.[30] We shall return to this difficulty when we reach the second pole of otherness, that of the other as foreign. What must now retain our attention is the necessity to distinguish between body and flesh, if we are to be able to proceed to the derivation of a unique kind of alter ego starting from the ego. In other words, what is meaningful for us is the very production of this distinction at this crucial moment of the enterprise of the constitution of objective nature on the basis of intersubjectivity. The fact that a phenomenology of constitution fails to account for the constitution of the otherness of the foreign is one thing. However, the fact that in order to constitute a *foreign* subjectivity, it is necessary to formulate the idea of *ownness* that is precisely flesh in its difference with respect to the body is something else again: the latter interests us here.

Myself as flesh, before the constitution of the alter ego, is what the strategy of the intersubjective constitution of nature obliges us to think. That we owe to this impossible enterprise the formation of the ontological concept of flesh is indeed the divine surprise. As we know, the methodological decision rests in the reduction to the sphere of ownness from

---

29. Moving back before the *Cartesian Meditations,* Didier Franck in *Chair et Corps. Sur la phénoménologie de Husserl* (Paris: Éd. de Minuit, 1981) sees in the theme of *Leibhaft* (embodied givenness), as early as Husserl's *Ideas* 1, the necessary antecedent of the problematic of the flesh: "Embodied givenness, which defines evidence in general (before all critique and hence before any problem of apodicticity, for example) must not be taken as a metaphor, a manner of speaking, a figure proper to Husserl's style" (p. 19). The theme of embodiment is also held to have preceded that of the flesh.

30. Cf. my analysis of the "Fifth Cartesian Meditation" in *Husserl: An Analysis of his Phenomenology,* trans. Edward G. Ballard and Lester E. Embree (Evanston, Ill.: Northwestern University Press, 1967), pp. 115–42.

which would be excluded all objective predicates indebted to intersubjectivity. The flesh would then prove to be the pole of reference of all bodies
belonging to this nature (ownness).[31]

Let us leave aside here the derivation of the alter ego through pairing
one flesh with another; let us ponder the phenomenological trait of the
flesh that designates it as a paradigm of otherness. The fact that the flesh
is most originally mine and of all things that which is closest, that its
aptitude for feeling is revealed most characteristically in the sense of touch,
as in Maine de Biran—these primordial features make it possible for flesh
to be the organ of desire, the support of free movement; but one cannot
say that they are the object of choice or desire. I, as this man: this is the
foremost otherness of the flesh with respect to all initiative. Otherness
here signifies primordiality with respect to any *design*. Starting from this
otherness, I can *reign over*. Primordiality, however, is not a reign. Ontologically, the flesh precedes the distinction between the voluntary and the
involuntary. It can, of course, be characterized by the "I can"; the "I can,"
however, does not derive from the "I want" but provides a ground for it. The
flesh is the place of all the passive syntheses on which the active syntheses
are constructed, the latter alone deserving to be called works (*Leistungen*):
the flesh is the matter (*hulē*) in resonance with all that can be said to be
hulē in every object perceived, apprehended. In short, it is the origin of all
"alteration of ownness."[32] From the above, it results that selfhood implies
its own "proper" otherness, so to speak, for which the flesh is the support.[33] In this sense, even if the otherness of the stranger can—by some
impossibility—be derived from the sphere of ownness, the otherness of
the flesh would still precede it.

The question then arises whether Husserl's great discovery, supported

31. Here I shall quote this crucial text in the "Fifth Meditation," with reference to Didier
Franck's translation: "Among the bodies belonging to this 'Nature' and included in my peculiar ownness, I then find my *animate organism* [*meinen Leib*, which Franck renders as *chair*,
'flesh'] as *uniquely* singled out—namely as the only one of them that is not just a body but
precisely an animate organism [*chair*, 'flesh']: the sole object within my abstract world-stra-
tum to which, in accordance with experience, I ascribe *fields of sensation* (belonging to it,
however, in different manners—a field of tactual sensations, a field of warmth and coldness,
and so forth), the only object 'in' which I '*rule and govern*' *immediately*, governing particularly
in each of its organs" (E. Husserl, *Cartesian Meditation*, trans. Dorion Cairns [The Hague:
M. Nijhoff, 1969], p. 97; passage cited and translated by Didier Franck, *Chair et Corps*,
pp. 93–94).
32. "L'Altération du propre" is the title of one of the chapters of Didier Franck's work
Chair et Corps, pp. 109ff.
33. Didier Franck discusses the connection between selfhood and self-givenness in
par. 46 of the *Cartesian Meditations* in *Chair et Corps*, p. 111.

by the distinction between flesh and body, can be dissociated from what above we termed its strategic role in transcendental phenomenology at the time of the *Cartesian Meditations*. I believe so. In addition to the problem, to which we shall return later, of the derivation of the status of the foreign starting from the sphere of ownness on the basis of the unparalleled passive synthesis formed by the "pairing" of the ego and the alter ego, one can find in Husserl's unpublished manuscripts investigations and developments on the difference (and the relation) between flesh and body, relatively independent of the problematic of the intersubjective constitution of nature common to all. What is said about the distinction between *here* and *there*, insofar as these are irreducible to any localization through objective points of reference, belongs preeminently to this phenomenological ontology of the flesh. In these texts dealing with the objective nonspatiality of the flesh, one finds an unexpected echo of Wittgenstein's reflections on the nonbelonging of the subject to the system of his objects and on the implications of this paradox concerning the notion of *anchoring*, which we encountered early on in the course of these studies. To say that the flesh is absolutely here, and so heterogeneous with respect to any set of geometric coordinates, is equivalent to saying that it is nowhere in terms of objective spatiality. And the "over there," where I could be if I transported myself there—outside of the question of knowing in what sense what is over there for me can "resemble the here for another"—has the same status of heterogeneity as the here of which it is the correlate. On the basis of the model of the problem of localizing the flesh, other problems relating to the primordial spatiality of the flesh could be posed. Among these, I shall note those related to the *environing world*, taken as the correlate of the body-flesh. What we read in the unpublished manuscripts about the world as practicable completes fortuitously what has just been said about the internal, as it were, spatiality of the flesh. At the same time, the notes on contact as a primitive form of sensing give new life to the entire Biranian problematic of existence-resistance and prompt us to shift our emphasis to the pole of the world in the spatiality of the flesh. As Jean-Luc Petit has established in the work we have quoted so many times, it is upon this prelinguistic relation between my flesh localized by the self and a world accessible or inaccessible to the "I can" that a semantics of action is finally to be constructed which will not lose its way in the endless exchange of language games.

Only as the ontology of the flesh breaks free as far as possible from the problematic of constitution that paradoxically required it can we face the inverse paradox to that posed by Strawson's theory of basic particulars: namely, not what it means that a body is my body, that is, flesh, but that

the flesh is also a body among bodies. It is here that phenomenology finds
its limit, at least the phenomenology that intends to derive the objective
aspects of the world from a nonobjectifying primordial experience, principally by means of intersubjectivity. The problem we called the reinscription of phenomenological time in cosmological time in *Time and Narrative*
finds a series of equivalences here: just as it was necessary to invent the
calendar to correlate the lived now with the anonymous instant and to
draw up the geographic map to correlate the charnel here with an indifferent place, and thereby to inscribe the proper name—my name—in the
civil register, it is necessary, as Husserl himself states, to *make* the flesh
part of the world (*mondaneiser*) if it is to appear as a body among bodies. It
is here that the otherness of others as foreign, other than me, seems to
have to be, not only interconnected with the otherness of the flesh that
I am, but held in its way to be prior to the reduction to ownness. For
my flesh appears as a body among bodies only to the extent that I am
myself an other among all the others, in the apprehension of a common
nature, woven, as Husserl says, out of the network of intersubjectivity—
itself, unlike Husserl's conception, founding selfhood in its own way. It
is because Husserl thought of the other than me only as another me,
and never of the self as another, that he has no answer to the paradox
summed up in the question: How am I to understand that my flesh is also
a body?

Should we not then turn to *Being and Time* to develop an ontology of
the flesh that takes into account both the flesh's intimacy to the self and its
opening onto the world? This is the second side of the paradox mentioned
above, namely that it is Husserl and not Heidegger who opened the way
for this ontology, although the general framework of thought in *Being and
Time* appears better suited to this sort of undertaking; in substituting the
encompassing structure of being-in-the-world for the problem of the
constitution of a world in and through consciousness, in calling Dasein,
being-there, the being that does not belong to the ensemble of beings
present-at-hand, did not Heidegger, in principle, free the problematic of
one's own body from the trial of a reduction to ownness, within the general reduction of all being "taken for granted"? By moving regressively
from the sense of inclusive "worldliness" to the sense of "in," did he not
indicate the philosophical place of the flesh? Furthermore, did he not accord a place for state-of-mind, or mood (*Befindlichkeit*), beyond any psychology of affects in the existential constitution of the there (§29)?[34] And

34. In a sense, the Heideggerian theory of state-of-mind can be interpreted as crowning
the Biranian enterprise. The analytic of Dasein is directed straightaway to that which, for
Maine de Biran, remained peripheral to the analysis of effort, namely the recognition of

did he not perceive, at the heart of every state-of-mind, the blatant fact of the impossibility of getting out of a condition into which no one has ever entered, inasmuch as birth itself, as Hannah Arendt expresses so eloquently, has never, properly speaking, been the experience of entering into the world but that of already having been born and of finding oneself already there?

From these preliminary remarks, one could conclude that, if there is an existential category especially appropriate to an investigation of the self as flesh, it would be that of *thrownness*, thrown-there. If we are willing to admit that this expression does not suggest any fall from some higher place, in the gnostic manner, but the *facticity* on the basis of which Dasein becomes a burden for itself, then the character of the weight of existence immediately signifies being delivered over to oneself, hence an opening, by virtue of which all the affective tones express both the self-intimacy of being-there and the manners of appearing in the world. The notion of a thrown-project, even in the sense of fallen, deteriorated (or *échu*, in Martineau's translation of Heideggerian *Verfallen*), indeed carries to the level of concept the strangeness of human finiteness, insofar as it is sealed by embodiment, hence what we call here primary otherness, in order to distinguish it from the otherness of the foreign. One could even say that the link, in the same existentiale of state-of-mind, of the burdensome character of existence and of the task of having-to-be, expresses what is most crucial in the paradox of an otherness constitutive of the self and in this way reveals for the first time the full force of the expression "oneself as another."

And yet, despite having set into place a conceptual apparatus that seems so well suited to developing an ontology of the flesh, we have to admit that Heidegger has not developed the notion of the flesh as a distinct existentiale. I see several reasons for this silence. The first has to do with what can be termed the phenomenological impetus of the ontology of Dasein. For having placed too great an emphasis on fear (*Being and Time*, §30) and finally on the anxiety stemming from being-toward-death, does

---

external existence as the resistance of things in the experience of the active sense of touch. For Maine de Biran, indeed, it was necessary to start first with the tie between effort and resistance before positing on the edge of the experience of the active body, immanent to the desiring self, the tactile experience of reality. By making the existentiale being-in-the-world the framework for the entire analysis, Heidegger opens the way for an ontology of the flesh, in which the latter gives itself to be thought not only as the embodiment of "I am" but as the practical meditation of that being-in-the-world that we are in each case. This conjunction between flesh and world is held to allow us to think of the properly passive modalities of our desires and our moods as the sign, the symptom, the indication of the contingent character of our insertion in the world.

one not neglect the instructions that a phenomenology of suffering would be most apt to dispense? Only in the work of Michel Henry do we find this phenomenology practiced. Next, if we remain within the framework sketched out by the ontology of being-in-the-world, we may wonder if the phenomenology of spatiality, so propitiously begun in Husserl, receives the attention it deserves in Heidegger. To be sure, paragraph 24 of *Being and Time* is specifically devoted to the spatiality of Dasein and underscores the irreducibility of this spatiality to geometric space as a system of indifferent places. Why, then, did Heidegger not grasp this opportunity to reinterpret the Husserlian notion of flesh (*Leib*), which he could not have been unaware of, in terms of the analytic of Dasein? The answer we can give to this question perhaps touches an essential point: as is suggested by the earlier paragraphs dealing with the spatiality of the world—"the environment of the environing world" (*l'ambiance du monde ambiant* in Martineau's translation)—the spatial dimension of being-in-the-world appears to involve mainly the inauthentic forms of care. Dasein's spatiality, to be sure, is not that of a being present-at-hand, or even that of a being ready-to-hand, but it is against the backdrop of the spatiality of available and manipulable things that Dasein's spatiality is made, with painstaking effort, to stand out. If the theme of embodiment appears to be stifled, if not repressed, in *Being and Time,* this is doubtless because it must have appeared too dependent on the inauthentic forms of care—let us say, of preoccupation—that make us tend to interpret ourselves in terms of the objects of our care.[35] We may then wonder if it is not the unfolding of the problematic of temporality, triumphant in the second section of *Being and Time,* that prevented an *authentic* phenomenology of spatiality—and along with it, an ontology of the flesh—from being given its chance to develop. It is as though temporality were the exclusive theme of a meditation on authentic existence, as though the authentic features of spatiality were finally to be derived from those of temporality. Lastly, one may wonder whether Heidegger saw the resources that could be found in a philosophy of being that would substitute the transcendental of the act for that of substance, as is demanded by a phenomenology of acting and suffering. This final remark forms a bridge between the reflections made in this section and those of the section preceding it in the present study. It is

35. What is said about the reinterpretation of the *pathē* in book 2 of Aristotle's *Rhetoric* moves in this direction: "It is not an accident that the earliest systematic Interpretation of affects that has come down to us is not treated in the framework of 'psychology'. Aristotle investigates the *pathē* [affects] in the second book of his *Rhetoric*. Contrary to the traditional orientation, according to which rhetoric is conceived as the kind of thing we 'learn in school', this work of Aristotle must be taken as the first systematic hermeneutic of the everydayness of Being with one another" (*Being and Time*, p. 178).

the entire forefront of the ontology of selfhood that must move in accordance with the three dimensions of otherness.

b. The Otherness of Other People

The second signification contained in the metacategory of otherness—the otherness of other people—is closely tied to the modalities of *passivity* that the phenomenological hermeneutic of the self has come across repeatedly throughout the earlier studies concerning the relation of the self to the other than self. A new dialectic of the Same and the Other is produced by this hermeneutic, which, in many ways, attests that here the Other is not only the counterpart of the Same but belongs to the intimate constitution of its sense. Indeed, on the properly phenomenological level, the multiple ways in which the other than self affects the understanding of the self by itself marks, precisely, the difference between the *ego* that posits itself and the *self* that recognizes itself only through these very affections.

There is not a single one of our analyses in which this specific passivity of the self affected by the other than self is not announced. Even on the linguistic plane, the speaker's self-designation appeared to be intertwined, to employ a familiar term of Husserlian terminology, to the speech situation by virtue of which every participant is affected by the speech addressed to him or to her. Listening to speech then becomes an integral part of discourse inasmuch as it is itself addressed to another.

In the second phase of our work, the self-designation of the agent of action appeared to be inseparable from the ascription by another, who designates me in the accusative as the author of my actions. In this exchange between ascription in the second person and self-designation, one can say that the reflexive recovery of this being-affected by the ascription pronounced by others is intertwined with the intimate ascription of action to oneself. This intertwining is expressed on the grammatical plane by the omnipersonal character of the self, which circulates among all the pronouns. The affection of the self by the other than self is the basis for this ordered exchange between the grammatical persons.

It is, once again, the same exchange between the affected self and the affecting other that governs, on the narrative plane, the way the reader of a story assumes the roles held by the characters, which are most often constructed in the third person, inasmuch as they enter into the plot at the same time as the action recounted. Reading, as the milieu in which the transfer between the world of the narrative—and hence the world of the literary characters as well—and the world of the reader takes place, constitutes a privileged place and bond for the affection of the reading subject. The reader's catharsis, we might say—freely borrowing some of the categories from H. R. Jauss's aesthetics of reception—occurs only if it proceeds from a prior *aisthēsis,* which the reader's struggle with the text transforms into *poiēsis.*[36] It thus appears that the affection of the self by the other than self finds in *fiction* a privileged milieu for thought experiments that cannot be eclipsed by the "real" relations of interlocution and interaction. Quite the opposite, the reception of works of fiction contributes to the imaginary and symbolic constitution of the actual exchanges of words and actions. Being-affected in the fictive mode is therefore incorporated into the self's being-affected in the "real" mode.

It is finally on the ethical plane that the affection of the self by the other displays the specific features that belong as much to the properly ethical plane as to the moral plane of obligation. The very definition of ethics that we have proposed—living well with and for others in just institutions—cannot be conceived without the project of living well being affected by solicitude, both that which is exerted and that which is received. Prior to any consideration of the justice of the exchanges, the dialectic of self-esteem and friendship can be entirely rewritten in terms of a dialectic of action and affection. In order to be the "friend of oneself"—in accordance with Aristotelian *philautia*—one must already have entered into a relation of friendship with others, as though friendship for oneself were a self-affection rigorously correlative to the affection by and for the other as friend. In this sense, friendship forms the bed of justice, as the virtue "for others," following another of Aristotle's sayings. The passage from ethics to morality—from the optative mode of living well to the imperative mode of obligation—occurred, in the study that followed, under the protection of the Golden Rule, to which we thought we gave full credit by assigning to it the merit of interposing the commandment at the very intersection of the asymmetrical relation between doing and undergoing (the good you would want to be done to you, the evil you would hate to be done to you). Acting and suffering then seem to be distributed between two different protagonists: the agent and the patient, the latter appearing as the potential victim of the former. But because of the reversibility of the roles, each agent is the patient of the other. Inasmuch as one is affected by the power over one exerted by the other, the agent is invested with the responsibility of an action that is placed from the very outset under the rule of reciprocity, which the rule of justice will transform into a rule of equality. Since each protagonist holds two roles, being both agent and patient, the formalism of the categorical imperative requires the "matter" of a *plurality* of acting beings each affected by forces exerted reciprocally.

The question here is that of determining what new figure of otherness is called for by this affection of the *ipse* by the other than self and, by

36. Jauss, "La Jouissance esthétique."

implication, what dialectic of the Same and the Other replies to the demand for a phenomenology of the self *affected* by the other than self.

I should like to show essentially that it is impossible to construct this dialectic in a unilateral manner, whether one attempts, with Husserl, to derive the alter ego from the ego, or whether, with Lévinas, one reserves for the Other the exclusive initiative for assigning responsibility to the self. A two-pronged conception of otherness remains to be constructed here, one that does justice in turn to the primacy of self-esteem and also to the primacy of the convocation to justice coming from the other. What is at stake here, as we shall soon see, is a formulation of otherness that is homogeneous with the fundamental distinction between two ideas of the Same—the Same as *idem* and the Same as *ipse*—a distinction upon which our entire philosophy of selfhood (*ipseity*) has been based.

We cannot take up our examination of the "Fifth Cartesian Meditation" where we left it at the point of the reduction to the sphere of ownness, a reduction to which we owed the beginnings of an ontology of the flesh, without first expressing some concern about whether the reduction to ownness is capable of being thought nondialectically, that is, without the simultaneous interference of the *foreign*. To be sure, Husserl, like everyone, knows that we are not alone and that we deny our transcendental solitude by the sole fact that we name it and address it to some partner in the discourse of the *Cartesian Meditations*. Like each of us, he understands, prior to any philosophy, the word "other" as meaning other than me. Having said this, the fifth meditation stems from the bold stroke of the preceding meditation, a stroke by which the meditating ego reduces this common knowledge to the status of a prejudice, and so holds it to be unfounded.[37] The meditating ego will therefore begin by suspending, hence by rendering entirely problematic, all that ordinary experience owes to others in order to discern that which, in experience reduced to the sphere of ownness, makes the positing of others just as apodictic as the positing of itself. This movement of thought is entirely comparable to Descartes's hyperbolic doubt, except that it is not based on the hypothesis of any evil

---

37. The "Fourth Cartesian Meditation" says that the ego "as the active and affected subject of consciousness, lives in all processes of consciousness and is related, through them, to all object-poles" (Husserl, *Cartesian Meditations*, p. 66). It is therefore the determination of thoughts as acts and the play between passivity and activity that results from this that, on principle, singularizes the ego. Moreover, the ego of the fourth meditation proves to be the substratum of its dispositions, its convictions, its permanent properties—in short, of what, since Aristotle, is called *hexis, habitus;* through this, the ego has a *style,* namely the character of a person. Even more fundamentally, the ego is that to which all thoughts, in the broadest sense of the word, belong, and it makes all transcendencies modalities of its interiority. The ego then allows itself to be thought as a *monad,* and phenomenology as transcendental egology.

genius; instead it consists in an operation foreign to any ordinary suspicion: it is a philosophical act, belonging to the family of founding acts. As we shall see later, it is by a comparable, though opposite, hyperbole that E. Lévinas will initiate his conception of radical otherness. As concerns the *epokhē* practiced here by Husserl, within the general *epokhē* that inaugurates phenomenology, it is held to leave a remainder that owes nothing to others, namely the sphere of ownness, to which belongs the ontology of the flesh discussed above. Allow me to stress here the fact that this sphere of ownness is entirely dependent, as to its sense, on the reduction forcibly performed within the reduction. The only path then left open is that of constituting the senses of the other "in" (German, *in*) and "on the basis of" (*aus*) the sense of the I. In an instant we shall say what phenomenological discovery we owe to this bold stroke, a discovery that amounts to a veritable rebellion as regards any project of constitution, if constitution signifies a foundation in and through the I. But first it must be said that all the arguments that are intended to "constitute" the other in and on the basis of the sphere of ownness are circular, doubtless because the constitution of the thing tacitly remains the model for this constitution.

The fact that the other is presupposed from the very outset is confirmed, a first time, by the *epokhē* with which the analysis begins: in one way or another, I have always known that the other is not an object of thought but, like me, a subject of thought, that he perceives me as other than himself, that together we intend the world as a common nature, that together, as well, we build communities of persons capable of behaving, in their turn, on the scene of history as personalities of a higher order. This tenor of meaning precedes the reduction to ownness. Next, the presupposition of the other is a second time—and more secretly—contained in the formation of the very sense of the sphere of ownness. In the hypothesis that I am alone, this experience could never be totalized without the help of the other who helps me to gather myself together, strengthen myself, and maintain myself in my identity.[38] In this sphere of ownness, transcendence reduced in this way to immanence would deserve even less to be called a world; the world has no meaning before the constitution of a common nature. Finally, and most especially, my own body, my flesh, cannot serve as the first *analogon* for an analogical transfer if it is not already held to be a body among bodies. Husserl himself speaks here, as we

---

38. A psychoanalytic conception, like that of Heinz Kohut, called "self-analysis," amply confirms this; without the support of self-objects (in the psychoanalytic sense of the term), the self would lack cohesiveness, self-confidence, self-esteem—in short, it would lack true "narcissism." In other words, the flesh in danger of fragmentation needs the help of the other for its identification. As a result, the flesh remains forever "incompletely constituted" (D. Franck, *Chair et Corps*, p. 130).

have already mentioned, of the process of "making into a world," by which I identify myself with one of the things of nature, namely a physical body. Making into a world consists in an authentic intertwining (*Verflechtung*) by which I perceive myself as a thing in the world. Given this, has the die not already been cast? To say that my flesh is also a body, does this not imply that it appears in just this way to the eyes of others? Only a flesh (for me) that is a body (for others) can play the role of first *analogon* in the analogical transfer from flesh to flesh.

And yet, through a paradox similar to that we mentioned in the preceding section, the failure of the constitution of others, as a constitution belonging to the foundational aim characteristic of an ultimately egological transcendental phenomenology, provided the opportunity for an authentic discovery, parallel to that of the difference between flesh and body—one, moreover, related to the latter—namely the discovery of the paradoxical character of the other's mode of *givenness:* intentionalities that are directed to the other as foreign, that is, as other than me, *go beyond* the sphere of ownness in which they are nevertheless rooted.

Husserl gave the name "appresentation" to this givenness in order to express, on the one hand, that unlike representations in signs or images, the givenness of the other is an authentic givenness and, on the other hand, that unlike the orginary, immediate givenness of the flesh to itself, the givenness of the other never allows me to live the experiences of others and, in this sense, can never be converted into originary presentation. This has also been said elsewhere about memory: the series of memories of others can never find a place in the series of my own memories. In this sense, the gap can never be bridged between the presentation of my experience and the appresentation of your experience.

To this twofold negative characterization, Husserl adds the positive feature that constitutes his genuine discovery. Appresentation, he says, consists in an "apperceptive transfer from my [flesh]" (*Cartesian Meditations,* §50, p. 110), more precisely, in an "analogizing apprehension" (p. 111) whose origin lies in the body of the other perceived "over there": an analogizing apprehension by virtue of which the other's body is apprehended as flesh, for the same reason as my own. One may ask, along with D. Franck, "by virtue of *what* can a body *over there* that, as such, is presented as immanent transcendence, receive the sense of flesh and, thanks to this sense, appresent another *ego* whose transcendence is of a higher order" (*Chair et Corps,* p. 125)? In truth, apprehending a body over there as flesh *is* appresentation itself as such. If we seek an argument here, we find only a circle: appresentation presupposes itself, and in this it constitutes not only a paradox in relation to the constitution of things but also an enigma that can only be twisted in every direction. Do we make any progress by characterizing in terms of "pairing" (*Paarung*) the grasp of the body over there as flesh? A new idea is, of course, introduced, the idea of forming a couple between one flesh and another. We indeed understand that only an embodied ego, that is, an ego that is its own body, can be paired with the flesh of another ego. But what does "being paired with" mean? What if we stress the resemblance included in the notion of pairing? This is perfectly legitimate, but on the condition of distinguishing the analogical transfer from any discursive use of comparison. In this respect, appresentation differs not only from apprehending through signs or images and from originary intuition but also from any inference through which one would conclude, for example, a resemblance between mental experiences based upon an objective resemblance between expressions.[39] Instead, "passive syntheses" are to be compared to this analogical grasping, if it is not to be a form of inference. The transfer by which my flesh forms a pair with another flesh is a prereflexive, predicative operation, but this is an unparalleled passive synthesis—the most primitive perhaps, and one that is found intertwined with all the other "passive syntheses." Moreover, the assimilation of one term to another, which appears to be implied by the notion of analogizing grasp, has to be corrected by the idea of a fundamental dissymmetry, tied to the gap we mentioned earlier between appresentation and originary presentation. Never will pairing allow us to cross the barrier that separates appresentation from intuition. The notion of appresentation, therefore, combines similarity and dissymmetry in a unique manner.

So, one may ask, what has been gained by introducing the notions of appresentation, analogical apprehension, and pairing? If they cannot take the place of a constitution in and through the ego, they at least serve to point up an enigma that we can localize: the kind of transgression of the sphere of ownness constituted by appresentation is valid only within the limits of a transfer of *sense:* the sense of ego is transferred to another body, which, as flesh, also contains the sense of ego. Whence the perfectly adequate expression of alter ego in the sense of "a second flesh" ("seconde chair propre," in D. Franck's expression, *Chair et Corps,* p. 135). Resemblance and dissymmetry have a bearing on the sense of ego and on that of alter ego. Kept within these limits, Husserl's discovery is ineffaceable. Later we shall see that it bears all its fruits only in conjunction with the

---

39. In this regard, the role Husserl assigns to the *concordant* grasp of sketches is not to be understood in terms of a reasoning process that draws a conclusion for the concordance of appresentations based upon that of presentations. This involves instead a relation of *indication* in which the interpretation is made immediately, much as the reading of symptoms. The style of confirmation to which this reading of indications belongs involves the same neither-nor discourse characteristic of appresentation: neither primordial intuition nor discursive inference.

movement coming from the other toward me. However, if this second movement has priority in the ethical dimension, the movement from the ego toward the alter ego maintains a priority in the gnoseological dimension. In this dimension, the analogical transfer indicated by Husserl is an authentically productive operation, to the extent that it transgresses the very program of phenomenology, in transgressing the experience of one's own flesh. If it does not create otherness, which is always presupposed, it confers upon it a specific meaning, namely the admission that the other is not condemned to remain a stranger but can become *my counterpart,* that is, someone who, *like* me, says "I." The resemblance based on the pairing of flesh with flesh works to reduce a distance, to bridge a gap, in the very place where it creates a dissymmetry. That is what is signified by the adverb "like": like me, the other thinks, desires, enjoys, suffers. If it is objected that the transfer of sense does not produce the sense of *alter* in alter ego but the sense of ego, it must be replied that this is indeed the case in the gnoseological dimension. The sense of *ego* in alter ego is the one we have presupposed in all our studies concerning the self-designation of any person other than myself—in language, in action, in narrative, and in moral imputation. Ultimately, this transfer of sense can receive the form of a citation, by virtue of which "he thinks," "she thinks," signifies "he/she says in his/her heart: I think." This is the marvel of analogical transfer.

It is here that the analogical transfer from myself to the other intersects with the inverse movement of the other toward me. It intersects with the latter but does not abolish it, even if it does not presuppose it.

This movement of the other toward me is sketched out again and again in the works of Emmanuel Lévinas. At the origin of this movement lies a break. And this break occurs at the point of articulation of phenomenology and of the ontology of the "great kinds," the Same and the Other. This is why we have reserved until this moment the encounter with the work of Emmanuel Lévinas. From a critical perspective, this work is, in fact, directed against a conception of the identity of the Same, to which the otherness of the Other is diametrically opposed, but at a level of radicality where the distinction I propose between two sorts of identity, that of *ipse* and that of *idem,* cannot be taken into account: to be sure, this is not the result of some phenomenological or hermeneutical negligence but because, in Lévinas, the identity of the Same is bound up with an ontology of totality that my own investigation has never assumed or even come across. It results that the self, not distinguished from the I, is not taken in the sense of the self-designation of a subject of discourse, action, narrative, or ethical commitment. A pretension dwells within it, one more radical than that driving the Fichtean, then Husserlian ambition of universal constitution and radical self-grounding; this pretension expresses a will to closure, more precisely a state of separation, that makes otherness the equivalent of radical exteriority.

In what way is Husserl concerned by this breaking effect? He is concerned to the extent that phenomenology and its major theme of intentionality belong to a philosophy of *representation* that, according to Lévinas, cannot help but be idealist and solipsistic. To represent something to oneself is to assimilate it to oneself, to include it in oneself, and hence to deny its otherness. The analogical transfer, which is the major contribution of the *Cartesian Meditations,* does not escape this reign of representation. It is therefore in a nongnoseological domain of thought that the other attests to himself. This domain is fundamentally that of ethics. When the face of the other raises itself before me, above me, it is not an appearance that I can include within the sphere of my own representations. To be sure, the other appears, his face makes him appear, but the face is not a spectacle; it is a voice.[40] This voice tells me, "Thou shall not kill." Each face is a Sinai that prohibits murder. And me? It is in me that the movement coming from the other completes its trajectory: the other constitutes me as responsible, that is, as capable of responding. In this way, the word of the other comes to be placed at the origin of my acts. Self-imputation, the central theme of the preceding three studies, is now inscribed within an asymmetrical dialogic structure whose origin lies outside me.

The question raised by this conception of the Other is not posed on the level of descriptions, however admirable they may be, which still belong to what could be called an alternative phenomenology, a different hermeneutic, one that could ultimately be situated as an extension of Kantian ethics. In a sense, Lévinas does break with representation, just as Kant maintains practical reason outside the realm of theoretical reason. However, whereas Kant placed respect for the law above respect for persons, with Lévinas the face singularizes the commandment: it is in each case for the first time that the Other, a particular Other, says to me: "Thou shall not kill." Lévinas's philosophy, as was suggested above, arises as an effect of a break that occurs at the very point where what we have just called an alternative phenomenology is joined to a reworking of the "great kinds" of the Same and the Other. Because the Same signifies totalization and separation, the exteriority of the Other can no longer be expressed in the language of relation. The Other absolves itself from relation, in the same movement by which the Infinite draws free from Totality. But how are we

40. Lévinas, "The Face Speaks," in *Totality and Infinity: An Essay on Exteriority,* trans. A. Lingis (Pittsburgh: Duquesne University Press, 1969), p. 67. And again: "The eye does not shine; it speaks" (ibid.).

to think the irrelation implied by this otherness in its movement of absolution?

It appears to me that the break effect related to this thought of absolute otherness stems from the use of *hyperbole,* one worthy of Cartesian hyperbolic doubt and diametrically opposed to the hyperbole by which we characterized above the reduction to ownness in Husserl. By hyperbole, it must be strongly underscored, we are not to understand a figure of style, a literary trope, but the systematic practice of *excess* in philosophical argumentation. Hyperbole appears in this context as the strategy suited to producing the effect of a break with regard to the idea of exteriority in the sense of absolute otherness.

Hyperbole, in fact, simultaneously reaches both poles, the Same and the Other. It is remarkable that *Totality and Infinity* begins by establishing an ego possessed by the desire to form a circle with itself, to identify itself. Even more than in *Time and the Other,*[41] which speaks of the ego "encumbered" by the self, the ego before the encounter with the other (it would be better to say, the ego before it is broken into by the other) is a stubbornly closed, locked up, separate ego. The theme of *separation,* as bound up as it is with phenomenology—with a phenomenology of egotism—already bears the mark of hyperbole: hyperbole expressed in the virulence of a declaration such as this: "In separation . . . the I is ignorant of the Other" (*Totality and Infinity,* p. 62). For an ego such as this, incapable of the Other, the *epiphany* of the face (still a phenomenological theme) signifies an absolute exteriority, that is, a nonrelative exteriority (a theme belonging to the dialectic of the "great kinds").

To the hyperbole of separation, on the side of the Same, replies the hyperbole of epiphany on the side of the Other. Epiphany expresses something different than phenomenon. The "evincing" of the face lies apart from the vision of forms and even from the sensuous hearing of voices. This is because the Other, according to *Totality and Infinity,* is not some interlocutor but a paradigmatic figure of the type of a master of justice. In this sense, the assertion that speech "is a teaching" (p. 67) is hyperbolic. The hyperbole is at once that of Elevation and that of Exteriority. Elevation—the face of the Other—it has been said, summons me as though from Sinai. Exteriority—the teaching of the face—unlike the maieutics of Plato's *Meno,* awakens no reminiscence. Separation has made interiority sterile. Since the initiative belongs wholly to the Other, it is in the accusative—a mode well named—that the I is met by the injunction and made

41. Emmanuel Lévinas, *Time and the Other,* trans. Richard A. Cohen (Pittsburgh: Duquesne University Press, 1987), p. 56.

capable of answering, again in the accusative: "It's me here!"[42] Hyperbole, in *Totality and Infinity,* culminates in the affirmation that the teaching of the face reestablishes no primacy of relation with respect to the terms. No middle ground, no between, is secured to lessen the utter dissymmetry between the Same and the Other.

Lévinas's *Otherwise than Being* employs even greater hyperbole, to the point of paroxysm. A preparatory work of demolition finishes off the ruins of "representation," of the "theme," of the "Said," in order to open up, beyond "Saying" (*Dire*) the era of "Retraction" (*Dédire*). In the name of this retraction the *assignment of responsibility* withdraws from the language of manifestation, from its expression, and from its theme. As retraction, the assignment of responsibility adopts the figure of hyperbole, in a range of excess never before attained. In this way the assignment of responsibility is carried back to a past more ancient than any past of memory, which would still be able to be taken up in a present consciousness. The injunction comes from that which is prior to any beginning, any *arkhē:* the retraction of the *arkhē* is named *an-archy.* Also participating in hyperbole is the evocation of being-assigned, which is not to be considered the other side of any activity, and hence of "a responsibility that is justified by no prior commitment" (p. 102). After this, the language becomes more and more excessive: "obsession of the Other," "persecution by the Other," and finally, and especially, "substitution of the I for the Other." Here, the work reaches its paroxysm: "Under accusation by everyone, the responsibility for everyone goes to the point of substitution. A subject is a hostage" (p. 112). This expression, the most excessive of all, is thrown out here in order to prevent the insidious return of the self-affirmation of some "clandestine and hidden freedom" maintained even within the passivity of the self summoned to responsibility. The paroxysm of the hyperbole seems to me to result from the extreme—even scandalous—hypothesis that the Other is no longer the master of justice here, as is the case in *Totality and Infinity,* but the offender, who, as an offender, no less requires the gesture of pardon and expiation. There is no doubt that this is just where Lévinas wants to lead the reader: "The overemphasis of openness is responsibility for the other to the point of substitution, where the for-the-other proper to disclosure, to monstration to the other, turns into the for-the-other proper to responsibility. This is the thesis of the present work" (p. 113). Indeed, it is only here that the abyss hollowed out between otherness and identity is bridged: "We have to speak here of expiation as uniting identity and alterity" (p. 118).

42. Hyperbole: "the accusative form, which is a modification of no nominative form" (Lévinas, *Otherwise than Being,* p. 124).

Paradoxically, it is the hyperbole of separation, on the side of the Same, that appears to me to lead the hyperbole of exteriority, on the side of the other, to an impasse, unless the preeminently ethical movement of the other toward the self is made to intersect with (as we have termed it) the gnoseological movement from the self toward the other. In truth, what the hyperbole of separation renders unthinkable is the distinction between self and I, and the formation of a concept of selfhood defined by its openness and its capacity for discovery.

Now the theme of exteriority does not reach the end of its trajectory, namely awakening a responsible response to the other's call, except by presupposing a capacity of reception, of discrimination, and of recognition that, in my opinion, belongs to another philosophy of the Same than that to which the philosophy of the Other replies. If interiority were indeed determined solely by the desire for retreat and closure, how could it ever hear a word addressed to it, which would seem so foreign to it that this word would be as nothing for an isolated existence? One has to grant a capacity of reception to the self that is the result of a reflexive structure, better defined by its power of reconsidering preexisting objectifications than by an initial separation. Even more important, must we not join to this capacity of reception a capacity of discernment and recognition, taking into account the fact that the otherness of the Other cannot be summed up in what seems to be just one of the figures of the Other, that of the master who teaches, once we have to consider as well the figure of the offender in *Otherwise than Being*? And what are we to say of the Other when he is the executioner? And who will be able to distinguish the master from the executioner, the master who calls for a disciple from the master who requires a slave? As for the master who teaches, does he not ask to be recognized in his very superiority? In other words, must not the voice of the Other who says to me: "Thou shalt not kill," become my own, to the point of becoming my conviction, a conviction to equal the accusative of "It's me here!" with the nominative of "Here I stand"? Finally, to mediate the opening of the Same onto the Other and the internalization of the voice of the Other in the Same, must not language contribute its resources of communication, hence of reciprocity, as is attested by the exchange of personal pronouns mentioned so many times in the preceding studies, an exchange that reflects a more radical one, that of question and answer in which the roles are continually reversed? In short, is it not necessary that a dialogue superpose a relation on the supposedly absolute distance between the separate I and the teaching Other? [43]

Finally in the theme of *substitution,* in which the force of the hyperbole

43. Cf. Francis Jacques, *Dialogiques II* (Paris: PUF, 1984).

culminates, expressing the philosophy of otherness in its greatest vehemence, I perceive a sort of reversal of the reversal performed in *Totality and Infinity*. The assignment of responsibility, stemming from the summons by the Other and interpreted in terms of the most total passivity,[44] is reversed in a show of abnegation in which the self attests to itself by the very movement with which it removes itself. Who, in fact, is obsessed by the Other? Who is hostage to the Other if not a Same no longer defined by separation but by its contrary, Substitution?[45] I find confirmation of this interpretation of the theme of substitution in the role assigned, under the guidance of this very theme, to the category of testimony.[46] We indeed see to what testimony is given: to the absolute, to be sure, hence to the Elevated, named "the glory of the infinite," and to Exteriority, with respect to which the face is like a trace. In this sense, "there is no testimony . . . only of the Infinite" (*Otherwise than Being*, p. 146). But *who* testifies, if not the Self, distinguished henceforth from the I by virtue of the idea of the assignment of responsibility? "The self is the very fact of being exposed under the accusation that cannot be assumed, where the ego supports the others, unlike the certainty of the ego that rejoins itself in freedom" p. 118). Testimony is therefore the mode of truth of this auto-exhibition of the Self, the inverse of the certainty of the ego. Is this testimony so far removed from what we have constantly called attestation? To be sure, Lévinas never speaks of the attestation *of self,* the very expression being suspected of leading back to the "certainty of the ego." It remains that, through the form of the accusative, the first person is indirectly involved and that the accusative cannot remain "nonassumable," to borrow an expression quoted above, under pain of stripping all meaning from the very theme of substitution, under the aegis of which Lévinas reassumes the theme of testimony.

From this confrontation between Husserl and Lévinas results the suggestion that there is no contradiction in holding the movement from the Same toward the Other and that from the Other toward the Same to be dialectically complementary. The two movements do not annihilate one another to the extent that one unfolds in the gnoseological dimension of

44. In the paragraph devoted to the "responsible subject that is not absorbed in being" (Lévinas, *Otherwise than Being*, pp. 135–36), we read this: "In responsibility, the same, the ego, is me, summoned, provoked, as irreplaceable, and thus accused as unique in the supreme passivity of one that cannot slip away without fault" (p. 135).

45. The strange reversal made here, on the plane of the same, through the theme of substitution finds its consecration in the expression that attracted our attention above: "We have to speak here of expiation as uniting identity and alterity" (ibid., p. 118).

46. I devote a detailed analysis to the category of testimony in Lévinas by way of a confrontation with Heidegger and with Jean Nabert, the latter being certainly the more unexpected of the two, in "Emmanuel Lévinas, penseur du temoignage," in *Répondre d'autrui, Emmanuel Lévinas* (Neuchâtel: La Baconnière, 1989).

sense, the other in the ethical dimension of injunction. The assignment of responsibility, in the second dimension, refers to the power of self-designation, transferred, in accordance with the first dimension, to every third person assumed to be capable of saying "I." Was not this *intersecting* dialectic of oneself and the other than self anticipated in the analysis of the promise? If another were not counting on me, would I be capable of keeping my word, of maintaining myself?

c. Conscience

To hold conscience—in the sense of the German *Gewissen*—to be the place of an original form of the dialectic between selfhood and otherness is an enterprise fraught with difficulties.

First challenge: if the metaphor of the voice and the call seems to add a novel dimension to the concepts around which our basic concepts of ethics have been organized, is not this surplus of meaning necessarily concretized in notions as *suspect* as "bad" and "good" conscience? This challenge will provide the opportunity to put to the test the claim that the attestation of selfhood is inseparable from an exercise of *suspicion*.

Second challenge: assuming that one can free it from the yoke of prejudice tied to "good" and "bad" conscience, does not conscience itself denote a phenomenon distinct from the attestation of our power-to-be? The issue here, in the presence of this nonmoral version of conscience, will be to make more precise phenomena such as *injunction* or *debt*, which seem to be indicated by the metaphor of the voice.

Third challenge: if the injunction or the debt constitutes the ultimate requisite of conscience, is the portion of otherness that can be discerned there anything different from the otherness of other people, possibly in forms that our preceding investigation did not do justice to? In short, what authorizes our assigning a distinct place to the phenomenon of conscience on the plane of the "great kinds" of the Same and the Other?

The first challenge forces us to enter the problematic of conscience by the gate of *suspicion*. There is no reason to regret this, to the extent that the phenomenon of conscience maintains a sure kinship with attestation, which we said above mingles together being-true and being-false. Conscience is, in truth, that place par excellence in which illusions about oneself are intimately bound up with the veracity of attestation. The suspicion concerns, most precisely, the alleged surplus of meaning that the idea of conscience appears to superimpose on the major concept of ethics: the wish to live well (with all the additions with which we are familiar), obligation, and conviction. After all, our three studies on ethics were all conducted on the basis of common notions, the Golden Rule being the most striking example, without our having to erect conscience as a supplementary agency. There is, nonetheless, a problem inasmuch as conscience, without adding anything to the tenor of meaning of the guiding concepts of ethics, reinscribes these concepts within the dialectic of the Same and the Other, under the guise of a specific modality of passivity. It is of this unprecedented passivity that the metaphor of the voice, at once inside me and higher than me, serves as the symptom or the clue.

In the chapter of *Being and Time* entitled "Gewissen," which we shall analyze at greater length when we consider the second challenge proposed above, Heidegger described perfectly this moment of otherness that distinguishes conscience. Far from being foreign to the constitution of selfhood, this otherness is closely related to its emergence, inasmuch as, under the impetus of conscience, the self is made capable of taking hold of itself in the anonymity of the "they." This implication of conscience in the opposition between the self and the "they" does not exclude another type of relation between being-self and being-with, to the extent that the "they" is already an inauthentic modality of being-with and that, moreover, this retreat into the hidden heart offers to the other the vis-à-vis that he or she has a right to expect, that is, the self. Now how does the self free itself from the "they"? Here is found the feature that distinguishes the phenomenon of conscience, namely the sort of call (*Ruf*) or appeal (*Anruf*) that is indicated by the metaphor of the voice. In this intimate conversation, the self appears to be called upon and, in this sense, to be *affected* in a unique way. Unlike the dialogue of the soul with itself, of which Plato speaks, this affection by another voice presents a remarkable dissymmetry, one that can be called vertical, between the agency that calls and the self called upon. It is the vertical nature of the call, equal to its interiority, that creates the enigma of the phenomenon of conscience.

The authenticity of this phenomenon can only be reconquered with difficulty, not really at the expense of the metaphoric nature of the expression "voice of conscience"—metaphor, in my opinion, not excluding a genuine capacity for discovery[47]—but by moving against the current of moralizing interpretations that actually conceal its force of discovery.

It is here that the test of suspicion is shown to be beneficial in order to recover the capacity for discovery belonging to the metaphor of the voice. To do this, we have to mobilize the force of denunciation resonating, before the Nietzschean thunderbolt, in Hegel's warning shot.

We indeed find a virulent critique of the misinterpretation of conscience in the pages that the *Phenomenology of Spirit* devotes to the "moral view of the world";[48] what follows in chapter 6 attests to the fact that the authentic

47. Cf. *The Rule of Metaphor*, seventh study.
48. Hegel, *Phenomenology of Spirit*, pp. 383ff. pp. 642ff.

phenomenon of conscience is not carried along with the fall of the moral vision of the world. Instead, *Gewissen* belongs to a higher-order dialectic in which acting consciousness and judging consciousness confront one another: the "pardon" resulting from the mutual recognition of the two antagonists who admit the limits of their viewpoints and renounce their partiality denotes the authentic phenomenon of conscience. It is along the path of this recognition that the critique of the moral vision of the world is found.

It is noteworthy that this bitter critique attacks "postulates" wholly invented for the purpose and in which it is difficult to recognize not only what Kant termed "postulate" in the "Dialectic of Practical Reason" but even more so the features of Kantian formalism, reduced, as we accomplished above, to implementing the test of universalization. The artifice of the Hegelian construction is not, however, to be deplored; as an artifice it takes its place among the excesses, transgressions, and hyperboles of all sorts that nourish moral reflection and, perhaps, philosophical reflection in general. Moreover, the fact that this is a vision *of the world* that is mobilized by moralism is of the greatest importance. The first postulate, indeed, is that morality, while requiring that duty be done—hence, become real—dismisses the whole of nature as insignificant, through its condemnation of desire, which is nature in us. The second postulate maintains that, unable to produce any harmony between the ought and the is, morality postpones indefinitely the moment of satisfaction which the agent nonetheless seeks in the effectivity of action. Finally, the third postulate concerns the fact that since this agreement between form and content is never given here below, it is cast into another consciousness, that of a holy legislator situated outside of the world.

Little matter, once again, that Hegel misrepresents Kant, and probably Fichte as well, in constructing his postulates.[49] For us what is essential is that it produced a strategy of dismantling applied to the "dissemblance" (*die Verstellung*) to which the entire section that follows in the *Phenomenology* is devoted. Consciousness, indeed, is caught up here in a disappearing act, as it is tracked from one untenable position to the next, attempting to escape the contradictions in the moral vision of the world concealed by these postulates. How can action be taken seriously if the satisfaction of action is just a lure? How can duty be what ought-to-*be* if actuality endlessly slips away? How can autonomy remain the sovereign moral principle if the reconciliation with reality is sent off into another world? It is therefore with "contempt" that we say good-bye to a *hypocrisy* that the dissem-

---

49. M. Gueroult, "Les Déplacements (*Vertellungen*) de la conscience morale kantienne selon Hegel," in *Hommage à Jean Hyppolite* (Paris: PUF, 1971), pp. 47–80.

blances have not been able to conceal. Now this entire critique makes sense only from the perspective of the subsequent moment of the spirit, already present in a negative manner, or in filigree, in the dissemblance. This is why Hegel placed the three moments—the moral vision of the world, dissemblance or equivocal displacement, and the dialectic of the beautiful soul and the hero of action, culminating in the moment of reconciliation and pardon—under the heading "Spirit That Is Certain of Itself: Morality."[50] It is this journey of the critique of the moral vision of the world toward the point where *Gewissen* is equivalent to certainty of self that confines Hegel's effort to a warning shot before Nietzsche's thunderbolt.[51]

50. Hegel, *Phenomenology of Spirit*, p. 364.

51. A critique that is just as acerbic as that of judging consciousness can be read in the second part of Hegel's *Philosophy of Right*, concerned with morality (*Moralität*), which, as we know, is subordinated to ethical life (*Sittlichkeit*), which itself culminates in the theory of the state. The subjective will, "abstract, restricted, and formal" (§108, p. 76), is the theme of the second part, whose critical tendency must not be exaggerated. For the subjective will also has its right, which is at the very least that of seeing the project of the will recognized as *mine* (§114, p. 79). The critique of conscience is placed at the precise point where the demand for the right proper to the subjective will becomes autonomous with respect to any common aim, whether it be that of the family, of civil society, or of the state. It is noteworthy that Hegel associated conscience with the idea of the Good in the third section of part 2. It is, to be sure, in favor of the Good that the will decides within the limits of its subjectivity, but to a Good biased by the subjective perspective as such, permeated by the sense of duty (§133, p. 89). The antinomies of purely formal duty denounced in the *Phenomenology of Spirit* and to which the *Philosophy of Right* expressly refers, return here. The sole arbitrator of the fulfilment of formal and abstract duty is then conscience (§136, p. 90), left to the solitude and arbitrariness of its inner heart. In an addition to §136, we read: "But conscience is this deepest inward solitude with oneself where everything external and every restriction has disappeared" (p. 254). It is the absence of contents, which ethical life alone can bring, that condemns conscience to this solitude and this arbitrariness: "Here at the abstract standpoint of morality, conscience lacks this objective content and so its explicit character is that of infinite abstract self-certainty [*Gewissheit*], which at the same time is for this very reason the self-certainty of *this* subject" (§137, p. 91). Then, even the difference between good and evil is abolished: "Once self-consciousness has reduced all otherwise valid duties to emptiness and itself to the sheer inwardness of the will, it has become the potentiality of either making the absolutely universal its principle, or equally well of elevating above the universal the self-will of private particularity, taking that as its principle and realizing it through its actions, i.e., it has become potentially evil. [Observation:] To have a conscience, if conscience is only formal subjectivity, is simply to be on the verge of slipping into evil; in independent self-certainty, with its independence of knowledge and decision, both morality and evil have their common root" (§139, p. 92). It should, however, be noted that in the framework of this incisive critique, a place is reserved for "true conscience" (§137, p. 90). But this is nothing other than ethical "disposition." This is doubtless one of the major differences between the *Philosophy of Right* and the *Phenomenology of Spirit*: in the latter, conscience went beyond itself in the religious character of forgiveness; in the *Philosophy of Right*, conscience, left with its own conviction as sole criterion, is absorbed by politics, which confers objective determinations upon it that it essentially lacks. But what happens when the ethical life of a people is

From the second essay of the *Genealogy of Morals,* entitled "'Guilt' [*Schuld*], 'Bad Conscience' [*schlechtes Gewissen*] and the Like,"[52] I should like to retain just one point—the parallel presented here with the Hegelian critique of "dissemblance." To be sure, the genealogical turn of the Nietzschean critique can be contrasted with the teleological turn of the Hegelian critique.[53] The profound kinship between the two critiques is confessed, however, by Nietzsche himself when he characterizes "bad" conscience as falsifying interpretation and his own vision of "grand innocence" as authentic interpretation. It is, moreover, a problem in Nietzsche to determine whether the reference, assured by the genealogical method, to "strong" or "weak" Life, reaches the ultimate referent of a terminal deciphering, and if it is true that, in interpretation, there is no literal meaning that could be set in opposition to a figurative meaning.

The essay seems to leave a place for a concept of conscience that would be neutral, through the praise given to the *promise,* the antidote of forgetting, held to be "an active and . . . positive faculty of repression."[54]

---

basically corrupted? Is it not then in the conscience of those who resist it, those who are no longer intimidated by lies and fear, that the integrity of ethical life itself finds refuge? Hegel believed he had superseded all recourse to conscience: "As one of the commoner features of history (e.g. in Socrates, the Stoics, and others), the tendency to look deeper into oneself and to know and determine from within oneself what is right and good appears in ages when what is recognized as right and good in contemporary manners cannot satisfy the will of better men" (§138, p. 92). The cruel twentieth century has taught us that it is not so. But this does not prevent the fact that, left to its own judgment, conscience will never be rid of the tendency to confuse good and evil, and that this very confusion remains the fate of conscience left solely to itself: it is what we must continue to understand in the admirable §139 of the *Philosophy of Right,* in which Hegel ventures to write that it is in the very "inwardness of the will" that evil lies (p. 93).

52. Friedrich Nietzsche, *On the Genealogy of Morals,* trans. Walter Kaufmann and R. J. Hollingdale (New York: Vintage Books, 1967).

53. In and of itself, the genealogical method is truly comprehensible only in its relation with the philosophical method (*Philosophenbuch*), which we saw at work in the critique of the cogito (cf. Introduction). Without the reference to what I then called the tropological reduction, one runs the risk of reducing the genealogical method to a genetic explanation, one conducted, moreover, in the spirit of a rather primitive view of biology. One then forgets that the genealogical method produces an intersection between a semiology of textual origin and a symptomatology of medical origin. This is why we find in it a sort of denunciation of the metaphoric transfer and of the metonymic inversion that the *Philosophenbuch* placed under the heading (in this recalling Hegel) of *Verstellung,* of displacement-dissemblance.

54. "To breed an animal *with the right to make promises*—is this not the paradoxical task that nature has set itself in the case of man? is this not the real problem regarding man?" (Nietzsche, *Genealogy of Morals,* p. 57). A disturbing note, however, colors this praise: this responsible animal is also a predictable and, hence, a calculable animal (p. 58). This is the price of a *free* will, that of an "autonomous" and "supramoral" individual, for "'autonomous' and 'moral' are mutually exclusive" (p. 59).

This self-mastery—this "mnemotechnics"!—has behind it a long history of torment and torture which it shares with the asceticism that the third essay will connect to the evildoing of priests.[55] And if moral conscience as such calls for vigilance, bad conscience, on its part, requires a complete dismantling, which begins with the evocation of synonyms as weighted down by their meaning, especially in German, as *Schuld* (guilt), *Schulden* (debt), and *Vergeltung* (requital). We have, then, the clear world, in one sense, of the creditor and the debtor and, in another sense, the shadowy world of anger and vengeance. For the most archaic manner of recovering a debt is to do violence to the debtor: "Without cruelty there is no festival: thus the longest and most ancient part of human history teaches—and in punishment there is so much that is *festive!*" (*Genealogy of Morals*, p. 67).

Should we be struck by Nietzsche's authoritarian tone, as he proclaims that he has discovered the "origin" of "the moral conceptual world," "its beginnings" (p. 65)? What are we to say about this *Vorzeit*, about the ancient times—"this prehistory [which] is in any case present in all ages or may always reappear" (p. 71)? A strange proleptic, so to speak, archaeology indeed in which prehistory and the future interact with each other! And are we to take at face value the praise of suffering which the cruelty of punishment is held to make meaningful?[56] What is important, it seems, is that the training of the responsible animal is no longer credited to "free will" and to "the absolute spontaneity of man in good and evil," "that philosophers' invention, so bold and so fateful" (p. 69). This is the anti-Cartesian, anti-Kantian point of the entire tirade, which combines the mysterious complexity of punishment with the apparent simplicity of the relation between debtor and creditor.[57] What counts here is the polemical point, all the reversals made by the genealogical method being intended to destroy teleology with the weapons of archaeology. To state the origin is to abolish the aim and its alleged rationality. There is no intelligible aim for punishment, but instead a dark and mysterious origin.

The trap held out by the Nietzschean text is that of a new dogmatism,

55. "But how did that other [*diese andere*] 'somber thing,' the consciousness of guilt, the 'bad conscience,' come into the world?" (ibid., p. 62).

56. "'Every evil the sight of which edifies a god is justified': thus spoke the primitive logic of feeling" (ibid., p. 69).

57. Nietzsche's most positive message on this point is the apology of the *active* affects in contrast to the *reactive* affects like resentment, to which the sense of justice is related, when it is attached to the victims' complaint rather than to the triumphant cry of the victors. Good conscience is that of the aggressive administrator of justice; bad conscience is that of the complainant, who has to denigrate the strong will that seeks power. This is the guiding thread of G. Deleuze's philosophical interpretation of Nietzsche (*Nietzsche et la philosophie*, 2d ed. [Paris: Presses Universitaires de France, 1967]).

the dogmatism of the will to power discussed in §12 (pp. 76ff.). We must not, however, overlook the observation that accompanies, as if in passing, the naming of the will to power, namely that the fluidity of the origin, in opposition to the alleged fixity of the aim, of the end, is the occasion for a "fresh interpretation" (*ein Neu-interpretieren*), of an "adaptation" (*ein Zurechtmachen*) (p. 77), which, in turn, testifies to what extent the subsequent significations assigned to punishment were added on later.[58] Nietzsche even indulges himself by proposing a dozen different ways in which punishment could be interpreted (*gedeutet*) and rearranged (*zurechtgemacht*) in relation to entirely different ends. Now is not this "overdetermination" (*überladen*) by utilities of all kinds—a genuine overdetermination in the Freudian sense of the term—turned against the biologic determinism that Nietzsche imposes on the reader in §§16–25 in the second essay of *Genealogy of Morals*?[59]

I shall say nothing, within the context of this study, about the meaning or the possibility of the *second innocence* proclaimed toward the end of the essay and to which all of Nietzsche's work contributes. All that matters to me here is the force of the suspicion, implicit in Hegel, explicit in Nietzsche, that conscience is equated with "bad conscience." The worst solution for destroying this equation would be to appeal to bad in the name of good conscience. This reversal of pro and con would remain captive to the same circular problematic, justification and judgments of indignation simply being replaced by self-justification and self-glorification.

In order to step outside the poisoned circle of "good" and "bad" conscience, there is always the temptation to relate the phenomenon of conscience, without any additional moral qualification, to the central phenomenon of *attestation*, which is just the other side of suspicion. It is then a matter of determining by means of what previously undetected feature the attestation of selfhood, with which we began, contributes in an un-

---

58. Allow me to interpolate here Nietzsche's parenthetic remark: "Today it is impossible to say for certain *why* people are really punished: all concepts in which an entire process is semiotically concentrated elude definition; only that which has no history is definable" (*Genealogy of Morals*, p. 80).

59. "Hostility, cruelty, joy in persecuting, in attacking, in change, in destruction—all this turned against the possessors of such instincts: *that* is the origin of the 'bad conscience'" (ibid., p. 85). "But thus began the gravest and uncanniest illness, from which humanity has not yet recovered, man's suffering *of man, of himself*" (ibid.). But this, Nietzsche says, is his "own hypothesis" which has its own "presuppositions" (§§16–17). In this way, the authoritarian tone of revelation continues to alternate with the hypothetical tone of an adventurous archaeology, to say nothing of the kind of eschatology toward which this archaeology veers: ". . . as if man were not a goal but only a way, an episode, a bridge, a great promise" (p. 85). And again: "The bad conscience is an illness, there is no doubt about that, but an illness as pregnancy is an illness" (p. 88).

precedented way to the dialectic of the Same and the Other. It is here that our investigation encounters the second challenge announced above, which could be placed under the heading of the "demoralizing" of conscience.

Removing conscience in this way from the false alternative of "good" and "bad" conscience finds its most radical formulation in Heidegger, in the section entitled "Conscience" (*Gewissen*) in part 2 of *Being and Time,* where it is summed up this way: "An authentic potentiality-for-Being is attested by the conscience" (p. 277). We are all the more attentive to Heidegger's analysis as we owe to him the starting point of this entire discussion of the metaphor of the voice. This potentiality-for-being attested by conscience is initially marked by no particular competence for distinguishing good from bad. Conscience, one could say, is in its own way "beyond good and evil." Here we come across one of the effects of the struggle led against the thought value of the neo-Kantians and, even more so, against that of Max Scheler in his *Formalism in Ethics and Non-formal Ethics of Values.* It is as though, by underscoring *Sein* in Dasein, one refrained from recognizing any primordially ethical force of the call, the "advocation" (to borrow from the translation proposed by E. Martineau) of the *Anruf.* Indeed, whether one considers the content or the origin of the call, nothing is implied that was not already named under the title of potentiality-for-being. Conscience says nothing: no commotion, no message, but a silent call. As for the caller, it is nothing other than Dasein itself: "In conscience *Dasein* calls itself" (p. 320). This is perhaps the most surprising moment of the analysis. It is in this complete immanence of Dasein to itself that Heidegger recognizes a certain dimension of superiority: "The call undoubtedly does not come from someone else who is with me in the world. The call comes *from* me and yet *from beyond me and over me* [*aus mir und doch über mich*]" (ibid.).[60]

If we confine ourselves to these formulations, it is not evident what the analysis of conscience contributes to that of the potentiality-for-being, if not the mark of primordiality and authenticity that conscience places on attestation. The novelty resides in the explication of the trait of strange(r)ness (following Martineau's *étrang[èr]eté*), by which conscience inscribes itself within the dialectic of Same and Other. A subtle compari-

---

60. It is not that all reference to others is lacking, but others are implied only with respect of the "they" and on the inauthentic level of concern: "The call reaches the they-self of concernful Being with Others" (Heidegger, *Being and Time,* p. 317). The major theme is the separation of the self from the "they": "Conscience summons Dasein's Self from its lostness in the 'they'" (p. 319). We shall return, in the context of the third challenge, to this absence in *Being and Time* of the development of authentic forms of being-with, upon which a different approach to the otherness of conscience could be grafted.

son is made between the strange(r)ness of the voice and the condition of fallenness (in the sense, too, of *échu* as a note falls due, or a lot falls to one) of thrownness. For it is indeed into existence that Dasein is thrown. The avowal of the passivity, of the nonmastery of affection, tied to being-called, is directed toward a meditation on nothingness, that is, on the radical nonchoice affecting being-in-the-world, considered in its facticity.[61]

The introduction late in the discussion of the notion of *Schuld*—translated both "guilt" and "debt"—by no means restores any ethical connotation to this uncanniness. The accent falls heavily on *Sein* in *Schuldigsein:* "Where . . . shall we get our criterion for the primordial existential meaning of the 'Guilty!' [indebtedness]? From the fact that this 'Guilty!' [indebtedness] turns up as a predicate for the 'I am'" (*Being and Time,* p. 326). By stressing the ontology of guilt (of being-in-debt), Heidegger dissociates himself from what common sense most readily attaches to the idea of debt, namely that it is owed to someone else—that one is responsible as a debtor—finally, that being with one another is public. And this is indeed what Heidegger intends to reduce to its just portion. Ontology stands guard on the threshold of ethics. Heidegger hammers out his demands: first, inquire in principle into Dasein's *being*-guilty (being-in-debt) (p. 328); hence, first of all, into a mode of being. In this way, he sets out of consideration the everyday phenomena of debt, of indebtedness, which are "related to our concernful Being with Others" (ibid.). Being-in-debt, therefore, does not result from indebtedness (*Verschuldung*)—but the other way around. If some failing is revealed here, it is not evil—war, Lévinas would say—but an ontological trait prior to any ethics: "Being-the-basis of a nullity [*Grundsein einer Nichtigkeit*]" (p. 329).[62] There is no clearer way of abolishing the primacy of ethics: "The primordial 'Being-guilty' [being-in-debt] cannot be defined by morality, since morality already presupposes it for itself" (p. 332). Unfortunately, Heidegger does not show how one could travel the opposite path—from ontology toward ethics. And yet this appears to be promised in paragraph 59, where Heidegger enters into a debate with the "ordinary" interpretation of conscience. In this sense, attestation gives rise to a certain set of criteria, at

61. "What could be more alien to the 'they', lost in the manifold 'world' of its concern, than the Self which has been individualized down to itself in uncanniness and been thrown into the 'nothing'?" (ibid., pp. 321–22). This is why the caller is not anyone, since the call comes from the very uncanniness (strange[r]ness) of the condition of throwness and fallenness: "a call which comes *from* uncanniness," that is, from "thrown individualization" (p. 325).

62. And again: "This means that *Dasein as such is guilty* [in debt], if our formally existential definition of 'guilt ['debt'] as 'Being-the-basis of a nullity' is indeed correct" (ibid., p. 331).

least as far as a critique of common sense. From this results a critique of the notions of "good" and "bad" conscience in terms resembling those we have used. The notion of "bad" conscience is first struck with the mark of "everydayness": it comes, in fact, too late, after-the-fact (it is reactive, Nietzsche would say); it thus lacks the prospective character inherent in care. Nothing is to be gained, then from *re*morse, from *re*pentance. As for "good" conscience, it is dismissed as hypocritical, for who can say, "I am good"? Heidegger does not even want to hear of conscience referred to as admonishment, warning, in the name of that curious argument that conscience would thereby become once again a prisoner of the "they" (p. 339). In all of this, Heidegger's critique of common sense is clearly to be compared with Nietzsche's *Genealogy of Morals*. He therefore rejects together Kant's deontological viewpoint, the Schelerian theory of values, and, by the same token, the critical function of conscience. All of this remains within the province of concern, which lacks the central phenomenon—the call of one's ownmost possibilities. Here, attestation is truly a kind of understanding, but one that cannot be reduced to knowing something. The meaning of attestation is now sealed: "calling forth and summoning us to Being-guilty [being-in-debt]" (p. 341).

The final word on conscience has not yet been stated. The connection asserted between attestation and *resoluteness* seems to lead the notion of conscience back to the field of ethics. We are familiar, in this regard, with the tie between resoluteness and being-toward-death. What resoluteness contributes in its own right is the intention of being-a-whole sealed by being-toward-death. The transition from one notion to the other occurs through the expression "wanting to have a conscience" (p. 342), whence proceeds the final formulation: "*This reticent self-projection upon one's own-most Being-guilty* [being-in-debt], *in which one is ready for anxiety*—we call '*resoluteness*'" (p. 343). We note how careful Heidegger is here to avoid the vocabulary of acting, which appears to him as either in opposition to suffering, which thrown-being also rejects, or in opposition to the theoretical, which would destroy the complete unity of Dasein splintering it into "distinct behaviors." Attestation-conscience, however, is inscribed in the problematic of *truth*, as opening and disclosing: "In resoluteness we have now arrived at the truth of Dasein which is most primordial because it is *authentic*" (p. 343). But cut off from the demands of others and from any properly moral determination, resoluteness remains just as indeterminate as the call to which it seems to reply. The expression "letting oneself be summoned out of one's lostness in the 'they'" (p. 345), returns here. But fundamental ontology refrains from making any pronouncements about the orientation of action: "In resoluteness the issue for Dasein is its ownmost potentiality-for-Being, which, as something thrown, can project itself only upon definite factical possibilities" (p. 346). It is as though the philosopher were referring his reader to a moral situationism destined to fill the silence of an indeterminate call.[63]

To this demoralization of conscience, I would oppose a conception that closely associates the phenomenon of *injunction* to that of *attestation*. Being-enjoined would then constitute the moment of otherness proper to the phenomenon of conscience, in accordance with the metaphor of the voice. Listening to the voice of conscience would signify being-enjoined by the Other. In this way, the rightful place of the notion of *debt* would be acknowledged, a notion that was too hastily ontologized by Heidegger at the expense of the ethical dimension of indebtedness. But how are we to avoid falling back into the trap of "bad" and "good" conscience, from which we are protected by Hegel, Nietzsche, and Heidegger, each in his own way? A remark made earlier with respect to the metaphor of the *court* put us on the right path. Is it not because the stage of morality has been dissociated from the triad ethics-morality-conviction, then hypostatized because of this dissociation, that the phenomenon of conscience has been correlatively impoverished and that the revealing metaphor of the voice has been eclipsed by the stifling voice of the court? In fact, it is the entire triad presented in the three preceding studies that offers itself here to a reinterpretation in terms of otherness. I am called to live well with and for others in just institutions: this is the first injunction. However, following a suggestion mentioned above, one borrowed from Franz Rosenzweig in *The Star of Redemption* (bk. 2), there is a form of commandment that is not yet a law: this commandment, if it can be called such, can be heard in the tone of the *Song of Songs,* in the plea that the lover addressed to the beloved: "Thou, love me!" It is because violence taints all the relations of interaction, because of the power-over exerted by an agent on the patient of the action, that the commandment becomes law, and the law, prohibition: "Thou shalt not kill." It is at this point that the sort of short-circuit between conscience and obligation takes place, from which results the reduction of the voice of conscience to the verdict of the court. We must not stop moving up the slope leading from this injunction-prohibition back to the injunction to live well. This is not all: we must not stop the trajectory of ethics at the point of imperative-injunction but continue to follow its

---

63. This is indeed what appears to be suggested by the following text and by the note on Karl Jaspers to which it refers: "To present the factical existentiell possibilities in their chief features and interconnections, and to Interpret them according to their existential structure, falls among the tasks of a thematic existential anthropology" (ibid., p. 348). And the note: "In the direction of such a problematic, Karl Jaspers is the first to have explicitly grasped the task of a doctrine of world-views and carried it through. Cf. his *Psychologie der Weltanschauungen*" (p. 496).

course all the way to moral choices in situation. The injunction then meets up with the phenomenon of *conviction,* which we saw was restricted by Hegel to the field of subjective morality. This is not false, if we are willing to note that it is always alone that, in what we called the tragic character of action, we make up our minds. In measuring up to conviction in this way, conscience attests to the passive side: "Here I stand! *I cannot do otherwise!*" But, if we agree to follow our reasoning concerning the ethics of decision in situation, the moment of conviction is not a substitute for the test of the rule; it arises at the end of a conflict, which is a conflict of duties. In addition, the moment of conviction marks, in my opinion, a recourse to the as yet unexplored resources of ethics, beneath morality and yet through it. It was for this reason that I believed I could call upon the most singularizing features of Aristotelian *phronēsis* in order to emphasize the tie connecting conviction to its ethical ground, through the level of imperatives. How, then, can we help but echo Heidegger's remark, related by Gadamer, when the former was commenting on Aristotle's ethics: "But *phronēsis* is *Gewissen!*"[64] If we keep in mind the definition of *phronēsis,* which includes right rule in the choice of the *phronimos,* one can no longer concur with the Heidegger of *Being and Time* that the voice says nothing but is restricted to directing Dasein back to its ownmost potentiality for being. Conscience, as attestation-injunction, signifies that these "ownmost possibilities" of Dasein are primordially structured by the optative mood of living well, which mood governs in a secondary fashion the imperative of respect and links up with the conviction belonging to moral judgment in situation. If this is so, the passivity of being-enjoined consists in the situation of listening in which the ethical subject is placed in relation to the voice addressed to it in the second person. To find oneself called upon in the second person at the very core of the optative of living well, then of the prohibition to kill, then of the search for the choice appropriate to the situation, is to recognize oneself as being enjoined to *live well with and for others in just institutions and to esteem oneself as the bearer of this wish.* The otherness of the Other is then the counterpart, on the dialectical level of the "great kinds," to this passivity specific to being-enjoined.

Now, what more is there to say about the otherness of this Other? Here we find ourselves confronting the third challenge stated at the start of this meditation: is not this Other, in one way or another, other people? Whereas Heidegger relates the otherness of the call to strange(r)ness and to the nothingness of thrown-being, fallen or deteriorated, and finally reduces the otherness of conscience to the encompassing otherness of being-in-the-world, which we recentered earlier around the flesh, there is a

64. Cf. above, n. 15.

strong temptation to compare, by contrast, the otherness of the injunction to that of other people.

The fact that conscience is the voice of the Other in the sense of others is something that Hegel enabled us to think, to the extent that conscience is tied to the reconciliation of two as yet partial figures of mind: judging consciousness and acting consciousness. In this way, the phenomenon of split consciousness crosses through the entire *Phenomenology of Spirit,* from the moment of the desire of the other, passing through the dialectic of master and slave, all the way to the double figure of the beautiful soul and the hero of action. It is important, however, that the ultimate reconciliation leaves us puzzled with respect to the identity of that other in "openly confessing itself by the vision of itself in the other" (p. 407). Does not the mention of pardon already mark the entrance into the sphere of religion? Hegel leaves his reader in a state of suspense when he writes: "The word of reconciliation is the objectively existent Spirit, which beholds the pure knowledge of itself qua universal essence, in its opposite, in the pure knowledge of itself qua absolutely self-contained and exclusive individuality—a reciprocal recognition which is absolute Spirit" (p. 408.).[65] Hegel, the philosopher of mind, leaves us here in a state of indecision, halfway between an anthropological reading and a theological reading.

The ultimate equivocalness with respect to the status of the Other in the phenomenon of conscience is perhaps what needs to be preserved in the final analysis. It is decided in a clearly anthropological sense in Freudian metapsychology: moral conscience is another name for the superego, which itself is made up of (sedimented, forgotten, and to a large extent, repressed) identifications with parental and ancestral figures. Although set on the plane of science, psychoanalysis concurs here with innumerable popular beliefs that the voices of our ancestors continue to make themselves heard among the living and in this way ensure, not only the transmission of wisdom, but its intimate personal reception at every stage. This dimension, which could be called *generational,* is an undeniable component of the phenomenon of injunction and, all the more so, of that of indebtedness.[66]

To this *genetic* explanation—legitimate in its own sphere—it could be objected that it does not exhaust the phenomenon of injunction and even

---

65. And again: "The reconciling *Yes,* in which the two 'I's let go their antithetical *existence,* is the *existence* of the 'I' which has expanded into a duality, and therein remains identical with itself, and, in its complete externalization and opposite, possesses the certainty of itself: it is God manifested in the midst of those who know themselves in the form of pure knowledge" (*Phenomenology of Spirit,* p. 409).

66. Allow me to refer here to the pages of *Time and Narrative* 3 dealing with the category of debt as a structure of historicity (pp. 143, 156–57, 189–92).

less so that of indebtedness. If, on the one hand, the self were not constituted primordially as a receptive structure for the sedimentation of the
superego, the internalization of ancestral voices would be unthinkable, and
the ego, as a primitive agency, could not even perform the function of
mediator, or better of intercessor, which Freud accords to it among the
three masters that fight over its allegiance—the id, the superego, and external reality.[67] The aptitude for being-affected through the mode of injunction does seem to constitute the condition of the possibility of the
empirical phenomenon of identification, which is far from exhibiting the
sort of transparency that is too readily ascribed to it. On the other hand,
the generational model of conscience contains another even more impene-
trable enigma: the figure of the ancestor, beyond relatives whether close
or distant, begins a movement of infinite regress in which the Other progressively loses—from generation to generation!—the initial, presumed
familiarity. Ancestors are removed from the realm of representation, as is
confirmed by their capture in myths and cults.[68] A *pietas* of a unique kind
unites in this way the living and the dead. This *pietas* reflects the circle in
which we finally revolve: whence does the ancestor draw the authority of
his voice, if not from his presumedly privileged tie to the Law, immemorial just as he is? Thus the injunction itself precedes itself, through the
intercession of the ancestor, the generational figure of the Other.

What has just been said about the Freudian superego, as the word of
ancestors resonating in my head, constitutes a good preface for the remarks with which I shall conclude this meditation on the otherness of
conscience. I shall reserve them for the reduction, which seems to me to
result from the work of Emmanuel Lévinas as a whole, of the otherness of
conscience to the otherness of other people. To the reduction of being-in-
debt to the strange(r)ness tied to the facticity of being-in-the-world, characteristic of the philosophy of Martin Heidegger, Emmanuel Lévinas opposes a symmetrical reduction of the otherness of conscience to the
externality of the other manifested in his face. In this sense, there is no
other modality of otherness for Lévinas than *this* externality. The model
of all otherness is the other person. To these alternatives—either Heidegger's strange(r)ness or Lévinas's externality—I shall stubbornly oppose
the original and originary character of what appears to me to constitute
the third modality of otherness, namely *being enjoined as the structure of
selfhood.*

<hr/>

67. "The Ego and the Id," trans. James Strachey, *The Standard Edition of the Complete
Psychological Works of Sigmund Freud,* vol. 19 (London: Hogarth Press, 1961), pp. 3–66.
   68. François Wahl, "Les Ancêtres, ça ne se représente pas," in *L'Interdit de la représenta-
tion,* 1981 Montpellier conference (Paris: Éd. du Seuil, 1984), pp. 31–62.

To justify the irreducible character of this third modality of otherness, I shall return to the objections that I have just raised to the genetic explanation given by Freud of the agency of the superego, taking into account the difference in context. On the one hand, if the injunction coming from the other is not part and parcel of self-attestation, it loses its character of injunction, for lack of the existence of a being-enjoined standing before it as its respondent. If one eliminates this dimension of auto-affection, one ultimately renders the metacategory of conscience superfluous; the category of the other suffices. To Heidegger, I objected that attestation is primordially injunction, or attestation risks losing all ethical or moral significance. To Lévinas, I shall object that the injunction is primordially attestation, or the injunction risks not being heard and the self not being affected in the mode of being-enjoined. The profound unity of self-attestation and of the injunction coming from the other justifies the acknowledgment, in its irreducible specificity, of the modality of otherness corresponding, on the plane of the "great kinds," to the passivity of conscience on the phenomenological plane.

On the other hand, sharing Lévinas's conviction that the other is the necessary path of injunction,[69] allow me to stress, more than he would want to, the need to maintain a certain equivocalness of the status of the Other on the strictly philosophical plane, especially if the otherness of conscience is to be held irreducible to that of other people. To be sure, Lévinas does not fail to say that the face is the trace of the Other. The category of the trace seems in this way to correct as well as to complete that of epiphany. Perhaps the philosopher as philosopher has to admit that one does not know and cannot say whether this Other, the source of the injunction, is another person whom I can look in the face or who can stare at me, or my ancestors for whom there is no representation, to so great an extent does my debt to them constitute my very self, or God—living God, absent God—or an empty place. With this aporia of the Other, philosophical discourse comes to an end.

*

Allow me to conclude on a tone of Socratic irony. Is it necessary to leave in such a state of dispersion the three great experiences of passivity—the experience of one's own body, of others, and of conscience—which introduced the three modalities of otherness on the plane of the "great kinds"?

---

69. In this respect the distance is not as great as it may seem between the theme of forgiveness at the end of the chapter on "Spirit" (*Geist*) of the *Phenomenology of Spirit* and the theme of substitution in *Otherwise than Being*, except for the fact, itself not negligible, that in Hegel reciprocity wins out, whereas in Lévinas an asymmetry favors the other.

This dispersion seems to me on the whole well suited to the very idea of otherness. Only a discourse other than itself, I will say, plagiarizing the *Parmenides,* and without adventuring any further into the thicket of speculation, is suited to the metacategory of otherness, under penalty of otherness suppressing itself in becoming the same as itself.

INDEX

Act, illocutionary, 43, 45; locutionary, 43; perlocutionary, 43. *See also* Force, illocutionary

Actant, 145–46

Action, 155, 303; and agent, 88–96, 245; analytic philosophy of, 17, 20, 115n; conceptional schema of, 57–61; semantics of (agentless), 56–57, 73–87

Action dans la philosophie analytique, L', 67n, 301n

"Actions, Reasons, and Causes" (Davidson), 74, 81

Aesthetics (Hegel), 243

After Virtue (Ricoeur), 158, 160n.25

Agapē, 25

"Analytic of Pure Practical Reason" (Kant), 209

Anchoring, 49, 51–54

Anscombe, G. E. M., 67–80 passim, 105–6, 153; *Intention*, 62, 67–73, 80n.23; parable of man pumping water, 71n

Antigone (Sophocles), 241–49, 256, 258

Apel, Karl Otto, 221, 280–82

Arendt, Hannah, 58–60, 194, 196–97, 256

Aristote et la question du monde (Brague), 187n, 307n.10

Aristotle, 121, 141, 214, 259, 290, 298, 300, 304, 352; on action and agent, 89–96; and being (ontology), 20, 302, 311, 317; on friendship, 181–94, 330; Heidegger's reinterpretation of, 311, 313; on justice, 198–202, 234, 257, 261; *Metaphysics*, 299, 303; on narrative, 143; *Nichomachean Ethics*, 89–94, 101, 172–88; on passions, 97; *Physics*, 91; *Poetics*, 143, 157; and the questions "Who?" "What?" "Why?" 71–72; *Rhetoric*, 97;

on tragedy, 152, 157; on voluntary vs. involuntary, 99, 101

Arkhē, 90, 92

Aron, Raymond, 107

Ascription, 88–107; aporias of, 96–112

Attestation, 21–23, 73n.13, 129, 297–356 passim. *See also* Doubt

Auctoritas, 197n.40

Augustine, 89; *Confessions*, 82; and Kant, 217n.31

Austin, J. L., 84, 301; *How to Do Things with Words*, 42–43

Autonomy vs. Heteronomy, 210, 216; and conflict. *See* Conflict

Babylonian Talmud, 219

Beauchamp, Paul, 23

Beginning, absolute vs. relative, 105–7

Being and Time (Heidegger), 64, 308, 322–29, 342

Being-as-substance, 20

Benjamin, Walter: "The Storyteller," 163–64

Bergson, Henri, 27

Bernanos, G., 36

Bible, citation of books: Leviticus, 219; Luke, 219; Matthew, 219; Song of Songs, 194n.32, 351

Bios, 152, 157, 177

Birth of Tragedy (Nietzsche), 11

Blue Notebook (Wittgenstein), 51

Bouleusis, 90

Brague, Rémi, 187, 313; *Aristote et la question du monde*, 187n, 307n.10

Braudel, Fernand: *L'Identité de la France*, 123

Bremond, Claude, 144–45; *Logique du récit*, 144

Buddenbrooks (Mann), 161